BARRON'S

AP® Psychology

WITH 3 PRACTICE TESTS

NINTH EDITION

Allyson J. Weseley, Ed.D.
AP Psychology Teacher
Roslyn High School, Roslyn, New York

Robert McEntarffer, Ph.D.
Assessment Specialist and AP Psychology Teacher
Lincoln Public Schools, Lincoln, Nebraska

To Kristin, Esme, and Guy.—R.M.

To Sara, Kate, and Eli.—A.W.

About the Authors
Rob McEntarffer taught AP Psychology at Lincoln Southeast High School in Lincoln, NE for 13 years and Psychology at Nebraska Wesleyan University for 7 years. He earned his teaching certificate in psychology at the University of Nebraska, a master's degree in educational psychology, and a Ph.D. in education. He has extensive experience in scoring the Advanced Placement Psychology free-response questions, having served as a Reader, Table Leader, and as the high school Question Leader. He is past chair of the national organization Teachers of Psychology in Secondary Schools, worked with the committee on the National Standards for the Teaching of High School Psychology, and is involved in writing assessment materials for high school–and college level–introductory psychology textbooks. He works as an assessment specialist for his school district.

Allyson Weseley has taught AP Psychology and run a Behavioral Science Research Program at Roslyn High School in Roslyn Heights, NY for over 25 years. Her students have enjoyed great success on the AP exam, with a 100 percent passing rate and well over 80 percent earning 5's. She earned an undergraduate degree in Psychology at Princeton University, a master's degree from the Harvard Graduate School of Education, and a doctorate from Columbia University's Teachers College. Dr. Weseley has served as a Reader and Table Leader for the AP Psychology exam, published a number of psychology-related activities, led several psychology teacher workshops, and served on the board of Teachers of Psychology in the Secondary Schools.

All inquiries should be addressed to:
Published by Kaplan, Inc., d/b/a Barron's Educational Series
750 Third Avenue New York, N.Y 10017
www.barronseduc.com

ISBN: 978-1-5062-6208-6

10 9 8 7 6 5 4 3 2 1

Kaplan, Inc., d/b/a Barron's Educational Series print books are available at special quantity discounts to use for sales promotions, employee premiums, or educational purposes. For more information or to purchase books, please call the Simon & Schuster special sales department at 866-506-1949.

Contents

UNIT 2: BIOLOGICAL BASES OF BEHAVIOR

UNIT 3: SENSATION AND PERCEPTION

UNIT 4: LEARNING

UNIT 5: COGNITIVE PSYCHOLOGY

UNIT 6: DEVELOPMENTAL PSYCHOLOGY

UNIT 7: MOTIVATION, EMOTION, AND PERSONALITY

UNIT 8: CLINICAL PSYCHOLOGY

UNIT 9: SOCIAL PSYCHOLOGY

PRACTICE TESTS

Updates in this Edition

This edition of Barron's AP* Psychology is updated to match changes to the College Board course description for the AP Psychology course. Changes to this edition include:

- Additions to the Barron's Essential 5 ("Use what psychology teaches you about cognition")
- Detail added to "Introduction: Using this Book" regarding the recent changes in the course exam description
- Additional suggestions added to "Using Psychology to Study Psychology" (in "Introduction: Using this Book")
- Content chapters reorganized into the 9 College Board AP Psychology units
- Summary provided for each new AP Psychology unit
- Content summaries and multiple choice items aligned with changes to the College Board AP Psychology curriculum
- Updated material in "Test-Taking Strategies" ("Finally, Remember to Apply Some of What You've Learned About Psychology to How You Study")
- New Skills section in "Test taking strategies"

As you review the content in this book to work toward earning that **5** on your AP PSYCHOLOGY exam, here are five things that you **MUST** know above everything else:

1 **Know the psychological perspectives.** Psychological researchers study the mind and behavior from different "perspectives." Each perspective uses some unique research methods, concepts, and vocabulary to describe and explain thinking and behavior. Knowing the vocabulary and concepts associated with each perspective can help you better understand psychological theories and quickly narrow down possible answers to exam questions. For instance, if a question uses the term *classical conditioning*, you should be able to immediately identify the question as belonging in the "behavioral" area of psychology and look for answers that include other behavioral terms or key individuals. The psychological perspectives are introduced in Chapter 1 and form the basis for the discussion of personality, psychological disorders, and treatment of psychological disorders found in Chapters 11, 12, and 13, respectively.

2 **Know your terms.** Psychological terms refer to specific concepts, and it is important that you don't confuse these terms with "pop" psychological ideas or the casual ways nonpsychologists use the same words. For example:

- To a psychologist, people diagnosed with antisocial personality disorder (Chapter 12) are not shy or unfriendly, but rather callous and unfeeling toward others.
- "Learning" in psychological terms refers to much more than learning in school and is divided into many specific kinds of learning such as classical and operant conditioning. You can read more about this in Chapter 6.

You should make sure that you understand the specific, scientific meaning of psychological terms. Most of the multiple-choice items on the exam (which determine the majority of your final score) measure your knowledge and ability to apply psychological terminology.

3 **Psychology is a science.** Psychological researchers use the scientific method to gather data and test hypotheses about the mind and behavior instead of relying on intuition, what the majority of people believe, or "common sense." Often what people refer to as "common sense" offers contradictory ideas. Regarding attraction, common sense tells us both that "opposites attract" and that "birds of a feather flock together." Psychological researchers carefully gather data about topics like attraction to reach conclusions rather than relying on intuition or belief. Chapter 2 ("Methods") describes in detail how psychologists gather data and test hypotheses. Understanding research methodology is vital to your performance on the exam and your understanding of the science of psychology.

4 **Application is key.** The AP Psychology test is designed to measure your knowledge of psychological concepts and ability to apply these concepts. Exam items (especially the free-response questions) usually require you to go beyond defining terms by applying them to a scenario or making connections between different concepts. However, the AP Psychology exam is not designed to measure your writing ability or ability to express your knowledge in creative or unique ways. The measurement goals of this exam are to assess your knowledge of psychological concepts and your ability to apply this knowledge.

5 **Use what psychology teaches you about cognition (Chapter 7) to improve your study habits.** You have been a student for many years, and no doubt you've received advice about how to study and have developed your own study habits. Use what psychology teaches you about cognition to improve your study habits. Studying for the AP Psychology exam is an opportunity for you to modify your study methods based on the research findings about the effectiveness of different encoding and recall techniques. For example:

- Memory research clearly indicates that "distributed practice" (spacing your studying over a span of days or weeks) is much more effective than "massed practice" ("cramming" all your studying just before the test).
- Memory techniques like chunking, mnemonic devices, and context cues can dramatically improve your ability to recall sets of terms and save you hours of study time.
- The information-processing model predicts that focusing on the meaning, context, and application of psychological ideas will increase your ability to recall and use psychological ideas.
- Research indicates that students can (and should) take advantage of "retrieval practice" (also known as the "testing effect"): you should interrupt your reading and studying with frequent small "tests" of your knowledge. Use the practice questions at the end of each chapter to test your knowledge.

Introduction: Using This Book

The purpose of this book is to provide you with the best possible preparation for the AP Psychology exam. Becoming familiar with the structure of the test is an essential part of this preparation. Therefore, following this introduction we include an overview of the exam.

After the overview of the exam, we include a diagnostic test to help you gauge how best to prepare for the exam. You may wish to take this test after you have been exposed to all the information provided by your class but before you begin to study. The Multiple-Choice Error Analysis Sheet is intended to help you identify your areas of relative strength and weakness. Notice that we organize the Multiple-Choice Error Analysis Sheet according to the chapter titles you can find in the textbook you used in your AP Psychology class. This should help you use information from the diagnostic test to determine what chapters to review in the textbook. For each of the 14 chapters, compute the percentage of questions you answered correctly. In this test, the number of questions on a topic is indicative of the amount of attention it typically receives on the exam. Therefore, you should spend the most time studying the areas on which many questions were asked and you got a relatively low percentage of them correct.

After the diagnostic test, we review the terms and concepts measured on the AP Psychology test. This review is organized in 9 units that are comprised of 14 chapters. The College Board recently revised the way they organized materials for the AP Psychology course. The textbook you use for your AP Psychology course probably includes about 14 chapters. The College Board grouped these chapters into 9 overall units. For each unit, the College Board describes topics, learning targets, and examples for specific content in the unit that may be assessed on the test. (Your AP Psychology instructor can provide more information about these units.) We are not reproducing these topics, learning targets, and examples in this review book, but the content of this book corresponds closely to these new descriptions.

We devote most of the book to a review of the main areas of psychology. The content is organized in such a way that it mirrors the format of the exam. These areas and their relative coverage on the AP exam are listed in the table below. Notice that this table lists the 9 units the College Board uses to organize their materials, the percentage of items you can expect on the test from that unit, and the 14 chapters from most textbooks that are included in that unit.

College Board Unit	% of Items on the AP Psychology Test	Textbook Chapter
Scientific Foundations	10-14%	History and Approaches Methods
Biological Bases of Behavior	8-10%	Biological Bases of Behavior States of Consciousness
Sensation and Perception	6-8%	Sensation and Perception
Learning	7-9%	Learning
Cognitive Psychology	13-17%	Cognition Testing and Individual Differences
Developmental	7-9%	Developmental Psychology
Motivation, Emotion, and Personality	11-15%	Motivation and Emotion Personality
Clinical Psychology	12-16%	Abnormal Psychology Treatment of Psychological Disorders
Social Psychology	8-10%	Social Psychology

Because this is a review book, our aim is to include only that information you need to know for the exam. Nonetheless, some of this information is particularly important, and we convey that fact by highlighting such material as **Tips**. Important terms and people appear at the beginning of each chapter and are set in **bold** in the text. They can also be found in the index.

Skills

Starting with the 2020 AP Psychology test, the College Board began "keying" multiple choice items to one of 3 skills, in addition to which content area the item is addressing. We include more information about these skills in Chapter 15 ("Test-Taking Strategies" section).

Skill 1 - Concept Understanding: applying concepts, theories, and perspectives in context. *Note: all the multiple choice items in this review book assess your ability to apply psychological concepts.*
Skill 2 - Data Analysis: understanding and making inferences based on numerical data. *Note: We include information at the beginning of Chapter 2, "Methods" that will help you answer Data Analysis questions.*
Skill 3 - Scientific Investigation: analyzing and explaining examples of research studies. *Note: We include information at the beginning of Chapter 2, "Methods" that will help you answer Data Analysis questions.*

Names

The College Board names many psychologists in their most recent revision of their course description, and all those researchers are described in this review book. However, we recommend that you do NOT spend a large part of your study time memorizing all these names. The AP Psychology exam primarily focuses on psychological concepts and ideas, not people. We included a list of the most significant psychologists in the "Fabulous 15" section and suggest that you focus your study on those individuals.

Practice Questions, Test Tips, and Practice Exams

Multiple-choice practice questions and explanations of the correct answers are provided at the end of each review chapter. We recommend that you first review the material in the chapter and then answer all the review questions in order to test your comprehension. (This is called "retrieval practice" and it's one of the most effective studying techniques according to cognitive psychologists. You'll learn more about why this technique is so effective in Chapter 7.)

To help prepare you for the exam, Chapter 15 presents a group of testing tips and Chapter 16 focuses on how to answer the free-response questions. We included a discussion of how best to approach the essays and also provide a number of examples of the kinds of essay questions likely to appear on the exam. We also include model essay answers to give you an idea of what the readers of the exam are looking for.

At the end of the book we included two full-length practice exams. Keep in mind that taking a practice exam under actual testing conditions (all at once and within the time limit) is always best. Every exam includes an explanation of the correct answers as well as an Error Analysis Sheet.

Using Psychology to Study Psychology

Research by cognitive and educational psychologists indicates that the following three principles might be the most powerful ideas students can use to make their studying more efficient and effective. This book is designed to help you use these principles.

Distributed Practice

Studies consistently show that spreading your studying out over a period of time is much more effective than "massing" your studying just before you have to use the information (that is, cramming for a test). This book begins with a diagnostic test. You can use this practice exam to "diagnose" what chapters you already know well and which chapters you need to study thoroughly. You can use this assessment of your strengths and weaknesses to plan your study schedule, spreading your studying across a period of time.

Depth of Processing

Encoding the meaning of terms, that is, deeply processing about what psychological terms and concepts *mean* to you, thinking about them in your own words and attaching your own personal examples to them, are effective ways to study and retain information. In this book, we provide multiple examples of the terms and concepts discussed. Information that is deeply processed is more likely to be encoded into long term memory. The more you "personalize" the terms and examples, thinking about how they apply to you and your own life, the more likely you'll be to remember those ideas on the exam. Remember, learning is an *active*, not a *passive*, activity. The more you involve yourself in the process by thinking about how the terms and theories apply to you and your life (this is also called the "self-reference effect"), the better you'll remember the content in this book (and you'll reduce your overall study time!).

Retrieval Practice

Recent research indicates that interrupting your studying with frequent small quizzes about the content is very effective. Students who frequently answer questions about the content they are studying are more likely to remember the content, even if they don't answer the questions correctly. This book is designed to help you take advantage of the power of retrieval practice (also called the "testing effect"). The chapters in this book are 10 to 20 pages long and each ends with 15 practice questions. Treat these practice questions like a "mini-test" after you are done studying each chapter. Try to answer the questions without looking back at the chapter or looking ahead at the correct answers. Even if you don't feel ready for the quiz at the end of the chapter, or if you get many of the items wrong, the experience of taking the test and thinking about your answers will help you learn and remember the terms and concepts.

Finally, the book includes an index that will be helpful to you anytime you come across a term or person you know is important, but do not remember. It will refer you to a page or pages that discuss that term or person.

Overview of the AP Psychology Exam

The AP Psychology exam has two parts: a multiple-choice section and a free-response section. You will have two hours to complete the whole test. The multiple-choice portion of the exam contains 100 five-choice (A to E) questions. You will have 70 minutes to complete this section.

The score for the multiple-choice section of the AP exam is based on the number of questions answered correctly. No points are deducted for questions answered incorrectly or left blank. Since there is no "guessing penalty," you should make sure you answer every multiple-choice question on the exam. Chapter 15 describes important tips for answering AP Psychology multiple-choice questions.

The free-response section of the test consists of two questions, and you must answer them both. Unlike most other AP exams, you will not be given a choice of topics. You will have 50 minutes to complete this portion of the exam. Some students find writing two full essays in such a short amount of time to be difficult. Chapter 16 includes some helpful suggestions for tackling this section of the exam.

Your overall composite score (ranging from 1 to 5) on the exam will take into account your performance on both the multiple-choice and free-response sections, with the multiple-choice section counting for twice as much. This means that two-thirds of your score depends on your performance on the multiple-choice questions, and the other one-third of your score is based on the quality of your essays.

Each year, the exact breakdown of the percentage of people who earn each score differs. More information on score breakdowns in past years is available from the College Board (see the College Board website: *www.collegeboard.org/ap*).

Diagnostic Test

This diagnostic test is designed to provide you with a realistic experience of what taking the multiple-choice section of the AP Psychology exam will be like. These items were written to accurately reflect the content represented on the AP Psychology exam, and the items are written at a difficulty level similar to items on the actual exam. In addition, you can analyze your correct and incorrect responses in order to decide how to allocate your study time. After you take this exam and score your responses, you can use the "Multiple-Choice Error Analysis Sheet" on page 33 to figure out what AP exam score your performance might correspond with, and which units of study you should focus on. Answer the following 100 multiple-choice items (remember to time yourself to make sure you stay within the 70-minute time limit!) and then use the scoring key.

ANSWER SHEET
Diagnostic Test

1. Ⓐ Ⓑ Ⓒ Ⓓ Ⓔ	26. Ⓐ Ⓑ Ⓒ Ⓓ Ⓔ	51. Ⓐ Ⓑ Ⓒ Ⓓ Ⓔ	76. Ⓐ Ⓑ Ⓒ Ⓓ Ⓔ
2. Ⓐ Ⓑ Ⓒ Ⓓ Ⓔ	27. Ⓐ Ⓑ Ⓒ Ⓓ Ⓔ	52. Ⓐ Ⓑ Ⓒ Ⓓ Ⓔ	77. Ⓐ Ⓑ Ⓒ Ⓓ Ⓔ
3. Ⓐ Ⓑ Ⓒ Ⓓ Ⓔ	28. Ⓐ Ⓑ Ⓒ Ⓓ Ⓔ	53. Ⓐ Ⓑ Ⓒ Ⓓ Ⓔ	78. Ⓐ Ⓑ Ⓒ Ⓓ Ⓔ
4. Ⓐ Ⓑ Ⓒ Ⓓ Ⓔ	29. Ⓐ Ⓑ Ⓒ Ⓓ Ⓔ	54. Ⓐ Ⓑ Ⓒ Ⓓ Ⓔ	79. Ⓐ Ⓑ Ⓒ Ⓓ Ⓔ
5. Ⓐ Ⓑ Ⓒ Ⓓ Ⓔ	30. Ⓐ Ⓑ Ⓒ Ⓓ Ⓔ	55. Ⓐ Ⓑ Ⓒ Ⓓ Ⓔ	80. Ⓐ Ⓑ Ⓒ Ⓓ Ⓔ
6. Ⓐ Ⓑ Ⓒ Ⓓ Ⓔ	31. Ⓐ Ⓑ Ⓒ Ⓓ Ⓔ	56. Ⓐ Ⓑ Ⓒ Ⓓ Ⓔ	81. Ⓐ Ⓑ Ⓒ Ⓓ Ⓔ
7. Ⓐ Ⓑ Ⓒ Ⓓ Ⓔ	32. Ⓐ Ⓑ Ⓒ Ⓓ Ⓔ	57. Ⓐ Ⓑ Ⓒ Ⓓ Ⓔ	82. Ⓐ Ⓑ Ⓒ Ⓓ Ⓔ
8. Ⓐ Ⓑ Ⓒ Ⓓ Ⓔ	33. Ⓐ Ⓑ Ⓒ Ⓓ Ⓔ	58. Ⓐ Ⓑ Ⓒ Ⓓ Ⓔ	83. Ⓐ Ⓑ Ⓒ Ⓓ Ⓔ
9. Ⓐ Ⓑ Ⓒ Ⓓ Ⓔ	34. Ⓐ Ⓑ Ⓒ Ⓓ Ⓔ	59. Ⓐ Ⓑ Ⓒ Ⓓ Ⓔ	84. Ⓐ Ⓑ Ⓒ Ⓓ Ⓔ
10. Ⓐ Ⓑ Ⓒ Ⓓ Ⓔ	35. Ⓐ Ⓑ Ⓒ Ⓓ Ⓔ	60. Ⓐ Ⓑ Ⓒ Ⓓ Ⓔ	85. Ⓐ Ⓑ Ⓒ Ⓓ Ⓔ
11. Ⓐ Ⓑ Ⓒ Ⓓ Ⓔ	36. Ⓐ Ⓑ Ⓒ Ⓓ Ⓔ	61. Ⓐ Ⓑ Ⓒ Ⓓ Ⓔ	86. Ⓐ Ⓑ Ⓒ Ⓓ Ⓔ
12. Ⓐ Ⓑ Ⓒ Ⓓ Ⓔ	37. Ⓐ Ⓑ Ⓒ Ⓓ Ⓔ	62. Ⓐ Ⓑ Ⓒ Ⓓ Ⓔ	87. Ⓐ Ⓑ Ⓒ Ⓓ Ⓔ
13. Ⓐ Ⓑ Ⓒ Ⓓ Ⓔ	38. Ⓐ Ⓑ Ⓒ Ⓓ Ⓔ	63. Ⓐ Ⓑ Ⓒ Ⓓ Ⓔ	88. Ⓐ Ⓑ Ⓒ Ⓓ Ⓔ
14. Ⓐ Ⓑ Ⓒ Ⓓ Ⓔ	39. Ⓐ Ⓑ Ⓒ Ⓓ Ⓔ	64. Ⓐ Ⓑ Ⓒ Ⓓ Ⓔ	89. Ⓐ Ⓑ Ⓒ Ⓓ Ⓔ
15. Ⓐ Ⓑ Ⓒ Ⓓ Ⓔ	40. Ⓐ Ⓑ Ⓒ Ⓓ Ⓔ	65. Ⓐ Ⓑ Ⓒ Ⓓ Ⓔ	90. Ⓐ Ⓑ Ⓒ Ⓓ Ⓔ
16. Ⓐ Ⓑ Ⓒ Ⓓ Ⓔ	41. Ⓐ Ⓑ Ⓒ Ⓓ Ⓔ	66. Ⓐ Ⓑ Ⓒ Ⓓ Ⓔ	91. Ⓐ Ⓑ Ⓒ Ⓓ Ⓔ
17. Ⓐ Ⓑ Ⓒ Ⓓ Ⓔ	42. Ⓐ Ⓑ Ⓒ Ⓓ Ⓔ	67. Ⓐ Ⓑ Ⓒ Ⓓ Ⓔ	92. Ⓐ Ⓑ Ⓒ Ⓓ Ⓔ
18. Ⓐ Ⓑ Ⓒ Ⓓ Ⓔ	43. Ⓐ Ⓑ Ⓒ Ⓓ Ⓔ	68. Ⓐ Ⓑ Ⓒ Ⓓ Ⓔ	93. Ⓐ Ⓑ Ⓒ Ⓓ Ⓔ
19. Ⓐ Ⓑ Ⓒ Ⓓ Ⓔ	44. Ⓐ Ⓑ Ⓒ Ⓓ Ⓔ	69. Ⓐ Ⓑ Ⓒ Ⓓ Ⓔ	94. Ⓐ Ⓑ Ⓒ Ⓓ Ⓔ
20. Ⓐ Ⓑ Ⓒ Ⓓ Ⓔ	45. Ⓐ Ⓑ Ⓒ Ⓓ Ⓔ	70. Ⓐ Ⓑ Ⓒ Ⓓ Ⓔ	95. Ⓐ Ⓑ Ⓒ Ⓓ Ⓔ
21. Ⓐ Ⓑ Ⓒ Ⓓ Ⓔ	46. Ⓐ Ⓑ Ⓒ Ⓓ Ⓔ	71. Ⓐ Ⓑ Ⓒ Ⓓ Ⓔ	96. Ⓐ Ⓑ Ⓒ Ⓓ Ⓔ
22. Ⓐ Ⓑ Ⓒ Ⓓ Ⓔ	47. Ⓐ Ⓑ Ⓒ Ⓓ Ⓔ	72. Ⓐ Ⓑ Ⓒ Ⓓ Ⓔ	97. Ⓐ Ⓑ Ⓒ Ⓓ Ⓔ
23. Ⓐ Ⓑ Ⓒ Ⓓ Ⓔ	48. Ⓐ Ⓑ Ⓒ Ⓓ Ⓔ	73. Ⓐ Ⓑ Ⓒ Ⓓ Ⓔ	98. Ⓐ Ⓑ Ⓒ Ⓓ Ⓔ
24. Ⓐ Ⓑ Ⓒ Ⓓ Ⓔ	49. Ⓐ Ⓑ Ⓒ Ⓓ Ⓔ	74. Ⓐ Ⓑ Ⓒ Ⓓ Ⓔ	99. Ⓐ Ⓑ Ⓒ Ⓓ Ⓔ
25. Ⓐ Ⓑ Ⓒ Ⓓ Ⓔ	50. Ⓐ Ⓑ Ⓒ Ⓓ Ⓔ	75. Ⓐ Ⓑ Ⓒ Ⓓ Ⓔ	100. Ⓐ Ⓑ Ⓒ Ⓓ Ⓔ

Diagnostic Test

PART I

1 Hour and 10 Minutes

DIRECTIONS: Each of the questions or incomplete statements below is followed by five suggested answers or completions. Select the one that is best in each case.

1. Rocco is a fun-loving, easygoing fellow. He rarely gets angry or upset and never seems to be in a rush. Rocco would best be described as having
   (A) an internal locus of control.
   (B) a Type B personality.
   (C) an Oedipus complex.
   (D) an introverted temperament.
   (E) self-actualized.

2. Tamil wants to see whether listening to Mozart will improve students' performance on geometry exams. It is most important that her experimental group consist of
   (A) students who already listen to Mozart.
   (B) students randomly assigned to listen to Mozart.
   (C) students randomly assigned not to listen to Mozart.
   (D) students who have already completed geometry.
   (E) students who have never studied geometry.

3. The space between the dendrites of one neuron and the terminal buttons of another is the
   (A) node of Ranvier.
   (B) axon.
   (C) medulla.
   (D) synapse.
   (E) myelin sheath.

4. Which of the following factors helps most to explain the increasing rate of obesity in the United States over the last 100 years?
   (A) the changing gene pool
   (B) the sedentary nature of modern jobs
   (C) the growth in popularity of the cities
   (D) the increase in the length of the workday
   (E) the lack of opportunities to exercise

5. Learned taste aversions generally result from
   (A) negative reinforcement.
   (B) shaping.
   (C) insight learning.
   (D) classical conditioning.
   (E) operant conditioning.

6. Creativity is most closely associated with
   (A) using algorithms.
   (B) divergent thinking.
   (C) functional fixedness.
   (D) excellent recall ability.
   (E) telegraphic speech.

7. Which theory of motivation best explains why some people enjoy dangerous hobbies such as skydiving and bungee jumping?
   (A) drive reduction theory
   (B) incentive theory
   (C) arousal theory
   (D) sociobiology
   (E) Maslow's hierarchy of needs

8. After finishing work on a big English project, Leo's room is a mess. His parents are furious and, without letting him explain, prohibit him from using his car or his cell phone for a month. Using this information, which parenting style are Leo's parents most likely using?
   (A) authoritative
   (B) indulgent
   (C) neglectful
   (D) authoritarian
   (E) democratic

9. Calinda is usually a hardworking, frugal single mother of two. Sometimes, however, she says her name is Meelo, a pop star, and instead of working she goes on spending sprees at local boutiques. On other occasions, she has been known to say that she is an eight-year-old boy named Curtis. Calinda's symptoms are most typical of
   (A) conversion disorder.
   (B) dissociative identity disorder.
   (C) schizophrenia.
   (D) post-traumatic stress disorder.
   (E) bipolar disorder.

10. Dr. Li thinks that Tony's anxiety is due primarily to unresolved issues with his mother from his youth. Dr. Li would best be labeled a
    (A) psychoanalyst.
    (B) biomedical psychologist.
    (C) behaviorist.
    (D) cognitive psychologist.
    (E) humanistic psychologist.

11. Which of the following types of approaches is used by the greatest number of clinical psychologists in the United States?
    (A) eclectic
    (B) psychodynamic
    (C) humanistic
    (D) client-centered
    (E) systematic desensitization

12. If Marie Curie, James Madison, and Mahatma Gandhi had all taken an intelligence test and scored poorly, most people would doubt that the test was
    (A) projective.
    (B) standardized.
    (C) valid.
    (D) normed.
    (E) reliable.

13. The easiest and most common technique used to gather information about people's personalities is by
    (A) administering projective tests.
    (B) observing people's behavior.
    (C) using brain scans.
    (D) asking people to fill out self-report inventories.
    (E) using free association and dream analysis.

14. Saluja decides she wants to try hanging out with a new group of friends. She used to be on the debate team but now tries out for the spring musical. Which of Erikson's stages is she most likely to be in?

(A) generativity versus stagnation
(B) intimacy versus isolation
(C) autonomy versus shame and doubt
(D) initiative versus guilt
(E) identity versus role confusion

15. Daniel is learning that five pennies spread out on his desk are the same number of coins as five pennies in a pile. According to Piaget, how old is Daniel likely to be?

(A) 1 year
(B) 2 years
(C) 4 years
(D) 8 years
(E) 13 years

16. Which part of the nervous system is most active in the exhaustion stage of Selye's GAS?

(A) somatic
(B) peripheral
(C) central
(D) parasympathetic
(E) sympathetic

17. Your knowledge of skills such as how to tie your shoes or ride a bicycle is thought to be stored in which part of the brain?

(A) hippocampus
(B) cerebral cortex
(C) medulla
(D) amygdala
(E) cerebellum

18. Zach is leaving for college and wants to teach his parents how to program their DVR before he goes. What reinforcement schedule would be the most effective to teach them this new skill?

(A) continuous reinforcement
(B) fixed ratio
(C) fixed interval
(D) variable ratio
(E) variable interval

19. Which of the following is an opiate?

(A) cocaine
(B) amphetamines
(C) heroin
(D) nicotine
(E) caffeine

20. Which structure is found in the middle ear?

(A) stirrup
(B) auditory nerve
(C) cochlea
(D) organ of Corti
(E) pinna

21. Mr. Kan is making soup. After tasting it, he decides it needs more salt and slowly adds some until he can first detect that the soup is saltier than it was before. The amount of salt Mr. Kan needs to add depends on his

(A) absolute threshold.
(B) perceptual set.
(C) difference threshold.
(D) olfactory sensitivity.
(E) gate-control theory.

22. Which type of scan uses X-ray technology to examine the structure of the brain?

(A) PET
(B) MRI
(C) CAT
(D) EEG
(E) fMRI

23. To safeguard participants' rights, prior to collecting any data, researchers are supposed to seek approval from

(A) the American Psychological Association.
(B) at least two licensed psychiatrists.
(C) an institutional review board.
(D) at least one psychiatrist and one psychologist.
(E) everyone on the research team.

DIAGNOSTIC TEST

24. Which of the following is the best example of basic research?

    (A) a first-grade teacher tests two different methods of teaching reading
    (B) a psychologist investigates how effective a new therapeutic approach is for treating phobias
    (C) a campaign manager commissions a poll to see how popular her candidate's stand on various issues is
    (D) a developmental psychologist explores how children's use of language changes as they age
    (E) a social psychologist studies how charities can convince people to donate more generously

25. An extra chromosome on the 21st pair is associated with

    (A) Alzheimer's disease.
    (B) Down syndrome.
    (C) Tay-Sachs disease.
    (D) Klinefelter's syndrome.
    (E) fetal alcohol syndrome.

26. Three-year-old Emma went to see a New York Yankees game in Yankee Stadium. From her seat in the bleachers, the players looked like tiny men, but as she walked toward the field, the players seemed to grow in size, as if by magic. Emma's belief that the men grew larger is best explained by

    (A) damage to her fovea.
    (B) place theory.
    (C) incomprehension about how to use the Gestalt principles of perception.
    (D) her inability to use binocular cues.
    (E) the fact that she is still developing size constancy.

27. Infants teach their parents to hold them a lot by crying whenever they are put down. When they are picked up, the babies stop crying. The parents are learning to pick up their babies via

    (A) insight learning.
    (B) positive reinforcement.
    (C) negative reinforcement.
    (D) latent learning.
    (E) punishment.

28. Which of the following sentences illustrates overgeneralization?

    (A) Toby is the fastest boy in the world.
    (B) Homey don't play that game.
    (C) Dani goed to the store.
    (D) Only human beings have the ability to used language.
    (E) All dogs have fur.

29. What theory suggests that using the term "girls" to refer to women might affect the way those people think about women?

    (A) the linguistic relativity hypothesis
    (B) social learning theory
    (C) the nativist theory of language
    (D) signal detection theory
    (E) arousal theory

30. Jenna invited Mari to a Ben Folds concert. Mari loves Ben Folds but loathes Jenna. What type of conflict is Mari experiencing?

    (A) approach-approach
    (B) avoidance-avoidance
    (C) approach-avoidance
    (D) multiple approach-avoidance
    (E) None, she should just go to the concert.

31. Wilhelm Wundt's early work led to the theory of

    (A) functionalism.
    (B) Gestalt psychology.
    (C) trephination.
    (D) repression.
    (E) structuralism.

32. Which type of personality theorist would most likely be criticized for underestimating the impact of the environment?

(A) trait
(B) behaviorist
(C) cognitive
(D) psychodynamic
(E) social-cognitive

33. Which of the following seems to be least heritable?

(A) hair color
(B) heart disease
(C) religious beliefs
(D) conscientiousness
(E) extraversion

34. Mohammed is trying to develop a test that will predict how great someone's potential is to be a prizefighter. This type of test would be best described as a (an)

(A) power test.
(B) speed test.
(C) achievement test.
(D) aptitude test.
(E) individual test.

35. Before you see a question on the AP Psychology exam, it is usually pretested on a group of college students taking an introductory course in psychology. This group of people are referred to as the

(A) standardization sample.
(B) validity testers.
(C) test population.
(D) basis for comparison.
(E) trial group.

36. Which of the following is a somatic symptom disorder?

(A) narcissistic personality disorder
(B) masochism
(C) generalized anxiety disorder
(D) psychogenic amnesia
(E) conversion disorder

37. Dr. Hernandez believes that poverty lies at the root of most of her inner-city clients' mental illnesses. This perspective is best labeled

(A) humanistic.
(B) sociocultural.
(C) biomedical.
(D) cognitive.
(E) behavioral.

38. A man calls Janie soliciting money for a charity that fights AIDS. He asks if they can count on Janie to contribute $100. Having never contributed to this charity before, Janie is taken aback by the amount and refuses. The representative of the charity then asks if Janie would be willing to make a $25 donation. What technique is the man representing the charity using?

(A) door-in-the-face
(B) lowballing
(C) norms of reciprocity
(D) self-fulfilling prophecy
(E) foot-in-the-door

39. Elsa hates her boss, but, in order to be successful at work, she goes out of her way to be nice to him. According to cognitive dissonance theory, Elsa's behavior is likely to

(A) make her resent her boss.
(B) lead her to displace her hostility onto others.
(C) cause her to work below her potential.
(D) result in more positive feelings about her boss.
(E) produce psychological problems in other aspects of her life.

40. ECT is most likely to be used to treat

(A) schizophrenia.
(B) phobias.
(C) depression.
(D) antisocial personality disorder.
(E) ECT is no longer an accepted medical treatment.

41. Which of the following types of therapies would be classified as insight therapy?
    (A) psychopharmacology
    (B) psychosurgery
    (C) flooding
    (D) token economy
    (E) client-centered therapy

42. Keela's car breaks down. A woman driving by would be most likely to help her
    (A) if the weather is bad.
    (B) if they are on a highly trafficked road.
    (C) if the driver is a highly religious woman.
    (D) if they are on a desolate country road.
    (E) if the driver is in a bad mood and can therefore sympathize with Keela.

43. Which of the following is a common symptom of depression?
    (A) eating more than usual
    (B) working harder than usual
    (C) abandoning old hobbies and picking up new ones
    (D) making a new group of friends
    (E) feeling closer to one's family

44. Kevin is hoping to find a mate who will love and support him despite all his faults. Carl Rogers might say that Kevin recognizes the importance of
    (A) narcissism.
    (B) reciprocal determinism.
    (C) thematic apperception.
    (D) self-actualization.
    (E) unconditional positive regard.

45. One drawback of cross-sectional research is that
    (A) differences between groups can be due to age or to cohort effects.
    (B) it takes a long time to complete this type of research.
    (C) participants are particularly likely to drop out during the study.
    (D) it is more expensive than most other kinds of research.
    (E) it is only effective with participants in certain socioeconomic strata.

46. Which of the following people demonstrates the most achievement motivation?
    (A) Joey is a carpenter who is anxious to find a life partner with whom to settle down.
    (B) Paula wants to make enough money as a doctor that she can work part-time and still support herself comfortably.
    (C) Nino works in an office-supply store. He frequently volunteers to come in early or stay late and prides himself on being a good worker.
    (D) Luther is in high school. He studies constantly because his parents give him $10 for every A he brings home, and Luther is saving up to buy a car.
    (E) Rula works 80 hours a week at a corporate law firm she hates because she needs to support her extravagant lifestyle.

47. Research has shown that gay and heterosexual men differ in that
    (A) homosexual men do not make good parents.
    (B) some of their brain structures differ in size.
    (C) heterosexual men are less likely to have suffered traumatic experiences as children.
    (D) the mothers of gay men are unusually domineering.
    (E) heterosexual men have more conflict with their parents.

48. In the past when Nuara's computer wouldn't print, she remedied the situation by restarting the computer. One day Nuara's printer came unplugged, but instead of checking the connections, she repeatedly restarted the computer. Nuara's behavior can best be explained by
    (A) proactive interference.
    (B) functional fixedness.
    (C) belief bias.
    (D) framing.
    (E) mental set.

49. According to the partial reinforcement effect,
   (A) highly desirable rewards are more effective than partial ones.
   (B) it is essentially impossible to find a reinforcer that influences everyone.
   (C) behaviors will be more resistant to extinction if they were reinforced intermittently.
   (D) punishment is most effective when it is divorced entirely from any signs of reinforcers.
   (E) people prefer certain types of reinforcement.

50. During a typical night of sleep, the average adult spends the most time in
   (A) stage 1.
   (B) stage 2.
   (C) stage 3.
   (D) stage 4.
   (E) REM.

51. Paul stared out the window as the train he was on raced through the countryside. He noticed that the telephone poles near the tracks seemed to fly by while the houses in the distance seemed to move slowly. This apparent difference in speed of movement is known as
   (A) texture gradient.
   (B) motion parallax.
   (C) stroboscopic motion.
   (D) the phi phenomenon.
   (E) relative speed.

52. In vision, the goal of accommodation is
   (A) to focus the image on the retina.
   (B) to maximize the amount of light that gets through the pupil.
   (C) to decrease the size of the blind spot.
   (D) to protect the lens.
   (E) to help the eyes rotate.

53. Farnaz randomly selected 50 new mothers to interview out of the 362 new mothers who gave birth in Random City's Central Hospital during the summer of 2011. What is Farnaz's population?
   (A) new mothers in Random City hospitals
   (B) new mothers in urban areas in the United States
   (C) new mothers throughout the world
   (D) the 50 new mothers with whom Farnaz speaks
   (E) the 362 new mothers at Central Hospital that summer

54. Sabrina finds a strong negative correlation between hours spent meditating and reported stress levels. Her findings indicate that
   (A) if a person meditates daily, she or he will not experience any stress.
   (B) people who meditate a lot tend to have higher stress levels.
   (C) meditation lowers stress levels in humans.
   (D) people with low stress levels meditate more than people with high stress levels.
   (E) the failure to meditate is a major cause of stress in humans.

55. In the early 20th century in the United States, which of the following perspectives was most prominent?
   (A) biological
   (B) behaviorist
   (C) psychoanalytic
   (D) Gestalt
   (E) cognitive

56. In which of the following groups would you expect to find the greatest standard deviation in IQ scores?
    (A) the graduating class of Princeton University
    (B) a special program for children who suffer from severe intellectual disability
    (C) elementary school students in a large public school system
    (D) the entering class of an elite preparatory school in India
    (E) girls who attend a small, single-sex private high school

57. Which of the following is a hormone?
    (A) dopamine
    (B) endorphins
    (C) insulin
    (D) GABA
    (E) acetylcholine

58. Gonzo raised his hand to answer his teacher's question. Which part of his nervous system most directly allowed him to perform this behavior?
    (A) parasympathetic
    (B) somatic
    (C) autonomic
    (D) sympathetic
    (E) central

59. Which part of the brain is most important in regulating an animal's sex drive?
    (A) amygdala
    (B) hypothalamus
    (C) pituitary gland
    (D) medulla
    (E) hippocampus

60. Five-year-old Olivia has never been outside of her neighborhood in New York City. Walking home from school one day, Olivia saw a cow standing in the middle of a cement ball field. To recognize the cow, Olivia most likely had to rely on
    (A) signal detection theory.
    (B) perceptual set.
    (C) bottom-up processing.
    (D) difference threshold.
    (E) brightness constancy.

61. After staring at a painting of a red and yellow parrot in a birdcage for a full minute, Saju turns his gaze to an empty birdcage painted on a white wall. What will he see in the empty cage?
    (A) the red and yellow parrot
    (B) a red and green parrot
    (C) a green and blue parrot
    (D) a blue and yellow parrot
    (E) nothing, just an empty cage

62. In Tolman's experiment on latent learning, latent learning was shown by
    (A) the rats whose performance declined steadily throughout the trials.
    (B) the rats whose progress improved steadily throughout the trials.
    (C) the rats whose progress improved markedly once a reward was introduced.
    (D) the rats whose progress declined markedly once a reward was introduced.
    (E) the rats whose progress never improved significantly.

63. According to the contingency theory of classical conditioning,
    (A) stronger URs result in better learning.
    (B) the more pleasant the CR, the more likely it will be learned.
    (C) the more times you pair a CS and US, the stronger the conditioning that will result.
    (D) people learn best when the US precedes the CS.
    (E) strength of conditioning depends on the extent to which the CS reliably predicts the US.

64. Which statement about memory is true?

(A) People can correctly gauge the accuracy of their memories.
(B) Children initially have accurate memories of their first few years of life but forget them as they age.
(C) Older people are worse at all types of memory tasks than are younger people.
(D) Memories are like stored video images.
(E) There is no one place in the brain where memories are stored.

65. Kelsey is an attractive 20-something with many friends. She is struggling to make a name for herself in Hollywood as an actress. Although she gets enough work to support herself, she does mostly commercials and small roles in minor films. Abraham Maslow would say that Kelsey is still striving to meet her need

(A) to self-actualize.
(B) for safety.
(C) for esteem.
(D) to belong.
(E) for power.

66. When a newborn baby is sleeping, which reflex will be elicited by a sudden noise or touch?

(A) Babinski
(B) plantar
(C) rooting
(D) Moro
(E) grasping

67. Kate, a newborn baby, probably most likes to look at

(A) her cousin's toy robot.
(B) pastel colored blocks.
(C) her stuffed sheep.
(D) cartoons on television.
(E) her own face.

68. Roscoe works for a nasty and abusive boss but tells everyone what a wonderful woman she is. Psychoanalysts would say that Roscoe is using which of the following defense mechanisms?

(A) displacement
(B) reaction formation
(C) projection
(D) sublimation
(E) intellectualization

69. In a normal distribution, approximately what percentage of people's scores fall between the *z* scores of -2 and $+2$?

(A) 25
(B) 50
(C) 75
(D) 82
(E) 95

70. The typical age of onset for schizophrenia is

(A) at birth.
(B) during childhood.
(C) during young adulthood.
(D) during middle age.
(E) after age 70.

71. Research suggests that genetic and other biological factors play the greatest role in causing

(A) simple phobias.
(B) agoraphobia.
(C) dissociative identity disorder.
(D) bipolar disorder.
(E) conversion disorder.

72. Armand is the president of his local chapter of the National Rifle Association (NRA). He incorrectly believes that only a tiny fringe element of Americans favor stronger gun control laws. Armand's mistake is best explained by

(A) deindividuation.
(B) the just-world bias.
(C) norms of reciprocity.
(D) the false consensus effect.
(E) outgroup bias.

73. Dr. Lupin challenges her depressed clients' beliefs that their lives are hopeless and without purpose and gives them homework assignments in which the clients are required to engage in the activities that used to bring them joy. What type of therapy is Dr. Lupin using?

    (A) existential
    (B) rational emotive behavior therapy
    (C) Gestalt
    (D) psychoanalytic
    (E) modeling

74. Milgram's obedience studies showed that

    (A) members of minority groups were better able to stand up to authority figures than Caucasians.
    (B) absolute obedience was best achieved under explicit threats.
    (C) most people would obey an authority figure's order to harm a stranger.
    (D) people would follow orders up to a point but almost all refused to do something illegal or immoral.
    (E) women are far more obedient than men are.

75. If Artie always seems to act competitively, even in situations where others do not, people are likely to make what kind of attribution about the cause of Artie's competitiveness?

    (A) fundamental
    (B) situation-stable
    (C) situation-unstable
    (D) person-stable
    (E) person-unstable

76. Which of the following is one of the main advantages of group therapy?

    (A) The client develops lasting friendships with all the other members of the group.
    (B) The success rate of group therapy is higher.
    (C) It reduces the financial burden of therapy.
    (D) Group therapists generally have more years of training than individual therapists.
    (E) The therapy usually takes less time.

77. Tom is a Type A individual who is seeking short-term, focused psychotherapy to help him make his lifestyle healthier. With what kind of therapist do you think Tom would be happiest?

    (A) behaviorist
    (B) psychodynamic
    (C) sociocultural
    (D) humanistic
    (E) somatic

78. Which of the following is an example of hostile aggression?

    (A) Billy shoots a deer in order to feed his family supper.
    (B) Joe beats up a man at an ATM because he wants to steal his money.
    (C) Lula screams at her cat to scare him off the kitchen table.
    (D) Tutti hits her younger brother because she's angry at her mother.
    (E) Mike pushes another man out of the way to grab the shirt he wants off the sale rack.

79. According to Howard Gardner, which of the following is a type of intelligence?

    (A) naturalist
    (B) practical
    (C) experiential
    (D) fluid
    (E) general

80. Dr. Kraysin rejects the Big Five model of personality because she believes that people are so different it is impossible to describe them all with a common set of traits. What kind of trait theory would Dr. Kraysin favor?

(A) cognitive
(B) psychodynamic
(C) idiographic
(D) sociocultural
(E) individual

81. Drinking alcohol while pregnant increases the chance that the child

(A) will be born with an addiction to alcohol.
(B) will have a low birth weight.
(C) will suffer from intellectual disability.
(D) will grow up to be a drug dealer.
(E) will have heart disease.

82. Supporters of attachment parenting argue that babies like to be held all the time and that parents should seek to maximize the amount of physical contact they have with their babies. Such research is most in line with the findings of

(A) Gilligan.
(B) Piaget.
(C) Harlow.
(D) Freud.
(E) Kohlberg.

83. Isabella fondly remembers the first time she went skydiving. This information is an example of

(A) declarative memory.
(B) semantic memory.
(C) implicit memory.
(D) eidetic memory.
(E) procedural memory.

84. According to the James-Lange theory of emotion

(A) a specific physiological reaction to an event triggers the recognition of a specific emotion.
(B) the thalamus is the key part of the brain involved in emotion.
(C) an initial emotion leads to the expression of the antagonistic emotion and that second emotion grows stronger with repetition.
(D) emotions are expressed the same way across different cultures.
(E) different emotions result from different interpretations of similar physiological responses.

85. Which of the following is an example of observational learning?

(A) a girl learns to howl by watching wolves on a television show
(B) a parrot learns to say "mama" by listening to its owner
(C) a student learns to type through the process of trial and error
(D) a kitten learns to chase birds by copying its mother
(E) a boy learns to make his bed after his parents reward him with money

86. Which of the following is an example of discrimination?

(A) Jessica continues to talk during class even after being publicly reprimanded by the teacher.
(B) Melissa has learned to dig for earthworms only after it rains.
(C) Franz always bounces the basketball three times before shooting a free throw.
(D) After his father yells at and punishes him, Helmut winces when he hears a man yell on television.
(E) Mr. Black wants his students to call him by his first name and not to raise their hands. Weeks into the semester after having given up these habits, some of Mr. Black's students still occasionally raise their hands.

87. In a normal distribution,

(A) 95 percent of the scores fall within one standard deviation of the mean.
(B) everyone scores within three standard deviations of the mean.
(C) the mean is always greater than the median.
(D) the mean, median, and mode are all equal.
(E) the standard deviation is always less than 1.0.

88. When a neuron initially depolarizes,

(A) sodium ions flow into the cell.
(B) chloride ions flow into the cell.
(C) magnesium ions flow into the cell.
(D) potassium ions flow out of the cell.
(E) strontium ions flow out of the cell.

89. The part of the brain most responsible for making decisions is the

(A) thalamus.
(B) amygdala.
(C) hippocampus.
(D) prefrontal cortex.
(E) corpus callosum.

90. Which of the following cognitive tendencies is most closely related to the problem of experimenter bias?

(A) the availability heuristic
(B) functional fixedness
(C) the representative heuristic
(D) confirmation bias
(E) overconfidence

91. As Mobu walked to homeroom, he passed dozens of his classmates in the hallway. What they were wearing that day was briefly in Mobu's

(A) short-term memory.
(B) iconic memory.
(C) long-term memory.
(D) echoic memory.
(E) working memory.

92. Tiger lilies appear orange because they

(A) reflect orange light.
(B) absorb orange light.
(C) transduce orange light.
(D) reflect red light and absorb yellow light.
(E) reflect yellow light and absorb red light.

93. Your knowledge of who the first president of the United States was is usually found in which level of your consciousness?

(A) conscious
(B) nonconscious
(C) preconscious
(D) subconscious
(E) unconscious

94. Karl is so consumed by his fears of sexual inadequacy that he has not been on a date in over two years. To which of the following would a psychoanalyst be most likely to attribute Karl's problem?

(A) an overly strong libido
(B) the reality principle
(C) the preconscious
(D) an anal expulsive personality
(E) a phallic fixation

95. Banu scored 130 on the WISC. What is his z score and approximately what percentile is he in?

(A) −2, 2nd
(B) −2, 16th
(C) 0, 50th
(D) 2, 90th
(E) 2, 98th

96. Which of the following is a positive symptom of schizophrenia?

(A) flat affect
(B) greater sensitivity toward others
(C) catatonia
(D) reduced depression
(E) hallucinations

97. Broca's area is usually located in which part of the cortex?

(A) left frontal lobe
(B) right frontal lobe
(C) left temporal lobe
(D) right temporal lobe
(E) right parietal lobe

98. Dr. Soo is a psychiatrist who wants to prescribe a drug for one of her patients who is suffering from GAD. Which of the following drugs is she most likely to prescribe?

(A) tricyclic antidepressants
(B) Thorazine
(C) Haldol
(D) lithium
(E) Valium

99. One possible explanation for group polarization is

(A) outgroup bias.
(B) self-fulfilling prophecy.
(C) self-serving bias.
(D) the fundamental attribution error.
(E) diffusion of responsibility.

100. Which is typical of a positively skewed distribution?

(A) The mean is higher than the median.
(B) The mean is lower than the median.
(C) There are more high scores than low scores.
(D) The mode is higher than the median but lower than the mean.
(E) The mode is lower than the median but higher than the mean.

PART II

50 minutes

DIRECTIONS: You have 50 minutes to answer the *two* questions that follow. Your answer should present an argument rather than a list of facts. Make sure to incorporate psychological terminology into your answers whenever possible.

1. Professor Willborn recently completed a naturalistic observation study on people who play violent video games. She submitted her work for publication and one of the reviewers suggested that she further investigate the relationship between violent video games and attitudes toward real-world violence using a different research method. Professor Willborn is considering using the experimental method or the correlational method for the follow-up study. Answer the following questions about **both** research methods:
   - What variables would Professor Willborn examine in her experimental study? What variables would Professor Willborn examine in her correlational study? (Use specific terminology associated with the variables if appropriate.)
   - How could Professor Willborn operationally define at least one of the variables in her experimental study? How could Professor Willborn operationally define at least one of the variables in her correlational study? (Do not define the same variable for both methods.)
   - How could Professor Willborn organize her participants to gather data in her experimental study? How could Professor Willborn organize her participants to gather data in her correlational study?
   - What kind of conclusion would Professor Willborn be able to form based on the results of her experimental study? What kind of conclusion would Professor Willborn be able to form based on the results of her correlational study?

2. One of the important contributions of psychology has been to identify aspects of thinking and experiences outside of conscious awareness. Define each of the terms below *and* provide an example showing how each concept describes an influence on behavior that people are not consciously aware of.
   - Selective attention
   - Cognitive dissonance
   - Fundamental attribution error
   - Perceptual set
   - Sensory memory

ANSWER KEY
Diagnostic Test

Part I

1. **B**	26. **E**	51. **B**	76. **C**
2. **B**	27. **C**	52. **A**	77. **A**
3. **D**	28. **C**	53. **E**	78. **D**
4. **B**	29. **A**	54. **D**	79. **A**
5. **D**	30. **C**	55. **B**	80. **C**
6. **B**	31. **E**	56. **C**	81. **C**
7. **C**	32. **A**	57. **C**	82. **C**
8. **D**	33. **C**	58. **B**	83. **A**
9. **B**	34. **D**	59. **B**	84. **A**
10. **A**	35. **A**	60. **C**	85. **D**
11. **A**	36. **E**	61. **C**	86. **B**
12. **C**	37. **B**	62. **C**	87. **D**
13. **D**	38. **A**	63. **E**	88. **A**
14. **E**	39. **D**	64. **E**	89. **D**
15. **D**	40. **C**	65. **C**	90. **D**
16. **D**	41. **E**	66. **D**	91. **B**
17. **E**	42. **D**	67. **E**	92. **A**
18. **A**	43. **A**	68. **B**	93. **C**
19. **C**	44. **E**	69. **E**	94. **E**
20. **A**	45. **A**	70. **C**	95. **E**
21. **C**	46. **C**	71. **D**	96. **E**
22. **C**	47. **B**	72. **D**	97. **A**
23. **C**	48. **E**	73. **B**	98. **E**
24. **D**	49. **C**	74. **C**	99. **E**
25. **B**	50. **B**	75. **D**	100. **A**

ANSWERS EXPLAINED

Part I

1. **(B)** Being easygoing, slow to anger, and relaxed are qualities of a Type B personality. If Rocco had an internal locus of control he would believe that he controls what happens to him. The Oedipus complex is the Freudian idea that boys desire their mothers and see their fathers as rivals for their mothers' love. Temperament is one's inborn style of relating to the world, and someone with an introverted temperament would be shy, unlike Rocco. Maslow and other humanistic theorists believe people have self-actualized when they have reached their full potentials.

2. **(B)** The experimental group is the one that gets the treatment involved in the independent variable; therefore, the group that listens to Mozart is the experimental group. It doesn't matter whether the experimental group already listens to Mozart or has studied geometry so long as students are randomly assigned to the experimental and control groups.

3. **(D)** The space between two neurons is called the synapse. The nodes of Ranvier and myelin sheath both help increase the speed of neural transmission. Myelin is a fatty substance that insulates the axon, and the nodes of Ranvier are gaps between sections of myelin over which the impulse can jump. The axon carries the impulse between the soma and terminal branches. The medulla is the part of the brain that regulates involuntary behaviors such as breathing and heart rate.

4. **(B)** Jobs in the early 21st century are far more likely to involve sitting at a desk than they were 100 years ago, making it more difficult to burn calories at work. Significant changes in the gene pool are unlikely. Urban areas have not markedly increased in popularity, and people who live in cities tend to walk more than people who live in suburban areas. Working longer hours doesn't make people gain weight, and there are an ever-increasing number of ways to exercise.

5. **(D)** A learned taste aversion typically occurs when a novel taste (CS) is paired with an unpleasant reaction such as nausea (US). Negative reinforcement and shaping are terms generally associated with operant conditioning (learning by associating one's behaviors with certain consequences). Insight learning typically occurs when one has a sudden realization about how to solve a problem.

6. **(B)** Divergent thinking is a term frequently associated with creativity. While convergent thinking involves the pursuit of one answer to a problem, often in a particular way, divergent thinking promotes more open-ended, innovative thought. Algorithms are formulaic approaches to problem-solving that guarantee correct answers. Functional fixedness, the inability to think of a novel use for an object, is an obstacle to creativity. Having excellent recall ability is not necessarily related to being creative. Telegraphic speech, also known as the two-word stage of language, is common around age two.

7. **(C)** Arousal theory suggests that some people who have a high optimal level of arousal would pursue dangerous activities like skydiving. The other theories of motivation have difficulty explaining such actions.

8. **(D)** Authoritarian parents tend to make harsh rules and implement them without exception. Authoritative parents are more flexible with the creation and implementation of rules; this style of parenting has also been termed "democratic." Indulgent and neglectful parents typically eschew rules, the former because they want to be kind and the latter because they don't pay enough attention to their children's needs.

9. **(B)** Calinda may suffer from dissociative identity disorder, formerly known as "multiple personality disorder." This disorder, while questioned by some, manifests itself in breaks in consciousness and memory as the sufferer shifts from one personality to another. Conversion disorder is a type of somatoform disorder in which someone complains of a physical problem (e.g., deafness) for which no organic cause can be found. Schizophrenia, often confused with dissociative identity disorder, does not involve multiple personalities. Rather, someone with schizophrenia suffers from profoundly disordered thought. Post-traumatic stress disorder is an anxiety disorder that typically plagues people who have experienced tragic events like wars and natural disasters. Bipolar disorder is a type of affective disorder in which people alternate between periods of mania and depression.

10. **(A)** Psychoanalysts stress the pivotal role of childhood experiences and how they can manifest themselves later as anxiety and other types of problems. Biomedical psychologists are more likely to focus on the importance of biological factors such as hormones and neurotransmitters. Behaviorists believe that experience would have an important impact on anxiety, but they would not credit events from one's youth as being particularly powerful. Cognitive psychologists emphasize the influence of the way people process information, while humanistic psychologists stress the effect of people's needs and how they feel about themselves.

11. **(A)** Most clinicians are eclectic, meaning that they draw from a number of different perspectives.

12. **(C)** Since Curie, Madison, and Gandhi are all thought of as intelligent, an intelligence test on which they scored poorly would be criticized as lacking validity. A test that lacks validity does not test what it is supposed to test. Projective tests are typically used by psychodynamic psychologists to measure personality. It is possible for a test to be standardized, normed, and reliable, but still not valid.

13. **(D)** The easiest and most common technique used to measure personality is a self-report inventory. Self-report inventories are typically questionnaires on which people answer close-ended questions. Some of the other methods are more difficult to employ (e.g., observing behavior and using brain scans). Projective tests, free association, and dream analysis are used mainly by psychoanalysts.

14. **(E)** Saluja is probably in the identity versus role confusion stage during which adolescents try on a variety of roles in an effort to define themselves. The other choices are all stages that Erikson proposed occur at other times during one's life.

15. **(D)** Daniel is learning conservation of number, a skill that Piaget believed children learn in the concrete operational stage (ages 8–12).

16. **(D)** Selye's GAS (general adaptation syndrome) consists of three stages: alarm, resistance, and exhaustion. If a stressor wears a person out, she or he reaches exhaustion and the parasympathetic nervous system returns the body to homeostasis.

17. **(E)** Procedural knowledge, your knowledge of how to perform skills such as tying your shoes, is thought to be stored in the cerebellum.

18. **(A)** It is easier for people and animals to learn new things when they are reinforced continuously. If something is reinforced every time, it is easier to form a link between the action and its consequences. Partial reinforcement schedules, however, are more resistant to extinction.

19. **(C)** Heroin is an opiate. Opiates are drugs that relieve pain. All the other drugs listed are stimulants.

20. **(A)** The stirrup is one of the ossicles, the three bones in the middle ear. The auditory nerve connects the cochlea to the brain. The cochlea is the structure in the inner ear in which the organ of Corti can be found. The pinna is the fleshy part of the outer ear.

21. **(C)** Difference threshold, or just-noticeable difference, is the amount a stimulus needs to be changed in order for a person to detect a difference. Absolute threshold is the smallest amount of a stimulus necessary for one to detect its presence. If you were to add salt to a plain glass of water until someone could first taste it, you would be testing absolute threshold. Since the soup already had some salt, this question is about difference threshold.

22. **(C)** A CAT or CT scan uses X-rays taken from 180 different angles to create a computerized image that can depict the structure of the brain. MRIs can also show the structure of the brain, but they do so by using magnetic fields. An even more advanced technology is the fMRI, which uses magnetic fields to show both structure and function. EEGs show brain function by measuring electrical activity, and PET scans show brain function by measuring the metabolism of glucose.

23. **(C)** The purpose of institutional review boards (IRBs) is to make sure researchers treat participants ethically. All research conducted at registered research institutions and/or intended for publication must be approved by an IRB prior to any interaction with participants. None of the other people or groups listed in the choices would be permitted to stand in as a replacement.

24. **(D)** Basic research, as opposed to applied research, seeks to expand knowledge without a clear practical use. Choices A, B, C, and E all have clear, intended applications. Although learning about how children's use of language changes could yield knowledge that would ultimately have a practical impact, such an application is not its immediate goal.

25. **(B)** Down syndrome is caused by an extra chromosome on the 21st pair. Klinefelter's syndrome results when a boy has an extra X chromosome (XXY). Alzheimer's and Tay-Sachs are due to genetic (not chromosomal) abnormalities. Fetal alcohol syndrome is caused by a mother drinking alcohol during her pregnancy.

26. **(E)** We know that when objects get closer to us they do not grow larger because, through experience, we have learned size constancy. Damage to the fovea would impair vision, and an inability to use binocular cues would limit depth perception. The Gestalt principles of perception (e.g., similarity, proximity) are thought to be inborn. Place theory is a theory about how we recognize pitch.

27. **(C)** Negative reinforcement is when a behavior (e.g., picking up a baby) is strengthened because it results in the removal of an aversive stimulus (e.g., crying). Insight learning, in this case, would involve parents suddenly realizing that holding their babies is a good thing. Positive reinforcement is when a behavior is strengthened by the addition of a pleasant stimulus; if babies applauded their parents when picked up, they would be positively reinforcing them. Latent learning is learning that occurs in the absence of reinforcement. Punishment is when a behavior becomes less likely due to the addition of an unpleasant stimulus; if we rephrased the question and asked how the parents were learning to avoid putting their babies down, the answer would be punishment.

28. **(C)** According to Noam Chomsky, children's innate language acquisition device enables them to decode grammatical rules amazingly quickly. Sometimes, in the process, they apply the rules when it is incorrect to do so; that is, they overgeneralize. A child who understands the idea that the past tense in English is often denoted by the addition of *-ed* therefore might add *-ed* to irregular verbs like *go*.

29. **(A)** Whorf's linguistic relativity hypothesis holds that language influences (or, in its initial pronouncement, determines) thought. Therefore, referring to women as "girls" could affect the way people think about women. Bandura's social learning theory explains how people learn by modeling the behavior of others. The nativist theory of language refers to Chomsky's school of belief that human beings are wired in such a way that we learn language quickly and easily. Signal detection is a perceptual theory and arousal theory has to do with motivation.

30. **(C)** An approach-avoidance conflict is when one is attracted to and repelled by different features of the same thing. In this case, Mari is attracted to the idea of seeing Ben Folds but repelled by spending the evening with Jenna. In an approach-approach conflict, one must choose between two attractive alternatives. In an avoidance-avoidance conflict, one must choose between two unattractive alternatives. In a multiple approach-avoidance conflict, one must choose between several options, each of which has an attractive and unattractive feature.

31. **(E)** Wundt's goal was to identify the basic cognitive structures people used; hence, his theory is known as *structuralism*. William James's theory of functionalism turned attention to how these structures function in our lives. Gestalt psychology focused on the importance of the whole. Trephination was an ancient practice of putting holes in people's skulls in order to let evil spirits escape. Repression is a key part of Freudian theory.

32. **(A)** Trait theorists contend that personality is the expression of a person's established characteristics, an explanation that makes it difficult to explain the effect that different situations can have on behavior. Behaviorists, conversely, stress the impact of the environment, and cognitive psychologists emphasize the role of one's way of thinking. Social-cognitive theorists believe that the interaction between environment and cognition gives rise to personality. Finally, psychodynamic theorists emphasize the role of unconscious processes and early childhood experiences.

33. **(C)** Heritability refers to the extent to which the variation of a factor in the population can be explained by genetic differences. Physical traits (e.g., hair color) tend to be more heritable than personality traits (e.g., conscientiousness) and there is virtually no evidence that attitudes (e.g., religious beliefs) are heritable at all.

34. **(D)** A test that measures potential is an aptitude test. A power test is comprised of items in increasing level of difficulty and is intended to ascertain the highest level at which one can perform, whereas a speed test contains many easy items and is meant to discern how fast one can solve the problems. Achievement tests measure what someone has learned. Individual tests, as opposed to group tests, are given to one person at a time.

35. **(A)** A standardization sample is a group of people who take a test to help establish norms and therefore standardize it. Introductory psychology students in college are thought to be similar to the high school students taking AP Psychology, so their performance is used to standardize the test. The other choices are made-up distractors.

36. **(E)** Somatoform disorders are marked by physical complaints in the absence of physical causes. A diagnosis of conversion disorder typically results when no organic (physical) cause can be found for a physical complaint such as paralysis of a limb, blindness, or deafness. Narcissistic personality disorder is, not surprisingly, a type of personality disorder; masochism is a paraphilia; generalized anxiety disorder is classified as an anxiety disorder; and psychogenic amnesia is a type of dissociative disorder.

37. **(B)** Dr. Hernandez's belief that poverty can help trigger mental illness emphasizes the role of society and culture in psychological illness. Humanistic psychologists stress the importance of fulfilling one's needs, biomedical psychologists focus on the impact of neurochemicals, cognitive psychologists put primacy on the influence of how one thinks, and behaviorists emphasize the effect of the environment.

38. **(A)** Door-in-the-face is a compliance technique in which one begins with a request that is likely to be perceived as too large and follows up with a smaller request that will surely be seen as more reasonable. Lowballing is when unattractive features of a decision are hidden until after someone agrees. Norms of reciprocity is the idea that people feel obliged to treat others as those others have treated them. Self-fulfilling prophecy is when one person's expectations of someone else elicit behavioral confirmation in the second person. Foot-in-the-door is when one asks first for a trivial favor and then follows up with a larger request. That people acquiesce to the small favor makes it more likely that they will say "yes" to the more substantial second request.

39. **(D)** Cognitive dissonance theory posits that it is stressful to hold a thought (e.g., I hate my boss) that contradicts one's actions (e.g., I am really nice to my boss). The stress motivates people to reduce the dissonance by bringing their beliefs into line with their actions. Therefore, since Elsa cannot change her behavior, she is likely to change her beliefs about her boss.

40. **(C)** ECT (electroconvulsive therapy) is most commonly used to treat depression. In some patients, severe depression that has not responded to drug therapy has been found to be relieved by ECT.

41. **(E)** Client-centered therapy is a type of humanistic therapy pioneered by Carl Rogers. Humanistic therapies emphasize the importance of the clients' understanding of their problems, insight, and free will to change. Somatic therapies like psychopharmacology and psychosurgery, and behaviorist techniques like flooding and token economies, do not depend on or value the clients' insights.

42. **(D)** Bystander intervention studies have shown that the fewer people around, the more likely it is that someone will help another person in need. One reason posited for this phenomenon is diffusion of responsibility, the idea that when others are present, any single person experiences a decreased feeling of responsibility to help. Interestingly, religious beliefs have not been found to predict helping behavior. People are more likely to help, however, when they are in good moods, an idea known as the "feel-good, do-good phenomenon."

43. **(A)** One of the most common symptoms of depression is a disruption in eating habits, either by eating too much or eating too little. When depressed, people tend to lose interest in almost anything—work, hobbies, friends, and even family.

44. **(E)** Rogers asserted that we all need unconditional positive regard; unconditional positive regard comes from people whose love and support is not conditional on our behaving a particular way. Narcissism means self-love. Reciprocal determinism is Bandura's theory that people's traits, environments, and behaviors interact to shape their personalities. Thematic apperception is the name of a projective personality test. Self-actualization is Maslow's idea that people strive to be the best they can be.

45. **(A)** Cross-sectional research seeks to identify the impact of aging by comparing different age groups at the same time. However, while it is possible that 20-year-olds and 50-years-olds differ due to the number of years they have been alive, it is also possible that differences between the groups are due to the experience of growing up at the time that they did; such differences are known as cohort effects. Choices B, C, and D are drawbacks to longitudinal research, and the effectiveness of cross-sectional research does not seem to be linked to the socioeconomic background of the participants.

46. **(C)** Achievement motivation is typically defined as a person's drive to be successful in work or school. Achievement motivation is more closely linked to how good a job one seeks to do than to the type of job (e.g., doctor) that one has. People with high achievement seek to do their best, not merely to make money or gain other extrinsic rewards, but because they want to challenge themselves.

47. **(B)** Simon LeVay's research has shown that a group of cells in the hypothalamus of heterosexual men is typically larger than the cluster in gay men, while part of the corpus callosum in gay men is typically larger than the same area in heterosexual men. Recent studies have debunked the myths that gay men and lesbians do not make good parents, were likely to have been abused as children, and that gay men have domineering mothers.

48. **(E)** Our tendency to approach problems in ways that have been successful for us in the past is known as mental set. Proactive interference is when something we learned first interferes with our ability to remember something we learned later. Functional fixedness is the tendency to overlook novel uses for items we are accustomed to using in a particular way. Belief bias is when people's preexisting beliefs interfere with their logical reasoning. Framing is the finding that the way in which the same information is presented can impact the way we perceive it.

49. **(C)** The partial reinforcement effect is the idea that behaviors reinforced intermittently, as opposed to continuously, will be more resistant to extinction as it will be more difficult to unlearn the connection between behavior and reinforcement.

50. **(B)** People spend approximately 50 percent of their time asleep in stage 2. Approximately 25 percent is spent in REM, 20 percent in deep sleep (stages 3 and 4), and only about 5 percent in stage 1.

51. **(B)** Motion parallax is a depth cue. Nearby objects appear to move faster as we pass them than do objects that are far away. Texture gradient is also a depth cue; we can see more texture in objects that are close by than in those that are far away. Stroboscopic motion is what movies use to create the appearance of motion. The phi phenomenon explains why we perceive the light in a movie marquee or traffic sign as moving. Relative speed is a made-up distractor.

52. **(A)** Accommodation is the process by which the lens changes shape (flattens or thickens) to focus an image on the retina.

53. **(E)** The population is every case that could have been included in the study. Only the 362 new mothers who gave birth at Central Hospital could possibly have been selected. The 50 mothers with whom Farnaz speaks is the sample, not the population.

54. **(D)** A correlation shows a relationship but not necessarily a cause-and-effect relationship. Therefore, choices C and E are incorrect. A negative correlation is when the presence of one variable (e.g., hours spent meditating) predicts the absence of a second variable (e.g., stress); therefore, choice D is correct, and choice B is incorrect. Finally, choice A is wrong for several reasons including that it does not suggest an inverse relationship between the variables and that when research is done on a group of people, one cannot infer anything about particular individuals.

55. **(B)** During the early 1900s in the United States, behaviorism was the dominant psychological perspective. More recently, with technological advances that have made it possible to study the internal workings of the body and mind, the biological and cognitive perspectives have become increasingly prominent. Psychoanalytic psychology's heyday was around the turn of the 20th century, but it never achieved the prominence in the United States that it had in Europe. Gestalt psychology originated in Germany in the late 19th century.

56. **(C)** Standard deviation is measure of variability. The greater the standard deviation, the more varied or diverse the group. We would expect a lot of variability in the IQ scores of students in a large public school system. Conversely, we would expect all the other groups to have less variability as they are narrower groups who are unlikely to differ from one another as much in terms of IQ.

57. **(C)** Insulin is a hormone secreted by the pancreas and used to turn glucose in the bloodstream into glycogen in the liver. Dopamine, endorphins, GABA, and acetylcholine are all neurotransmitters.

58. **(B)** Raising your hand to answer a question is a voluntary motor movement controlled by the somatic nervous system. The parasympathetic and sympathetic systems are the two parts of the autonomic nervous system; they control involuntary functions such as heart rate and digestion. The central nervous system includes the brain and spinal cord. Although they would have played a role in telling Gonzo to raise his hand, taking that action was ultimately enabled by the motor neurons in his somatic system.

59. **(B)** The hypothalamus controls motivated behaviors such as eating and having sex. The amygdala is important in fear and other emotions. The pituitary gland is the master gland of the endocrine system. The medulla is the part of the brain that regulates involuntary processes like breathing. The hippocampus is important in memory.

60. **(C)** Bottom-up processing is when an object is perceived only by examining the object itself. Signal detection theory and perceptual set are theories about how one's expectations and past experiences can impact perception. Since Olivia's experience is limited to the concrete jungle of New York City where cows are unusual and she saw the cow in a place one would not have expected to see a cow, her perception of the cow would have relied on bottom-up processing. Difference threshold is the amount a stimulus needs to change in order for someone to perceive that it has changed. Brightness constancy is our knowledge that the relative brightness of objects stays the same even as the level of overhead illumination changes.

61. **(C)** The opponent process theory of color vision explains that some of the cells that help us to see color are organized in opponent pairs: red and green, blue and yellow, black and white. If we fatigue one half of the pair and then look at a white surface that reflects all wavelengths of light, we will see an image in the opponent colors (a negative color afterimage). Hence, the red of the original parrot is seen as green and the yellow appears blue.

62. **(C)** Latent learning is learning that occurs in the absence of a reward even though it may not be evidenced until a reward is present. Tolman had three groups of rats: one that was rewarded every time they finished a maze, one that was never rewarded, and one that was only rewarded on the second half of the trials. Tolman found that this third group performed like the unrewarded group until the reward was introduced and then showed a tremendous improvement as soon as they could earn a reward. He concluded that the rats had learned during the first half of the trials but simply not had any reason to hurry to finish the maze since there was no reward; thus, their learning had been latent or hidden.

63. **(E)** Rescorla's contingency theory of classical conditioning modified the original contiguity theory by saying that learning didn't simply depend on the number of times a CS and US were paired but rather the degree to which the CS reliably predicted the US. The US can be said to be contingent upon the CS when the CS reliably predicts the US.

64. **(E)** Memories are stored all over the brain, which casts doubt on recent movies in which people can get unpleasant memories erased. People do not have a good sense of whether or not their memories are accurate. Young children's brains are not developed enough to form clear, explicit memories. Older people are worse than young people at some types of memory tasks (such as recall tasks), but not all; remember, exercise caution before choosing extreme answer choices that contain words like *all.* Contrary to what many people believe, memories are not like video images we can replay at will; rather, we may reconstruct and alter them each time we recall them to mind.

65. **(C)** Maslow's hierarchy of needs begins with physiological needs, and then moves to safety needs, belongingness needs, esteem needs, and, finally, self-actualization. Since Kelsey can support herself and lives in a relatively safe place, the first two levels of need are probably fulfilled. Her many friends probably fulfill her need to belong. Kelsey is struggling to make a name for herself as an actress, which reflects a need to achieve something and be respected; these are esteem needs.

66. **(D)** The Moro reflex is also known as the startle reflex. The Babinski reflex is babies' tendency to spread their toes when the bottom of the foot is scratched; the plantar reflex is the opposite tendency in adults. The rooting reflex is when, in response to feeling a touch to its cheek, a baby will turn its head to find a nipple. Grasping is when the infant will curl its finger around an object placed in its palm.

67. **(E)** Newborns love to look at human faces. Real faces are preferable to most anything.

68. **(B)** Reaction formation is a defense mechanism in which one expresses the opposite of what one feels; Roscoe feels hate but professes love. Displacement is when one takes out one's feelings on a less threatening target than the cause. Projection is when one attributes one's own undesirable traits to others. Sublimation is when one channels one's sexual energy into more acceptable pursuits. Intellectualization is when one deals with a problem in a distant, detached manner.

69. **(E)** Ninety-five percent of the scores in a normal distribution fall between the z scores of -2 and $+2$. Z scores measure the distance from the mean in units of standard deviation. The percent of scores falling under each area of the normal curve is predetermined; there's no way around memorizing it: 68 percent within one standard deviation, 95 percent within two standard deviations, and 99 percent within three standard deviations.

70. **(C)** The age of onset for schizophrenia is usually in the early 20s.

71. **(D)** Bipolar disorder has been linked to an excess of acetylcholine receptors. The manic phase responds well to lithium, and the depressed phase responds well to antidepressant medications. In addition, much research suggests that bipolar disorder runs in families. Though we may be predisposed to develop certain phobias more easily than others, phobias are well explained by and treated from other perspectives, particularly the behaviorist perspective. The existence of dissociative identity disorder is hotly debated; those who believe in its existence generally posit a traumatic event in childhood as a cause. Conversion disorders have become increasingly uncommon in the United States; such a change argues against a genetic cause as the gene pool remains relatively stable. Further, a conversion disorder involves a physical complaint in the absence of a physical symptom and is therefore unlikely to have a biological cause.

72. **(D)** The false consensus effect is the tendency of people to overestimate the number of people who share their views. Deindividuation is a loss of self-restraint under conditions of anonymity and arousal. The just-world bias is people's belief that good things happen to good people, and bad things happen to bad people. Norms of reciprocity is the idea that we feel obligated to treat others as they have treated us. Outgroup bias refers to the negative attitudes people often have toward people who do not belong to the same groups that they do.

73. **(B)** Dr. Lupin's approach is a cognitive-behavioral one; she challenges her clients' beliefs (cognitive) and gives them homework assignments to practice new behaviors (behavioral). Rational emotive behavior therapy (REBT), developed by Albert Ellis, does just that. Modeling is the closest alternative, but it involves the observation and imitation of behaviors. Existential and Gestalt therapies are humanistic approaches. Psychoanalysis involves probing patients' unconscious in order to discover the repressed roots of their complaints.

74. **(C)** Milgram showed that the majority of participants were willing to deliver an electric shock of sufficient voltage to kill someone; thus, most were willing to do something immoral and illegal. Members of minority groups were not compared to Caucasians. No explicit threats were used. Women and men behaved similarly.

75. **(D)** If Artie acts competitively in situations where others do not (low consensus), people are likely to attribute his behavior to something in himself (a person attribution) rather than something in the situation. If Artie always acts this way (high consistency), people are likely to make a stable (as opposed to unstable) attribution.

76. **(C)** Group therapy tends to be less expensive than individual therapy as the cost is shared by the members of the group. Some people may make friends with others in their group, but it is highly unlikely that they develop lasting friendships with *all* the other people in their group and making such friendships is not the goal of seeking therapy. Another asset of group therapy, albeit not a choice in this question, is that people come to understand that many people have the same kind of problems as they do. Few clear differences exist between group and individual therapy in terms of success rate, length of therapists' training, and time spent in therapy.

77. **(A)** Behaviorist therapies tend to be relatively brief and focus on replacing behaviors that make clients unhappy with ones that will make them happier. Psychodynamic therapies tend to be long, in part, because they involve a search for the underlying cause of a patient's issues, a search that often involves a discussion of someone's entire life. Since people from the sociocultural perspective see society as the cause of mental illness, short-term therapy that focuses on the individual is difficult. Humanistic therapies tend not to be as focused as behaviorist ones; they may focus on more abstract issues such as how to find meaning in one's life rather than on how to alter a particular behavior. Somatic therapies are not psychotherapies; most commonly they involve changing one's biochemistry via drugs.

78. **(D)** Hostile aggression is aggression for its own sake rather than aggression that is instrumental in attaining a goal. In all the other choices, the goal of the aggression is to gain something (e.g., supper, money). In choice D, the aggression is intended to accomplish nothing other than serve as an outlet for Tutti's anger.

79. **(A)** Howard Gardner has posited the existence of eight different types of intelligence (naturalist, bodily-kinesthetic, musical, interpersonal, intrapersonal, spatial, linguistic, and logical-mathematical). Practical and experiential are types of intelligence discussed by Sternberg. Fluid intelligence (as opposed to crystallized intelligence) tends to decline as one ages. General intelligence (g) is Spearman's concept of a single factor that underlies all types of intelligence.

80. **(C)** There are two kinds of trait theorists: idiographic theorists who believe that we need different sets of traits to describe different people and nomothetic theorists who believe all people can be described with one set of fundamental traits. None of the other choices refer to trait theorists.

81. **(C)** Drinking alcohol while pregnant may lead the baby to be born with fetal alcohol syndrome (FAS). FAS children tend to suffer from intellectual disability. They are not born addicted to alcohol and are unlikely to become drug dealers. The main cause of low birth weight is mothers who smoke. FAS children are not particularly likely to develop heart disease.

82. **(C)** Harry Harlow studied baby monkeys and is credited with demonstrating the importance of contact comfort. Harlow's work suggested that infants crave the physical comfort of a body. Gilligan is known for her work challenging Kohlberg's theory of development as gender biased. Piaget developed a stage theory of cognitive development. Freud's best-known contributions are his stage theory of psychosexual development and treatment technique of psychoanalysis.

83. **(A)** Isabella's memory of the first time she went skydiving is a declarative or explicit memory because it is a conscious memory she can actively recall. It is also an example of an episodic memory, but that term is not a choice. Semantic memory is our memory for facts. Implicit memory, as opposed to explicit memory, contains memories we don't even realize we have. Eidetic memory is another name for photographic memory. Procedural memory is memory for how to do things such as take a foul shot or play the piano.

84. **(A)** The James-Lange theory of emotion asserts that events cause distinct physiological responses in our bodies that were then recognized as particular emotions. For instance, hitting a home run alters your body in a specific way that tells you that you feel excited and happy. This theory is often confused with Schachter's two-factor theory described in choice E. Schachter's theory holds that the physiological response to most events is similar, a general kind of arousal. The particular emotion is discerned by a cognitive process of appraisal that follows. The Cannon-Bard theory posits that the thalamus plays a central role in the process of identifying emotions. Choice C describes the opponent process theory of emotion. Choice D refers to Paul Ekman's work that showed that throughout the world most people recognize emotions similarly; for example, a smile is seen as a sign of happiness.

85. **(D)** Observational learning is when one member of a species observes a behavior in another member of that species and then copies it. The same species aspect of the definition means that a girl howling like a wolf and a parrot imitating its owner saying "mama" are not examples of observational learning. The other two choices involve no observation or imitation.

86. **(B)** Discrimination in operant conditioning is learning that a behavior will only result in reinforcement under certain conditions. Since earthworms are easier to find after it rains, Melissa has learned to discriminate between the good and bad times to dig for earthworms.

87. **(D)** In a normal distribution, the mean, median, and mode are equal. Ninety-five percent of the scores fall within two standard deviations of the mean. The normal curve is asymptotic, which means it never hits the axis so we cannot say that everyone falls within any number of standard deviations from the mean. The standard deviation can be less than or more than 1; it depends upon what is being measured.

88. **(A)** When a neuron depolarizes, sodium ions flow into the cell. Sodium ions carry a positive charge, and their influx helps change the charge of the cell from negative to positive. The negative charge of the cell at rest is due, largely, to the presence of many chloride ions in the cell; this number does not increase during depolarization. Potassium ions also carry a positive charge and flow into the cell when it is depolarized. Neither magnesium nor strontium plays a role in this process.

89. **(D)** The prefrontal cortex plays an important role in decision-making. Decision-making is a highly complex cognitive skill, which should serve as an indication that the answer will probably involve the cortex.

90. **(D)** Experimenter bias refers to the idea that researchers' beliefs in their own hypotheses may cause them inadvertently to influence the results of the research so as to confirm those hypotheses. Confirmation bias refers to a similar tendency in all people to pay more attention to information that supports their preexisting beliefs than to information that refutes them. The availability heuristic is the tendency to draw conclusions about the frequency of something based on how easy it is to recall it to memory. Functional fixedness is the tendency not to recognize that a familiar object can be used in a novel way. The representative heuristic is the tendency to reason by similarity and, in the process, to underweight base rate probability. For instance, people might believe that a tall, very thin, attractive woman would be more likely to be a supermodel than a librarian. Overconfidence is people's tendency to be excessively confident in their decisions.

91. **(B)** Iconic memory is the name given to our visual, sensory memory. It has a large capacity but lasts only for a fraction of a second. Short-term memory holds only about seven items and lasts for about 30 seconds. Long-term memory is thought to be essentially limitless in both capacity and duration. Echoic memory is the auditory sensory memory; it lasts three to four seconds. When we are actively processing information, it is in our working memories.

92. **(A)** Objects appear the color of the wavelengths of light that they reflect.

93. **(C)** Your knowledge that George Washington was the first president of the United States is usually found in your preconscious. Now that I have caused you to think about Washington, the information is in your conscious. The nonconscious controls your body processes such as heart rate and digestion. Information in your subconscious affects how you process information and includes implicit memories. The unconscious is a term used mostly by psychodynamic theorists to refer to troubling thoughts that we have actively pushed out of our conscious minds.

94. **(E)** Freud suggested that, while going through the psychosexual stages, people could get fixated. People who have phallic fixations typically have issues of either over- or underconfidence about their sexual prowess. A strong libido would cause Karl to seek dating, or at least sex, frequently. The ego is guided by the reality principle. The preconscious refers to information about which one is not thinking but that could be called to the conscious mind easily. Someone with an anal expulsive personality is usually extremely messy and disorganized.

95. **(E)** Scores on the WISC are normally distributed. The WISC has a mean of 100 and a standard deviation of 15. Banu, therefore, scored two standard deviations above the mean: $(130 - 100)/15 = 2$. Z scores are a measure of the distance from the mean in units of standard deviation, so Banu has a z score of $+2$, making possible answers D and E. Percentile is a measure of the percent of test takers who scored at or below a particular score. We know that 50 percent of the test takers scored at or below the mean. We know that an additional 34 percent of scores fall between the mean and one standard

deviation above the mean, and we know that another 13.5 percent of scores fall between one and two standard deviations above the mean. Adding these numbers together tells us that Banu scored at the 97.5th percentile, making the answer E.

96. **(E)** Positive symptoms of schizophrenia are ones that are related to excesses rather than deficits. Having hallucinations, perceiving sensory stimulation when none exists, is a positive symptom. Flat affect and catatonia are negative symptoms since they are deficits in emotion and movement, respectively. Greater sensitivity to others and reduced depression are positive things, but they are not symptoms of schizophrenia.

97. **(A)** Broca's area is typically in the left frontal lobe. Broca's area controls our ability to use our mouths to form the words we wish to say. In most people, language functions are controlled mostly by the left hemisphere. The frontal lobe has many important functions relating to movement; it also houses the motor cortex.

98. **(E)** GAD, generalized anxiety disorder, results in the client experiencing a constant, low-level feeling of tension. Such feelings can be treated with mild sedatives such as Valium. Tricyclic antidepressants are most often used to treat depression. Thorazine and Haldol are typically used to treat schizophrenia. Lithium has been shown to be helpful in treating the manic phase of bipolar disorder.

99. **(E)** Group polarization is the phenomenon that, given time together to discuss something, groups of like-minded individuals will often come to hold more extreme ideas than those with which they entered the group. One possible reason for this phenomenon is that in the group, the responsibility for the extreme decision seems to be divided among the group's members. Outgroup bias is the prejudice people feel against members of other groups. Self-fulfilling prophecy is the idea that one person's expectations about another person can influence the second person's behavior. Self-serving bias is the tendency to take greater responsibility for successful outcomes than unsuccessful ones. The fundamental attribution error is the tendency to underestimate the influence of situational factors on other people's behavior.

100. **(A)** In a positively skewed distribution, there are more low scores than high scores. Typically, one or several unusually high scores, or outliers, skew the distribution. As a result, the mean is pulled up, toward the extreme scores, and is therefore higher than the median. Outliers generally have no effect on the mode, the most frequently occurring score, so it is difficult to make a general statement about the relationship of skew to the mode.

Multiple-Choice Error Analysis Sheet

After checking your answers on the practice test, use the tables below to analyze your results.

The first table below indicates what overall AP exam score is mostly likely for different ranges of scores on the multiple-choice section of the test. Performance on the free-response questions will influence the overall score, but performance on the multiple-choice section is a good predictor of the overall exam score. Note that this exam is different than many exams you are used to: getting 75% correct on an exam in your AP Psychology class would probably worry you and your teacher, but getting 70 out of the 100 multiple-choice items correct on the AP Psychology exam is likely to earn you an overall score of a 4! (Note: This table changes for each test each year, so the table below is an approximation based on recently released exams.)

Number of Multiple-Choice Items Correct	Overall Exam Score You Would Most Likely Receive
88–100	5
74–87	4 or 5
60–73	3 or 4
45–59	2 or 3
30–44	1
0–29	1

Use the table below to "diagnose" your performance on the practice test: You can classify your errors by topic area, which will give you an idea about what your "stronger" and "weaker" chapters might be. By circling the numbers of the questions you answered incorrectly in the table below, you can get a picture of which chapters you might need to focus your study on.

Chapter	Question Numbers								
History and Approaches	24	31	55						
Methods	2	23	53	54	56	100			
Biological Bases of Behavior	3	22	25	57	58	59	88	89	97
Sensation and Perception	20	21	26	51	52	60	61	92	
States of Consciousness	19	50	93						
Learning	5	18	27	49	62	63	85	86	
Cognition	6	17	28	29	48	64	83	90	91
Motivation and Emotion	4	7	16	30	46	47	65	84	
Developmental Psychology	8	14	15	45	66	67	81	82	
Personality	1	13	32	33	44	68	80	94	
Testing and Individual Differences	12	34	35	69	79	87	95		
Abnormal Psychology	9	10	36	37	43	70	71	96	
Treatment of Psychological Disorders	11	40	41	73	76	77	98		
Social Psychology	38	39	42	72	74	75	78	99	

Part II

Question 1 Scoring Rubric

DIRECTIONS: This is an 8-point question. Each bullet represents two possible points. You earn 1 point for answering the question about the experimental method and 1 point for answering the question about the correlational method.
You would need to describe the follow-up studies and address the questions somewhere in your descriptions.
You do *not* need to define terms in your answer, and definitions alone will not score. The question asks you to answer questions about how Professor Willborn could use the experimental and correlational method to study the relationship between violent video games and attitudes toward real-world violence.

Point 1

What variables would Professor Willborn examine in her experimental study?

Awarded if you identified playing violent video games as the independent variable in the experiment and attitude toward real-world violence as the dependent variable. The reviewer suggested that the follow-up study investigate the relationship between playing violent video games and attitudes toward real-world violence, so playing violent video games is the only valid independent variable and attitude toward real-world violence is the only valid dependent variable for an experimental study on this research question.

Point 2

What variables would Professor Willborn examine in her correlational study?

Awarded if you identified playing violent video games and attitudes toward real-world violence as the two variables to be correlated. The terms independent variable and dependent variable are not usually associated with correlational studies.

Point 3

How could Professor Willborn operationally define at least one of the variables in her experimental study?

Awarded if you explained a possible operational definition for either playing violent video games or attitude toward real-world violence. There are multiple ways to operationally define these variables, and the point will be awarded if you describe any of the ways to measure this behavior (e.g., self-reports of video game playing, observations of video game playing) or this attitude (e.g., a survey, interview, physiological measure while watching a media portrayal of real-world violence, etc.).

Point 4

How could Professor Willborn operationally define at least one of the variables in her correlational study?

Awarded if you explained a possible operational definition for either playing violent video games or attitude toward real-world violence. There are multiple ways to operationally define these variables, and the point will be awarded if you describe any of the ways to measure this behavior (e.g., self-reports of video game playing, observations of video game playing) or this attitude (e.g., a survey, interview, physiological measure while watching a media portrayal of real-world violence, etc.). Note: You cannot earn point 4 if you operationally define the same variable as the variable defined for point 3.

Point 5

How could Professor Willborn organize her participants to gather data in her experimental study?

You must explain that participants are organized into at least two separate groups differing by the independent variable (playing violent video games). You may use the term "control group" and "experimental group" but need to clearly show that the groups are different based on the independent variable.

Point 6

How could Professor Willborn organize her participants to gather data in her correlational study?

Awarded if you explained how two pieces of data (the two variables: playing violent video games and attitude toward real-world violence) are gathered from each participant in the correlational study. You will *not* be awarded the point if you implied that participants are divided into separate groups based on the independent variable.

Point 7

What kind of conclusion would Professor Willborn be able to form based on the results of her experimental study?

Awarded if you explained that the experimental study could lead to a causal inference about the relationship between the independent variable and the dependent variable. You can explain this conceptually or through an example of a causal conclusion based on this study.

Point 8

What kind of conclusion would Professor Willborn be able to form based on the results of her correlational study?

Awarded if you explained that the correlational study could lead to predictions about the relationship between the variables. You will *not* be awarded the point if you implied that correlational studies can lead to causal inferences about the relationship between the variables. You can describe how the study might indicate that one variable increases as the other variable increases (positive correlation), one variable decreases as the other variable increases (negative correlation), or that the study might establish no statistical relationship between the variables (no or zero correlation). You can also use correlation coefficients (r values) correctly to gain the point.

Sample Essay

Professor Willborn should redesign her study as an experiment or a correlation. These methods are considered to get better data than naturalistic observation studies.

When she redesigns her study as an experiment, Professor Willborn would have to assign the variables correctly. In every experiment, there is an independent variable and a dependent variable. In this study, the independent variable is video games and the dependent variable is how violent the video games are and what that does to the player's attitude toward violence. So what she could do is find a sample of people willing to do her experiment, get them all to play violent video games in her lab under controlled conditions, and then observe them to figure out whether they enjoyed the violence in the video games or not. In this way the dependent variable is operationally defined by getting everyone to play violent video games in a controlled way that she can measure. She could organize her participants to gather her data by making sure they are all present and ready for the testing, and again by measuring them carefully. Also, she should probably set up this experiment in a double-blind way. Since the people playing the games don't know what she's testing, they wouldn't be biased and change their natural reactions. In the end, after doing all this, Professor Willborn should be able to conclude whether playing violent video games causes people to change their attitudes about real-world violence. It might turn out that playing violent video games causes people to not care as much about violence they see in their lives.

When she redesigns her study as a correlational study, Professor Willborn should try to correlate the important variables to figure out whether they correlate or not. In her study, just like in the experimental study, she would choose the variables "playing violent video games" and "attitude toward real-world violence" as the variables she will correlate. She could operationally define these variables by being careful how she observes them. If she observes them in a controlled way in her lab, then they will be operationally defined. What she would have to do is, again, have people play violent video games in her lab in a controlled way. But in the correlational study, she would organize her people to get her data by interviewing them after she times how long they play the games to see if their attitude toward real-world violence has changed. She would use these interviews to figure out if their attitude toward real-world violence changed after playing the video games. Then she could look at how long they played the games and how much their attitude changed. After she got all her data, she should be able to figure out if there is a correlation between playing video games and attitude change. She might find a positive correlation, which means that the people who played violent video games the most also changed their attitudes the most. Correlation does not imply causation, but she might find this correlation relationship between these variables in this study.

This might be a lot of work for Professor Willborn, but if she really wants to figure out what playing violent video games does to people, she's going to have to do something like this. Psychological studies are often complicated and take a lot of time.

Sample Essay Scoring

Notice that the first paragraph of this (fictional) student's essay does not score any points. This student introduces the topic with a short paragraph, which is fine but does not answer any part of the essay question directly. It's not necessary to provide an introduction paragraph in your AP Psychology essay—just dive into answering the question in order. This student chooses to answer all of the questions about the experimental design in one paragraph and all of the questions about the correlational method in a separate paragraph. This organization works well. The student could have also chosen to answer the questions in paragraphs grouped by the pairs of questions listed within the question.

The points this fictional student essay scores and doesn't score are:

Point 1

What variables would Professor Willborn examine in her experimental study?

Does *not* score, because the student incorrectly identifies the independent variable as video games. The rubric requires that students identify the independent variable as playing violent video games. Defining the independent variable as video games is too vague to score.

Point 2

What variables would Professor Willborn examine in her correlational study?

Scores in the second sentence of the third paragraph when the student identifies the two variables to be correlated correctly: "the variables playing violent video games and attitude toward real-world violence as the variables she will correlate."

Point 3

How could Professor Willborn operationally define at least one of the variables in her experimental study?

Does *not* score. The student does not explain specific operational definitions of either variable. Stating that "being careful how she observes them . . . in a controlled way in her lab" is not specific enough to earn the point for operational definitions. The student does not provide possible operational definitions of both variables, so the point is not awarded.

Point 4

How could Professor Willborn operationally define at least one of the variables in her correlational study?

Does *not* score. The student says "She could operationally define these variables by being careful how she observes them. If she observes them in a controlled way in her lab, then they will be operationally defined." This statement is too vague to score, because it does not meet the rubric requirement to provide a possible operational definition for either variable in the study.

Point 5

How could Professor Willborn organize her participants to gather data in her experimental study?

Does *not* score. The student never mentions organizing participants into groups based on the independent variable. What the student says about organizing participants is too vague and not relevant to creating control and experimental groups in the study.

Point 6

How could Professor Willborn organize her participants to gather data in her correlational study?

Scores when the student says "organize her people to get her data by interviewing them after she times how long they play the games to see if their attitude toward real-world violence has changed." The student meets the rubric requirement by describing how data on the two variables could be gathered from each participant.

Point 7

What kind of conclusion would Professor Willborn be able to form based on the results of her experimental study?

Scores when the student says "playing violent video games causes people to change their attitudes about real-world violence." This statement states a causal conclusion about the variables clearly, which meets the requirement of the rubric.

Point 8

What kind of conclusion would Professor Willborn be able to form based on the results of her correlational study?

Scores when the student says "She might find a positive correlation which means that the people who played violent video games the most also changed their attitudes the most." The student states and explains the positive correlation that might be found between the variables. The student goes on to clearly demonstrate knowledge about the difference between causal and correlational influences, but the point was already scored when the student explained the potential positive correlation conclusion.

Overall, this essay scores 5 of the 8 possible points.

Question 2 Scoring Rubric

DIRECTIONS: This is a 10-point question. Each definition of the 5 terms counts for 1 point, and each description of how the concept demonstrates a nonconscious influence is 1 point.

You do not need to use the exact words used to define the terms, but must communicate the meaning of the definition provided in the rubric.

You should use examples for the description points that describe an influence on behavior out of our conscious awareness. Examples alone will *not* score the definition points, but will score on the description points.

Point 1

Definition, selective attention

Awarded if you defined selective attention as the process of focusing on something in the environment, and as a consequence that information is encoded into memory. You may be more specific about the process, stating that selective attention determines what information from sensory memory is encoded into short-term memory, but that level of detail is not needed to score the point.

Point 2

Description, selective attention

Awarded if you provided an example that explains how selective attention is often not deliberate. Some aspect of our consciousness that we are not aware of often determines what we pay attention to, and consequently what information is encoded into memory through selective attention.

Point 3

Definition, Cognitive Dissonance

Awarded if you defined cognitive dissonance as the tension that exists when our attitudes do not match our behaviors.

Point 4

Description, cognitive dissonance

Awarded if you provided an example that describes how we are not aware of cognitive dissonance and its subsequent effects on our attitudes and behaviors. The example must clearly show that we are not consciously aware of either the tension created by cognitive dissonance or how we change our attitudes or behavior to relieve the dissonance.

Point 5

Definition, fundamental attribution error

Awarded if you defined the fundamental attribution error as the tendency to overestimate the importance of dispositional (such as personality) factors and underestimate the role of situational factors when we judge the behaviors of others. Both dispositional and situational factors need to be referred to in the definition.

Point 6

Description, fundamental attribution error

Awarded if you provided an example that shows we are not consciously aware of attributing behavior as being caused by inner dispositions rather than being caused by the situation. The example must clearly show how this error is not purposeful or a matter of choice. The error occurs and we are not consciously aware of having committed it.

Point 7

Definition, perceptual set

Awarded if you defined perceptual set as a predisposition to perceiving sensations in a certain way. Valid definitions must include the words or appropriate synonyms for perception and sensation.

Point 8

Description, perceptual set

Awarded if you provided an example that shows how perceptual sets determine how we perceive sensations without our choice or conscious awareness of their effects. The example must clearly show how perceptual sets create perceptions out of sensations instead of a conscious choice about how to perceive sensations.

Point 9

Definition, sensory memory

Awarded if you defined sensory memory as the split-second holding area for incoming sensory information. Scorable definitions must include the concept that sensory memory lasts a very short period of time and all sensory information flows into sensory memory.

Point 10

Description, sensory memory

Awarded if you provided an example that shows how sensory events are automatically encoded into sensory memory for a split second without our choice or awareness. The example must include the idea that we are not aware of encoding these sensory events and we do not choose which sensory events are encoded in sensory memory.

Sample Essay

Psychology is a very important subject that has discovered many important things. We all need to pay attention to psychology and psychology theories because they matter to us and to our loved ones.

One of the most important contributions of psychology has been to identify aspects of thinking and experiences outside of conscious awareness. What this means is that psychology helps us figure out what we think even if we don't really know why we think it.

Perceptual sets are things that determine what we perceive. They are like rules that help our brains figure out what to do with what we see, hear, etc. How this applies to this question is that we don't really know what these rules are, and these perceptual set rules determine how we see the world around us even though we aren't aware of them.

Cognitive dissonance are things that really bother us about what we think. If we think something bad about a friend then it's going to bother us even if we aren't aware of why it's bothering us.

Selective attention is when you pay attention to something so you remember it better later. We all choose to pay attention to certain things and then those things get encoded into memory a lot better. Sometimes you don't even know why you pay attention to something (like a loud bang or someone saying your name), but because of selective attention you are going to remember those things better even though you didn't know or choose what to pay attention to.

Sensory memory is our memory for sensory things. It applies to this question because we don't choose what senses to pay attention to. Everything that happens around us ends up in sensory memory at least for a little while, so that happens outside our conscious awareness.

The fundamental attribution error is when you attribute something to someone without being consciously aware of it. You might think they are mean or nice or rich or poor but you don't really choose to think that way about them. It's just automatic, like stereotyping.

All of these concepts and theories are very important to psychology and to figuring out why we do what we do, even if we aren't aware of doing them.

Sample Essay Scoring

Notice that the first two paragraphs of this (fictional) student's essay do not score any points. This is a good example of a student who tries to introduce the topic and provide a transition into answering the question. These writing techniques are useful in most other contexts, but remember that answering the AP Psychology essay question is a unique experience unlike a lot of other writing you do. Don't worry about writing an introductory paragraph or easing the reader into the topic. Just dive in and answer the question.

Also, notice that this (fictional) student answers the points out of order. This way of organizing is not necessarily a problem because readers are trained to look for scorable points wherever they occur in a student essay. But you aren't doing yourself or the AP reader any favors by going out of order. The readers are using a scoring rubric that is written in the order provided by the question, and you make their lives easier by going in order, and there is a slight chance they may miss a scorable part of your essay by not doing that.

The points this (fictional) student essay scores and doesn't score are:

Point 1

Definition, selective attention

Scores when student says in the fifth paragraph: "Selective attention is when you pay attention to something so you remember it better later." This definition matches the rubric definition. Notice that the student gives what might be incorrect information in the next sentence: "We all choose to pay attention to certain things and then those things get encoded into memory a lot better." The point is already awarded, so the reader doesn't worry about whether this next sentence indicates that the student thinks that selective attention is always under our control.

Point 2

Description, selective attention

Scores in the fifth paragraph when the students says: "Sometimes you don't even know why you pay attention to something (like a loud bang or someone saying your name), but because of selective attention you are going to remember those things better." This statement and example indicates that the student understands that selective attention is not always under our conscious control, and meets the rubric requirement.

Point 3

Definition, cognitive dissonance

Does *not* score. The student tries to define cognitive dissonance in the fourth paragraph, but the definition "Cognitive dissonance are things that really bother us about what we think" does not meet the rubric requirement that it must be a dissonance between our attitudes and behaviors.

Point 4

Description, cognitive dissonance

Does *not* score. The example provided about stereotyping is not specific enough to cognitive dissonance to match the rubric or score the point.

Point 5

Definition, fundamental attribution error

Does *not* score. The student defines fundamental attribution error in paragraph seven as "when you attribute something to someone without being consciously aware of it." This definition is not specific enough to score the point. The rubric requires that a definition of this concept address situational factors and dispositional factors in some way, and the definition the student provided does not address these factors.

Point 6

Description, fundamental attribution error

Does *not* score. The student may be trying to address this point with the example in paragraph seven, but the example just describes an automatic thought about another person, not an example of the fundamental attribution error being committed. The student establishes clearly that the thought is "automatic" and nonconscious, but the example is not specific enough to the fundamental attribution error to match the rubric.

Point 7

Definition, perceptual set

Scores in the third paragraph when the student says: "They are like rules that help our brains figure out what to do with what we see, hear, etc." This definition matches the rubric requirement for the definition, since it implies that perceptual sets are predispositions to perceiving sensations in certain ways. Notice that the first sentence comes close to a valid definition, but the student uses the word "things," which is too vague because it does not establish that these "things" are cognitive rules, predispositions, and so on.

Point 8

Description, perceptual set

Scores in the third paragraph when the student says: "we don't really know what these rules are, and these perceptual set rules determine how we see the world around us even though we aren't aware of them." This example matches the rubric requirement that students need to describe how perceptual sets determine perceptions without our conscious choice or awareness.

Point 9

Definition, sensory memory

Does *not* score. The student defines sensory memory in a very vague way in paragraph six, and the definition does not match the rubric requirement. The student does not say that sensory memory is a split-second holding area, and "sensory things" is too vague to imply sensory information.

Point 10

Description, sensory memory

Scores in the sixth paragraph when the student says: "Everything that happens around us ends up in sensory memory at least for a little while, so that happens outside our conscious awareness." This is a good example of how a student may not be able to define a concept well, but does understand the concept well enough to apply it to lack of conscious awareness. The student describes how all sensory events are encoded into sensory memory for a short time without our conscious awareness. This matches the rubric requirement well and scores the point.

Overall, this essay scores 5 points out of 10.

UNIT 1

Scientific Foundations

This first unit focuses on the historical origins of the science of psychology, current psychological perspectives, and the research methods psychologists use to gather data about human thinking and behavior. You will find the content from this unit in the textbook you use in your AP Psychology class in the "History and Research Methods" chapter.

History and Approaches

1

Key Terms

- Introspection
- Structuralism
- Functionalism
- Psychoanalytic theory
- Behaviorism
- Humanist perspective
- Psychoanalytic perspective
- Biopsychology (or neuroscience) perspective
- Evolutionary (or Darwinian) perspective
- Behavioral perspective
- Cognitive perspective
- Social-cultural (or sociocultural) perspective

Key People

- Wilhelm Wundt
- William James
- Mary Whiton Calkins
- Margaret Floy Washburn
- G. Stanley Hall
- Max Wertheimer
- Sigmund Freud
- John B. Watson
- Ivan Pavlov
- B. F. Skinner
- Abraham Maslow
- Carl Rogers
- Charles Darwin
- Jean Piaget

HISTORY OF PSYCHOLOGY

One way to think about the history of psychology is to organize the various theorists and theories into "waves," or schools of thought. Each wave is a way of thinking about human thought and behavior that dominated the field for a certain period of time until a new way of looking at psychology started to dominate the field.

Wave One—Introspection

Archaeologists and historians find evidence that humans have always thought about our thought and behavior, so in a way, the study of psychology is as old as our species. Archaeologists find evidence of trephination—Stone Age humans carving holes through the skull to release evil spirits. Greek philosophers such as Plato and Democritus theorized about the relationship between thought and behavior. However, thinking about psychology is different than studying it scientifically. Many psychologists specializing in the history of the science date the beginning of scientific psychology to the year 1879. In that year, **Wilhelm Wundt** (1832–1920) set up the first psychological laboratory in an apartment near the university at

Wilhelm Wundt

William James

Mary Whiton Calkins

Margaret Floy Washburn

Leipzig, Germany. Wundt trained subjects in **introspection**—the subjects were asked to record accurately their cognitive reactions to simple stimuli. Through this process, Wundt hoped to examine basic cognitive structures. He eventually described his theory of **structuralism**—the idea that the mind operates by combining subjective emotions and objective sensations. In 1890, **William James** (1842–1910) published *The Principles of Psychology*, the science's first textbook. James examined how these structures Wundt identified function in our lives (James's theory is called **functionalism**). Another early pioneer in the new science of psychology was **Mary Whiton Calkins** (1863–1930), who studied with William James and went on to become president of the American Psychological Association. **Margaret Floy Washburn** (1871–1939) was the first woman to earn a PhD in psychology. Another student of William James, **G. Stanley Hall** (1844–1924), pioneered the study of child development and was the first president of the American Psychological Association. Introspective theories were important in establishing the science of psychology, but they do not significantly influence current psychological thinking.

G. Stanley Hall

Wave Two—Gestalt Psychology

While Wundt and James were experimenting with introspection, another group of early psychologists were explaining human thought and behavior in a very different way. **Gestalt psychologists** like **Max Wertheimer** (1880–1943) argued against dividing human thought and behavior into discrete structures. **Gestalt psychology** tried to examine a person's total experience because the way we experience the world is more than just an accumulation of various perceptual experiences. Gestalt theorists demonstrated that whole experience is often more than just the sum of the parts of the experience. A painting can be represented as rows and columns of points of color, but the experience of the painting is much more than that. Therapists later incorporated Gestalt thinking by examining not just a client's difficulty but the context in which the difficulty occurs. Like the introspective theories, other than the contribution to specific forms of therapy and the study of perception, Gestalt psychology has relatively little influence on current psychology.

Max Wertheimer

Wave Three—Psychoanalysis

If you ask someone to name a famous psychologist, he or she will most likely name **Sigmund Freud** (1856–1939). Freud revolutionized psychology with his psychoanalytic theory. While treating patients for various psychosomatic complaints, Freud believed he discovered the **unconscious mind**—a part of our mind over which we do not have conscious control that determines, in part, how we think and behave. Freud believed that this hidden part of ourselves builds up over the years through **repression**—the pushing down into the unconscious events and feelings that cause so much anxiety and tension that our conscious mind cannot deal with them. Freud believed that to understand human thought and behavior truly, we must examine the unconscious mind through dream analysis, word association, and other psychoanalytic therapy techniques. While many therapists still use some of Freud's basic ideas in

Sigmund Freud

helping clients, Freud has been criticized for being unscientific and creating unverifiable theories. Freud's theories were and are widely used by various artists. Many of Freud's terms moved from being exclusively used by psychologists to being used in day-to-day speech (e.g., **defense mechanism**).

John B. Watson

Wave Four—Behaviorism

John B. Watson (1878–1958) studied the pioneering conditioning experiments of **Ivan Pavlov** (1849–1936). Watson then declared that for psychology to be considered a science, it must limit itself to observable phenomena, not unobservable concepts like the unconscious mind. Watson along with others wanted to establish **behaviorism** as the dominant paradigm of psychology. Behaviorists maintain that psychologists should look at only behavior and causes of behavior—**stimuli** (environmental events) and **responses** (physical reactions)—and not concern themselves with describing elements of consciousness. Another behaviorist, **B. F. Skinner** (1904–1990), expanded the basic ideas of behaviorism to include the idea of **reinforcement**—environmental stimuli that either encourage or discourage certain responses. Skinner's intellectual influence lasted for decades. Behaviorism was the dominant school of thought in psychology from the 1920s through the 1960s.

Ivan Pavlov

Wave Five—Multiple Perspectives

Currently, there is no one way of thinking about human thought and behavior that all or even most psychologists share. Many psychologists describe themselves as **eclectic**—drawing from multiple perspectives. As psychology develops in the new century, perhaps one way of thinking will become dominant. For now, though, psychologists look at thought and behavior from multiple perspectives.

B. F. Skinner

PSYCHOLOGICAL PERSPECTIVES

As described in the section about the history of psychology, different contemporary psychologists look at human thought and behavior from different perspectives. Contemporary perspectives can be placed into eight broad categories.

Humanist Perspective

Partially in reaction to the perceived reductionism of the behaviorists, some psychologists tried to describe some mysterious aspects of consciousness again. The **humanists**, including theorists **Abraham Maslow** (1908–1970) and **Carl Rogers** (1902–1987), stressed individual choice and free will. This contrasts with the **deterministic** behaviorists, who theorized that all behaviors are caused by past conditioning. Humanists believe that we choose most of our behaviors and these choices are guided by physiological, emotional, or spiritual needs. A humanistic psychologist might explain that an introverted person may choose to limit social contact with others because he or she finds that social needs are better satisfied by contact with a few close friends rather than large groups. Humanistic theories are not easily tested by the scientific method. Some psychological historians view it as more of a historical perspective than a current one. However, some therapists find humanistic ideas helpful in aiding clients to overcome obstacles in their lives.

Abraham Maslow

Carl Rogers

Psychoanalytic Perspective

The **psychoanalytic perspective**, as described previously, continues to be a part, if a controversial one, of modern psychology. Psychologists using this perspective believe that the **unconscious** mind—a part of our mind that we do not have conscious control over or access to—controls much of our thought and action. Psychoanalysts would look for impulses or memories pushed into the unconscious mind through **repression**. This perspective thinks that to understand human thought and behavior, we must examine our **unconscious** mind through dream analysis, word association, and other psychoanalytic therapy techniques. A psychoanalytic psychologist might explain that an introverted person avoids social situations because of a repressed memory of trauma in childhood involving a social situation, perhaps acute embarrassment or anxiety experienced (but not consciously remembered) at school or a party.

Biopsychology (or Neuroscience) Perspective

Biopsychologists explain human thought and behavior strictly in terms of biological processes. Human **cognition** and reactions might be caused by effects of our **genes**, **hormones**, and **neurotransmitters** in the brain or by a combination of all three. A biopsychologist might explain a person's tendency to be **extroverted** as caused by genes inherited from their parents and the genes' effects on the abundance of certain neurotransmitters in the brain. Biopsychology is a rapidly growing field. Some scientists wonder if the future of psychology might be a branch of the science of biology. (See also Chapter 3, "Biological Bases of Behavior.")

Evolutionary (or Darwinian) Perspective

Evolutionary psychologists (also sometimes called **sociobiologists**) examine human thoughts and actions in terms of **natural selection**. Some psychological traits might be advantageous for survival, and these traits would be passed down from the parents to the next generation. A psychologist using the evolutionary perspective (based on **Charles Darwin's** (1809–1882) theory of natural selection) might explain a person's tendency to be extroverted as a survival advantage. If a person is outgoing, he or she might make friends and allies. These connections could improve the individual's chances of survival, which increases the person's chances for passing this trait for extroversion down to his or her children. The evolutionary perspective is similar to (and in some ways a subset of) the biopsychology perspective.

Charles Darwin

Behavioral Perspective

Behaviorists explain human thought and behavior in terms of **conditioning**. Behaviorists look strictly at observable behaviors and human and animal responses to different kinds of stimuli. A behaviorist might explain a person's tendency to be extroverted in terms of reward and punishment. Was the person rewarded for being outgoing? Was the person punished for withdrawing from a situation or not interacting with others? A behaviorist would look for environmental conditions that caused an extroverted response in the person (see also Chapter 6, "Learning").

Cognitive Perspective

Jean Piaget

Cognitive psychologists examine human thought and behavior in terms of how we interpret, process, and remember environmental events. In this perspective, the rules that we use to view the world are important to understanding why we think and behave the way we do. In Chapter 9, "Developmental Psychology," you will learn about **Jean Piaget's** (1896–1980) cognitive developmental theory, which focuses on how our cognitions develop in stages as we mature. A cognitive psychologist might explain a person's tendency to be extroverted in terms of how he or she interprets social situations. Does the individual interpret others' offers for conversation as important ways to get to know someone or important for his or her own life in some way? To a cognitive psychologist, an extroverted person sees the world in such a way that being outgoing makes sense.

Social-Cultural (or Sociocultural) Perspective

Social-cultural psychologists look at how our thoughts and behaviors vary between cultures. They emphasize the influence culture has on the way we think and act. A social-cultural psychologist might explain a person's tendency to be extroverted by examining his or her culture's rules about social interaction. How far apart do people in this culture usually stand when they have a conversation? How often do people touch each other while interacting? How much value does the culture place on being part of a group versus being an individual? These cultural norms would be important to a sociocultural psychologist in explaining a person's extroversion.

Biopsychosocial Perspective

This modern perspective acknowledges that human thinking and behavior results from combinations of biological ("bio"), psychological ("psycho"), and social ("social") factors. Psychologists who emphasize the biopsychosocial perspective view other perspectives as too focused on specific influences on thinking and behavior (sometimes called "being reductionistic"). A biopsychosocial psychologist would agree with a cognitive psychologist about the influence of how we remember and interpret events, but would point out that biological and social influences are equally responsible for our decisions. The biopsychosocial perspective might explain extroversion by focusing on the combination of several influences: a genetic tendency for extroversion (similar to the biopsychological explanation), how a person has been conditioned toward extroverted behavior, and how social pressures, such as conformity, influence his or her extroverted behaviors.

Summary

If you ask psychologists which of these perspectives they most agree with, they might say that each perspective has valid explanations depending on the specific situation. This point of view, sometimes called **eclectic**, claims that no one perspective has all the answers to the variety of human thought and behavior. Psychologists use various perspectives in their work depending on which point of view fits best with the explanation. In the future, some perspectives might be combined or new perspectives might emerge as research continues.

PRACTICE QUESTIONS

Directions: Each of the questions or incomplete statements below is followed by five suggested answers or completions. Select the one that is best in each case.

1. You are at a lecture about the history of psychology and the speaker states that Wilhelm Wundt's theory of structuralism was the first scientific psychological theory. On what historical fact might the speaker be basing her or his argument?
   (A) Wundt was internationally known at the time, and this lent credence to his theory in the scientific community.
   (B) Wundt studied under Ivan Pavlov for his graduate training, and Pavlov required scientific methods to be used.
   (C) Structuralism was based on the results of his introspection experiments, so it is, at least in part, empirical.
   (D) Structuralism was based on careful anecdotes gathered from Wundt's extensive clinical career.
   (E) Wundt was the first person to study psychology in an academic setting.

2. Sigmund Freud's theory of the unconscious mind
   (A) was revolutionary because it was the first comprehensive explanation of human thought and behavior.
   (B) resulted from discoveries about the human brain obtained by cadaver dissection.
   (C) is outdated and has no relevance for modern psychology.
   (D) focused entirely on human males' sex drive.
   (E) depends on the idea that humans can remember events but not be consciously aware of the memory.

3. In what way might a behaviorist disagree with a cognitive psychologist about the cause of aggression?
   (A) A behaviorist might state that aggression is caused by memories or ways we think about aggressive behavior, while a cognitive psychologist might say aggression is caused by a past repressed experience.
   (B) A behaviorist might state that aggression is a behavior encouraged by our genetic code, while a cognitive psychologist might state that aggression is caused by memories or ways we think about aggressive behavior.
   (C) A behaviorist might state that aggression is caused by past rewards for aggressive behavior, while a cognitive psychologist might believe aggression is caused by an expressed desire to fulfill certain life needs.
   (D) A behaviorist might state that aggression is caused by past rewards for aggressive behavior, while a cognitive psychologist might believe aggression is caused by memories or ways we think about aggressive behavior.
   (E) A behaviorist would not disagree with a cognitive psychologist about aggression because they both believe that aggressive behavior is caused by the way we cognitively process certain behaviors.

4. Dr. Marco explains to a client that his feelings of hostility toward a coworker are most likely caused by the way the client interprets the coworker's actions and the way he thinks that people should behave at work. Dr. Marco is most likely working from what perspective?
   (A) behavioral
   (B) cognitive
   (C) psychoanalytic
   (D) humanist
   (E) social-cultural

5. The research methodology Wilhelm Wundt used is called
   (A) introspection.
   (B) structuralism.
   (C) naturalistic observation.
   (D) inferential.
   (E) scientific.

6. Which of the following psychologists wrote the first psychology textbook?
   (A) William James
   (B) Wilhelm Wundt
   (C) B. F. Skinner
   (D) John Watson
   (E) Albert Bandura

7. Which of the following psychologists was part of the Gestalt group of psychologists?
   (A) Carl Rogers
   (B) Wilhelm Wundt
   (C) B. F. Skinner
   (D) John B. Watson
   (E) Max Wertheimer

8. Which of the following concepts is most integral to Sigmund Freud's psychoanalytic theory?
   (A) trephining
   (B) structuralism
   (C) the unconscious mind
   (D) the concept of Gestalt
   (E) behaviorism

9. Sigmund Freud's psychoanalytic theory has been criticized for being
   (A) appropriate for female patients, but not male patients.
   (B) only applicable to research settings, not therapy settings.
   (C) based on large groups, not individual cases.
   (D) unscientific and unverifiable.
   (E) too closely tied to behavioristic thought.

10. John B. Watson relied on the pioneering work of __________ in establishing behaviorism as a paradigm of psychology.

(A) B. F. Skinner
(B) Wilhelm Wundt
(C) William James
(D) Ivan Pavlov
(E) Sigmund Freud

11. B. F. Skinner introduced the idea of __________ to the paradigm of behaviorism.

(A) unconscious thinking
(B) reinforcement
(C) conditioning
(D) defense mechanisms
(E) introspection

12. Which of the following psychologists might have described himself as a humanist?

(A) B. F. Skinner
(B) William James
(C) Abraham Maslow
(D) John Watson
(E) Ivan Pavlov

13. Symbolic dream analysis might be an important research technique to a psychologist from which of the following perspectives?

(A) behaviorist
(B) biopsychologist
(C) psychoanalytic
(D) evolutionary
(E) structuralist

14. Behaviorists explain human thought and behavior as a result of

(A) past conditioning.
(B) unconscious behavioral impulses.
(C) natural selection.
(D) biological processes.
(E) individual choice.

15. A therapist who says that she uses whatever psychological perspective "works best" for each patient might be best described as

(A) social-cultural.
(B) humanist.
(C) eclectic.
(D) psychoanalytic.
(E) functionalist.

ANSWER KEY

1. **C**	6. **A**	11. **B**
2. **E**	7. **E**	12. **C**
3. **D**	8. **C**	13. **C**
4. **B**	9. **D**	14. **A**
5. **A**	10. **D**	15. **C**

ANSWERS EXPLAINED

1. **(C)** Scientific research is empirical by nature, and Wundt based the theory of structuralism on the results of experimentation. Wundt's reputation and the academic setting are not relevant to the scientific nature of his theory. Wundt did not study under Pavlov nor was he a clinical psychologist.

2. **(E)** The unconscious mind contains memories of events or feelings of which we are not consciously aware. It was not the first comprehensive theory. Freud did not use cadaver dissection to formulate the theory. While the sex drive figures prominently in the theory, the theory is not focused entirely on sex. While some psychologists would dispute much of Freud's theory, many therapists still find the idea of the unconscious mind relevant.

3. **(D)** Behaviorists look at what behaviors we are rewarded for, and cognitive psychologists explain our behavior through the way we interpret events. The rest of the answers are explanations of other psychological perspectives incorrectly applied to behaviorism or cognitive theory.

4. **(B)** The cognitive perspective emphasizes the role of interpretation of others' actions and best fits the given scenario. The other perspectives would emphasize other types of explanations.

5. **(A)** Wundt used the technique of introspection to research his theory of structuralism. He did not use naturalistic observation and inferential and scientific are general terms that might be applied to many different types of research.

6. **(A)** William James wrote the first psychology textbook, *The Principles of Psychology*, in 1890.

7. **(E)** Wertheimer is the only psychologist in this list who was included as part of the Gestalt group in the text.

8. **(C)** The unconscious mind is an integral concept in Freudian theory. Memories and impulses are repressed into the unconscious mind and this drives our later behaviors. The other concepts mentioned do not relate to psychoanalytic theory.

9. **(D)** Freud did not use the scientific method and many of his conclusions cannot be tested. The theory was based on individual male and female cases in therapeutic settings, and is not tied closely to behaviorism.

10. **(D)** Watson referred to the conditioning experiments Ivan Pavlov did with dogs. B. F. Skinner came after Watson chronologically, and the other psychologists mentioned are not part of the behaviorist paradigm.

11. **(B)** Skinner added the idea of reinforcing events, such as rewards and punishments, to the basic idea of behaviorism. Unconscious thinking and defense mechanisms are concepts from the psychoanalytic perspective. Conditioning is a general term used before Skinner did his research. Introspection was a technique used by Wundt.

12. **(C)** Maslow is the only psychologist in this list included in the section on humanism in the text. Skinner, Pavlov, and Watson are behaviorists.

13. **(C)** The idea that dreams contain symbols is central to the psychoanalytic perspective, and not any of the other perspectives listed.

14. **(A)** Behaviorists explain human thought and behavior as a result of conditioning in our pasts, either classical conditioning or operant conditioning. This conditioning restricts (or eliminates) the idea of personal choice, and behaviorists do not usually refer to biological causes and evolutionary theory (like natural selection). The unconscious mind is a concept from psychoanalytic theory.

15. **(C)** The eclectic perspective claims that no one perspective can best explain all human behaviors and a therapist who works with many different perspectives to help individual patients is in some sense eclectic, not any of the other specific perspectives listed.

2 Methods

Key Terms

- Hindsight bias
- Applied research
- Basic research
- Hypothesis
- Independent variable
- Dependent variable
- Theory
- Operational definition
- Validity
- Reliability
- Sampling
- Sample
- Population
- Representative sample
- Random sampling
- Stratified sampling
- Experiment—laboratory and field
- Confounding variables—participant- and situation-relevant
- Random assignment
- Controls
- Group matching
- Experimenter bias
- Double-blind procedure
- Single-blind procedure
- Response or participant bias
- Social desirability
- Hawthorne effect
- Placebo method
- Correlations—positive and negative
- Survey method
- Response rate
- Naturalistic observation
- Case study method
- Descriptive statistics
- Frequency distribution
- Measures of central tendency—mean, median, mode
- Extreme scores or outliers
- Positive versus negative skew
- Measures of variability—range, standard deviation, variance
- *z* score
- Normal curve
- Correlation coefficient
- Scatter plot
- Line of best fit/regression line
- Inferential statistics
- Sampling error
- *p* value
- Statistical significance
- Institutional Review Board (IRB)
- Coercion
- Informed consent
- Anonymity
- Confidentiality
- Debriefing

Note about Skills: Content in this chapter is relevant to one of the skills the College Board identified to be measured on the AP Psychology test. Specifically, in this chapter you will learn about what the College Board calls Skill 3–Scientific Investigation: analyzing and explaining examples of research studies. As you study the terms and ideas in this chapter, test yourself with the questions at the end of the chapter to make sure that you are able to use the relevant vocabulary to analyze and critique psychological research studies.

RESEARCH METHODS

Psychology is a science, and it is therefore based on research. Though people are often guided effectively by their common intuition, sometimes it leads us astray. People have the tendency upon hearing about research findings (and many other things) to think that they knew it all along; this tendency is called **hindsight bias**. After an event occurs, it is relatively easy to explain why it happened. The goal of scientific research, however, is to predict what will happen in advance.

An understanding of research methods is fundamental to psychology. Because of that, you are more likely to see a free-response (or essay) question on this topic than on any other.

Sometimes psychologists conduct research in order to solve practical problems. For instance, psychologists might compare two different methods of teaching children to read in order to determine which method is better or they could design and test the efficacy of a program to help people quit smoking. This type of research is known as **applied research** because it has clear, practical applications. Other psychologists conduct **basic research**. Basic research explores questions that are of interest to psychologists but are not intended to have immediate, real-world applications. Examples of basic research would include studying how people form their attitudes about others and how people in different cultures define intelligence.

Terminology

Hypotheses and Variables

Although some research is purely descriptive, most psychological research is guided by hypotheses. A **hypothesis** expresses a relationship between two variables. Variables, by definition, are things that can vary among the participants in the research. For instance, religion, stress level, and height are variables. According to an experimental hypothesis, the **dependent variable** depends on the **independent variable**. In other words, a change in the independent variable will produce a change in the dependent variable. For instance, consider the hypothesis that watching violent television programs makes people more aggressive. In this hypothesis, watching television violence is the independent variable since the hypothesis suggests that a change in television viewing will result in a change in behavior. In testing a hypothesis, researchers manipulate the independent variable and measure the dependent variable. Hypotheses often grow out of theories. A **theory** aims to explain some phenomenon and allows researchers to generate testable hypotheses with the hope of collecting data that support the theory.

Researchers not only need to name the variables they will study, they need to provide **operational definitions** of them. When you operationalize a variable, you explain how you will measure it. For instance, in the hypothesis above, what programs will be considered violent? What behaviors will be considered aggressive? These and many other questions need to be answered before the research commences. The operationalization of the variables raises many issues about the validity and reliability of the research.

TIP

When writing about research, students often describe the goal as proof of the hypothesis. However, proving a hypothesis is impossible. Rather, research aims to gather data that either supports or disproves a hypothesis.

Validity and Reliability

Good research is both valid and reliable. Research is **valid** when it measures what the researcher set out to measure; it is accurate. Research is **reliable** when it can be replicated; it is consistent. If the researcher conducted the same research in the same way, the researcher would get similar results.

Sampling

Before one can begin to investigate a hypothesis, one needs to decide who or what to study. The individuals on which the research will be conducted are called **participants** (or subjects), and the process by which participants are selected is called **sampling**. In order to select a **sample** (the group of participants), one must first identify the **population** from which the sample will be selected. The population includes anyone or anything that could possibly be selected to be in the sample.

The goal in selecting a sample is that it be **representative** of a larger population. If I conduct my research about television violence using only my own psychology students, I cannot say much about how viewing violent television affects other people. My students may not be representative of a larger population. I would be better off specifying a larger and more diverse population, the whole student body of 1,000, for example, and then randomly selecting a sample of 100. The definition of **random selection** is that every member of the population has an equal chance of being selected. Random selection increases the likelihood that the sample represents the population and that one can generalize the findings to the larger population.

Note that psychologists use the term **random** differently than laypeople. If I choose my sample by standing in front of the library on a Wednesday morning and approaching people in a way I feel is random, I have not used random sampling. Perhaps, without realizing it, I was less likely to approach people I did not know or people wearing college sweatshirts. Since they would not stand an equal chance of being selected for the study, the selection process is not random. In addition, the method just described would not yield a representative sample of the school's population. Not everybody will walk past the library on Wednesday morning. People who do not will have no chance of being selected for the study and therefore are not part of the population. Random selection is best done using a computer, a table of random numbers, or that tried-and-true method of picking names out of a hat.

TIP

Selecting a sample randomly maximizes the chance that it will represent the population from which it was drawn and allows researchers to draw generalizations about the population based on their findings about their sample.

Even if I randomly select a sample of 100 people from the school's population of 1,000, clearly the sample will probably not perfectly reflect the composition of the school. For instance, if the school has exactly 500 males and 500 females in it, what are the chances that my random sample will have the same 1:1 ratio? Although we could compute those odds, that is not necessary. Clearly, the larger the sample, the more likely it is to represent the population. A sample of all 1,000 students guarantees that it is perfectly representative, and a sample of 1 person guarantees that it is far from representative. So why not use all 1,000 students? The downside of a large sample is time and money. Also, realizing that the populations psychologists study are often much larger than 1,000 people is important. Therefore, for research to use large, but not prohibitively large, samples is considered optimum. Statistics can be used to determine how large a sample should be in order to represent a population of any particular size. If asked on the Advanced Placement examination to design your own research, you should specify the size of your sample and avoid using samples of extreme sizes.

One additional action can be taken to increase the likelihood that a sample will represent the larger population from which it was chosen. **Stratified sampling** is a process that allows a researcher to ensure that the sample represents the population on some criteria. For instance, if I thought that participants of different racial groups might respond differently, I would want to make sure that I represented each race in my sample in the same proportion that it appears in the overall population. In other words, if 500 of the 1,000 students in a school are Caucasian, 300 are African American, and 200 are Latino, in a sample of 100 students I would want to have 50 Caucasians, 30 African Americans, and 20 Latinos. To that end, I could first divide the names of potential participants into each of the three racial groups, and then I could choose a random subsample of the desired size from each group.

Experimental Method

Experiments can be divided into laboratory experiments and field experiments. **Laboratory experiments** are conducted in a lab, a highly controlled environment, while **field experiments** are conducted out in the world. The extent to which laboratory experiments can be controlled is their main advantage. The advantage of field experiments is that they are more realistic.

Psychologists' preferred method of research is the **experiment** because only through a carefully controlled experiment can one show a causal relationship. An experiment allows the researcher to manipulate the independent variable and control for **confounding variables**. A confounding variable is any difference between the experimental and control conditions, except for the independent variable, that might affect the dependent variable. In order to show that the violent television programs cause participants' aggression, I need to rule out any other possible cause. An experiment can achieve this goal by randomly assigning participants to conditions and by using various methods of control to eliminate confounding variables.

TIP

Students often equate all research with experiments. As described in the text, many different kinds of research can be conducted, but only experiments can identify cause-and-effect relationships.

Assignment is the process by which participants are put into a group, experimental or control. **Random assignment** means that each participant has an equal chance of being placed into any group. The benefit of random assignment is that it limits the effect of **participant-relevant confounding variables**. If participants were given the opportunity to choose whether to be in the group watching the violent television or not, it is highly unlikely that the two groups would be comprised of similar people. Perhaps violent people prefer violent television and would therefore select the experimental group. Even if one were to assign people to groups based on a seemingly random criterion (when they arrived at the experiment or where they were sitting in the room), one might open the door to confounding variables. Using random assignment diminishes the chance that participants in the two groups differ in any meaningful way, or, in other words, it **controls** for participant-relevant variables.

TIP

Random assignment controls for participant-relevant confounding variables. Students sometimes confuse random assignment and random sampling. While both involve randomization, sampling is the process of choosing the research participants from the population, and it happens before assignment. Assignment is the process of dividing participants into groups (for example, experimental and control), and it cannot be done until after you have identified the sample.

Note that when we talk about differences between groups, we are referring to the group average. A single very aggressive subject will not throw off the results of the entire group. The idea behind random assignment is that, in general, the groups will be equivalent.

If one wanted to ensure that the experimental and control groups were equivalent on some criterion (e.g., sex, IQ scores, age), one could use **group matching**. If one wanted to group match for sex, one would first divide the sample into males and females and then randomly assign half of each group to each condition. Group matching would not result in the same number of males and females within each group. Rather, half of the males and half of the females would be in each of the groups.

Situation-relevant confounding variables can also affect an experiment. For the participants to be equivalent is not enough. The situations into which the different groups are put must also be equivalent except for the differences produced by the independent variable. If the experimental group watches violent television in a large lecture hall while the control group watches other programs in a small classroom, their situations are not equivalent. Therefore, any differences found between the groups may possibly be due not to the independent variable, as hypothesized, but rather to the confounding variables. Other situation-relevant variables include the time of day, the weather, and the presence of other people in the room. Making the environments into which the two groups are placed as similar as possible **controls** for situation-relevant confounding variables.

Experimenter bias is a special kind of situation-relevant confounding variable. Experimenter bias is the unconscious tendency for researchers to treat members of the experimental and control groups differently to increase the chance of confirming their hypothesis. Note that experimenter bias is not a conscious act. If researchers purposely distort their data, it is called fraud, not experimenter bias. Experimenter bias can be eliminated by using a **double-blind procedure**. A double blind occurs when neither the participants nor the researcher are able to affect the outcome of the research. A double blind can be accomplished in a number of ways. The most common way is for the researcher to have someone blind to the participants' condition interact with the participants. A **single blind** occurs when only the participants do not know to which group they have been assigned; this strategy minimizes the effect of **demand characteristics** as well as certain kinds of **response** or **participant bias**. Demand characteristics are cues about the purpose of the study. Participants use such cues to try to respond appropriately. Response or subject bias is the tendency for subjects to behave in certain ways (for example, circle the midpoint on a scale or pick the right-hand option more than the left-hand one). One kind of response bias, the tendency to try to give answers that reflect well upon them, is called **social desirability**.

TIP

Equivalent environments control for situation-relevant confounding variables.

Experiments typically involve at least one **experimental group** and a **control group**. The experimental group is the one that gets the treatment operationalized in the independent variable. The control group gets none of the independent variable. It serves as a basis for comparison. Without a control group, knowing whether changes in the experimental group

TIP

Double blinds eliminate both experimenter and subject bias.

are due to the experimental treatment or simply to any treatment at all is impossible. In fact, merely selecting a group of people on whom to experiment has been determined to affect the performance of that group, regardless of what is done to those individuals. This finding is known as the **Hawthorne effect**.

Continuing with the television example, the experimental group would be the participants who view violent television, while the control group would view some other type of television, perhaps a comedy. If I were really designing an experiment, I would have to be much more specific in operationally defining my independent variable. I would need to identify exactly what program(s) each group would watch and for how long. Many experiments involve much more complicated designs. In our example, additional groups would view other types of films or groups would view differing amounts of violent content.

One important method of control is known as the **placebo method**. Whenever participants in the experimental group are supposed to ingest a drug, participants in the control group are given an inert but otherwise identical substance. This technique allows researchers to separate the physiological effects of the drug from the psychological effects of people thinking they took a drug (called the **placebo effect**).

Sometimes using participants as their own control group is possible, a procedure known as **counterbalancing**. For instance, if I wanted to see how frustration affected performance on an IQ test, I could have my participants engage in a task unlikely to cause frustration, test their IQ, and then give them a frustrating task and test their IQs again. However, this procedure creates the possibility of **order effects**. Participants may do better on the second IQ test simply by virtue of having taken the first IQ test. This problem can be eliminated by using **counterbalancing**. I can counterbalance by having half the participants do the frustrating task first and half the participants do the not-frustrating task first and then switching.

TIP

Students sometimes believe that a control group is the only possible method of control. Remember that although it is an extremely important and obviously named type of control, using control groups is but one of many such methods.

Correlational Method

A **correlation** expresses a relationship between two variables without ascribing cause. Correlations can be either positive or negative. A **positive correlation** between two things means that the presence of one thing predicts the presence of the other. A **negative correlation** means that the presence of one thing predicts the absence of the other. See the statistics section for more information about correlations.

TIP

Correlation does not imply causation.

Sometimes psychologists elect not to use the experimental method. Sometimes testing a hypothesis with an experiment is impossible. Suppose, for example, I want to test the hypothesis that boys are more likely to call out in class than girls. Clearly, I cannot randomly assign subjects to conditions. Boys are boys, and girls are girls. The assignment of the independent variable, in this case, has been predetermined. As a result, I will never be able to isolate the cause of the calling out behavior. It could be a biological difference or one of many social influences that act differently upon the sexes from birth onward. If I seek to control all other aspects of the research process, as I would in an experiment, I will have conducted an **ex post facto study**.

An even more popular research design is the **survey method**. The survey method, as common sense suggests, involves asking people to fill out surveys. To contrast the survey method with the experimental method, return to the question about whether there is a relationship between watching violence on television and aggressive behavior. The original hypothesis, that *"watching violent television programs makes people more aggressive,"* cannot be tested using the survey method, because only an experiment can reveal a cause-effect relationship. However, one could use the survey method to investigate whether there is a relationship between the two variables, watching violence on television and aggressive behavior. In the survey method, neither of the variables is manipulated. Therefore, while there are two variables, there is no independent or dependent variable.

> **TIP**
>
> Students often confuse the use of surveys to measure the dependent variable in an experiment with the survey method. While surveys can be used as part of the experimental method, the survey method, as described, is a kind of correlational research in which the researcher does not manipulate the independent variable.

Using the survey method means that one can no longer control for participant-relevant confounding variables. Some people watch a lot of violent television, and others do not. In all likelihood, these two groups of people would differ in a number of other ways as well. The survey method does not enable the researcher to determine which of these differences cause a difference in violent behavior.

Although controlling for situation-relevant confounding variables using the survey method is possible (by bringing all the participants to one place at one time to fill out the survey), it is rarely done. One of the advantages of the survey method is that conducting research by mailing surveys for people to fill out at their convenience is easy. However, if people fill out the surveys in different places, at different times of day, by taking different amounts of time, and so on, the research will be plagued by confounding variables. Thus, again, determining what causes a difference in violent behavior becomes impossible. In addition, obtaining a random sample when one sends out a survey is difficult because relatively few people will actually send it back (low **response rate**), and these people are unlikely to make up a representative sample.

Naturalistic Observation

Sometimes researchers opt to observe their participants in their natural habitats without interacting with them at all. Such unobtrusive observation is called **naturalistic observation**. The goal of naturalistic observation is to get a realistic and rich picture of the participants' behavior. To that end, control is sacrificed.

> **TIP**
>
> Students often confuse naturalistic observation with field experiments. Both involve doing research out in the world. However, in naturalistic observation, the researchers do not impact the behavior of the participants at all. In contrast, in field experiments, as in all experiments, the researcher has manipulated the independent variable and attempted to eliminate as many confounding variables as possible.

Case Studies

One final research method we will mention is the **case study method**. The case study method is used to get a full, detailed picture of one participant or a small group of participants. For instance, clinical psychologists often use case studies to present information about a person suffering from a particular disorder. While case studies allow researchers to get the richest possible picture of what they are studying, the focus on a single individual or small group means that the findings cannot be generalized to a larger population.

STATISTICS

Note about Skills: Content in this chapter is relevant to one of the skills the College Board identified to be measured on the AP Psychology test. Specifically, in this section you will learn about what the College Board calls Skill 2–Data Analysis: understanding and making inferences based on numerical data. As you study the terms and ideas in this chapter, test yourself with the questions at the end of the chapter to make sure that you are able to use the statistical terms and processes to analyze data from psychological studies and recognize valid conclusions based on those data.

Descriptive Statistics

Descriptive statistics, as the name suggests, simply describe a set of data. For instance, if you were interested in researching what kinds of pets your schoolmates have, you might summarize that data by creating a **frequency distribution** that would tell you how many students had dogs, cats, zebras, and so on. Graphing your findings is often helpful. Frequency distributions can be easily turned into line graphs called **frequency polygons** or bar graphs known as **histograms**. The *y*-axis (vertical) always represents frequency, while whatever you are graphing, in this case, pets, is graphed along the *x*-axis (horizontal).

You are probably already familiar with at least one group of statistical measures called measures of **central tendency**. Measures of central tendency attempt to mark the center of a distribution. Three common measures of central tendency are the **mean**, **median**, and **mode**. The mean is what we usually refer to as the average of all the scores in a distribution. To compute the mean, you simply add up all the scores in the distribution and divide by the number of scores. The median is the central score in the distribution. To find the median of a distribution, simply write the scores down in ascending (or descending) order and then, if there are an odd number of scores, find the middle one. If the distribution contains an even number of scores, the median is the average of the middle two scores. The mode is the score that appears most frequently. A distribution may, however, have more than one mode. A distribution is bimodal, for instance, if two scores appear equally frequently and more frequently than any other score.

The mean is the most commonly used measure of central tendency, but its accuracy can be distorted by **extreme scores** or **outliers**. Imagine that 19 of your 20 friends drive cars valued at $12,000 but your other friend has a Maserati valued at $120,000. The mean value of your cars is $17,400. However, since that value is in excess of everyone's car except one person's, you would probably agree that it is not the best measure of central tendency in this case. When a distribution includes outliers, the median is often used as a better measure of central tendency.

Unless a distribution is symmetrical, it is skewed. Outliers skew distributions. When a distribution includes an extreme score (or group of scores) that is very high, as in the car example above, the distribution is said to be **positively skewed**. When the skew is caused by a particularly low score (or group of scores), the distribution is **negatively skewed**. A positively skewed distribution contains more low scores than high scores; the skew is produced by some aberrantly high score(s). Conversely, a negatively skewed distribution contains more high scores than low scores. In a positively skewed distribution, the mean is higher than the median because the outlier(s) have a much more dramatic effect on the mean than on the median. Of course, the opposite is true in a negatively skewed distribution (see Fig. 2.1).

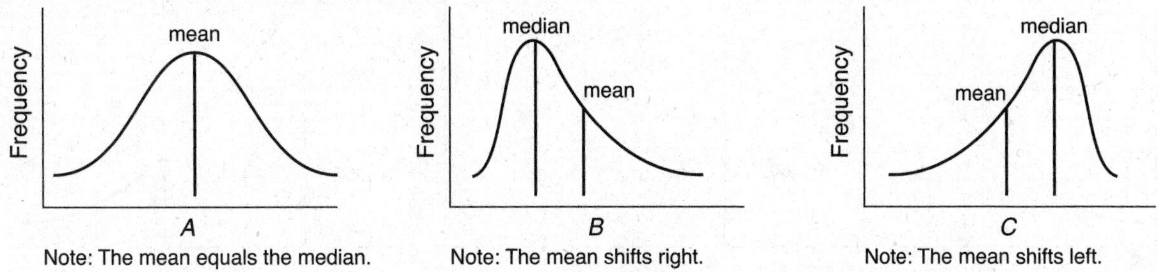

Figure 2.1 *A*, symmetrical distribution; *B*, positively skewed distribution; *C*, negatively skewed distribution.

Measures of variability are other types of descriptive statistical measures. Again, you may be familiar with some of these measures, such as the **range**, **variance**, and **standard deviation**. Measures of variability attempt to depict the diversity of the distribution. The range is the distance between the highest and lowest score in a distribution. The variance and standard deviation are closely related; standard deviation is simply the square root of the variance. Both measures essentially relate the average distance of any score in the distribution from the mean. The higher the variance and standard deviation, the more spread out the distribution.

Sometimes, being able to compare scores from different distributions is important. In order to do so, you can convert scores from the different distributions into measures called ***z* scores**. *Z* scores measure the distance of a score from the mean in units of standard deviation. Scores below the mean have negative *z* scores, while scores above the mean have positive *z* scores. For instance, if Clarence scored a 72 on a test with a mean of 80 and a standard deviation of 8, Clarence's *z* score would be −1. If Maria scored an 84 on that same test, her *z* score would be +0.5.

Often in psychology you will see reference to the **normal curve**. The normal curve is a theoretical bell-shaped curve for which the area under the curve lying between any two *z* scores has been predetermined. Approximately 68 percent of scores in a normal distribution fall within one standard deviation of the mean, approximately 95 percent of scores fall within two standard deviations of the mean, and almost 99 percent of scores fall within three standard deviations of the mean. Knowing that the normal curve is symmetrical, and knowing the three numbers given above will allow you to calculate the approximate percentage of scores falling between any given *z* scores. For instance, approximately 47.5 percent (95/2) of scores fall between the *z* scores of 0 and +2 (see Fig. 2.2).

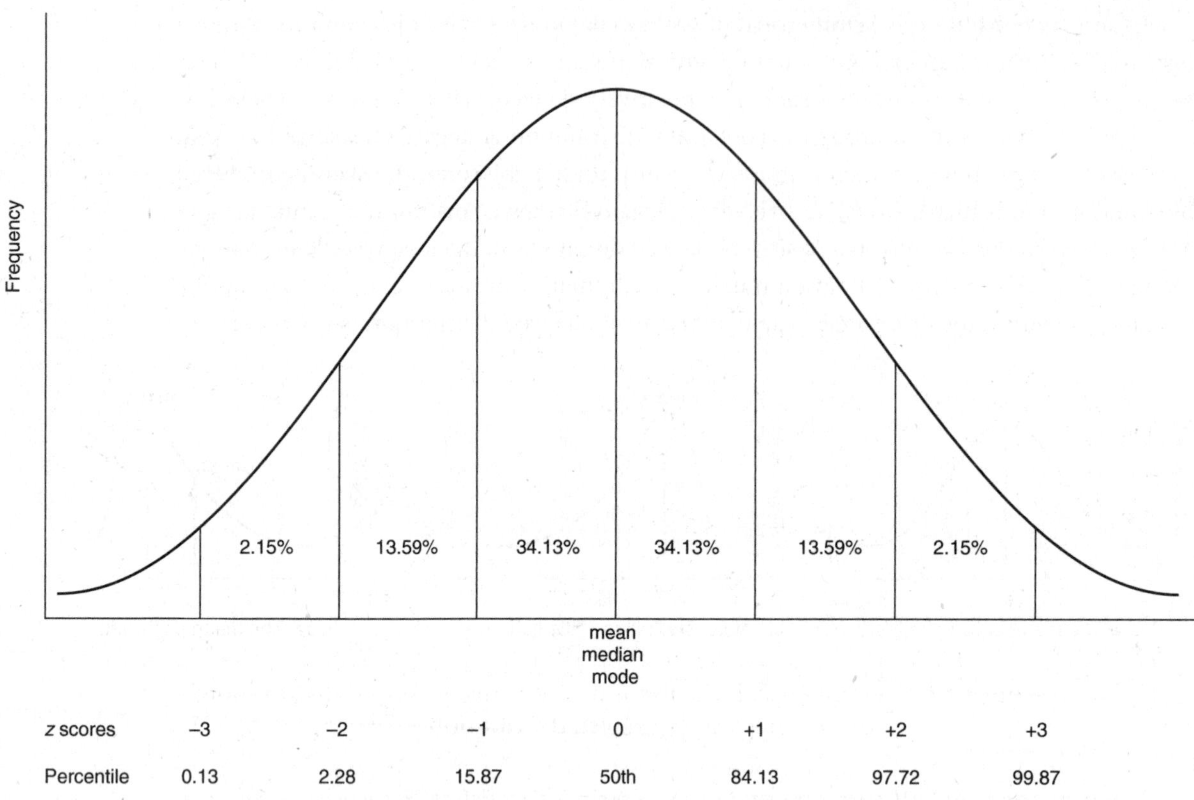

Figure 2.2 The normal distribution.

While *z* scores measure the distance of a score away from the mean, **percentiles** indicate the distance of a score from 0. Someone who scores in the 90th percentile on a test has scored better than 90 percent of the people who took the test. Similarly, someone who scores at the 38th percentile scored better than only 38 percent of the people who took the test. A clear relationship exists between percentiles and *z* scores when dealing with the normal curve. Someone who scores at the 50th percentile has a *z* score of 0, and someone who scores at the 98th percentile has an approximate *z* score of +2.

Correlations

A **correlation** measures the relationship between two variables. As explained earlier, correlations can be either positive or negative. If two things are positively correlated, the presence of one thing predicts the presence of the other. In contrast, a negative correlation means that the presence of one thing predicts the absence of the other. When no relationship exists between two things, no correlation exists. As an example, one would suspect that a positive correlation exists between studying and earning good grades. Conversely, one would suspect that a negative correlation might occur between cutting classes and earning good grades. Finally, it is likely that there is no correlation between the number of stuffed animals one owns and earning good grades.

Correlations may be either strong or weak. The strength of a correlation can be computed by a statistic called the **correlation coefficient**. Correlation coefficients range from −1 and +1 where −1 is a perfect negative correlation and +1 is a perfect positive correlation. Both −1 and +1 denote equally strong correlations. The number 0 denotes the weakest possible correlation—no correlation—which means that knowing something about one variable tells you nothing about the other.

A correlation may be graphed using a **scatter plot**. A scatter plot graphs pairs of values, one on the *y*-axis and one on the *x*-axis. For instance, the number of hours a group of people study per week could be plotted on the *x*-axis while their GPAs could be plotted on the *y*-axis. The result would be a series of points called a scatter plot. The closer the points come to falling on a straight line, the stronger the correlation. The **line of best fit**, or **regression line**, is the line drawn through the scatter plot that minimizes the distance of all the points from the line. When the line slopes upward, from left to right, it indicates a positive correlation. A downward slope evidences a negative correlation. The scatter plot depicting the data set given in Table 2.1 is graphed in Figure 2.3.

TIP

Students often believe strong correlations correspond to positive numbers. Do not forget that −.92 is exactly as strong a correlation as +.92.

Table 2.1 The Relationship Between Hours Studied and GPA

Name	Hours Studied	GPA
Teresa	15	3.8
Raoul	17	3.8
Todd	4	1.3
Lucy	11	3.1
Aaron	8	2.4
Pam	12	3.3
Laticia	14	3.9
Greg	9	2.5
Megan	5	0.6

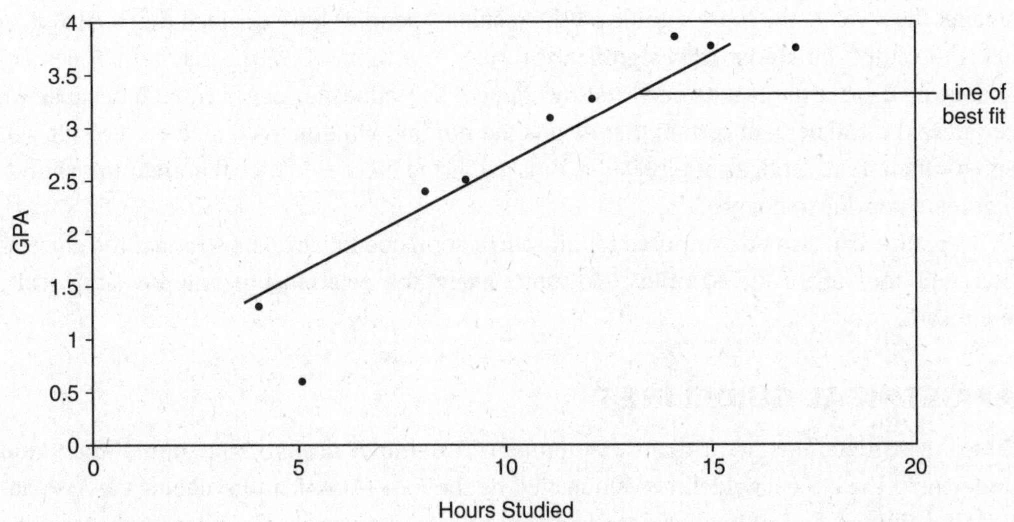

Figure 2.3 Scatter plot showing the correlation between hours studied and GPA.

TIP

As discussed previously, a correlation, no matter how strong, does not indicate a causal relationship.

Inferential Statistics

Whereas descriptive statistics provide a way to summarize information about the sample studied, the purpose of **inferential statistics** is to determine whether or not findings can be applied to the larger population from which the sample was selected. Remember that one of the primary goals in selecting a sample is that the sample represents the population from which it was picked. If a sample does not represent the larger population, one cannot infer anything about the larger population from the sample. Guaranteeing that a sample is representative of a population is impossible. The extent to which the sample differs from the population is known as **sampling error**.

Say that you ran an experiment testing the effects of sugar consumption on short-term memory. You randomly assigned your 50 subjects to either a control group that was given a sugar-free lollipop or to the experimental group that was given a seemingly identical lollipop that contained sugar. You then tested the participants' ability to recall 15 one-syllable nouns. If the experimental group remembered an average of 7 words and the control group remembered an average of 6.9 words, would you be comfortable concluding that sugar does, in fact, enhance short-term memory? Your gut reaction is probably to say that the 0.1 difference in the example is too small to allow us to draw such a conclusion. What if the experimental group consisted of just one person who recalled all 15 words while the control group contained one person who remembered only 5 words? You would probably be similarly reluctant to draw any conclusions even given this enormous difference in the number of words recalled due to the tiny sample size.

In both cases, you would be correct to be skeptical. The differences between the groups are likely due to sampling error and chance. The purpose of inferential statistics is to help psychologists decide when their findings can be applied to the larger population. Many different inferential statistical tests exist such as t-tests, chi square tests, and ANOVAs. They all take into account both the magnitude of the difference found and the size of the sample. However, what is most important for you to know is that all these tests yield a ***p* value**. The *p* value gives the probability that the difference between the groups is due to chance. The smaller the *p* value, the more significant the results. Scientists have decided that a *p* value of .05 is the cutoff for **statistically significant** results. A *p* value of .05 means that a 5 percent chance exists that the results occurred by chance. A *p* value can never equal 0 because we can never be 100 percent certain that results did not happen due to chance. As a result, scientists often try to replicate their results, thus gathering more evidence that their initial findings were not due to chance.

A *p* value can also be computed for any correlation coefficient. The stronger the correlation and the larger the sample, the more likely the relationship will be statistically significant.

APA ETHICAL GUIDELINES

Ethical considerations are a major component in research design. You should know and understand the ethical guidelines established by the APA (American Psychological Association) for human and animal research and be prepared to apply the concepts to specific research designs. Any type of academic research must first propose the study to the ethics board or **Institutional Review Board (IRB)** at the institution. The IRB reviews research proposals for ethical violations and/or procedural errors. This board ultimately gives researchers permission to go ahead with the research or requires them to revise their procedures.

Animal Research

Groups advocating the ethical treatment of animals are focusing more and more attention on how animals are treated in laboratory experiments. The APA developed strict guidelines about what animals and how animals can be used in psychological research. Ethical psychological studies using animals must meet the following requirements:

- The research must have a clear scientific purpose.
- The research must answer a specific, important scientific question.
- Animals chosen must be best-suited to answer the question at hand.
- Researchers must care for and house animals in a humane way.
- Researchers must acquire animal subjects legally. Animals must be purchased from accredited companies. If wild animals must be used, they need to be trapped in a humane manner.
- Researchers must design experimental procedures that employ the least amount of suffering feasible.

Human Research

Research involving human subjects must meet the following standards:

- **No coercion**—Participation should be voluntary.
- **Informed consent**—Participants must know that they are involved in research and give their consent. If the participants are deceived in any way about the nature of the study, the deception must not be so extreme as to invalidate the **informed consent**. The research the participants thought they were consenting to must be similar enough to the actual study to give the informed consent meaning. Also, researchers must be very careful about the trauma deception may cause (see "Risk," below).
- **Anonymity or confidentiality**—Participants' privacy must be protected. Their identities and actions must not be revealed by the researcher. Participants have **anonymity** when the researchers do not collect any data that enable them to match a person's responses with his or her name. In some cases, such as interview studies, a researcher cannot promise **anonymity** but instead guarantees **confidentiality**, that the researcher will not identify the source of any of the data.
- **Risk**—Participants cannot be placed at significant mental or physical risk. Typically, it is considered permissible for participants to experience temporary discomfort or stress, but activities that might cause someone long-term mental or physical harm must be avoided. This clause requires interpretation by the Review Board. Some institutions might allow a level of risk other boards might not allow. This consideration was highlighted by Stanley Milgram's obedience studies in the 1970s in which participants thought they were causing significant harm or death to other participants (see Chapter 14, "Social Psychology").
- **Debriefing**—After the study, participants should be told the purpose of the study and provided with ways to contact the researchers about the results. When research involves deception, it is particularly important to conduct a thorough **debriefing**.

PRACTICE QUESTIONS

Directions: Each of the questions or incomplete statements below is followed by five suggested answers or completions. Select the one that is best in each case.

1. Psychologists generally prefer the experimental method to other research methods because

   (A) experiments are more likely to support psychologists' hypotheses.
   (B) experiments can show cause-effect relationships.
   (C) it is easier to obtain a random sample for an experiment.
   (D) double-blind designs are unnecessary in an experiment.
   (E) experiments are more likely to result in statistically significant findings.

2. Theoretically, random assignment should eliminate

   (A) sampling error.
   (B) the need to use statistics.
   (C) concerns over validity.
   (D) many confounding variables.
   (E) the need for a representative sample.

3. Charlotte and Tamar are lab partners assigned to research who is friendlier, girls or boys. After conversing with their first 10 participants, they find that their friendliness ratings often differ. With which of the following should they be most concerned?

   (A) reliability
   (B) confounding variables
   (C) ethics
   (D) validity
   (E) assignment

4. Which of the following hypotheses would be most difficult to test experimentally?

   (A) People exposed to the color red will be more aggressive than those exposed to the color blue.
   (B) Exercise improves mood.
   (C) Exposure to violent television increases aggression.
   (D) Studying leads to better grades.
   (E) Divorce makes children more independent.

5. Professor Ma wants to design a project studying emotional response to date rape. He advertises for participants in the school newspaper, informs them about the nature of the study, gets their consent, conducts an interview, and debriefs them about the results when the experiment is over. If you were on the IRB, which ethical consideration would you most likely have the most concern about in Professor Ma's study?

(A) coercion
(B) deception
(C) confounding variables
(D) confidentiality
(E) clear scientific purpose

6. Some psychologists consider Stanley Milgram's obedience studies to be unethical because of which ethical consideration?

(A) improper sampling procedure
(B) risk of long-term harm
(C) clear scientific purpose
(D) debriefing
(E) anonymity

7. One of the principal differences between the ethical guidelines for human and animal research is:

(A) Human participants can be deceived for experimental purposes and animals cannot.
(B) Animals can be placed at much greater physical risk than human participants can.
(C) Human participants must be chosen much more carefully than animal subjects.
(D) If humans might physically suffer because of the study, the suffering must be minimal, in contrast to animal studies where any amount of suffering is ethical if it helps to further a clear scientific purpose.
(E) Environmental conditions for human studies must be monitored much more closely than they are in an animal study.

8. Lily scored 145 on an IQ test with a mean of 100 and a standard deviation of 15. What is her z score?

(A) −3
(B) −1.5
(C) +0.67
(D) 1.5
(E) +3

9. What is the median of the following distribution: 6, 2, 9, 4, 7, 3?

(A) 4
(B) 5
(C) 5.5
(D) 6
(E) 6.5

10. Emma scores a perfect 100 on a test that everyone else fails. If we were to graph this distribution, it would be

(A) symmetrical.
(B) normal.
(C) positively skewed.
(D) negatively skewed.
(E) a straight line.

11. José hypothesizes that a new drug he has just invented will enhance mice's memories. He feeds the drug to the experimental group and gives the control group a placebo. He then times the mice as they learn to run through a maze. In order to know whether his hypothesis has been supported, José would need to use

(A) scatter plots.
(B) descriptive statistics.
(C) histograms.
(D) inferential statistics.
(E) means-end analysis.

12. Which of the following is an example of random sampling?

I. Picking out of a hat to assign each of three classes to an experimental condition.
II. Having a computer generate a random list of 100 high school students.
III. Approaching any 50 students during sixth-period lunch.

(A) I only
(B) II only
(C) III only
(D) I and II
(E) I, II, and III

13. Vincenzo conducts an experiment to see whether fear makes mice run through mazes faster. He first selected a sample of 60 mice and then divided them into a control group and an experimental group. Which cannot be a confounding variable?

(A) how fast the mice are at the start
(B) when the mice run the maze
(C) the population from which he selected his subjects
(D) how frightened the mice are before the experiment
(E) where the mice run the maze

14. Olivia, a nursery school student, hypothesizes that boys have fights with the finger paints more than girls do. She tests her hypothesis by casually watching the finger-painting table for three days of nursery school. What method is she using?

    (A) field experiment
    (B) informal survey
    (C) case study
    (D) naturalistic observation
    (E) ethnography

15. Talia collects survey data that indicate that students who spend more time preparing for the AP test tend to score better than other students. Jen can now conclude that

    (A) studying improves exam grades.
    (B) a relationship exists between studying and exam grades.
    (C) a significant correlation exists between studying and exam grades.
    (D) anyone who does not study will do poorly on the exam.
    (E) better students tend to study more.

ANSWER KEY

1. **B**
2. **D**
3. **A**
4. **E**
5. **D**
6. **B**
7. **B**
8. **E**
9. **B**
10. **C**
11. **D**
12. **B**
13. **C**
14. **D**
15. **B**

ANSWERS EXPLAINED

1. **(B)** Psychologists generally prefer the experimental method to other research methods because experiments can show cause-effect relationships. The hallmarks of an experiment are the ability to manipulate the independent variable, randomly assign subjects to conditions, and eliminate (control for) differences between the conditions. When these steps are taken, disparities between the experimental and control groups can be attributed to the independent variable, the only thing that differed between the groups. No other research method allows for the control necessary to make such an attribution. None of the other statements are true.

2. **(D)** Random assignment should eliminate subject-relevant confounding variables (e.g., conscientiousness, IQ, hair color). Since it would be impossible to match participants on every possible dimension, many psychologists use random assignment. By taking advantage of the laws of probability, random assignment makes it likely that participants in the different conditions of an experiment will be equivalent. Random assignment does not relate to sampling or validity and has no impact on the need for statistics.

3. **(A)** Charlotte and Tamar's way of measuring friendliness is not reliable. Reliability refers to the consistency of a measure. Since they disagree so often, their measure is not consistent. In all likelihood, they need to operationalize their dependent variable more clearly. Reliability is sometimes confused with validity. Validity refers to the accuracy of a measure, which in this case is whether they are actually measuring friendliness.

4. **(E)** It would be extremely difficult to test whether parental divorce causes children to become more independent because it is essentially impossible to manipulate the independent variable, divorce. If we tried to recruit parents to be in our experiment and told them that half would be assigned to divorce and the other half to stay married, it is unlikely that any would consent to participate. If you wanted to compare children whose parents had divorced with children from intact families, you could conduct a quasi-experiment. In a quasi-experiment, the researcher is unable to manipulate the independent variable but tries to control as many other factors as possible. The other four examples are relatively easy to study experimentally as the independent variables (color, exercise, exposure to violent television, and studying) are not difficult to manipulate.

5. **(D)** Professor Ma would need to be particularly careful to ensure the participants' confidentiality in this study since it deals with a controversial and possibly embarrassing subject. There is no indication that Professor Ma coerced the participants or deceived them in any way. Confounding variables are a concern for the validity of the study but not an ethical consideration. The study does have a clear scientific purpose.

6. **(B)** Milgram's experiments involved considerable risk of long-lasting stress and anxiety for his subjects. The scientific purpose of Milgram's study is not disputed, and he debriefed participants and provided for anonymity of individual results.

7. **(B)** Within the limits imposed by the guidelines, researchers can physically harm animals if the harm is justified by the nature of the experiments. Deception is obviously not an issue applicable to animal research. Researchers must keep suffering to a minimum, so "any amount" is not an appropriate response (choice D). Animal subjects must be chosen carefully (from accredited commercial sources) and their environment must follow strict guidelines, so choices C and E are also incorrect.

8. **(E)** Lily's *z* score is +3. *Z* scores measure the distance of a score from the mean in units of standard deviation. Since the mean is 100 and the standard deviation is 15, Lily's score is 3 standard deviations above the mean.

9. **(B)** The median of the distribution is 5. The problem is easier if you put the scores in order: 2, 3, 4, 6, 7, 9. Since the distribution has an even number of scores, there is no middle score and you must average the two middle scores, 4 and 6.

10. **(C)** Emma's perfect score is an outlier and will therefore skew the distribution. Since it is a high score in a distribution of low scores, the distribution will be positively skewed.

11. **(D)** José needs to compare the performances of the two groups using inferential statistics to determine whether or not the experimental group's performance was significantly better. Scatter plots are used to graph correlations. José would certainly be interested in descriptive statistics as well, but he would not know whether or not his hypothesis had been supported until he used inferential statistics. Histograms are bar graphs, and means-end analysis is a problem-solving technique.

12. **(B)** Of the three methods presented, only having a computer generate a random list of names is an example of random sampling. The first example illustrates random assignment and not random sampling. Sampling is the process of choosing a group of participants from a population. Once sampling has been completed, one might assign the participants to conditions as described in I. Finally, approaching 50 students during a lunch period does not constitute random sampling even if the person who picks the people tries to do so randomly. Remember that the word *random* has a very specific meaning in the context of research. Random sampling means that all members of the population had an equal chance of being selected, and people are unable to be so scrupulously unbiased.

13. **(C)** A confounding variable is anything that differs between the control and experimental group besides the independent variable. How fast and frightened the mice are at the onset of the experiment are potential participant-relevant confounding variables. When and where the experiment takes place are possible situation-relevant confounding variables. However, the population from which Vincenzo selected his mice is not a confounding variable; they all came from the same population. True, the population can be flawed. For instance, it can be very homogeneous and thus fail to reflect how other mice would perform under similar conditions. However, such a flaw is not a confounding variable.

14. **(D)** Olivia is using naturalistic observation. As a student herself, she can observe the finger-painting table unobtrusively. She does not interact with the finger painters; she merely observes. Because Olivia does not manipulate an independent variable nor attempt to control any aspect of her study, she is not using any kind of experiment. She did not ask the participants questions as she would have if she were conducting a survey. She did not focus on a single participant or a small group of participants as she would have if she had been interested in putting together a case study. Finally, Olivia has not conducted ethnographic research. Ethnography is a type of research in which the researcher immerses himself or herself in another culture and then describes it. Ethnography is a method most commonly employed by anthropologists.

15. **(B)** Talia has established a relationship, or correlation, between the two variables she is studying. However, since she has not conducted an experiment, Talia does not know whether a cause-and-effect relationship occurs between studying and earning high grades on the exam. Therefore, Talia does not know if studying improves exam grades. Although Talia has found a correlation between studying and exam grades, whether or not that correlation is significant can be determined only through the use of inferential statistics. Even if the correlation were significant, it would not guarantee that if someone did not study, he or she would do poorly on the test. Finally, Talia's correlation does not tell us that better students study more. In fact, it tells us nothing about better students, not even what is meant by that term.

UNIT 2

Biological Bases of Behavior

The second AP Psychology unit shifts the focus from the history of psychology and research methods to the specific topic of the relationship between biology and behavior. The first part of the unit summarizes the structure and function of different parts of the brain (including neural anatomy and processes). The unit continues with a brief overview of how the biological systems of genetics and the endocrine system influence thinking and behavior. The unit ends by summarizing the application of biological psychology research to the specific topic of states of consciousness: how brain chemistry and other biological systems relate to sleep, dreams, and psychoactive drugs. You will find the content from this unit in the textbook you use in your AP Psychology class in the "Biological Psychology" and "States of Consciousness" chapters.

Biological Bases of Behavior 3

Key Terms

- Neuroanatomy
- Neuron
- Dendrites
- Cell body (also called the soma)
- Axon
- Myelin sheath
- Terminal buttons (also called end buttons, axon terminal, terminal branches of axon, and synaptic knobs)
- Neurotransmitters
- Synapse
- Receptor sites
- Threshold
- Action potential
- All-or-none principle
- Neural firing
- Excitatory neurotransmitters
- Inhibitory neurotransmitters
- Acetylcholine
- Dopamine
- Endorphins
- Serotonin
- GABA
- Glutamate
- Norepinephrine
- Afferent neurons (or sensory neurons)
- Efferent neurons (or motor neurons)
- Central nervous system
- Spinal cord
- Peripheral nervous system
- Somatic nervous system
- Autonomic nervous system
- Sympathetic nervous system
- Parasympathetic nervous system
- Accidents
- Lesions
- Electroencephalogram (EEG)
- Computerized axial tomography (CAT or CT scan)
- Magnetic resonance imaging (MRI scan)
- Positron emission tomography (PET scan)
- Functional MRI (fMRI)
- Hindbrain
- Medulla
- Pons
- Cerebellum
- Midbrain
- Reticular formation
- Forebrain
- Thalamus
- Hypothalamus
- Amygdala
- Hippocampus
- Limbic system
- Cerebral cortex
- Hemispheres
- Left hemisphere
- Right hemisphere
- Brain lateralization (or hemispheric specialization)
- Corpus callosum
- Lobes
- Association area
- Frontal lobes
- Broca's area
- Wernicke's area
- Motor cortex
- Parietal lobes
- Sensory cortex
- Occipital lobes
- Temporal lobes
- Brain plasticity
- Endocrine system
- Adrenal glands
- Monozygotic twins

Key People

- Roger Sperry
- Michael Gazzaniga
- Paul Broca
- Carl Wernicke
- Thomas Bouchard

OVERVIEW

The influence of biology (sometimes called the **neuroscience** or **biopsychological perspective**) is growing. Some researchers predict that someday psychology will be a specialty within the field of biology. An understanding of the biological principles relevant to psychology is needed not only for the AP exam but for any understanding of current psychological thinking.

NEUROANATOMY

Neuroanatomy refers to the study of the parts and function of neurons. **Neurons** are individual nerve cells. These cells make up our entire nervous system, from the brain to the neurons that fire when you stub your toe. Every neuron is made up of discrete parts (see Fig. 3.1).

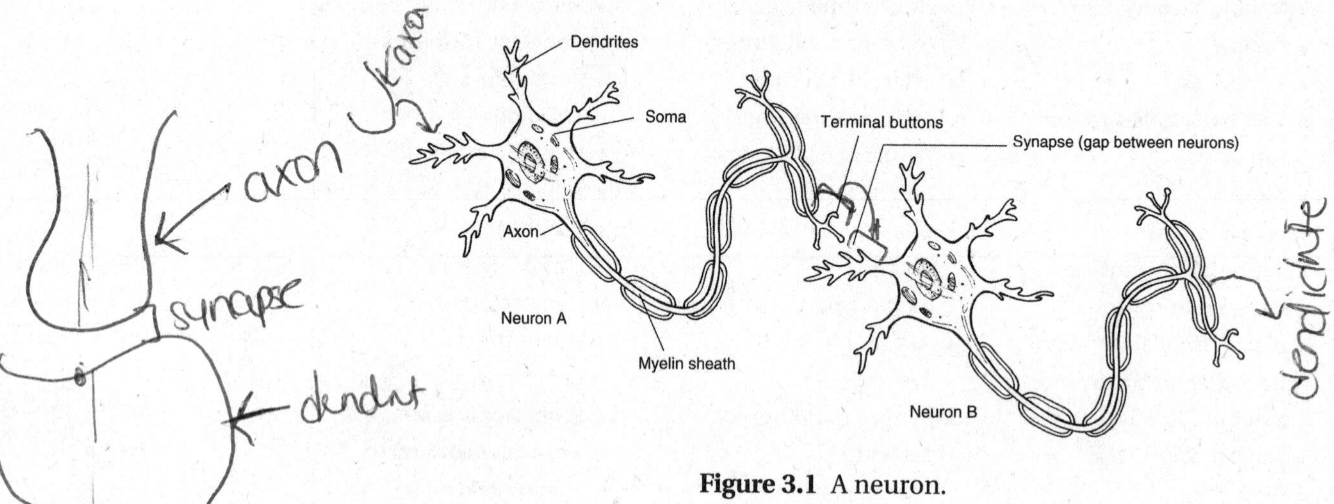

Figure 3.1 A neuron.

> **Dendrites** — rootlike parts of the cell that stretch out from the cell body. Dendrites grow to make synaptic connections with other neurons (see "Synapse," below).
>
> **Cell body** (also called the soma) — contains the nucleus and other parts of the cell needed to sustain its life.
>
> **Axon** — wirelike structure ending in the terminal buttons that extends from the cell body.
>
> **Myelin sheath** — a fatty covering around the axon of some neurons that speeds neural impulses.
>
> **Terminal buttons** (also called end buttons, terminal branches of axon, and synaptic knobs) — the branched end of the axon that contains neurotransmitters.
>
> **Neurotransmitters** — chemicals contained in terminal buttons that enable neurons to communicate. Neurotransmitters fit into receptor sites on the dendrites of neurons like a key fits into a lock.
>
> **Synapse** — the space between the terminal buttons of one neuron and the dendrites of the next neuron.

How a Neuron "Fires"

All of the different parts of the neuron work in sequence when a neuron transmits a message. In its resting state, a neuron has an overall slightly negative charge (−70mv) because mostly negative ions are within the cell and mostly positive ions are surrounding it. The cell membrane of the neuron is selectively permeable and prevents these ions from mixing. Visualize a two-neuron chain (see Fig. 3.1). The reaction begins when the terminal buttons of neuron A are stimulated and release neurotransmitters into the synapse. These neurotransmitters fit into **receptor sites** on the dendrites of neuron B. If enough neurotransmitters are received (this level is called the **threshold**), the cell membrane of neuron B becomes permeable and positive ions rush into the cell, bringing the charge within the cell to approximately +40mv. The change in charge spreads down the length of neuron B like a bullet from a gun. This electric message firing is called an **action potential**. It travels quickly: 120 meters per second. When the charge reaches the terminal buttons of neuron B, the buttons release their neurotransmitters into the synapse. The process may begin again if enough neurotransmitters are received by that next cell to pass the threshold. Notice that a neuron either **fires** completely or it does not fire; this is called the **all-or-none principle**. If the dendrites of a neuron receive enough neurotransmitters to push the neuron past its threshold, the neuron will fire completely every time. A neuron cannot fire a little or a lot; the impulse is the same every time.

> **TIP**
>
> Neural firing is an electrochemical process. Electricity travels within the cell (from the dendrites to the terminal buttons), and chemicals (neurotransmitters) travel between cells in the synapse. Electricity does not jump between the neurons.

Neurotransmitters

You already know that neurotransmitters are chemicals held in the terminal buttons that travel in the synaptic gap between neurons. It is important to understand that different types of neurotransmitters exist. Some neurotransmitters are **excitatory**, meaning that they excite the next cell into firing. Other neurotransmitters are **inhibitory**, meaning that they inhibit the next cell from firing. Each synaptic gap at any time may contain many different kinds of inhibitory and excitatory neurotransmitters. The amount and type of neurotransmitters received on the receptor sites of the neuron determine whether it will pass the threshold and fire. Researchers are identifying different types and functions of neurotransmitters every year. This ongoing research makes generalizing about what each neurotransmitter does difficult. However, Table 3.1 indicates some of the more important types and functions of neurotransmitters to psychologists.

Table 3.1 Neurotransmitters Important to Psychologists

Neurotransmitter	Function	Problems Associated with an Excess or Deficit
Acetylcholine	Motor movement	Lack of acetylcholine is associated with Alzheimer's disease
Dopamine	Motor movement and alertness	Lack of dopamine is associated with Parkinson's disease; an overabundance is associated with schizophrenia
Endorphins	Pain control	Involved in addictions
Serotonin	Mood control	Lack of serotonin is associated with clinical depression
GABA	Important inhibitory neurotransmitter	Seizures, sleep problems
Glutamate	Excitatory neurotransmitter, involved in memory	Migraines, seizures
Norepinephrine	Alertness, arousal	Depression

NERVOUS SYSTEM

We can sense the world because our nervous system brings information from our senses to our brain. Since a neuron fires in only one direction (from dendrite to terminal buttons), our body needs two sets of wires: one to take information to the brain and one to take instructions back from the brain to the muscles.

Afferent Neurons (or Sensory Neurons)

Afferent neurons take information from the senses to the brain. (You can think of *a*fferent nerves as taking information in *a*t the brain.)

Interneurons

Once information reaches the brain or spinal cord, interneurons take the messages and send them elsewhere in the brain or on to efferent neurons.

Efferent Neurons (or Motor Neurons)

Efferent neurons take information from the brain to the rest of the body. (You can think of *e*fferent nerves as carrying information that *e*xits the brain.)

Organization of the Nervous System

Our nervous system is divided into different categories based on function. The two main divisions are the **central nervous system** and the **peripheral nervous system**. These are then subdivided further (see Fig. 3.2).

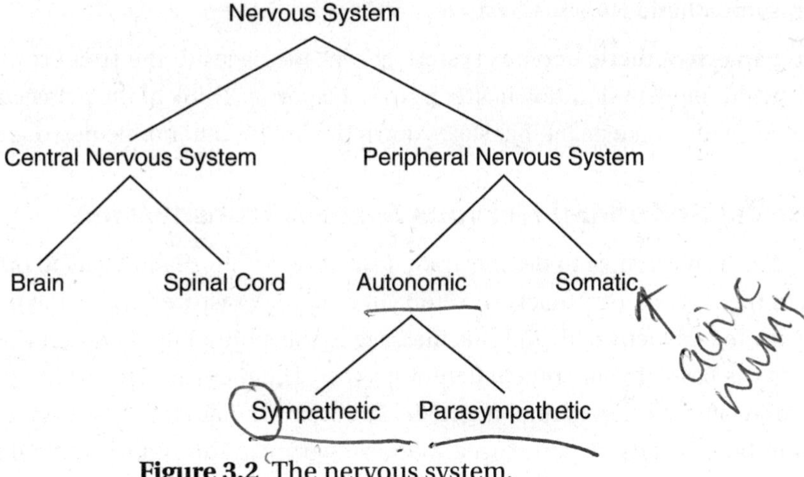

Figure 3.2 The nervous system.

The Central Nervous System

The central nervous system (CNS) consists of our brain and **spinal cord**—all the nerves housed within bone (the skull and vertebrae). Information about the structure and function of different parts of the brain is available in a later section. The spinal cord is a bundle of nerves that run through the center of the spine. It transmits information from the rest of the body to the brain.

The Peripheral Nervous System

The peripheral nervous system (PNS) consists of all the other nerves in your body—that is, all the nerves not encased in bone. The peripheral nervous system is divided into two categories: the somatic and the autonomic nervous systems.

Somatic Nervous System

The **somatic nervous system** controls our voluntary muscle movements. The motor cortex of the brain sends impulses to the somatic nervous system, which controls the muscles that allow us to move.

Autonomic Nervous System

The **autonomic nervous system** controls the automatic functions of our body—our heart, lungs, internal organs, glands, and so on. These nerves control our responses to stress—the fight or flight response that prepares our body to respond to a perceived threat. The autonomic nervous system is divided into two categories: the sympathetic and parasympathetic nervous systems.

Sympathetic Nervous System

The **sympathetic nervous system** mobilizes our body to respond to stress. This part of our nervous systems carries messages to the control systems of the organs, glands, and muscles that direct our body's response to stress. This is the alert system of our body. It accelerates some functions (such as heart rate, blood pressure, and respiration) but conserves resources needed for a quick response by slowing down other functions (such as digestion).

Parasympathetic Nervous System

The **parasympathetic nervous system** carries messages to the stress response system that causes our body to slow down after a stress response. Think of the parasympathetic nervous system as the brake pedal that slows down the body's autonomic nervous system.

Normal Peripheral Nervous System Transmission

Let us use an example to demonstrate how sensory information gets to our brain. While on a late-night quest for a snack, you stub your toe on a cast-iron coffee table. Sensory neurons in your toe are activated, and this message is transmitted up a neuron that runs from your toe to the base of your spine (afferent nerves). The message continues up your spinal cord on more afferent nerves until it enters your brain through the brainstem and is transmitted to the brain's sensory cortex (see the next section, "The Brain") and you know you have stubbed your poor little toe. Your motor cortex now sends impulses down the spinal cord to the muscles controlling your leg and foot (efferent nerves), causing you to hop up and down holding your damaged limb, muttering under your breath.

Reflexes: An Important Exception

Most sensory information and muscle movements are controlled by the process described above. However, humans have a few reflexes that work differently. Certain reactions occur the moment sensory impulses reach the spinal cord. If you stimulate the correct area just below your kneecap, your leg will jerk without your conscious control. This sensory information is processed by the spine, and the spine tells your leg to move. The information reaches your brain and you realize your knee has been stimulated but only after this reflex has occurred. Another important reflex occurs in response to intense heat or cold. If we touch an object that is very hot or cold, our spine will send back a message jerking us away from that object. This might help keep us from harming ourselves, so it has adaptive value (it might help us survive, and therefore this trait is passed on to our children).

THE BRAIN

Possibly the most relevant part of biology to psychologists is the brain. As far as we can tell, the brain controls most of human thought and behavior. Researchers know quite a bit about brain anatomy and function, but many mysteries still remain about how the brain functions. Studying how the brain works is challenging because we cannot simply observe brain function the way we might observe a heart beating. To our eyes, a brain thinking looks exactly like a brain not thinking. Researchers are discovering many new details about how the brain works through experimentation and the use of technology. However, we still have a long way to go before we really understand how the brain controls our thoughts and behavior.

Ways of Studying the Brain

As mentioned previously, the first challenge of brain research is creating a way of detecting brain function. The following describes some of the methods researchers use.

Accidents

Phineas Gage

In 1848, a railroad worker named Phineas Gage was involved in an **accident** that damaged the front part of his brain. Gage's doctor took notes documenting the brain damage and how Gage's behavior and personality changed after the accident. Accidents like this give researchers clues about brain function. Gage became highly emotional and impulsive after the accident. Researchers concluded that the parts of the brain damaged in the accident are somehow involved in emotional control.

Lesions

Lesioning is the removal or destruction of part of the brain. This is, of course, never done purely for experimental purposes. Sometimes doctors decide that the best treatment for a certain condition involves surgery that will destroy or incapacitate part of the brain. For example, a person may develop a brain tumor that cannot be removed without removing part of the surrounding brain. When these types of surgeries are performed, doctors closely monitor the patient's subsequent behavior for changes. Any time brain tissue is removed (lesioning), researchers can examine behavior changes and try to infer the function of that part of the brain.

A famous historical example of lesioning is the frontal lobotomy. In the past, this surgery was used (many historians say overused) to control mentally ill patients with no other treatment options. Researchers knew that lesioning part of the frontal lobe would make the patients calm and relieve some serious symptoms. Drug treatments have now replaced frontal lobotomies.

Electroencephalogram

An **electroencephalogram (EEG)** detects brain waves. Researchers can examine what type of waves the brain produces during different stages of consciousness and use this information to generalize about brain function. The EEG is widely used in sleep research to identify the different stages of sleep and dreaming.

Computerized Axial Tomography

A **computerized axial tomography (CAT or CT) scan** is a sophisticated X-ray. The CAT scan uses several X-ray cameras that rotate around the brain and combine all the pictures into a detailed three-dimensional picture of the brain's structure. Note that the CAT scan can show only the structure of the brain, not the functions or the activity of different brain structures. A doctor could use a CAT scan to look for a tumor in the brain, but would not get any information about how active different parts of the brain are.

Magnetic Resonance Imaging

The **magnetic resonance imaging (MRI)** is similar to a CAT scan in a way: both scans give you pictures of the brain. The MRI, however, uses different technology to create more detailed images. An MRI uses magnetic fields to measure the density and location of brain material. Since the MRI does not use X-rays like the CAT scan does, the patient is not exposed to carcinogenic radiation. Like the CAT scan, the MRI gives doctors information about only the structure of the brain, not the function.

Positron Emission Tomography

The **positron emission tomography (PET) scan** lets researchers see what areas of the brain are most active during certain tasks. A PET scan measures how much of a certain chemical (e.g., glucose) parts of the brain are using. The more glucose used, the higher the activity. Different types of scans are used for different chemicals such as neurotransmitters, drugs, and oxygen flow.

Functional MRI

Functional MRI (fMRI) is a new technology that combines elements of the? MRI and PET scans. An fMRI scan can show details of brain structure with information about blood flow in the brain, tying brain structure to brain activity during cognitive tasks.

Brain Structure and Function

All the different methods of studying the brain give researchers different types of information about brain structure and function. The brain is the most complicated organ in the body. (In some ways, it is the most complex object we know of.) Because of this complexity, we need to divide the brain into separate categories in order to keep track of the information. Researchers have categorized hundreds of different parts and functions of different parts of the brain. When you study the brain, think about three separate major categories or sections: the **hindbrain**, **midbrain**, and **forebrain**. Some evolutionary psychologists organize these categories into two major divisions: the "old brain" (hindbrain and midbrain) and the "new brain" (forebrain).

Hindbrain

The hindbrain consists of structures in the top part of the spinal cord. The hindbrain is our life support system; it controls the basic biological functions that keep us alive. Some of the important specific structures within the hindbrain are the medulla, pons, and cerebellum (refer to Fig. 3.3 for locations of these structures).

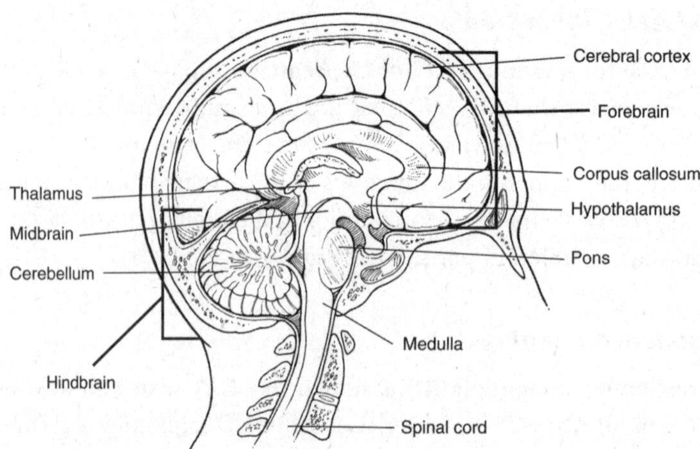

Figure 3.3 The brain.

Medulla

The **medulla** is involved in the control of our blood pressure, heart rate, and breathing. It is also known as the medulla oblongata and is located above the spinal cord.

> **TIP**
>
> Some of the descriptions of brain function may seem vague or redundant when you read about the functions of other structures. Remember that some of the ways in which the brain works are still being investigated and the functions are just summarized here for our purposes. Keep the areas and general functions in mind instead of spending your time trying to figure out exact specific functions and locations.

Pons

The **pons** (located just above the medulla and toward the front) connects the hindbrain with the midbrain and forebrain. It is also involved in the control of facial expressions.

Cerebellum

The **cerebellum** (located on the bottom rear of the brain) looks like a smaller version of our brain stuck onto the underside of our brain. Cerebellum means little brain. The cerebellum coordinates some habitual muscle movements, such as tracking a target with our eyes or playing the saxophone.

Midbrain

The midbrain is located just above the spinal cord but still below areas categorized as the forebrain. It is very small in humans, but this area of the brain controls some very important functions. In general, your midbrain coordinates simple movements with sensory information. For example, if you turn your head right now, your midbrain coordinates with muscles in your eyes to keep them focused on this text. Different parts of the midbrain are important in various muscle coordinations. For purposes of the AP test, though, you should remember that this area is between the hindbrain and the forebrain and integrates some types of sensory information and muscle movements. One specific structure in the midbrain you should be familiar with is the **reticular formation**. It is a netlike collection of cells throughout the midbrain that controls general body arousal and the ability to focus our attention. If the reticular formation does not function, we fall into a deep coma.

Forebrain

The various areas of the forebrain are very important to psychologists (and to students taking the AP Psychology test). Areas of the forebrain control what we think of as thought and reason. Notice in Figure 3.3 how large the forebrain is in comparison with the other areas. The size of our forebrain makes humans human, and most psychological researchers concentrate their efforts in this area of the brain. Specific areas of interest to us in the forebrain are the **thalamus**, **hypothalamus**, **amygdala**, and **hippocampus.** (The amygdala and hippocampus are not illustrated in Fig. 3.3.)

Thalamus

The thalamus is located on top of the brain stem. It is responsible for receiving the sensory signals coming up the spinal cord and sending them to the appropriate areas in the rest of the forebrain. (See the specific areas listed in the section, "Areas of the Cerebral Cortex," for examples of where some of these messages end up.)

Hypothalamus

The hypothalamus is a small structure right next to the thalamus. The small size of the hypothalamus doesn't mean that it is not important. The hypothalamus controls several metabolic functions, including body temperature, sexual arousal (libido), hunger, thirst, and the endocrine system (see the "Endocrine System" section later in this chapter). If you consider yourself a morning person or a night person, the hypothalamus might be involved, since it controls our biological rhythms.

Amygdala and Hippocampus

There are two arms surrounding the thalamus. These are called the hippocampus. Structures near the end of each hippocampal arm are called the amygdala. The amygdala is vital to our experiences of emotion, and the hippocampus is vital to our memory system. Memories are not permanently stored in this area of the brain, however. Memories are processed through this area and then sent to other locations in the cerebral cortex for permanent storage. Researchers now know that memories must pass through this area first in order to be encoded because individuals with brain damage in this area are unable to retain new information.

Cerebral Cortex

When most people think of the human brain, they think of and picture the **cerebral cortex.** The gray wrinkled surface of the brain is actually a thin (0.039-inch [1-mm]) layer of densely packed neurons. This layer covers the rest of the brain, including most of the structures we have described. When we are born, our cerebral cortex is full of neurons (more than we have now, actually) but the neurons are not yet well connected. As we develop and learn, the dendrites of the neurons in the cerebral cortex grow and connect with other neurons. This process forms the complex neural web you now have in your brain. The surface of the cerebral cortex is wrinkled (the wrinkles are called **fissures**) to increase the available surface area of the brain. The more wrinkles, the more surface area contained within our skull. If our cerebral cortex were not wrinkled, our skull would have to be 3 square feet (0.3 m^2) to hold all those neural connections!

> **TIP**
>
> These parts of the brain (thalamus, hypothalamus, amygdala, and hippocampus) are grouped together and called the **limbic system** because they all deal with aspects of emotion and memory. When you study the parts of the brain, grouping structures together according to function should help you remember them.

Hemispheres

The cerebral cortex is divided into two **hemispheres**: left and right. The hemispheres look like mirror images of one another, but they exert some differences in function. The **left hemisphere** gets sensory messages and controls the motor function of the right half of the body. The **right hemisphere** gets sensory messages and controls the motor function of the left half of the body. (This is called **contralateral control**.) Researchers are currently investigating other differences between the hemispheres, such as the possibility that the left hemisphere may be more active during logic and sequential tasks and the right during spatial and creative tasks. However, these generalizations need to be researched further before conclusions are drawn. This specialization of function in each hemisphere is called **brain lateralization** or **hemispheric specialization**. Most of this research in differences between the hemispheres is done by examining **split-brain patients**—patients whose **corpus callosum** (the nerve bundle that connects the two hemispheres, see Fig. 3.3) has been cut to treat severe epilepsy. The operation was pioneered by neuropsychologists **Roger Sperry** (1913–1994) and **Michael Gazzaniga** (1939–present). Split-brain patients also cannot orally report information only presented to the right hemisphere, since the spoken language centers of the brain are usually located in the left hemisphere.

Areas of the Cerebral Cortex

When you study the cerebral cortex, think of it as a collection of different areas and specific cortices. Think of the cerebral cortex as eight different **lobes**, four on each hemisphere: frontal, parietal, temporal, and occipital. Some of the major functions of these parts of the brain that are relevant to the AP test are mentioned here. Any area of the cerebral cortex that it is not associated with receiving sensory information or controlling muscle movements is labeled as an **association area**. Although specific functions are not known for each association area, these areas are very active in various human thoughts and behaviors. For example, association areas are thought to be responsible for complex, sophisticated thoughts like judgment and humor.

Frontal Lobes

The **frontal lobes** are large areas of the cerebral cortex located at the top front part of the brain behind the eyes (see Fig. 3.4). The anterior or front of the frontal lobe is called the **prefrontal cortex** and is thought to play a critical role in directing thought processes. It is said to act as the brain's central executive and is believed to be important in predicting consequences, pursuing goals, maintaining emotional control, and engaging in abstract thought. The story of Phineas Gage mentioned previously exemplifies some of the functions of the prefrontal cortex. Phineas Gage's limbic system was separated from his frontal lobes in an accident. Doctors reported that he lost control of his emotions and became impulsive and animalistic.

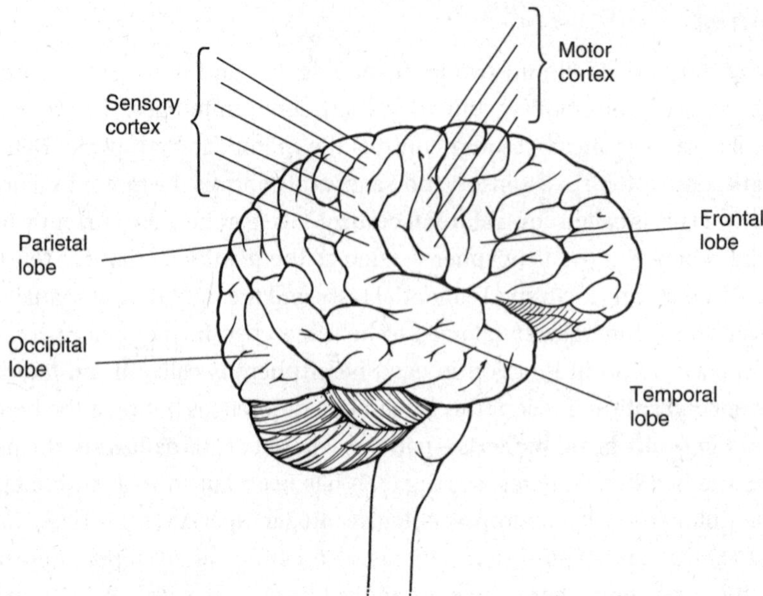

Figure 3.4 The lobes of the cerebral cortex.

In most people, the frontal lobe in the left hemisphere contains one of the two special areas responsible for language processing (some left-handed people's language centers are in the right hemisphere). **Broca's area** (**Paul Broca**, 1824–1880) is in the frontal lobe and is responsible for controlling the muscles involved in producing speech. Damage to this area can result in the loss of this ability. (The other area is **Wernicke's area** [**Carl Wernicke**, 1848–1905] and is located in the temporal lobe—see that section for more information.)

A thin vertical strip at the back of the frontal lobe (farthest from the eyes, see Fig. 3.4) is called the **motor cortex**. This part of the cerebral cortex sends signals to our muscles, controlling our voluntary movements. The top of the body is controlled by the neurons at the bottom of this cortex (by the ears), progressing down the body as you go up the cortex. So the top of the motor cortex controls the feet and toes of the body.

Parietal Lobes

The **parietal lobes** are located behind the frontal lobe but still on the top of the brain (see Fig. 3.4). The parietal lobes contain the **sensory cortex** (also known as the **somato-sensory cortex**), which is located right behind the motor cortex in the frontal lobe. The sensory cortex is a thin vertical strip that receives incoming touch sensations from the rest of our body. The sensory cortex is organized similarly to the motor cortex. The top of the sensory cortex receives sensations from the bottom of the body, progressing down the cortex to the bottom, which processes signals from our face and head.

TIP

The term *occipital* looks like the word *optical* to some students. Thinking about this might help you remember the primary function of the occipital lobe!

Occipital Lobes

Our **occipital lobes** are at the very back of our brain, farthest from our eyes. This is somewhat counterintutive since one of the major functions of this lobe is to interpret messages from our eyes in our visual cortex. Impulses from the retinas in our eyes are sent to the visual cortex to be interpreted. Impulses from the right half of each retina are processed in the visual cortex in the right occipital lobe. Impulses from the left part of each retina are sent to the visual cortex in our left occipital lobe.

Temporal Lobes

The **temporal lobes** process sound sensed by our ears. Sound waves are processed by the ears, turned into neural impulses, and interpreted in our auditory cortices. The auditory cortex is not lateralized like the visual cortices are. Sound received by the left ear is processed in the auditory cortices in both hemispheres. The second language area is located in the temporal lobe. (The first was Broca's area in the frontal lobe.) Wernicke's area interprets both written and spoken speech. Damage to this area would affect our ability to understand language. Our speech might sound fluent but lack the proper syntax and grammatical structure needed for meaningful communication.

Brain Plasticity

Researchers know some of the functions of different areas of the cerebral cortex, but they have also discovered that the brain is somewhat plastic or flexible. While these cortices and lobes usually perform the functions already mentioned, other parts of the brain can adapt themselves to perform other functions if needed. You already know that the cerebral cortex is made up of a complex network of neurons connected by dendrites that grow to make new connections. Since dendrites grow throughout our lives, if one part of the brain is damaged, dendrites might be able to make new connections in another part of the brain that would be able to take over the functions usually performed by the damaged part of the brain. Dendrites grow most quickly in younger children. Researchers know that younger brains are more plastic and are more likely to be able to compensate for damage.

ENDOCRINE SYSTEM

Another part of human biology relevant to psychology is the **endocrine system**. This is a system of glands that secrete hormones that affect many different biological processes in our bodies. As mentioned previously, the endocrine system is controlled in the brain by the hypothalamus. The endocrine system is complex, but a few elements of the entire process are especially relevant to psychologists.

Adrenal Glands

The **adrenal glands** produce adrenaline, which signals the rest of the body to prepare for fight or flight. This response was mentioned earlier in connection with the autonomic nervous system—the part of our nervous system that controls involuntary responses, such as heart rate and blood pressure.

Ovaries and Testes

Women's ovaries and men's testes produce our sex hormones, estrogen for women and testosterone for men. Research shows that levels of these hormones in men and women may partially explain gender differences demonstrated in certain experiments and situations. See the Chapter 9, "Developmental Psychology," for examples of these differences.

GENETICS

Besides the functioning of the brain and nervous system, another biological factor that affects human thought and behavior is genetics. Most human traits, like body shape, introversion, or temper, result from the combined effects of nature (our genetic code) and nurture (the environment where we grow up and live). Psychological researchers attempt to determine how much nature and nurture contribute to human traits.

Basic Genetic Concepts

Every human cell contains 46 chromosomes in 23 pairs. The genetic material that makes up chromosomes is DNA—deoxyribonucleic acid. Certain segments of DNA control the production of specific proteins that control some human traits. These discrete segments are called genes. Genes can be dominant or recessive. If we inherit two recessive genes for a particular trait, that trait will be expressed. In any other combination of genes, the dominant trait is expressed. Psychological researchers investigate how different combinations of genes create tendencies for physical and behavioral traits.

Twins

Since identical twins (called **monozygotic twins** since they develop from one fertilized egg called a zygote) share all the same genetic material, researchers study them in order to examine the influence of genes on human traits. In one famous study, **Thomas Bouchard** found more than 100 identical twins who were given up for adoption and raised in different families. The study compared hundreds of traits and made conclusions about the relative influences of genetics and the environment on specific traits. For example, the study found a correlation coefficient of 0.69 on the IQ test for identical twins raised apart and a 0.88 for identical twins living together. This shows that the environment has some effect on IQ score, since twins raised in the same family have more similar IQs. However, the IQs of twins raised apart are still highly correlated, demonstrating that IQ is also heavily influenced by genetics. Twin studies like this one have been criticized in one important way, however. Even twins raised in separate families obviously share very similar physical appearances. This physical similarity may cause others to treat them in similar ways, creating the same **effective psychological environment** for both twins. This similarity in environment might explain the high correlations that Bouchard attributed to genetic influence.

Chromosomal Abnormalities

Our gender is determined by our twenty-third pair of chromosomes. Men have an X and Y chromosome, and women have two X chromosomes. Usually a man will contribute either an X chromosome to a child (resulting in a girl) or a Y (resulting in a boy). Occasionally, chromosomes will combine (or fail to) in an unusual way, resulting in a chromosomal abnormality. For example, babies with **Turner's syndrome** are born with only a single X chromosome in the spot usually occupied by the twenty-third pair. Turner's syndrome causes some physical characteristics, like shortness, webbed necks, and differences in physical sexual development.

Babies born with **Klinefelter's syndrome** have an extra X chromosome, resulting in an XXY pattern. The effects of this syndrome vary widely, but it usually causes minimal sexual development and personality traits like extreme introversion.

Other chromosomal abnormalities may cause intellectual disability. The most common type is **Down syndrome**. Babies with Down syndrome are born with an extra chromosome on the twenty-first pair. Some physical characteristics are indicative of Down syndrome: rounded face, shorter fingers and toes, slanted eyes set far apart, and some degree of intellectual disability.

PRACTICE QUESTIONS

Directions: Each of the questions or incomplete statements below is followed by five suggested answers or completions. Select the one that is best in each case.

1. Blindness could result from damage to which cortex and lobe of the brain?
   (A) visual cortex in the frontal lobe
   (B) visual cortex in the temporal lobe
   (C) sensory cortex in the parietal lobe
   (D) visual cortex in the occipital lobe
   (E) cerebral cortex in the occipital lobe

2. Paralysis of the left arm might be explained by a problem in the
   (A) motor cortex in the frontal lobe in the left hemisphere.
   (B) motor cortex in the frontal lobe in the right hemisphere.
   (C) sensorimotor cortex in the temporal lobe in the left hemisphere.
   (D) motor cortex in the parietal lobe in the left hemisphere.
   (E) motor cortex in the occipital lobe in the right hemisphere.

3. Deafness can result from damage to the inner ear or damage to what area of the brain?
   (A) connections between the auditory nerve and the auditory cortex in the frontal lobe
   (B) connections between the auditory nerve and the auditory cortex in the temporal lobe
   (C) connections between the areas of the sensory cortex that receive messages from the ears and the auditory cortex
   (D) connections between the hypothalamus and the auditory cortex in the temporal lobe
   (E) connections between the left and right sensory areas of the cerebellum

4. According to the theory of evolution, why might we call some parts of the brain the old brain and some parts the new brain?
   (A) Old brain parts are what exist in very young children, and the new brain develops later.
   (B) The old brain developed first according to evolution.
   (C) The old brain becomes more active as we grow older.
   (D) The new brain deals with new information, while the old brain deals with information gathered when we were children.
   (E) The old brain is most affected by age deterioration (dementias) while the new brain remains unaffected.

5. Which chemicals pass across the synaptic gap and increase the possibility the next neuron in the chain will fire?

(A) synaptic peptides
(B) inhibitory neurotransmitters
(C) adrenaline-type exciters
(D) excitatory neurotransmitters
(E) potassium and sodium

6. You eat some bad sushi and feel that you are slowly losing control over your muscles. The bacteria you ingested from the bad sushi most likely interferes with the use of

(A) serotonin.
(B) insulin.
(C) acetylcholine.
(D) thorazine.
(E) adrenaline.

7. The three major categories researchers use to organize the entire brain are the

(A) old brain, new brain, and cerebral cortex.
(B) lower, middle, and upper brain.
(C) hindbrain, midbrain, and forebrain.
(D) brain stem, limbic system, and cerebral cortex.
(E) neurons, synapses, and cerebral cortex.

8. A spinal reflex differs from a normal sensory and motor reaction in that

(A) a spinal reflex occurs only in response to extremely stressful stimuli.
(B) in a spinal reflex, the spine moves the muscles in response as soon as the sensory information reaches the spine, while usually the impulse must reach the brain before a response.
(C) in a normal sensory/motor reaction, the spine transmits the information through afferent nerve fibers, while reflex reactions are transmitted along special efferent nerves.
(D) spinal reflexes are part of the central nervous system response, while normal sensory/motor reactions are part of the peripheral nervous system.
(E) spinal reflexes occur only in animals because humans are born without instinctual responses.

9. Antidepressant drugs like Prozac are often used to treat mood disorders. According to what you know about their function, which neurotransmitter system do these types of drugs try to affect?

(A) serotonin
(B) adrenaline
(C) acetylcholine
(D) endorphins
(E) morphine

10. Which sentence most closely describes neural transmission?

    (A) An electric charge is created in the neuron, the charge travels down the cell, and chemicals are released that cross the synapse to the next cell.
    (B) A chemical change occurs within the cell, the change causes an electric charge to be produced, and the charge jumps the gap between the nerve cells.
    (C) The electric charge produced chemically inside a group of neurons causes chemical changes in surrounding cells.
    (D) Neurotransmitters produced in the hindbrain are transmitted to the forebrain, causing electric changes in the cerebral cortex.
    (E) Neural transmission is an electrochemical process both inside and outside the cell.

11. Dr. Dahab, a brain researcher, is investigating the connection between certain environmental stimuli and brain processes. Which types of brain scans is he most likely to use?

    (A) MRI and CAT
    (B) CAT and EKG
    (C) PET and EEG
    (D) EKG and CAT
    (E) lesioning and MRI

12. Split-brain patients are unable to

    (A) coordinate movements between their major and minor muscle groups.
    (B) speak about information received exclusively in their right hemisphere.
    (C) speak about information received exclusively in their left hemisphere.
    (D) solve abstract problems involving integrating logical (left-hemisphere) and spatial (right-hemisphere) information.
    (E) speak about information received exclusively through their left ear, left eye, or left side of their bodies.

13. When brain researchers refer to *brain plasticity,* they are talking about

    (A) the brain's ability to quickly regrow damaged neurons.
    (B) the surface texture and appearance caused by the layer known as the cerebral cortex.
    (C) the brain's versatility caused by the millions of different neural connections.
    (D) our adaptability to different problems ranging from survival needs to abstract reasoning.
    (E) new connections forming in the brain to take over for damaged sections.

14. Mr. Spam is a 39-year-old male who has been brought into your neurology clinic by his wife. She has become increasingly alarmed by her husband's behavior over the last four months. You recommend a CAT scan to look for tumors in the brain. Which two parts of the brain would you predict are being affected by the tumors?

    List of symptoms: vastly increased appetite, body temperature fluctuations, decreased sexual desire, jerky movements, poor balance when walking and standing, inability to throw objects, and exaggerated efforts to coordinate movements in a task

    (A) motor cortex and emotion cortex
    (B) somato-sensory cortex and hypothalamus
    (C) hypothalamus and cerebellum
    (D) cerebellum and medulla
    (E) thalamus and motor cortex

15. In most people, which one of following is a specific function of the left hemisphere that is typically not controlled by the right hemisphere?

    (A) producing speech
    (B) control of the left hand
    (C) spatial reasoning
    (D) hypothesis testing
    (E) abstract reasoning

ANSWER KEY

1. **D**
2. **B**
3. **B**
4. **B**
5. **D**
6. **C**
7. **C**
8. **B**
9. **A**
10. **A**
11. **C**
12. **B**
13. **E**
14. **C**
15. **A**

ANSWERS EXPLAINED

1. **(D)** The visual cortex is located in the occipital lobe. The other locations are incorrect for the visual cortex. The sensory cortex interprets touch stimuli, and the cerebral cortex is the term for the entire wrinkled surface of the brain, so those items are incorrect.

2. **(B)** The motor cortex (which is located in the frontal lobe) in the right hemisphere controls the left side of the body. The sensorimotor cortex (also known as the motor cortex) is in the frontal lobe, not the temporal lobe. The other locations for the motor cortex are also incorrect.

3. **(B)** The auditory cortex is located in the temporal lobe and is connected to the inner ear by the auditory nerve. Other locations given for the auditory cortex are incorrect. The sensory cortex, hypothalamus, and cerebellum are not involved in hearing.

4. **(B)** The old or reptilian brain exists in all mammals and is thought to have developed first. As humans evolved into primates, the cerebral cortex developed and grew larger, allowing us to solve more complex problems. All brain structures are present in children from birth. All parts of the brain might deal with new or old information. Dementia is not more likely to affect the old or new brain.

5. **(D)** Excitatory neurotransmitters increase the likelihood that the next neuron will fire. Inhibitory neurotransmitters actually decrease the chance the next neuron will fire when received by the cells' dendrites. Synaptic peptides and adrenaline-type exciters are not relevant to neuroanatomy (or any other anatomy—they are nonsense terms!). Potassium and sodium are integral in the process of depolarization but are not secreted from terminal buttons into the synaptic gap.

6. **(C)** Acetylcholine is the neurotransmitter involved in muscle control. Serotonin is also a neurotransmitter, but it would not be responsible for losing control over your muscles. Insulin is involved in hunger control. Thorazine is an antipsychotic drug prescribed by psychiatrists. Adrenaline is a hormone released by the adrenal glands in response to stressful situations.

7. **(C)** The hindbrain, midbrain, and forebrain are three of the traditional categories of brain structures. The new brain is synonymous with the cerebral cortex. The brain stem, limbic system, and cerebral cortex are divisions of the brain but not overall categories that include the entire brain. Neurons and synapses are parts of neuroanatomy, not major divisions of the brain.

8. **(B)** Spinal reflexes, such as the reflex that causes your leg to move when a doctor strikes your leg just below your kneecap, are controlled by the spine, not the brain. Stress is not relevant to the process, nor are afferent and efferent nerves. All spinal reflexes involve the peripheral nervous system. Humans do have some spinal reflexes; they are not limited to animals.

9. **(A)** Serotonin is the only neurotransmitter on the list that is identified as being involved in mood disorders. Adrenaline is a hormone released by the adrenal glands in response to stressful situations. Acetylcholine is a neurotransmitter that controls muscle movements. Endorphins are painkillers in the brain that might temporarily elevate mood but would not be responsible for long-term mood disorders. Morphine is a drug that interacts with our endorphins to alleviate pain.

10. **(A)** Neural firing involves an electric charge within the cell and chemical transmission between cells (across the synapse). It is electric within the cell and chemical between the cells. The electric charge does not jump the gap between neurons. The question refers to an individual neuron firing, not a group of neurons. Neurotransmitters are not confined to the hindbrain or the forebrain.

11. **(C)** The PET and EEG scans both give information about brain function (the PET measures brain activity, and the EEG measures brain waves). The MRI and CAT scans give information about brain structure, not function. An EKG is a medical test for heart function. Lesioning involves destroying brain tissue and would not be used in this type of research.

12. **(B)** Since the left hemisphere typically controls speech, split-brain patients are usually unable to talk about information exposed to only the right hemisphere. Their muscle coordination is usually normal (possible after a short adjustment period). Their ability to solve abstract problems is not affected. Visual information from the left part of each eye is transmitted to the right hemisphere, not the entire left eye. Both hemispheres receive auditory information from the left ear.

13. **(E)** Plasticity refers to the brain's ability to rewire itself to recover functions lost through some type of brain damage. This process occurs most quickly in children but can happen to a limited extent in adults. The brain does not quickly regrow neurons, it reconnects existing neurons in new ways. Plasticity has little to do with the texture and appearance of the cerebral cortex. The adaptability referred to in choice D is related to plasticity, but the correct answer, E, is a much more specific explanation.

14. **(C)** A tumor on the hypothalamus would explain the first three symptoms since the hypothalamus controls (at least in part) body temperature, libido, and hunger. The cerebellum coordinates some types of movements, including throwing objects and our sense of balance. The motor cortex controls voluntary muscle movements, but the specific movements described in the question are controlled by the cerebellum. The medulla controls our life-support functions, like heart rate and respiration. The thalamus directs signals coming in from the spinal cord to different parts of the brain.

15. **(A)** As mentioned previously in the analysis of split-brain patients, the left hemisphere typically controls speech. The left hand is controlled by the motor cortex in the right hemisphere. Some evidence indicates that the right hemisphere is more active in spatial reasoning. Both hemispheres are involved in hypothesis testing and abstract reasoning.

4 States of Consciousness

Key Terms

- Consciousness
- Levels of consciousness
- Conscious level
- Nonconscious level
- Preconscious level
- Subconscious level
- Unconscious level
- Sleep
- Sleep cycles
- Sleep stages
- REM sleep
- Sleep disorders
- Insomnia
- Narcolepsy
- Sleep apnea
- Night terrors
- Dreams
- Freudian dream interpretation
- Activation-synthesis dream theory
- Information-processing dream theory
- Psychoactive drugs
- Agonists
- Antagonists
- Tolerance
- Withdrawal
- Stimulants
- Depressants
- Hallucinogens (also called psychedelics)
- Opiates

Key People

- William James
- Sigmund Freud

OVERVIEW

While you are reading this text, you can probably become aware of your sense of consciousness. Early psychologists such as **William James**, author of the first psychology textbook, were very interested in consciousness. However, since no tools existed to examine it scientifically, the study of consciousness faded for a time. Currently, consciousness is becoming a more common research area due to more sophisticated brain imaging tools and an increased emphasis on cognitive psychology.

The historical discussion about consciousness centers on the competing philosophical theories of **dualism** and **monism**. Dualists believe humans (and the universe in general) consist of two materials: thought and matter. Matter is everything that has substance. Thought is a nonmaterial aspect that arises from, but is in some way independent of, a brain. Dualists argue that thought gives humans free will. Some philosophers maintain that thought is eternal and continues existing after the brain and body die. Monists disagree and believe everything is the same substance, and thought and matter are aspects of it. Thought is a by-product of brain processes and stops existing when the body dies.

This debate between the Dualists and Monists is a philosophical debate, not a scientific one. However, psychologists use research to describe some of the processes or elements of consciousness through experiments and theories/hypotheses. Psychologists define consciousness as our level of awareness about ourselves and our environment. We are conscious to the degree we are aware of what is going on inside and outside ourselves.

TIP

This psychological definition implies that consciousness is not like an on/off switch. We are not conscious or unconscious. Psychologists refer to different levels and different states of consciousness.

LEVELS OF CONSCIOUSNESS

Ironically, we experience different levels of consciousness in our daily life without being consciously aware of the experience. While you are reading this text, you might be tapping your pen or moving your leg in time to the music you are listening to. One level of consciousness is controlling your pen or leg, while another level is focused on reading these words. Research demonstrates other more subtle and complex effects of different levels of consciousness. The **mere-exposure effect** (also see Chapter 14) occurs when we prefer stimuli we have seen before over novel stimuli, even if we do not consciously remember seeing the old stimuli. For example, say a researcher shows a group of research participants a list of nonsense terms for a short period of time. Later, the same group is shown another list of terms and asked which terms they prefer or like best. The mere-exposure effect predicts that the group will choose the terms they saw previously, even though the group could not recall the first list of nonsense terms if asked. On some level, the group knows the first list.

A closely related concept is **priming**. Research participants respond more quickly and/or accurately to questions they have seen before, even if they do not remember seeing them. Another fascinating phenomenon that demonstrates levels of consciousness is **blind sight**. Some people who report being blind can nonetheless accurately describe the path of a moving object or accurately grasp objects they say they cannot see! One level of their consciousness is not getting any visual information, while another level is able to "see" as demonstrated by their behavior.

The concept of consciousness consisting of different levels or layers is well established. Not all researchers agree about what the specific levels are, but some of the possible types offered by researchers are shown in the chart on the following page.

Conscious level	The information about yourself and your environment you are currently aware of. Your conscious level right now is probably focusing on these words and their meanings.
Nonconscious level	Body processes controlled by your mind that we are not usually (or ever) aware of. Right now, your nonconscious is controlling your heartbeat, respiration, digestion, and so on.
Preconscious level	Information about yourself or your environment that you are not currently thinking about (not in your conscious level) but you could be. If I asked you to remember your favorite toy as a child, you could bring that preconscious memory into your conscious level.
Subconscious level	Information that we are not consciously aware of but we know must exist due to behavior. The behaviors demonstrated in examples of priming and mere-exposure effect suggest some information is accessible to this level of consciousness but not to our conscious level.
Unconscious level	Psychoanalytic psychologists believe some events and feelings are unacceptable to our conscious mind and are repressed into the unconscious mind. Many psychologists object to this concept as difficult or impossible to prove. See the section on psychoanalytic theory in Chapter 11 for more information about the unconscious.

SLEEP

As a student, sleep is probably a subject near and dear to you. Many studies show that a large percentage of high school and college students are sleep deprived, meaning they do not get as much sleep as their body wants. To a psychologist, referring to being asleep as being unconscious is incorrect. Sleep is one of the states of consciousness.

TIP

According to the psychological definition of *consciousness*, sleep is a state of consciousness because, while we are asleep, we are less aware of ourselves and our environment than we are when we are in our normal awake state. Other states of consciousness—drug-induced states, daydreaming, and so on—are states of consciousness for similar reasons.

Sleep Cycle

You may be familiar with the term **circadian rhythm**. During a 24-hour day, our metabolic and thought processes follow a certain pattern. Some of us are more active in the morning than others, some of us get hungry or go to the bathroom at certain times of day, and so on. Part of our circadian rhythm is our sleep cycle. Our sleep cycle is our typical pattern of sleep. Researchers using EEG machines can record how active our brains are during sleep and describe the different stages of sleep we progress through each night. Refer to Figure 4.1 for a graphic representation of the stages of a typical sleep cycle.

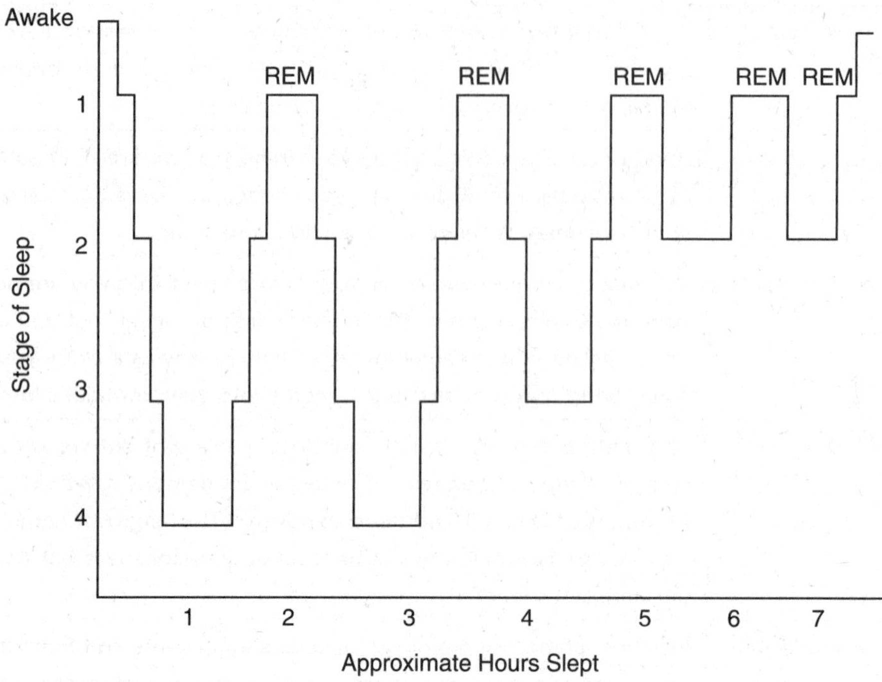

Figure 4.1 Stages of sleep.

As you can see in Figure 4.1, sleep is far from being a time of unconsciousness. We cycle through different stages of sleep during the night. Our brain waves and level of awareness change as we cycle through the stages. The period when we are falling asleep is called **sleep onset**. This is the stage between wakefulness and sleep. Our brain produces alpha waves when we are drowsy but awake. We might experience mild hallucinations (such as falling or rising) before actually falling asleep and entering stage 1. While we are awake and in stages 1 and 2, our brains produce theta waves, which are relatively high-frequency, low-amplitude waves. However, the theta waves get progressively slower and higher in amplitude as we go from wakefulness and through stages 1 and 2. In stage 2, the EEG starts to show sleep spindles, which are short bursts of rapid brain waves. From there, we move into stages 3 and 4, which are sometimes called delta sleep (also called slow-wave sleep) because of the delta waves that exist during these stages. The slower the wave (slow waves are low-frequency waves), the deeper the sleep and less aware we are of our environment. A person in delta sleep is very difficult to wake up. If you are awakened out of delta sleep, you may be very disoriented and groggy. Delta sleep seems to be very important in replenishing the body's chemical supplies, releasing growth hormones in children, and fortifying our immune system. A person deprived of delta sleep will be more susceptible to illness and will feel physically tired. Increasing exercise will increase the amount of time we spend in stages 3 and 4.

After a period of time in delta sleep, our brain waves start to speed up and we go back through stages 3 and 2. However, as we reach stage 1, our brain produces a period of intense activity, our eyes dart back and forth, and many of our muscles may twitch repeatedly. This is **REM—rapid eye movement**. This sleep stage is sometimes called **paradoxical sleep** since our brain waves appear as active and intense as they do when we are awake. The exact purposes of REM are not clear, but some effects are known. Dreams can occur in any stage of sleep but are far more likely to take place during REM sleep; especially detailed dreams. REM sleep deprivation interferes with memory. Individuals deprived of REM sleep will experience

REM rebound—experiencing more and longer periods of REM—the next time they are allowed to sleep normally. The more stress we experience during the day, the longer our periods of REM sleep will be.

Notice in Figure 4.1 that not only do we cycle through these approximately 90-minute stages about 4–7 times during the night, the cycle itself varies during the night. As we get closer to morning (or whenever we naturally awaken), we spend more time in stages 1 and 2 and in REM sleep and less in stages 3 and 4. Also, age affects the pattern. Babies not only spend more total time sleeping than we do (up to 18 hours), they also spend more time in REM sleep. As we age, our total need for sleep declines as does the amount of time we spend in REM sleep. Although research has not answered all the questions about sleep, details about our sleep cycle provide clues as to why we spend so much of our life in this altered state of consciousness.

Sleep Disorders

Many of us will experience a night, or perhaps a series of nights, of sleeplessness. These isolated periods of disruption in our sleep pattern give us an idea of the inconvenience and discomfort true sleep disorders can cause in people's lives. Sleep researchers identify and diagnose several sleep disorders.

Insomnia is far and away the most common sleep disorder, affecting up to 10 percent of the population. An insomniac has persistent problems getting to sleep or staying asleep at night. Most people will experience occasional bouts of insomnia, but diagnosed insomniacs have problems getting to sleep more often than not. Insomnia is usually treated with suggestions for changes in behavior: reduction of caffeine or other stimulants, exercise at appropriate times (not right before bedtime) during the day, and maintaining a consistent sleep pattern. Doctors and researchers encourage insomniacs to use sleeping pills only with caution, as they disturb sleep patterns during the night and can prevent truly restful sleep.

Narcolepsy occurs far more rarely than insomnia, occurring in less than 0.001 percent of the population. Narcoleptics suffer from periods of intense sleepiness and may fall asleep at unpredictable and inappropriate times. Narcoleptics may suddenly fall into REM sleep regardless of what they are doing at the time. One of my students suffered from narcolepsy from the time he was a preadolescent up until his graduation from high school. After he was finally diagnosed, he estimated that before his treatment he was drowsy almost his entire day except for two to three hours in the late afternoon. Narcolepsy can be successfully treated with medication and by changing sleep patterns, such as introducing naps at strategic times during the day.

Sleep apnea may be almost as common as insomnia and, in some ways, might be more serious. Apnea causes a person to stop breathing for short periods of time during the night. The body causes the person to wake up slightly and gasp for air, and then sleep continues. This process robs the person of deep sleep and causes tiredness and possible interference with attention and memory. Severe apnea can be fatal. Since these individuals do not remember waking up during the night, apnea frequently goes undiagnosed. Overweight men are at a higher risk for apnea. Apnea can be treated with a respiration machine that provides air for the person as he or she sleeps.

My mother tells me that I experienced **night terrors** as a child. I would sit up in bed in the middle of the night and scream and move around my room. Night terrors usually affect children, and most do not remember the episode when they wake up. The exact causes are not known, but night terrors are probably related in some way to **somnambulism** (sleep walking). They occur more commonly in children, and both phenomena occur during the first few hours of the night in stage 4 sleep. Most people stop having night terrors and episodes of somnambulism as they get older.

DREAMS

Dreams are the series of storylike images we experience as we sleep. Some people remember dreams frequently, sometimes more than one per night, while others are not aware of whether we dream or not. Some of us even report lucid dreams in which we are aware that we are dreaming and can control the storyline of the dream. Dreams are a difficult research area for psychologists because they rely almost entirely on self-reports. As mentioned previously, researchers know that if people are awakened during or shortly after an REM episode, they often report they were dreaming. Researchers theorize about the purposes and meanings of dreams. However, validating these theories is difficult with the limited access researchers currently have to dreams.

Sigmund Freud considered dreams an important tool in his therapy. Freudian psychoanalysis emphasizes dream interpretation as a method to uncover the repressed information in the unconscious mind. Freud said that dreams were wish fulfilling, meaning that in our dreams we act out our unconscious desires. This type of dream analysis emphasizes two levels of dream content. **Manifest content** is the literal content of our dreams. If you dream about showing up at school naked, the manifest content is your nudity, the room you see yourself in at school, the people present, and so on. More important to Freud was the **latent content**, which is the unconscious meaning of the manifest content. Freud thought that even during sleep, our ego protected us from the material in the unconscious mind (thus the term **protected sleep**) by presenting these repressed desires in the form of symbols. So showing up naked at school would represent a symbol in this type of analysis, perhaps of vulnerability or anxiety. This type of dream analysis is common. Check any bookstore, and you will find multiple dream interpretation books based on this theory. However, popularity does not imply validity. Researchers point out that this theory is difficult to validate or invalidate. How do we know which are the correct symbols to examine and what they mean? The validity of the theory cannot be tested. Consequently, this analysis is mostly used in psychoanalytic therapy and in pop psychology rather than in research.

The **activation-synthesis theory** of dreaming looks at dreams first as biological phenomena. Brain imaging proves that our brain is very active during REM sleep. This theory proposes that perhaps dreams are nothing more than the brain's interpretations of what is happening physiologically during REM sleep. Researchers know that our minds are very good at explaining events, even when the events have a purely physiological cause. **Split-brain patients** (see Chapter 3) sometimes make up elaborate explanations for behaviors caused by their operation. Dreams may be a story made up by a literary part of our mind caused by the intense brain activity during REM sleep. According to this theory, dreams, while interesting, have no more meaning than any other physiological reflex in our body.

The **information-processing theory** of dreaming falls somewhere in between the Freudian and activation-synthesis theories. This theory points out that stress during the day will increase the number and intensity of dreams during the night. Also, most people report their dream content relates somehow to daily concerns. Proponents of information processing theorize that perhaps the brain is dealing with daily stress and information during REM dreams. The function of REM may be to integrate the information processed during the day into our memories. Babies may need more REM sleep than adults because they process so much new information every day.

DRUGS

Psychoactive drugs are chemicals that change the chemistry of the brain (and the rest of the body) and induce an altered state of consciousness. Some of the behavioral and cognitive changes caused by these drugs are due to physiological processes, but some are due to expectations about the drug. Research shows that people will often exhibit some of the expected effects of the drug if they think they ingested it, even if they did not. (This is similar to the placebo effect.)

All psychoactive drugs change our consciousness through similar physiological processes in the brain. Normally, the brain is protected from harmful chemicals in the bloodstream by thicker walls surrounding the brain's blood vessels. This is called the **blood-brain barrier**. However, the molecules that make up psychoactive drugs are small enough to pass through the blood-brain barrier. These molecules either mimic or block naturally occurring neurotransmitters in the brain. The drugs that mimic neurotransmitters are called **agonists**. These drugs fit in the receptor sites on a neuron that normally receive the neurotransmitter and function as that neurotransmitter normally would. The drugs that block neurotransmitters are called **antagonists**. These molecules also fit into receptor sites on a neuron. However, instead of acting like the neurotransmitter, they simply prevent the natural neurotransmitters from using that receptor site. Other drugs prevent natural neurotransmitters from being reabsorbed back into a neuron, creating an abundance of that neurotransmitter in the synapse. One example of this kind of drug is Prozac, which is called a "selective serotonin reuptake inhibitor" because it prevents serotonin from being reabsorbed back into the neuron. No matter what mechanism they use, drugs gradually alter the natural levels of neurotransmitters in the brain. In some cases, the brain will produce less of a specific neurotransmitter if the amount of that neurotransmitter is being influenced by a psychoactive drug.

Agonists and Antagonists

Agonists	Drugs that occupy receptors and activate them.
Antagonists	Drugs that occupy receptors but do not activate them. Antagonists block receptor activation by agonists.

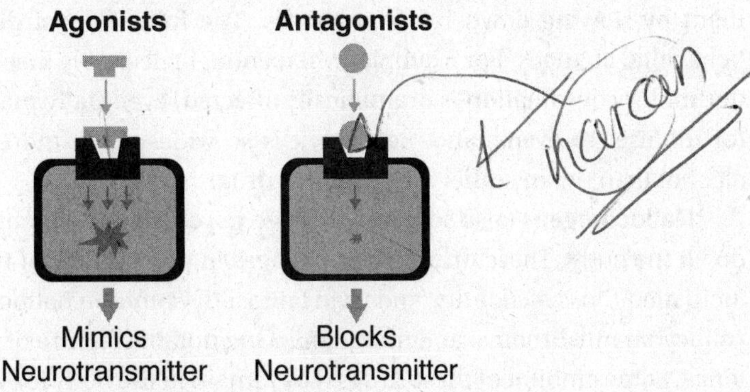

Figure 4.2 Agonists and antagonists.

This change causes **tolerance**, a physiological change that produces a need for more of the same drug in order to achieve the same effect. Tolerance will eventually cause **withdrawal** symptoms in users. Withdrawal symptoms vary from drug to drug. They range from the headache I might get if I do not consume any caffeine during the day to the dehydrating and potentially fatal night sweats (sweating profusely during sleep) a heroin addict experiences during withdrawal. Dependence on psychoactive drugs can be either psychological or physical or can be both. Persons psychologically dependent on a drug feel an intense desire for the drug because they are convinced they need it in order to perform or feel a certain way. Persons physically dependent on a substance have a tolerance for the drug, experience withdrawal symptoms without it, and need the drug to avoid the withdrawal symptoms.

Different researchers categorize psychoactive drugs in different ways, but four common categories are stimulants, depressants, hallucinogens, and opiates.

Caffeine, cocaine, amphetamines, and nicotine are common **stimulants**. Stimulants speed up body processes, including autonomic nervous system functions such as heart and respiration rate. This dramatic increase is accompanied by a sense of euphoria. The more powerful stimulants, such as cocaine, produce an extreme euphoric rush that may make a user feel extremely self-confident and invincible. All stimulants produce tolerance, withdrawal effects, and other side effects (such as disturbed sleep, reduced appetite, increased anxiety, and heart problems) to a greater or lesser degree that corresponds with the power of the drug.

TIP

Alcohol is categorized as a depressant because of its effect on our nervous system, even though some people report feeling more energized after ingesting a small amount of alcohol. This energizing effect is due to expectations about alcohol and because alcohol lowers inhibitions. Similarly, nicotine is a stimulant because it speeds up our nervous system, but some smokers smoke to relax.

Depressants slow down the same body systems that stimulants speed up. Alcohol, barbiturates, and anxiolytics (also called tranquilizers or antianxiety drugs) like Valium are common depressants. Obviously, alcohol is by far the most commonly used depressant and psychoactive drug. An euphoria accompanies the depressing effects of depressants, as does tolerance and withdrawal symptoms. In addition, alcohol slows down our reactions and judgment by slowing down brain processes. The inhibition of different brain regions causes behavioral changes. For example, when enough alcohol is ingested to affect the cerebellum, our motor coordination is dramatically affected, eventually making it difficult or impossible for the user to even stand. Because it is so widespread, more research has been done on alcohol than on any other psychoactive drug.

Hallucinogens (also sometimes called **psychedelics**) do not necessarily speed up or slow down the body. These drugs cause changes in perceptions of reality, including sensory hallucinations, loss of identity, and vivid fantasies. Common hallucinogens include LSD, peyote, psilocybin mushrooms, and marijuana. One notable feature of hallucinogens is their persistence. Some amount of these drugs may remain in the body for weeks. If an individual ingests the hallucinogen again during this time period, the new dose of the chemical is added to the lingering amount, creating more profound and potentially dangerous effects. This effect is sometimes called **reverse tolerance** because the second dose may be less than the first but cause the same or greater effects. Effects of hallucinogens are less predictable than those of stimulants or depressants.

Opiates such as morphine, heroin, methadone, and codeine are all similar in chemical structure to opium, a drug derived from the poppy plant. The opiates all act as agonists for endorphins and thus are powerful painkillers and mood elevators. Opiates cause drowsiness and a euphoria associated with elevated endorphin levels. The opiates are some of the most physically addictive drugs because they rapidly change brain chemistry and create tolerance and withdrawal symptoms.

Types of Psychoactive Drugs

Type of Drug	Main Effect	Examples
Stimulants	Arouse the autonomic nervous system	caffeine, cocaine, amphetamines, nicotine
Depressants	Slow down the autonomic nervous system	alcohol, barbiturates, tranquilizers
Hallucinogens	Cause sensory distortions	marijuana, LSD, peyote, mushrooms, psilocybin
Opiates	Relieve pain, elevate mood	codeine, morphine, heroin, methadone

PRACTICE QUESTIONS

Directions: Each of the questions or incomplete statements below is followed by five suggested answers or completions. Select the one that is best in each case.

1. Agonists are psychoactive drugs that
   (A) produce tolerance to the drug without the associated withdrawal symptoms.
   (B) mimic and produce the same effect as certain neurotransmitters.
   (C) mimic neurotransmitters and block their receptor sites.
   (D) enhance the effects of certain opiates like heroin.
   (E) make recovery from physical addiction more difficult.

2. In comparison with older people, babies
   (A) sleep more fitfully; they tend to wake up more often.
   (B) sleep more deeply; they spend more time in stage 3 and 4 sleep.
   (C) spend more time in the REM stage than other sleep stages.
   (D) spend more time in stage 1, which causes them to awaken easily.
   (E) sleep more than young adults, but less than people over 50.

3. Which of the following is the best analogy for how psychologists view consciousness?
   (A) the on/off switch on a computer
   (B) a circuit breaker that controls power to a house
   (C) a fuse that allows electricity to pass through until a short circuit occurs
   (D) a dimmer switch for a light fixture
   (E) the ignition switch on a car

4. During a normal night's sleep, how many times do we pass through the different stages of sleep?
   (A) 2
   (B) 2–3
   (C) 4–7
   (D) 8–11
   (E) 11–15

5. Deep or slow wave sleep is associated with which type(s) of brain waves?
   (A) alpha
   (B) beta
   (C) delta
   (D) alpha and beta
   (E) beta and delta

6. Activation-synthesis theory tries to explain
   (A) how consciousness emerges out of neural firings.
   (B) how psychoactive drugs create euphoric effects.
   (C) the origin and function of dreams.
   (D) how our mind awakens us after we pass through all the sleep stages.
   (E) how our consciousness synthesizes all the sensory information it receives.

7. Which of the following tends to increase during a typical night's sleep in an adult?
   (A) night terrors
   (B) deep sleep
   (C) delta waves
   (D) dreaming
   (E) sleeptalking

8. Which of the following two sleep disorders occur most commonly?
   (A) insomnia and narcolepsy
   (B) apnea and narcolepsy
   (C) night terrors and apnea
   (D) somnambulism and insomnia
   (E) apnea and insomnia

9. Marijuana falls under what category of psychoactive drug?
   (A) depressant
   (B) mood elevator
   (C) hallucinogen
   (D) stimulant
   (E) mood depressant

10. Night terrors and somnambulism usually occur during which stage of sleep?
    (A) stage 1, close to wakefulness
    (B) REM sleep
    (C) REM sleep, but only later in the night when nightmares usually occur
    (D) stage 4
    (E) sleep onset

11. Which neurotransmitter is affected by opiates?
    (A) serotonin
    (B) endorphins
    (C) dopamine
    (D) GABA
    (E) acetylcholine

12. In the context of this unit, the term *tolerance* refers to

    (A) treatment of psychoactive drug addicts by peers and other members of society.
    (B) the amount of sleep a person needs to function normally.
    (C) the need for an elevated dose of a drug in order to get the same effect.
    (D) the labeling of individuals automatically produced by the level of our consciousness.
    (E) the harmful side effects of psychoactive drugs.

13. The information-processing theory says that dreams

    (A) are meaningless by-products of how our brains process information during REM sleep.
    (B) are symbolic representations of the information we encode during the day.
    (C) are processed by one level of consciousness but other levels remain unaware of the dreams.
    (D) occur during REM sleep as the brain deals with daily stress and events.
    (E) occur only after stressful events, explaining why some people never dream.

14. Which level of consciousness controls involuntary body processes?

    (A) preconscious level
    (B) subconscious level
    (C) unconscious level
    (D) autonomic level
    (E) nonconscious level

15. Professor Bohkle shows a group of participants a set of geometric shapes for a short period of time. Later, Professor Bohkle shows the same group a larger set of shapes that includes the first set of geometric shapes randomly distributed among the other new images. When asked which shapes they prefer, the participants choose shapes from the first group more often than the new images, even though they cannot remember which images they had seen previously. This experiment demonstrates which concept?

    (A) priming
    (B) mere-exposure effect
    (C) shaping
    (D) fundamental-attribution error
    (E) primacy

ANSWER KEY

1. **B**	6. **C**	11. **B**
2. **C**	7. **D**	12. **C**
3. **D**	8. **E**	13. **D**
4. **C**	9. **C**	14. **E**
5. **C**	10. **D**	15. **B**

ANSWERS EXPLAINED

1. **(B)** Agonists fit into receptor sites for specific neurotransmitters and produce similar results. Choice C is a definition of antagonists. The other choices are incorrect distractions.

2. **(C)** Babies spend more time in REM. As we get older, the time spent in REM gradually decreases. The other choices are incorrect statements about the typical sleep patterns of infants.

3. **(D)** Psychologists define consciousness as our level of awareness of ourselves and our environment. A dimmer switch is the only analogy that implies a continuum from very dim to very bright with variations in between. Consciousness is not like an on/off switch as implied in the other choices.

4. **(C)** Most often, we cycle through the sleep stages around 5 to 6 times per night. The duration of a sleep cycle is approximately 90 minutes long.

5. **(C)** Delta waves indicate deep or slow wave sleep. Alpha and Beta waves indicate more shallow sleep stages.

6. **(C)** Activation-synthesis theory states that dreams are a meaningless by-product of brain processes during REM sleep. The other choices do not relate to this theory.

7. **(D)** Periods of REM sleep tend to lengthen in adults as the night goes on, correlating with higher rates of dreaming. Night terrors are highly unusual in adults and tend to occur during the periods of deep sleep that occur mostly in the first half of the night; delta waves are predominant during such periods of deep sleep. Sleeptalking is most common just as someone transitions from wakefulness into sleep and therefore is also more common at the beginning of the night.

8. **(E)** Research indicates that insomnia and apnea are the most common sleep disorders, even though apnea may be very underdiagnosed.

9. **(C)** Marijuana is a hallucinogen. Items B and E are not categories of psychoactive drugs.

10. **(D)** Sleepwalking and night terrors occur during stage 4 sleep and are unrelated to dreaming and REM sleep.

11. **(B)** Opiates mimic the effect of endorphins in the brain, producing the pain-killing and euphoric, dreamy state associated with these drugs.

12. **(C)** People who use psychoactive drugs get an increased tolerance for the drugs, meaning they need more of the drugs to get the same effect. In this context, tolerance has nothing to do with the treatment or labeling of others or with sleep.

13. **(D)** Information-processing theory states that REM sleep and dreaming reflect the brain processing the stresses and events of our recent experience. Choice A is a definition of the activation-synthesis theory of dreams. Dreams and symbolic representations, choice B, fits Freud's theory of dreams best. Choices C and E are incorrect distractors.

14. **(E)** Automatic functions like heart rate are controlled by the nonconscious level. The levels mentioned in the other choices control other parts of consciousness, except for the autonomic level, which is a created distracter and not a correct term.

15. **(B)** The mere-exposure effect occurs when we prefer stimuli we have seen before over novel stimuli, even if we do not consciously remember seeing the old stimuli. Priming refers to our ability to answer questions we have been exposed to before, even if we do not remember having seen the questions. Shaping is a concept in operant conditioning, primary-attribution error is a concept in social psychology that describes our tendency to attribute a person's behavior to his or her inner disposition rather than environment. Primacy is a concept from the memory chapter 7 "Cognition".

UNIT 3

Sensation and Perception

Unit 3 addresses research summarized in one (or possibly two) chapters in the textbook you use in your AP Psychology class: Sensation and Perception. Content in this chapter is closely related to some of the material in the Biological Bases of Behavior unit. In that unit, you learned about how neurons function and the different roles of parts of the brain. As you study sensation and perception, you'll learn how specialized neurons in our sensory organs operate and how sensations are transformed into perceptions in the brain.

5 Sensation and Perception

Key Terms

- Transduction
- Sensory adaptation
- Sensory habituation (also called perceptual adaptation)
- Cocktail-party phenomenon
- Sensation
- Perception
- Energy senses
- Chemical senses
- Vision
- Cornea
- Pupil
- Lens
- Retina
- Feature detectors
- Optic nerve
- Occipital lobe
- Visible light
- Rods and cones
- Fovea
- Blind spot
- Trichromatic theory
- Color blindness
- Afterimages
- Opponent-process theory
- Hearing
- Sound waves
- Amplitude
- Frequency
- Cochlea
- Pitch theories
- Place theory
- Frequency theory
- Conduction deafness
- Nerve deafness
- Touch
- Gate-control theory
- Taste (or gustation)
- Smell (or olfaction)
- Vestibular sense
- Kinesthetic sense
- Absolute threshold
- Subliminal messages
- Difference threshold
- Weber's law
- Signal detection theory
- Top-down processing
- Perceptual set
- Bottom-up processing
- Gestalt rules
- Proximity
- Similarity
- Continuity
- Closure
- Constancy
- Size constancy
- Shape constancy
- Brightness constancy
- Depth cues

Key People

- David Hubel
- Torsten Wiesel
- Ernst Weber
- Gustav Fechner
- Eleanor Gibson

OVERVIEW

Right now as you read this, your eyes capture the light reflected off the page or emitted by the screen in front of you. Structures in your eyes change this pattern of light into signals that are sent to your brain and interpreted as language. The sensation of the symbols on the page and the perception of these symbols as words allow you to understand what you are reading. All our senses work in a similar way. In general, our sensory organs receive stimuli.

These messages go through a process called **transduction**, which means the signals are transformed into neural impulses. These neural impulses travel first to the thalamus then on to different cortices of the brain (you will see later that the sense of smell is the one exception to this rule).

What we sense and perceive is influenced by many factors, including how long we are exposed to stimuli. For example, you probably felt your socks when you put them on this morning, but you stopped feeling them after a while. You probably stopped perceiving the feeling of your socks on your feet because of a combination of **sensory adaptation** (decreasing responsiveness to stimuli due to constant stimulation) and **sensory habituation** (our perception of sensations is partially due to how focused we are on them). What we perceive is determined by what sensations activate our senses and by what we focus on perceiving. We can voluntarily attend to stimuli in order to perceive them, as you are doing right now, but paying attention can also be involuntary. If you are talking with a friend and someone across the room says your name, your attention will probably involuntarily switch across the room. (This is sometimes called the **cocktail-party phenomenon**.)

These processes are our only way to get information about the outside world. The exact distinction between what is sensation and what is perception is debated by psychologists and philosophers. For our purposes, though, we can think of sensation as activation of our senses (eyes, ears, and so on) and perception as the process of understanding these sensations. We will review the structure and functions of each sensory organ and then explain some concepts involved in perception.

TIP

One of the ways to organize the different senses in your mind is by thinking about what they gather from the outside world. The first three senses listed here, vision, hearing, and touch, gather energy in the form of light, sound waves, and pressure, respectively. Think of these three senses as energy senses. The next two, taste and smell, gather chemicals. Think of these as chemical senses. The last two senses described, vestibular and kinesthetic, help us with body position and balance.

ENERGY SENSES

Vision

Vision is the dominant sense in human beings. Sighted people use vision to gather information about their environment more than any other sense. The process of vision involves several steps.

Step One: Gathering Light

Vision is a complicated process, and you should have a basic understanding of the structures and processes involved for the AP test. First, light is reflected off objects and gathered by the eye. Visible light is a small section of the electromagnetic spectrum that you may have studied in your science classes. The color we perceive depends on several factors. One is light intensity. It describes how much energy the light contains. This factor determines how bright the object appears. A second factor, light wavelength, determines the particular hue we see. Wavelengths longer than visible light are infrared waves, microwaves, and radio waves. Wavelengths shorter than visible light include ultraviolet waves and X-rays.

We see different wavelengths within the visible light spectrum as different colors. The colors of the visible spectrum in order from longest to shortest wavelengths are: red, orange, yellow, green, blue, indigo, and violet; you probably were taught the acronym *Roy G. Biv* to help you remember this order. When you mix all these colors of light waves together, you get white light or sunlight. Although we think of objects as possessing colors (a red shirt, a blue car), objects appear the color they do as a result of the wavelengths of light they reflect. A red shirt reflects red light and absorbs other colors. Objects appear black because they absorb all colors and white because they reflect all wavelengths of light.

Step Two: Within the Eye

When we look at something, we turn our eyes toward the object and the reflected light coming from it enters our eye. To understand the following descriptions, refer to Figure 5.1 for structures in the eye. The reflected light first enters the eye through the **cornea**, a protective covering. The cornea also helps focus the light. Then the light goes through the **pupil**. The pupil is like the shutter of a camera. The muscles that control the pupil (called the **iris**) open it (dilate) to let more light in and also make it smaller to let less light in. Through a process called **accommodation**, light that enters the pupil is focused by the *lens*; the lens is curved and flexible in order to focus the light. Try this: Hold up one finger and focus on it. Now, change your focus and look at the wall behind your finger. Then look at the finger again. You can feel the muscles changing the shape of your lens as you switch your focus. As the light passes through the lens, the image is flipped upside down and inverted. The focused inverted image projects on the **retina**, which is like a screen on the back of your eye. On this screen are specialized neurons that are activated by the different wavelengths of light.

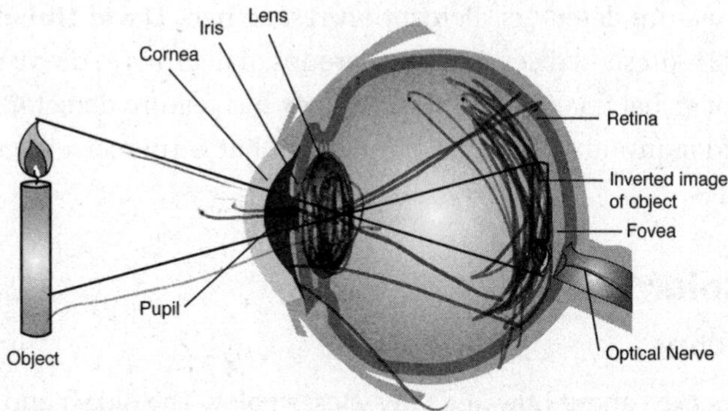

Figure 5.1 Cross section of the eye.

Step Three: Transduction

The term **transduction** refers to the translation of incoming stimuli into neural signals. This term applies not only to vision but to all our senses. In vision, transduction occurs when light activates the neurons in the retina. There are several layers of cells are in the retina.

The first layer of cells is directly activated by light. These cells are **cones**, cells that are activated by color, and **rods**, cells that respond to black and white. These cells are arranged in a pattern on the retina. Rods outnumber cones (the ratio is approximately twenty to one) and are distributed throughout the retina. Cones are concentrated toward the center of the retina. At the very center of the retina is an indentation called the **fovea** that contains the highest concentration of cones. If you focus on something, you are focusing the light onto your fovea and see it in color. Your peripheral vision, especially at the extremes, relies on rods and is mostly in black and white. Your peripheral vision may seem to be full color, but controlled experiments prove otherwise. (You can try this yourself. Focus on a spot in front of you and have a friend hold different colored pens in your peripheral vision. You will find you cannot determine the color of the pens until they get close to the center of your vision.)

If enough rods and cones fire in an area of the retina, they activate the next layer of bipolar cells. If enough bipolar cells fire, the next layer of cells, **ganglion cells**, is activated. The axons of the ganglion cells make up the optic nerve that sends these impulses to a specific region in the thalamus called the **lateral geniculate nucleus (LGN)**. From there, the messages are sent to the visual cortices located in the occipital lobes of the brain. The spot where the optic nerve leaves the retina has no rods or cones, so it is referred to as the **blind spot**. The optic nerve is divided into two parts. Impulses from the left side of each retina go to the left hemisphere of the brain. Impulses from the right side of each retina go to the right side of our brain. The spot where the nerves cross each other is called the **optic chiasm**.

You might have guessed that this is a simplified version of this process. Different factors are involved in why each layer of cells might fire, but this explanation is suitable for our purposes.

Step Four: In the Brain

You might remember from Chapter 2, "Biological Bases," that the visual cortex of the brain is located in the occipital lobe. Some researchers say it is at this point that sensation ends and perception begins. Others say some interpretation of images occurs in the layers of cells in the retina. Still others say it occurs in the LGN region of the thalamus. That debate aside, the visual cortex of the brain receives the impulses from the cells of the retina, and the impulses activate feature detectors. Perception researchers **David Hubel** (1926–2013) and **Torsten Wiesel** (1924–present) discovered that groups of neurons in the visual cortex respond to different types of visual images. The visual cortex has feature detectors for vertical lines, curves, motion, and many other features of images. What we perceive visually is a combination of these features.

Theories of Color Vision

Trichromatic Theory

Competing theories exist about how and why we see color. The oldest and simplest theory is **trichromatic theory** (also called the Young–Helmholtz Trichromatic [three color] theory). This theory hypothesizes that we have three types of cones in the retina: cones that detect the different colors blue, red, and green (the primary colors of light). These cones are activated in different combinations to produce all the colors of the visible spectrum. While this theory has some research support and makes sense intuitively, it cannot explain some visual phenomena, such as **afterimages** and **color blindness**. If you stare at one color for a while and then look at a white or blank space, you will see a color afterimage. If you stare at green, the afterimage will be red, while the afterimage of yellow is blue. Color blindness is similar. Individuals with dichromatic color blindness cannot see either red/green shades or blue/yellow shades. (The other type of color blindness is monochromatic, which causes people to see only shades of gray.) Another theory of color vision is needed to explain these phenomena.

Opponent-Process Theory

The opponent-process theory states that the sensory receptors arranged in the retina come in pairs: red/green pairs, yellow/blue pairs, and black/white pairs. If one sensor is stimulated, its pair is inhibited from firing. This theory explains color afterimages well. If you stare at the color red for a while, you fatigue the sensors for red. Then when you switch your gaze and look at a blank page, the opponent part of the pair for red will fire, and you will see a green afterimage. The opponent-process theory also explains color blindness. If color sensors do come in pairs and an individual is missing one pair, he or she should have difficulty seeing those hues. People with dichromatic color blindness have difficulty seeing shades of red and green or of yellow and blue.

TIP

Most researchers agree with a combination of trichromatic and opponent-process theory. Individual cones appear to correspond best to the trichromatic theory, while the opponent processes may occur at other layers of the retina. The important thing to remember is that both concepts are needed to explain color vision fully.

Hearing

Our auditory sense also uses energy in the form of waves, but sound waves are vibrations in the air rather than electromagnetic waves. Sound waves are created by vibrations, which travel through the air, and are then collected by our ears. These vibrations then finally go through the process of transduction into neural messages and are sent to the brain. Sound waves, like all waves, have **amplitude** and **frequency**. Amplitude is the height of the wave and determines the loudness of the sound, which is measured in decibels. Frequency refers to the length of the waves and determines pitch, measured in megahertz. High-pitched sounds have high frequencies, and the waves are densely packed together. Low-pitched sounds have low frequencies, and the waves are spaced apart.

Sound waves are collected in your outer ear, or pinna (see Fig. 5.2 for structures in the ear). The waves travel down the **ear canal** (also called the auditory canal) until they reach the **eardrum** or tympanic membrane. This is a thin membrane that vibrates as the sound waves hit it. Think of it as the head of a drum. This membrane is attached to the first in a series of three small bones collectively known as the ossicles. The eardrum connects with the **hammer** (or malleus), which is connected to the **anvil** (or incus), which connects to the **stirrup** (or stapes). The vibration of the eardrum is transmitted by these three bones to the **oval window**, a membrane very similar to the eardrum. The oval window membrane is attached to the **cochlea**, a structure shaped like a snail's shell filled with fluid. As the oval window vibrates, the fluid moves. The floor of the cochlea is the basilar membrane. It is lined with hair cells connected to the **organ of Corti**, which are neurons activated by movement of the hair cells. When the fluid moves, the hair cells move and transduction occurs. The organ of Corti fires, and these impulses are transmitted to the brain via the auditory nerve.

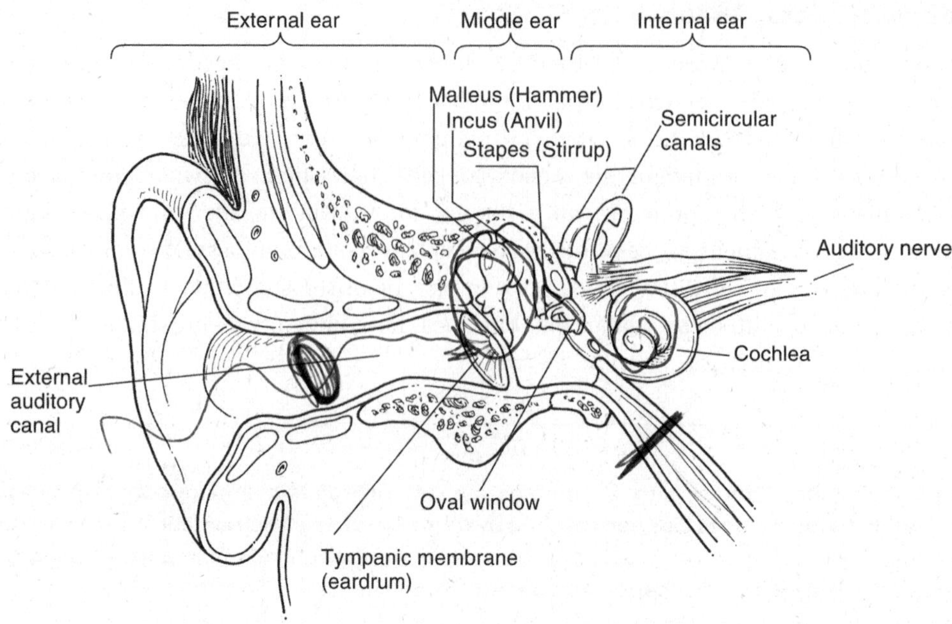

Figure 5.2 Cross section of the ear.

> **TIP**
> One way to remember amplitude and frequency is to imagine you are watching waves go by. Frequency is how frequently the waves come by. If they speed by quickly, the waves are high in frequency. Amplitude is how tall the waves are. The taller the waves, the more energy and the louder the noise.

Pitch Theories

The description of the hearing process above explains how we hear in general, but how do we hear different pitches or tones? As with color vision, two different theories describe the two processes involved in hearing pitch: place theory and frequency theory.

Place Theory

Place theory holds that the hair cells in the cochlea respond to different frequencies of sound based on where they are located in the cochlea. Some bend in response to high pitches and some to low. We sense pitch because the hair cells move in different places in the cochlea.

Frequency Theory

Research demonstrates that place theory accurately describes how hair cells sense the upper range of pitches but not the lower tones. Lower tones are sensed by the rate at which the cells fire. We sense pitch because the hair cells fire at different rates (frequencies) in the cochlea.

Deafness

An understanding of how hearing works explains hearing problems as well. **Conduction deafness** occurs when something goes wrong with the system of conducting the sound to the cochlea (in the ear canal, eardrum, hammer/anvil/stirrup, or oval window). For example, my mother-in-law has a medical condition that is causing her stirrup to deteriorate slowly. Eventually, she will need surgery to replace that bone in order to hear well. **Nerve** (or **sensorineural**) **deafness** occurs when the hair cells in the cochlea are damaged, usually by loud noise. If you have ever been to a concert, football game, or other event loud enough to leave your ears ringing, chances are you came close to or did cause permanent damage to your hearing. Prolonged exposure to noise that loud can permanently damage the hair cells in your cochlea, and these hair cells do not regenerate. Nerve deafness is much more difficult to treat since no method has been found that will encourage the hair cells to regenerate.

Touch

When our skin is indented, pierced, or experiences a change in temperature, our sense of touch is activated by this energy. We have many different types of nerve endings in every patch of skin, and the exact relationship between these different types of nerve endings and the sense of touch is not completely understood. Some nerve endings respond to pressure while others respond to temperature. We do know that our brain interprets the amount of indentation (or temperature change) as the intensity of the touch, from a light touch to a hard blow. We also sense placement of the touch by the place on our body where the nerve endings fire. Also, nerve endings are more concentrated in different parts of our body. If we want to feel something, we usually use our fingertip, an area of high nerve concentration, rather than the back of our elbow, an area of low nerve concentration. If touch or temperature receptors are stimulated sharply, a different kind of nerve ending called pain receptors will also fire. Pain is a useful response because it warns us of potential dangers.

Gate-control theory helps explain how we experience pain the way we do. Gate-control theory explains that some pain messages have a higher priority than others. When a higher priority message is sent, the gate swings open for it and swings shut for a low priority message, which we will not feel. Of course, this gate is not a physical gate swinging in the nerve, it is just a convenient way to understand how pain messages are sent. When you scratch an itch, the gate swings open for your high-intensity scratching and shuts for the low-intensity itching, and you stop the itching for a short period of time (but do not worry, the itching usually starts again soon!). Endorphins, or pain-killing chemicals in the body, also swing the gate shut. Natural endorphins in the brain, which are chemically similar to opiates like morphine, control pain.

CHEMICAL SENSES

Taste (or Gustation)

The nerves involved in the chemical senses respond to chemicals rather than to energy, such as light and sound waves. Chemicals from the food we eat (or whatever else we stick into our mouths) are absorbed by taste buds on our tongue (see Fig. 5.3). Taste buds are located on **papillae**, which are the bumps you can see on your tongue. Taste buds are located all over the tongue and some parts of the inside of the cheeks and roof of the mouth. Humans sense five different types of tastes: sweet, salty, sour, bitter, and umami ("savory" or "meaty" taste). Some taste buds respond more intensely to a specific taste and more weakly to others. People differ in their ability to taste food. The more densely packed the taste buds, the more chemicals are absorbed, and the more intensely the food is tasted. You can get an idea of how densely packed taste buds are by looking at the papillae on your tongue. If all the bumps are packed tightly together, you probably taste food intensely. If they are spread apart, you are probably a weak taster. What we think of as the flavor of food is actually a combination of taste and smell.

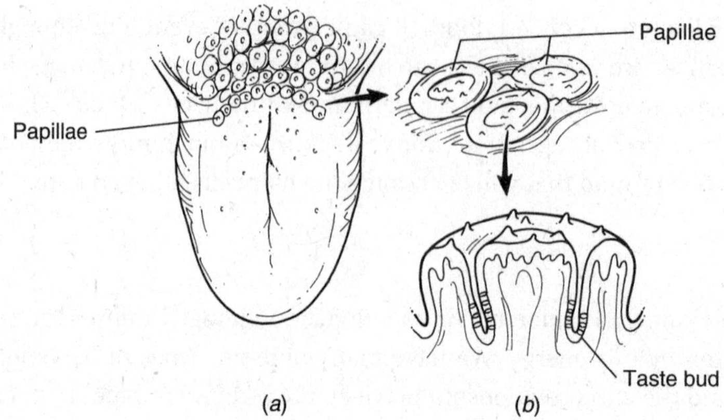

Figure 5.3 Taste sensors.

Smell (or Olfaction)

Our sense of smell also depends on chemicals emitted by substances. Molecules of substances, hot chocolate for example, rise into the air. Some of them are drawn into our nose. The molecules settle in a mucous membrane at the top of each nostril and are absorbed by receptor cells located there. The exact types of these receptor cells are not yet known, as they are for taste buds. Some researchers estimate that as many as 100 different types of smell receptors may exist. These receptor cells are linked to the **olfactory bulb** (see Fig. 5.4), which gathers the messages from the **olfactory receptor cells** and sends this information to the brain. Interestingly, the nerve fibers from the olfactory bulb connect to the brain differently than all the other senses do. The impulses from the other senses, except smell, go through the thalamus first before being sent to the cortex, but information from our sense of smell goes directly to the amygdala (emotional impulses) and then to the hippocampus (memory). This direct connection to the limbic system may explain why smell is such a powerful trigger for memories.

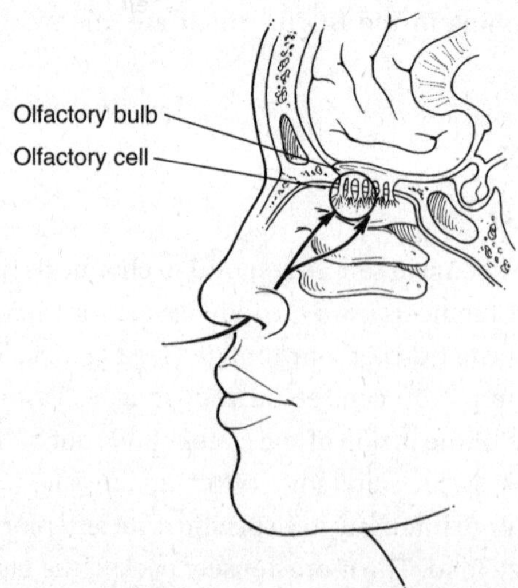

Figure 5.4 Cross section of the olfactory system.

BODY POSITION SENSES

Vestibular Sense

Our vestibular sense tells us about how our body is oriented in space. Three semicircular canals in the inner ear (see Fig. 5.2) give the brain feedback about body orientation. The canals are basically tubes partially filled with fluid. When the position of your head changes, the fluid moves in the canals, causing sensors in the canals to move. The movement of these hair cells activate neurons, and their impulses go to the brain. You have probably experienced the nausea and dizziness caused when the fluid in these canals is agitated. During an exciting roller-coaster ride, the fluid in the canals might move so much that the brain receives confusing signals about body position. This causes the dizziness and nauseous reaction.

Kinesthetic Sense

While our vestibular sense keeps track of the overall orientation of our body, our kinesthetic sense gives us feedback about the position and orientation of specific body parts. Receptors in our muscles and joints send information to our brain about our limbs. This information, combined with visual feedback, lets us keep track of our body. You could probably reach down with one finger and touch your kneecap with a high degree of accuracy because your kinesthetic sense provides information about where your finger is in relation to your kneecap.

See the following table for a summary of the senses and their associated receptors.

Table 5.1 Senses and Associated Receptors

Energy Senses	Vision	Rods, Cones (in Retina)
	Hearing	Hairlike cells in the cochlea
	Touch	Temperature, pressure, pain nerves (in the skin)
Chemical Senses	Taste (gustation)	Sweet, sour, salty, bitter, and umami taste buds (in papillae on the tongue)
	Smell (olfaction)	Smell receptors connected to the olfactory bulb (in the nose)
Body Position Senses	Vestibular sense	Hairlike cells in the three semicircular canals (in the inner ear)
	Kinesthetic sense	Receptors in muscles and joints

PERCEPTION

As stated before, perception is the process of understanding and interpreting sensations. Psychophysics is the study of the interaction between the sensations we receive and our experience of them. Researchers who study psychophysics try to uncover the rules our minds use to interpret sensations. We will cover some of the basic principles in psychophysics and examine some basic perceptual rules for vision.

Thresholds

Research shows that while our senses are very acute, they do have their limits. The **absolute threshold** is the smallest amount of stimulus we can detect. For example, the absolute threshold for vision is the smallest amount of light we can detect, which is estimated to be a single candle flame about 30 miles (48 km) away on a perfectly dark night. Most of us could detect a single drop of perfume a room away. Actually, the technical definition of absolute threshold is the minimal amount of stimulus we can detect 50 percent of the time, because researchers try to take into account individual variation in sensitivity and interference from other sensory sources. Stimuli below our absolute threshold is said to be **subliminal**. Some companies claim to produce subliminal message media that can change unwanted behavior. Psychological research does not support their claim. In fact, a truly subliminal message would not, by definition, affect behavior at all because if a message is truly subliminal, we do not perceive it! Research indicates some messages called subliminal (because they are so faint we do not report perceiving them) can sometimes affect behavior in subtle ways, such as choosing a word at random from a list after the word was presented subliminally. Evidence does not exist, however, that more complex subliminal messages such as "lose weight" or "increase your vocabulary" are effective. If these tapes do change behavior, the change most likely comes from the **placebo effect** rather than from the effect of the subliminal message.

So if we can see a single candle 30 miles (48 km) away, would we notice if another candle was lit right next to it? In other words, how much does a stimulus need to change before we notice the difference? The **difference threshold** defines this change. The difference threshold, sometimes called **just-noticeable difference**, is the smallest amount of change needed in a stimulus before we detect a change. This threshold is computed by **Weber's law**, named after psychophysicist **Ernst Weber** (Note: Some textbooks refer to this law as the Weber-Fechner law to honor the contributions of psychophysicist **Gustav Fechner**, 1801–1887). It states that the change needed is proportional to the original intensity of the stimulus. The more intense the stimulus, the more it will need to change before we notice a difference. You might notice a change if someone adds a small amount of cayenne pepper to a dish that is normally not very spicy, but you would need to add much more hot pepper to five-alarm chili before anyone would notice a difference. Further, Weber discovered that each sense varies according to a constant, but the constants differ between the senses. For example, the constant for hearing is 5 percent. If you listened to a 100-decibel tone, the volume would have to increase to 105 decibels before you noticed that it was any louder. Weber's constant for vision is 8 percent. So 8 candles would need to be added to 100 candles before it looked any brighter.

Perceptual Theories

Psychologists use several theories to describe how we perceive the world.

> **TIP**
>
> These perceptual theories are not competing with one another. Each theory describes different examples or parts of perception. Sometimes a single example of the interpretation of sensation needs to be explained using all of the following theories.

Signal Detection Theory

Real-world examples of perception are more complicated than controlled laboratory-perception experiments. After all, how many times do we get the opportunity to stare at a single candle flame 30 miles (48 km) away on a perfectly clear, dark night? **Signal detection theory** investigates the effects of the distractions and interference we experience while perceiving the world. This area of research tries to predict what we will perceive among competing stimuli. For example, will the surgeon see the tumor on the CAT scan among all the irrelevant shadows and flaws in the picture? Will the quarterback see the one open receiver in the end zone despite the oncoming lineman? Signal detection theory takes into account how motivated we are to detect certain stimuli and what we expect to perceive.

These factors together are called response criteria (also called **receiver operating characteristics**). For example, I will be more likely to smell a freshly baked rhubarb pie if I am hungry and enjoy the taste of rhubarb. By using factors like response criteria, signal detection theory tries to explain and predict the different perceptual mistakes we make. A **false positive** is when we think we perceive a stimulus that is not there. For example, you may think you see a friend of yours on a crowded street and end up waving at a total stranger. A **false negative** is not perceiving a stimulus that is present. You may not notice the directions at the top of a test that instruct you not to write on the test form. In some situations, one type of error is much more serious than the other, and this importance can alter perception. In the surgeon example mentioned previously, a false negative (not seeing a tumor that is present) is a more serious mistake than a false positive (suspecting that a tumor is there), although both mistakes are obviously important.

Top-Down Processing

When we use **top-down processing**, we perceive by filling in gaps in what we sense. For example, try to read the following sentence:

I _ope yo_ _et a 5 on t_ _ A_ e_am.

You should be able to read the sentence as "I hope you get a 5 on the AP exam." You perceived the blanks as the appropriate letters by using the context of the sentence. Top-down processing occurs when you use your background knowledge to fill in gaps in what you perceive. Our experience creates **schemata**, mental representations of how we expect the world to be. Our schemata influence how we perceive the world. Schemata can create a **perceptual set**, which is a predisposition to perceiving something in a certain way. If you have ever seen images in the clouds, you have experienced top-down processing. You use your background knowledge (schemata) to perceive the random shapes of clouds as organized shapes.

In the 1970s, some parent groups were very concerned about **backmasking**: supposed hidden messages musicians recorded backward in their music. These parent groups would play song lyrics backward and hear messages, usually threatening messages. Some groups of parents demanded an investigation about the effects of the backmasking. What was happening? Lyrics played backward are basically random noise. However, if you expect to hear a threatening message in the random noise, you probably will, much like expecting to see an image in the clouds. People who listened to the songs played backward and had schemata of this music as dangerous or evil perceived the threatening messages due to top-down processing.

Bottom-Up Processing

Bottom-up processing, also called **feature analysis**, is the opposite of top-down processing. Instead of using our experience to perceive an object, we use only the features of the object itself to build a complete perception. We start our perception at the bottom with the individual characteristics of the image and put all those characteristics together into our final perception. Bottom-up processing can be hard to imagine because it is such an automatic process. The feature detectors in the visual cortex allow us to perceive basic features of objects, such as horizontal and vertical lines, curves, motion, and so on. Our mind builds the picture from the bottom up using these basic characteristics. We are constantly using both bottom-up and top-down processing as we perceive the world. Top-down processing is faster but more prone to error, while bottom-up processing takes longer but is more accurate.

Principles of Visual Perception

The rules we use for visual perception are too numerous to cover completely in this book. However, some of the basic rules are important to know and understand for the AP psychology exam. One of the first perceptual decisions our mind must make is the **figure-ground relationship**. What part of a visual image is the figure and what part is the ground or background? Several optical illusions play with this rule. One example is the famous picture of the vase that if looked at one way is a vase but by switching the figure and the ground can be perceived as two faces (see Fig. 5.5).

Figure 5.5 Optical illusion.

Gestalt Rules

At the beginning of the twentieth century, a group of researchers called the Gestalt psychologists described the principles that govern how we perceive groups of objects. The Gestalt psychologists pointed out that we normally perceive images as groups, not as isolated elements. They thought this process was innate and inevitable. Several factors influence how we will group objects.

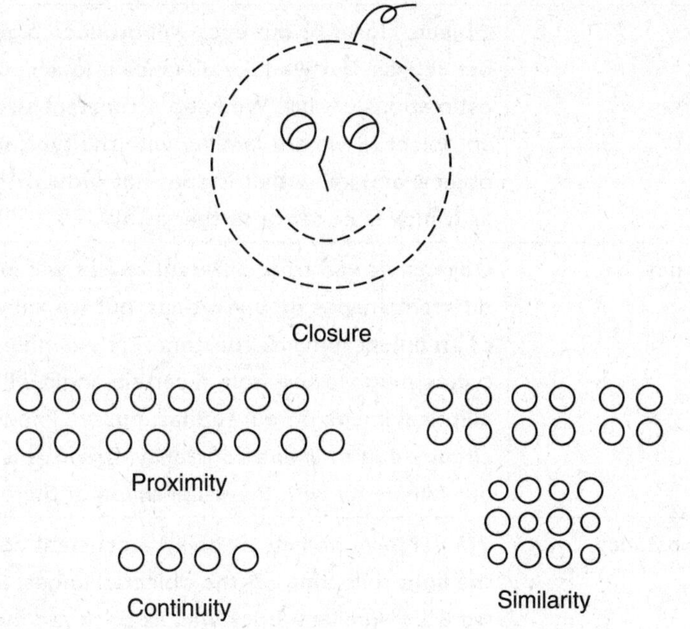

Proximity	Objects that are close together are more likely to be perceived as belonging in the same group.
Similarity	Objects that are similar in appearance are more likely to be perceived as belonging in the same group.
Continuity	Objects that are arranged in a continuous line or curve (such as a trail or a geometric figure) are more likely to be perceived as belonging in the same group.
Closure	Similar to top-down processing. Objects that make up a recognizable image are more likely to be perceived as belonging in the same group even if the image contains gaps that the mind needs to fill in.

Constancy

Every object we see changes minutely from moment to moment due to our changing angle of vision, variations in light, and so on. Our ability to maintain a constant perception of an object despite these changes is called **constancy**. There are several types of constancy.

Size constancy	Objects closer to our eyes will produce bigger images on our retinas, but we take distance into account in our estimations of size. We keep a constant size in mind for an object (if we are familiar with the typical size of the object) and know that it does not grow or shrink in size as it moves closer or farther away.
Shape constancy	Objects viewed from different angles will produce different shapes on our retinas, but we know the shape of an object remains constant. For example, the top of a coffee mug viewed from a certain angle will produce an elliptical image on our retinas, but we know the top is circular due to shape constancy. Again, this depends on our familiarity with the usual shape of the object.
Brightness constancy	We perceive objects as being a constant color even as the light reflecting off the object changes. For example, we will perceive a brick wall as brick red even as the daylight fades and the actual color reflected from the wall turns gray.

Perceived Motion

Another aspect of perception is our ability to gauge motion. Our brains are able to detect how fast images move across our retinas and to take into account our own movement. Interestingly, in a number of situations, our brains perceive objects to be moving when, in fact, they are not. A common example of this is the **stroboscopic effect**, used in movies or flip books. Images in a series of still pictures presented at a certain speed will appear to be moving. Another example you have probably encountered on movie marquees and with holiday lights, is the **phi phenomenon**. A series of lightbulbs turned on and off at a particular rate will appear to be one moving light. A third example is the **autokinetic effect**. If a spot of light is projected steadily onto the same place on a wall of an otherwise dark room and people are asked to stare at it, they will report seeing it move.

Depth Cues

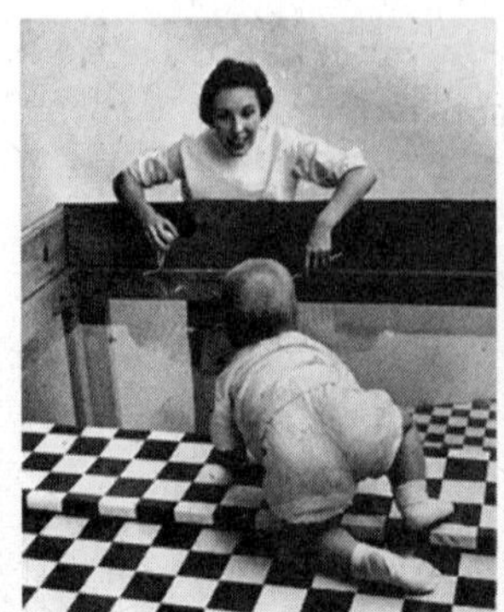

Visual Cliff

One of the most important and frequently investigated parts of visual perception is depth. Without depth perception, we would perceive the world as a two-dimensional flat surface, unable to differentiate between what is near and what is far. This limitation could obviously be dangerous. Researcher **Eleanor Gibson** used the **visual cliff experiment** to determine when human infants can perceive depth. An infant is placed onto one side of a glass-topped table that creates the impression of a cliff. Actually, the glass extends across the entire table, so the infant cannot possibly fall. Gibson found that an infant old enough to crawl will not crawl across the visual cliff, implying the child has depth perception. Other experiments demonstrate that depth perception develops when we are about three months old. Researchers divide the cues that we use to perceive depth into two categories: **monocular cues** (depth cues that do not depend on having two eyes) and **binocular cues** (cues that depend on having two eyes).

Monocular Cues

If you have taken a drawing class, you have learned monocular depth cues. Artists use these cues to imply depth in their drawings. One of the most common cues is **linear perspective**. If you wanted to draw a railroad track that runs away from the viewer off into the distance, most likely you would start by drawing two lines that converge somewhere toward the top of your paper. If you added a drawing of the train, you might use the **relative size cue**. You would draw the boxcars closer to the viewer as larger than the engine off in the distance. A water tower blocking our view of part of the train would be seen as closer to us due to the **interposition cue**; objects that block the view to other objects must be closer to us. If the train were running through a desert landscape, you might draw the rocks closest to the viewer in detail, while the landscape off in the distance would not be as detailed. This cue is called **texture gradient**; we know that we can see details in texture close to us but not far away. Finally, your art teacher might teach you to use **shadowing** in your picture. By shading part of your picture, you can imply where the light source is and thus imply depth and position of objects.

Binocular Cues

Other cues for depth result from our anatomy. We see the world with two eyes set a certain distance apart, and this feature of our anatomy gives us the ability to perceive depth. The finger trick you read about during the discussion of the anatomy of the eye demonstrates the first binocular cue—**binocular disparity** (also called **retinal disparity**). Each of our eyes sees any object from a slightly different angle. The brain gets both images. It knows that if the object is far away, the images will be similar, but the closer the object is, the more disparity there will be between the images coming from each eye. The other binocular cue is **convergence**. As an object gets closer to our face, our eyes must move toward each other to keep focused on the object. The brain receives feedback from the muscles controlling eye movement and knows that the more the eyes converge, the closer the object must be.

Effects of Culture on Perception

One area of psychology cross-cultural researchers are investigating is the effect of culture on perception. Research indicates that some of the perceptual rules psychologists once thought were innate are actually learned. For example, cultures that do not use monocular depth cues (such as linear perspective) in their art do not see depth in pictures using these cues. Also, some optical illusions are not perceived the same way by people from different cultures. For example, below is a representation of the famous Muller-Lyer illusion. Which of the following straight lines, *A* or *B*, appears longer to you?

Line *A* should look longer, even though both lines are actually the same length. People who come from noncarpentered cultures that do not use right angles and corners often in their building and architecture are not usually fooled by the Muller-Lyer illusion. Cross-cultural research demonstrates that some basic perceptual sets are learned from our culture.

Extrasensory Perception

Now that you've reviewed the senses and how the brain changes these sensations into perceptions, you can interpret the term **extrasensory perception (ESP)** in a more specific way than most people can: someone claiming to have "extrasensory perception" is claiming to perceive a sensation "outside" the senses discussed in this chapter. Psychologists are skeptical of ESP claims primarily because our senses are well understood, and researchers do not find reliable evidence that we can perceive sensations other than through our sight, smell, hearing, taste, touch, and vestibular/balance systems. Researchers who test ESP claims using rigorous experiments, such as double-blind studies, find other more likely explanations for supposed extrasensory phenomena. Usually ESP claims are better explained by such things as deception, magic tricks, or coincidence.

PRACTICE QUESTIONS

Directions: Each of the questions or incomplete statements below is followed by five suggested answers or completions. Select the one that is best in each case.

1. Our sense of smell may be a powerful trigger for memories because
   (A) we are conditioned from birth to make strong connections between smells and events.
   (B) the nerve connecting the olfactory bulb sends impulses directly to the limbic system.
   (C) the receptors at the top of each nostril connect with the cortex.
   (D) smell is a powerful cue for encoding memories into long-term memory.
   (E) strong smells encourage us to process events deeply so they will most likely be remembered.

2. The cochlea is responsible for
   (A) protecting the surface of the eye.
   (B) transmitting vibrations received by the eardrum to the hammer, anvil, and stirrup.
   (C) transforming vibrations into neural signals.
   (D) coordinating impulses from the rods and cones in the retina.
   (E) sending messages to the brain about orientation of the head and body.

3. In a perception research lab, you are asked to describe the shape of the top of a box as the box is slowly rotated. Which concept are the researchers most likely investigating?
   (A) feature detectors in the retina
   (B) feature detectors in the occipital lobe
   (C) placement of rods and cones in the retina
   (D) binocular depth cues
   (E) shape constancy

4. The blind spot in our eye results from
   (A) the lack of receptors at the spot where the optic nerve connects to the retina.
   (B) the shadow the pupil makes on the retina.
   (C) competing processing between the visual cortices in the left and right hemisphere.
   (D) floating debris in the space between the lens and the retina.
   (E) retinal damage from bright light.

5. Smell and taste are called ________ because ________
   (A) energy senses; they send impulses to the brain in the form of electric energy.
   (B) chemical senses; they detect chemicals in what we taste and smell.
   (C) flavor senses; smell and taste combine to create flavor.
   (D) chemical senses; they send impulses to the brain in the form of chemicals.
   (E) memory senses; they both have powerful connections to memory.

6. What is the principal difference between amplitude and frequency in the context of sound waves?
   (A) Amplitude is the tone or timbre of a sound, whereas frequency is the pitch.
   (B) Amplitude is detected in the cochlea, whereas frequency is detected in the auditory cortex.
   (C) Amplitude is the height of the sound wave, whereas frequency is a measure of how frequently the sound waves pass a given point.
   (D) Both measure qualities of sound, but frequency is a more accurate measure since it measures the shapes of the waves rather than the strength of the waves.
   (E) Frequency is a measure for light waves, whereas amplitude is a measure for sound waves.

7. Weber's law determines
   (A) absolute threshold.
   (B) focal length of the eye.
   (C) level of subliminal messages.
   (D) amplitude of sound waves.
   (E) just-noticeable difference.

8. Gate-control theory refers to
   (A) which sensory impulses are transmitted first from each sense.
   (B) which pain messages are perceived.
   (C) interfering sound waves, causing some waves to be undetected.
   (D) the gate at the optic chiasm controlling the destination hemisphere for visual information from each eye.
   (E) how our minds choose to use either bottom-up or top-down processing.

9. If you had sight in only one eye, which of the following depth cues could you NOT use?
   (A) texture gradient
   (B) convergence
   (C) linear perspective
   (D) interposition
   (E) shading

10. Which of the following sentences best describes the relationship between sensation and perception?
    (A) Sensation is a strictly mechanical process, whereas perception is a cognitive process.
    (B) Perception is an advanced form of sensation.
    (C) Sensation happens in the senses, whereas perception happens in the brain.
    (D) Sensation is detecting stimuli, perception is interpreting stimuli detected.
    (E) Sensation involves learning and expectations, and perception does not.

11. What function does the retina serve?

    (A) The retina contains the visual receptor cells that transform light into neural impulses.
    (B) The retina focuses light coming in the eye through the lens.
    (C) The retina determines how much light is let into the eye.
    (D) The retina determines which parts of the brain incoming light will be sent to.
    (E) The retina connects the two optic nerves and sends impulses to the left and right visual cortices.

12. Color blindness and color afterimages are best explained by what theory of color vision?

    (A) trichromatic theory
    (B) visible hue theory
    (C) opponent-process theory
    (D) dichromatic theory
    (E) binocular disparity theory

13. You are shown a picture of your grandfather's face, but the eyes and mouth are blocked out. You still recognize it as a picture of your grandfather. Which type of processing best explains this example of perception?

    (A) bottom-up processing
    (B) signal detection theory
    (C) top-down processing
    (D) opponent-process theory
    (E) gestalt replacement theory

14. What behavior would be difficult without our vestibular sense?

    (A) integrating what we see and hear
    (B) writing our name
    (C) repeating a list of digits
    (D) walking a straight line with our eyes closed
    (E) reporting to a researcher the exact position and orientation of our limbs

15. Which of the following sentences best describes the relationship between culture and perception?

    (A) Our perceptual rules are inborn and not affected by culture.
    (B) Perceptual rules are culturally based, so rules that apply to one culture rarely apply to another.
    (C) Most perceptual rules apply in all cultures, but some perceptual rules are learned and vary between cultures.
    (D) Slight variations in sensory apparatuses among cultures create slight differences in perception.
    (E) The processes involved in perception are genetically based, so genetic differences among cultures affect perception.

ANSWER KEY

1. **B**
2. **C**
3. **E**
4. **A**
5. **B**
6. **C**
7. **E**
8. **B**
9. **B**
10. **D**
11. **A**
12. **C**
13. **C**
14. **D**
15. **C**

ANSWERS EXPLAINED

1. **(B)** A nerve connects the olfactory bulb directly to the amygdala and hippocampus. This connection may explain why smell may be a powerful trigger for emotions and memories. This connection has nothing to do with learning, long-term memory, or deep processing. Smells are eventually communicated to the cortex, but that does not explain the special connection to memory.

2. **(C)** Hair cells inside the cochlea change the mechanical vibrations received at the oval window into neural signals that are transmitted to the brain. The cochlea is part of the ear, not the eye, so choices A and D are incorrect. The hammer, anvil, and stirrup transfer vibrations to the cochlea, not the other way around. The semicircular canals send messages to the brain about the orientation of the head and body.

3. **(E)** According to shape constancy, we know shapes remain constant even when our viewing angle changes. This experiment would not be investigating feature detectors, because the equipment required to measure the firing of feature detectors is not described. Placement of rods and cones in the retina would not affect perception of the top of the box. Binocular depth cues are probably not the target of the research because the researchers are not asking questions about depth.

4. **(A)** The spot where the optic nerve connects to the retina lacks rods and cones and is thus called the blind spot. Choices B and C are both incorrect statements about visual sensation/perception. Floating debris and retinal damage could cause blind spots. However, these do not occur in everyone, and the question implies the blind spot is present in everyone's eyes.

5. **(B)** We sense tastes and smells by absorbing chemicals. Energy senses are hearing, sight, and touch. Flavor senses and memory senses are not valid terms. Choice D is incorrect because all nerve impulses are sent by an electrochemical process.

6. **(C)** Amplitude is a measure of the height of the wave, creating the volume of the sound. Frequency is the measure of how quickly the waves pass a point, causing the pitch of the sound. The other choices are incorrect distractions.

7. **(E)** Weber's law calculates the difference threshold or the just-noticeable difference. It has nothing to do with sight, subliminal messages, or amplitude.

8. **(B)** Gate-control theory explains why some pain messages are perceived while others are not. This theory is specific to the sense of touch, so choices A, C, and D are incorrect. Choice E is incorrect because gate-control theory has to do with the perception of pain, not how we interpret sensations in general.

9. **(B)** All the other choices are monocular cues for depth, so they could be used by a person sighted in only one eye. Convergence is a binocular cue and would not work without two functioning eyes. When an object is close to our face and our eyes have to point toward each other slightly, our brain senses this convergence and uses it to help gauge distance.

10. **(D)** Sensation is the activation of our senses by stimuli, and perception is how we organize and interpret sensations. Choice A is incorrect because some sensation processes are more than mechanical. Choice B is too vague—advanced in what sense? Some researchers think part of perception may happen in the senses themselves, so choice C is incorrect. Choice E is false; perception involves learning and expectations.

11. **(A)** Visual receptors, rods and cones, are embedded in the retina, which is the back part of the eye. The rest of the items are incorrect because they describe functions the retina does not perform.

12. **(C)** The opponent-process theory explains these two phenomena, which the trichromatic theory cannot do. Visible hue is not a color vision theory. Dichromatic is a type of color blindness, not a theory of color vision. Binocular disparity is a depth cue.

13. **(C)** Your mind filled in the information from the picture by drawing on your experience. This is top-down processing. The example does not reflect bottom-up processing because information is being filled in, instead of an image being built from the elements present. Signal detection theory has to do with what sensations we pay attention to, not filling in missing elements in a picture. Opponent-process theory explains color vision. Gestalt theory might relate to this example because you are trying to perceive the picture as a whole, but there is no such term as gestalt replacement theory.

14. **(D)** Our vestibular sense helps with our sense of balance and orientation in space. Our vestibular sense has little to do with our sense of sight or hearing. Repeating digits would not be affected by the vestibular sense. Our kinesthetic sense gives us information about the position of our limbs.

15. **(C)** Most perceptual principles apply in all cultures. However, some perceptual sets are learned and will vary, so choices A and B are incorrect. Sensory apparatuses do not vary among cultures, and perception is not genetically based as implied in choice E.

UNIT 4

Learning

This unit focuses on content from one chapter in the textbook you use in your AP Psychology class: Learning. The title of this unit might confuse you at first because the content of the unit might not be what you think of when you see the word "learning." To psychologists, research into learning means research into how organisms are conditioned to perform different behaviors. Operant conditioning, classical conditioning, and cognitive learning research will help you explain different examples of human behaviors.

Learning

6

Key Terms

- Learning
- Acquisition
- Extinction
- Spontaneous recovery
- Generalization
- Discrimination
- Classical conditioning
- Unconditioned stimulus
- Unconditioned response
- Conditioned response
- Conditioned stimulus
- Aversive conditioning
- Second-order or higher-order conditioning
- Learned taste aversion
- Operant conditioning
- Law of effect
- Instrumental learning
- Skinner box
- Reinforcer, reinforcement
- Positive reinforcement
- Negative reinforce-ment
- Punishment
- Positive punishment
- Omission training
- Shaping
- Chaining
- Primary reinforcers
- Secondary reinforcers
- Generalized reinforcers
- Token economy
- Reinforcement schedules—FI, FR, VI, VR
- Continuous reinforcement
- Partial-reinforcement effect
- Instinctive drift
- Observational learn-ing or modeling
- Latent learning
- Insight learning

Key People

- Ivan Pavlov
- John B. Watson
- Rosalie Rayner
- John Garcia
- Robert Koelling
- Edward Thorndike
- B. F. Skinner
- Robert Rescorla
- Albert Bandura
- Edward Tolman
- Wolfgang Köhler

OVERVIEW

Psychologists differentiate between many different types of learning, a number of which we will discuss in this chapter. Learning is commonly defined as a long-lasting change in behavior resulting from experience. Although learning is not the same as behavior, most psychologists accept that learning can best be measured through changes in behavior. Brief changes are not thought to be indicative of learning. Consider, for example, the effects of running a marathon. For a short time afterward, one's behavior might differ radically, but we would not want to attribute this change to the effects of learning. In addition, learning must result from experience rather than from any kind of innate or biological change. Thus, changes in one's behavior as a result of puberty or menopause are not considered to be due to learning.

CLASSICAL CONDITIONING

Around the turn of the twentieth century, a Russian physiologist named **Ivan Pavlov** inadvertently discovered a kind of learning while studying digestion in dogs. Pavlov found that the dogs learned to pair the sounds in the environment where they were fed with the food that was given to them and began to salivate simply upon hearing the sounds. As a result, Pavlov deduced the basic principle of **classical conditioning**. People and animals can learn to associate neutral stimuli (e.g., sounds) with stimuli that produce reflexive, involuntary responses (e.g., food) and will learn to respond similarly to the new stimulus as they did to the old one (e.g., salivate).

The original stimulus that elicits a response is known as the **unconditioned stimulus** (US or UCS). The US is defined as something that elicits a natural, reflexive response. In the classic Pavlovian paradigm, the US is food. Food elicits the natural, involuntary response of salivation. This response is called the **unconditioned response** (**UR** or **UCR**). Through repeated pairings with a neutral stimulus such as a bell, animals will come to associate the two stimuli together. Ultimately, animals will salivate when hearing the bell alone. Once the bell elicits salivation, a **conditioned response (CR)**, it is no longer a neutral stimulus but rather a **conditioned stimulus (CS)**.

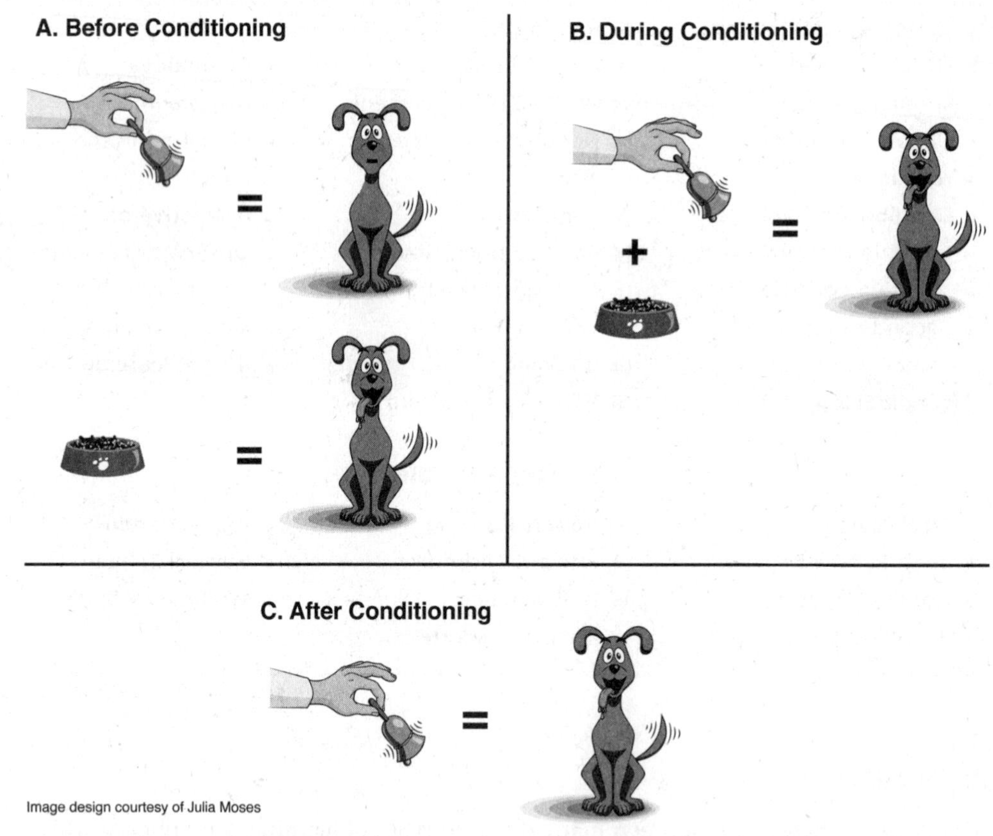

Figure 6.1. Prior to classical conditioning (A), a neutral stimulus like a bell elicits no reaction from a dog, but presenting the dog with food leads it to salivate. During conditioning (B), the bell is paired repeatedly with food, and the dog salivates to this combination. Once conditioning has occurred (C), merely ringing the bell will cause the dog to salivate.

Learning has taken place once the animals respond to the CS without a presentation of the US. This learning is also called **acquisition** since the animals have acquired a new behavior. Many factors affect acquisition. For instance, up to a point, repeated pairings of CSs and USs yield stronger CRs. The order and timing of the CS and US pairings also have an impact on the strength of conditioning. Generally, the most effective method of conditioning is to present the CS first and then to introduce the US while the CS is still evident. Now return to Pavlov's dogs. Acquisition will occur fastest if the bell is rung and, while it is still ringing, the dogs are presented with food. This procedure is known as **delayed conditioning**. Less effective methods of learning include:

- **Trace conditioning**—The presentation of the CS, followed by a short break, followed by the presentation of the US.
- **Simultaneous conditioning**—CS and US are presented at the same time.
- **Backward conditioning**—US is presented first and is followed by the CS. This method is particularly ineffective.

Of course, what can be learned can be unlearned. In psychological terminology, the process of unlearning a behavior is known as **extinction**. In terms of classical conditioning, extinction has taken place when the CS no longer elicits the CR. Extinction is achieved by repeatedly presenting the CS without the US, thus breaking the association between the two. If one rings the bell over and over again and never feeds the dogs, the dogs will ultimately learn not to salivate to the bell.

One fascinating and yet-to-be-adequately-explained part of this process is known as **spontaneous recovery**. Sometimes, after a conditioned response has been extinguished and no further training of the animals has taken place, the response briefly reappears upon presentation of the conditioned stimulus. This phenomenon is known as spontaneous recovery.

Often animals conditioned to respond to a certain stimulus will also respond to similar stimuli, although the response is usually smaller in magnitude. The dogs may salivate to a number of bells, not just the one with which they were trained. This tendency to respond to similar CSs is known as **generalization**. Subjects can be trained, however, to tell the difference, or **discriminate**, between various stimuli. To train the dogs to discriminate between bells, we would repeatedly pair the original bell with presentation of food, but we would intermix trials where we presented other bells that we did not pair with food.

Table 6.1 Basic Conditioning Phenomena in Pavlov's Work.

	Pavlov's Dog
Acquisition	The dog learns to salivate to the bell.
Extinction	The dog unlearns the bell-food connection and ceases to salivate to the bell.
Spontaneous Recovery	After extinction and a period of rest, the dog salivates when hearing the bell.
Generalization	The dog salivates to other bell-like noises.
Discrimination	The dog learns to salivate only to the sound of a specific bell.

Classical conditioning can also be used with humans. In one famous, albeit ethically questionable, study, **John B. Watson** and **Rosalie Rayner** conditioned a little boy named Albert to fear a white rat. Little Albert initially liked the white, fluffy rat. However, by repeatedly pairing it with a loud noise, Watson and Rayner taught Albert to cry when he saw the rat. In this example, the loud noise is the US because it elicits the involuntary, natural response of fear (UR) and, in Little Albert's case, crying. The rat is a neutral stimulus that becomes the CS, and the CR is crying in response to presentation of the rat alone. Albert also generalized, crying in response to a white rabbit, a man's white beard, and a variety of other white, fluffy things.

This example is an illustration of what is known as **aversive conditioning**. Whereas Pavlov's dogs were conditioned with something pleasant (food), baby Albert was conditioned to have a negative response to the white rat. Aversive conditioning has been used in a number of more socially constructive ways. For instance, to stop biting their nails, some people paint them with truly horrible-tasting materials. Nail biting therefore becomes associated with a terrible taste, and the biting should cease.

Once a CS elicits a CR, it is possible, briefly, to use that CS as a US in order to condition a response to a new stimulus. This process is known as **second-order** or **higher-order conditioning**. By using a dog and a bell as our example, after the dog salivates to the bell (first-order conditioning), the bell can be paired repeatedly with a flash of light, and the dog will salivate to the light alone (second-order conditioning), even though the light has never been paired with the food (see Table 6.2).

Table 6.2 First-Order and Second-Order Conditioning

	First-Order Conditioning
Training:	Presentation of bell + food = salivation
Acquisition:	Presentation of bell = salivation
Second-Order Conditioning (After First-Order Conditioning Has Occurred)	
Training:	Presentation of light + bell = salivation
Acquisition:	Presentation of light = salivation

Biology and Classical Conditioning

As is evident from its description, classical conditioning can be used only when one wants to pair an involuntary, natural response with something else. Once one has identified such a US, can a subject be taught to pair it equally easily with any CS? Not surprisingly, the answer is no. Research suggests that animals and humans are biologically prepared to make certain connections more easily than others. **Learned taste aversions** are a classic example of this phenomenon. If you ingest an unusual food or drink and then become nauseous, you will probably develop an aversion to the food or drink. Learned taste aversions are interesting because they can result in powerful avoidance responses on the basis of a single pairing. In addition, the two events (eating and sickness) are probably separated by at least several hours. Animals, including people, seem biologically prepared to associate strange tastes with feelings of sickness. Clearly, this response is adaptive (helpful for the survival of the species), because it helps us learn to avoid dangerous things in the future. Also interesting is how we seem to learn what, exactly, to avoid. Taste aversions most commonly occur with strong and unusual tastes. The food, the CS, must be **salient** in order for us to learn to avoid it. Salient stimuli are easily noticeable and therefore create a more powerful conditioned response. Sometimes taste aversions are acquired without good reason. If you were to eat some mozzarella sticks a few hours before falling ill with the stomach flu, you might develop an aversion to that popular American appetizer even though it had nothing to do with your sickness.

John Garcia and **Robert Koelling** performed a famous experiment illustrating how rats more readily learned to make certain associations than others. They used four groups of subjects in their experiment and exposed each to a particular combination of CS and US as illustrated in Table 6.3.

Table 6.3 Garcia and Koelling's Experiment Illustrating Biological Preparedness in Classical Conditioning

CS	US	Learned Response
Loud noise	Shock	Fear
Loud noise	Radiation (nausea)	Nothing
Sweet water	Shock	Nothing
Sweet water	Radiation (nausea)	Avoid water

The rats learned to associate noise with shock and unusual-tasting water with nausea. However, they were unable to make the connection between noise and nausea and between unusual-tasting water and shock. Again, learning to link loud noise with shock (e.g., thunder and lightning) and unusual-tasting water with nausea seems to be adaptive. The ease with which animals learn taste aversions is known as the Garcia effect.

OPERANT CONDITIONING

Whereas classical conditioning is a type of learning based on association of stimuli, **operant conditioning** is a kind of learning based on the association of consequences with one's behaviors. **Edward Thorndike** was one of the first people to research this kind of learning.

Thorndike conducted a series of famous experiments using a cat in a puzzle box. The hungry cat was locked in a cage next to a dish of food. The cat had to get out of the cage in order to get the food. Thorndike found that the amount of time required for the cat to get out of the box decreased over a series of trials. This amount of time decreased gradually; the cat did not seem to understand, suddenly, how to get out of the cage. This finding led Thorndike to assert that the cat learned the new behavior without mental activity but rather simply connected a stimulus and a response.

Thorndike put forth the **law of effect** that states that if the consequences of a behavior are pleasant, the stimulus-response (S-R) connection will be strengthened and the likelihood of the behavior will increase. However, if the consequences of a behavior are unpleasant, the S-R connection will weaken and the likelihood of the behavior will decrease. He used the term **instrumental learning** to describe his work because he believed the consequence was instrumental in shaping future behaviors.

B. F. Skinner, who coined the term operant conditioning, is the best-known psychologist to research this form of learning. Skinner invented a special contraption, aptly named a **Skinner box**, to use in his research of animal learning. A Skinner box usually has a way to deliver food to an animal and a lever to press or disk to peck in order to get the food. The food is called a **reinforcer**, and the process of giving the food is called **reinforcement**. Reinforcement is defined by its consequences; anything that makes a behavior more likely to occur is a reinforcer. Two kinds of reinforcement exist. **Positive reinforcement** refers to the addition of something pleasant. **Negative reinforcement** refers to the removal of something unpleasant. For instance, if we give a rat in a Skinner box food when it presses a lever, we are using positive reinforcement. However, if we terminate a loud noise or shock in response to a press of the lever, we are using negative reinforcement. The latter example results in **escape learning**. Escape learning allows one to terminate an aversive stimulus; **avoidance learning**, on the other hand, enables one to avoid the unpleasant stimulus altogether. If Sammy creates a ruckus in the English class he hates and is asked to leave, he is evidencing escape learning. An example of avoidance learning would be if Sammy cut English class.

TIP

Students often confuse negative reinforcement and punishment. However, any type of reinforcement results in the behavior being more likely to be repeated. The negative in negative reinforcement refers to the fact that something is taken away. The positive in positive punishment indicates that something is added. In negative reinforcement, the removal of an aversive stimulus is what is reinforcing.

Affecting behavior by using unpleasant consequences is also possible. Such an approach is known as **punishment**. By definition, punishment is anything that makes a behavior less likely. The two types of punishment are known as **positive punishment** (usually referred to simply as "punishment"), which is the addition of something unpleasant, and **omission training** or **negative punishment**, the removal of something pleasant. If we give a rat an electric shock every time it touches the lever, we are using punishment. If we remove the rat's food when it touches the lever, we are using omission training. Both procedures will result in the rat ceasing to touch the bar. Imagine that your parents decided to use operant conditioning principles to modify your behavior. If you did something your parents liked and they wanted to increase the likelihood of your repeating the behavior, your parents could use either of the types of reinforcement described in Table 6.4. On the other hand, if you did something your parents wanted to discourage, they could use either of the types of punishment described in Table 6.5.

Table 6.4 Reinforcement = A Consequence That Increases the Likelihood of a Behavior

Types	Mechanism	Examples
Positive reinforcement	Adds something pleasant	Parent gives child present as reward for cleaning room
Negative reinforcement	Removes something unpleasant	Parent stops yelling when child goes to clean room

Table 6.5 Punishment = A Consequence That Decreases the Likelihood of a Behavior

Types	Mechanism	Examples
Positive punishment	Adds something negative	Parent yells when child comes home after curfew
Omission training (also known as negative punishment)	Removes something pleasant	Parent takes away cell phone when child comes home after curfew

Punishment Versus Reinforcement

Generally, the same ends can be achieved through punishment and reinforcement. If I want students to be on time to my class, I can punish them for lateness or reward them for arriving on time. Punishment is operant conditioning's version of aversive conditioning. Punishment is most effective if it is delivered immediately after the unwanted behavior and if it is harsh. However, harsh punishment may also result in unwanted consequences such as fear and anger. As a result, most psychologists recommend that certain kinds of punishment (e.g., physical punishment) be used sparingly if at all.

You might wonder how the rat in the Skinner box learns to push the lever in the first place. Rather than wait for an animal to perform the desired behavior by chance, we usually try to speed up the process by using **shaping**. Shaping reinforces the steps used to reach the desired behavior. First the rat might be reinforced for going to the side of the box with the lever. Then we might reinforce the rat for touching the lever with any part of its body. By rewarding approximations of the desired behavior, we increase the likelihood that the rat will stumble upon the behavior we want.

Animals can also be taught to perform a number of responses successively in order to get a reward. This process is known as **chaining**. One famous example of chained behavior involved a rat named Barnabus who learned to run through a veritable obstacle course in order to obtain a food reward. Whereas the goal of shaping is to mold a single behavior (e.g., a bar press by a rat), the goal in chaining is to link together a number of separate behaviors into a more complex activity (e.g., running an obstacle course).

The terms acquisition, extinction, spontaneous recovery, discrimination, and generalization can be used in our discussion of operant conditioning, too. Using a rat in a Skinner box as our example, **acquisition** occurs when the rat learns to press the lever to get the reward. **Extinction** occurs when the rat ceases to press the lever because the reward no longer results from this action. Note that punishing the rat for pushing the lever is not necessary to extinguish the response. Behaviors that are not reinforced will ultimately stop and are said to be on an extinction schedule. **Spontaneous recovery** would occur if, after having extinguished the bar press response and without providing any further training, the rat began to press the bar again. **Generalization** would be if the rat began to press other things in the Skinner box or the bar in other boxes. **Discrimination** would involve teaching the rat to press only a particular bar or to press the bar only under certain conditions (e.g., when a tone is sounded). In the latter example, the tone is called a **discriminative stimulus**.

Table 6.6 Basic Conditioning Phenomena in Skinner's Work

	Rat in a Skinner Box
Acquisition	The rat learns to press the bar for food.
Extinction	The rat unlearns the bar-food connection and ceases to press the bar.
Spontaneous Recovery	After extinction and a period of rest, the rat presses the bar.
Generalization	The rat presses other objects that look like the bar.
Discrimination	The rat learns to press only a particular bar.

TIP

Students sometimes intuit that if there is no consequence to a behavior, its likelihood will be unchanged; remember, unless behaviors are reinforced, the likelihood of their recurrence decreases.

Not all reinforcers are food, of course. Psychologists speak of two main types of reinforcers: primary and secondary. **Primary reinforcers** are, in and of themselves, rewarding. They include things like food, water, and rest, whose natural properties are reinforcing. **Secondary reinforcers** are things we have learned to value such as praise or the chance to play a video game. Money is a special kind of secondary reinforcer, called a **generalized reinforcer**, because it can be traded for virtually anything. One practical application of generalized reinforcers is known as a **token economy**. In a token economy, every time people perform a desired behavior, they are given a token. Periodically, they are allowed to trade their tokens for any one of a variety of reinforcers. Token economies have been used in prisons, mental institutions, and even schools.

Intuitively, you probably realize that what functions as a reinforcer for some may not have the same effect on others. Even primary reinforcers, like food, will affect different animals in different ways depending, most notably, on how hungry they are. This idea, that the reinforcing properties of something depend on the situation, is expressed in the **Premack principle**. It explains that whichever of two activities is preferred can be used to reinforce the activity that is not preferred. For instance, if Peter likes apples but does not like to practice for his piano lesson, his mother could use apples to reinforce practicing the piano. In this case, eating an apple is the preferred activity. However, Peter's brother Mitchell does not like fruit, including apples, but he loves to play the piano. In his case, playing the piano is the preferred activity, and his mother can use it to reinforce him for eating an apple.

Reinforcement Schedules

When you are first teaching a new behavior, rewarding the behavior each time is best. This process is known as **continuous reinforcement**. However, once the behavior is learned, higher response rates can be obtained using certain partial-reinforcement schedules. In addition, according to the **partial-reinforcement effect**, behaviors will be more resistant to extinction if the animal has not been reinforced continuously.

Reinforcement schedules differ in two ways:

- What determines when reinforcement is delivered—the number of responses made (ratio schedules) or the passage of time (interval schedules).
- The pattern of reinforcement—either constant (fixed schedules) or changing (variable schedules).

A fixed-ratio (FR) schedule provides reinforcement after a set number of responses. For example, if a rat is on an FR-5 schedule, it will be rewarded after the fifth bar press. A variable-ratio (VR) schedule also provides reinforcement based on the number of bar presses, but that number varies. A rat on a VR-5 schedule might be rewarded after the second press, the ninth press, the third press, the sixth press, and so on; the average number of presses required to receive a reward will be five.

A fixed-interval (FI) schedule requires that a certain amount of time elapse before a bar press will result in a reward. In an FI-3 minute schedule, for instance, the rat will be reinforced for the first bar press that occurs after three minutes have passed. A variable-interval (VI) schedule varies the amount of time required to elapse before a response will result in reinforcement. In a VI-3 minute schedule, the rat will be reinforced for the first response made after an average time of three minutes.

TIP

Variable schedules are more resistant to extinction than fixed schedules, and all partial reinforcement schedules are more resistant to extinction than continuous reinforcement.

Variable schedules are more resistant to extinction than fixed schedules. Once an animal becomes accustomed to a fixed schedule (being reinforced after *x* amount of time or *y* number of responses), a break in the pattern will quickly lead to extinction. However, if the reinforcement schedule has been variable, noticing a break in the pattern is much more difficult. In effect, variable schedules encourage continued responding on the chance that just one more response is needed to get the reward.

TIP

Ratio schedules typically result in higher response rates than interval schedules.

Sometimes one is more concerned with encouraging high rates of responding rather than resistance to extinction. For instance, someone who employs factory workers to make widgets wants the workers to produce as many widgets as possible. Ratio schedules promote higher rates of responding than interval schedules. It makes sense that when people are reinforced based on the number of responses they make, they will make more responses than if the passage of time is also a necessary precondition for reinforcement as it is in interval schedules. Factory owners historically paid for piece work; workers were paid for each completed task rather than by the hour and were thus motivated to work as quickly as they could.

Biology and Operant Conditioning

Just as limits seem to exist concerning what one can classically condition animals to learn, limits seem to exist concerning what various animals can learn to do through operant conditioning. Researchers have found that animals will not perform certain behaviors that go against their natural inclinations. For instance, rats will not walk backward. In addition, pigs refuse to put disks into a banklike object and tend, instead, to bury the disks in the ground. The tendency for animals to forgo rewards to pursue their typical patterns of behavior is called **instinctive drift**.

Table 6.7 Schedules of Reinforcement

	Ratio	Interval
Fixed	Definition: Reinforcement is delivered after a set number of responses. Example: A restaurant gives you a free meal after the purchase of ten meals.	Definition: Reinforcement is delivered after a behavior is performed following the passage of a fixed amount of time. Example: Going to get lunch at a restaurant that opens promptly at noon.
Variable	Definition: Reinforcement is delivered after a variable number of responses. Example: Slot machines pay out on variable ratio schedules. Sometimes it takes just one pull to win but sometimes it takes hundreds.	Definition: Reinforcement is delivered after a behavior is performed following the passage of a variable amount of time. Example: Checking for your mail when your letter carrier's schedule is unpredictable.

COGNITIVE LEARNING

Radical behaviorists like Skinner assert that learning occurs without thought. However, cognitive theorists argue that even classical and operant conditioning have a cognitive component. In classical conditioning, such theorists argue that the subjects respond to the CS because they develop the expectation that it will be followed by the US. In operant conditioning, cognitive psychologists suggest that the subject is cognizant that its responses have certain consequences and can therefore act to maximize their reinforcement.

The Contingency Model of Classical Conditioning

The Pavlovian model of classical conditioning is known as the **contiguity model** because it postulates that the more times two things are paired, the greater the learning that will take place. Contiguity (togetherness) determines the strength of the response. **Robert Rescorla** revised the Pavlovian model to take into account a more complex set of circumstances. Suppose that dog 1, Rocco, is presented with a bell paired with food ten times in a row. Dog 2, Sparky, also experiences ten pairings of bell and food. However, intermixed with Sparky's ten trials are five trials in which food is presented without the bell and five more trials in which the bell is rung but no food is presented. Once these training periods are over, which dog will have a stronger salivation response to the bell? Intuitively, you will probably see that Rocco will, even though a model based purely on contiguity would hypothesize that the two dogs would respond the same since each has experienced ten pairings of bell and food.

TIP

Pavlov's contiguity model of classical conditioning holds that the strength of an association between two events is closely linked to the number of times they have been paired in time. Rescorla's contingency model of classical conditioning reflects more of a cognitive spin, positing that it is necessary for one event to reliably predict another for a strong association between the two to result.

Rescorla's model is known as the **contingency model** of classical conditioning and clearly rests upon a cognitive view of classical conditioning. *A* is contingent upon *B* when *A* depends upon *B* and vice versa. In such a case, the presence of one event reliably predicts the presence of the other. In Rocco's case, the food is contingent upon the presentation of the bell; one does not appear without the other. In Sparky's experience, sometimes the bell rings and no snacks are served, other times snacks appear without the annoying bell, and sometimes they appear together. Sparky learns less because, in her case, the relationship between the CS and US is not as clear. The difference in Rocco's and Sparky's responses strongly suggest that their expectations or thoughts influence their learning.

In addition to operant and classical conditioning, cognitive theorists have described a number of additional kinds of learning. These include observational learning, latent learning, abstract learning, and insight learning.

Observational Learning

As you are no doubt aware, people and animals learn many things simply by observing others. Watching children play house, for example, gives us an indication of all they have learned from watching their families and the families of others. Such **observational learning** is also known as **modeling** and was studied a great deal by **Albert Bandura** in formulating his social-learning theory. This type of learning is said to be species-specific; it only occurs between members of the same species.

Modeling has two basic components: observation and imitation. By watching his older sister, a young boy may learn how to hit a baseball. First, he observes her playing baseball with the neighborhood children in his backyard. Next, he picks up a bat and tries to imitate her behavior. Observational learning has a clear cognitive component in that a mental representation of the observed behavior must exist in order to enable the person or animal to imitate it.

A significant body of research indicates that children learn violent behaviors from watching violent television programs and violent adult models. Bandura, Ross, and Ross's (1963) classic Bobo doll experiment illustrated this connection. Children were exposed to adults who modeled either aggressive or nonaggressive play with, among other things, an inflatable Bobo doll that would bounce back up after being hit. Later, given the chance to play alone in a room full of toys including poor Bobo, the children who had witnessed the aggressive adult models exhibited strikingly similar aggressive behavior to that which they had observed. The children in the control group were much less likely to aggress against Bobo, particularly in the ways modeled by the adults in the experimental condition.

Latent Learning

Latent learning was studied extensively by **Edward Tolman**. Latent means hidden, and latent learning is learning that becomes obvious only once a reinforcement is given for demonstrating it. Behaviorists had asserted that learning is evidenced by gradual changes in behavior, but Tolman conducted a famous experiment illustrating that sometimes learning occurs but is not immediately evidenced. Tolman had three groups of rats run through a maze on a series of trials. One group got a reward each time it completed the maze, and the performance of these rats improved steadily over the trials. Another group of rats never got a reward, and their performance improved only slightly over the course of the trials. A third group of rats was not rewarded during the first half of the trials but was given a reward during the second half of the trials. Not surprisingly, during the first half of the trials, this group's performance was very similar to the group that never got a reward. The interesting finding, however, was that the third group's performance improved dramatically and suddenly once it began to be rewarded for finishing the maze.

Tolman reasoned that these rats must have learned their way around the maze during the first set of trials. Their performance did not improve because they had no reason to run the maze quickly. Tolman credited their dramatic improvement in maze-running time to latent learning. He suggested they had made a mental representation, or cognitive map, of the maze during the first half of the trials and evidenced this knowledge once it would earn them a reward.

Abstract Learning

Abstract learning involves understanding concepts such as "tree" or "same" rather than learning simply to press a bar or peck a disk in order to secure a reward. Some researchers have shown that animals in Skinner boxes seem to be able to understand such concepts. For instance, pigeons have learned to peck pictures they had never seen before if those pictures were of chairs. In other studies, pigeons have been shown a particular shape (e.g., square or triangle) and rewarded in one series of trials when they picked the same shape out of two choices and in another set of trials when they pecked at the different shapes. Such studies suggest that pigeons can understand concepts and are not simply forming S-R connections, as Thorndike and Skinner had argued.

Insight Learning

Wolfgang Köhler is well known for his studies of **insight learning** in chimpanzees. Insight learning occurs when one suddenly realizes how to solve a problem. You have probably had the experience of skipping over a problem on a test only to realize later, in an instant (we hope before you handed the test in), how to solve it.

Köhler argued that learning often happens in this sudden way due to insight rather than because of the gradual strengthening of the S-R connection suggested by the behaviorists. He put chimpanzees into situations and watched how they solved problems. In one study, Köhler suspended a banana from the ceiling well out of reach of the chimpanzees. In the room were several boxes, none of which was high enough to enable the chimpanzees to reach the banana. Köhler found the chimpanzees spent most of their time unproductively rather than slowly working toward a solution. They would run around, jump, and be generally upset about their inability to snag the snack until, all of a sudden, they would pile the boxes on top of each other, climb up, and grab the banana. Köhler believed that the solution could not occur until the chimpanzees had a cognitive insight about how to solve the problem.

Table 6.8 Famous Cognitive Learning Experiments

Researcher/Experiment	Major Finding	Take Home Message
Albert Bandura's Bobo Doll Experiments	Children exposed to an aggressive model imitated the model's behavior.	Aggression can be learned through observation.
Edward Tolman's Latent Learning Experiments	Rats that ran a maze repeatedly evidenced dramatic improvement following the introduction of a reward.	Rats learned their way around the maze, created and stored cognitive maps, and were able to use the maps when needed.
Wolfgang Kohler's Insight Learning Experiments	Chimpanzees solved problems suddenly rather than gradually.	Nonhuman animals are capable of insight.

PRACTICE QUESTIONS

Directions: Each of the questions or incomplete statements below is followed by five suggested answers or completions. Select the one that is best in each case.

1. Just before something scary happens in a horror film, they often play scary-sounding music. When I hear the music, I tense up in anticipation of the scary event. In this situation, the music serves as a(n)
   (A) US.
   (B) CS.
   (C) UR.
   (D) CR.
   (E) NR.

2. Try as you might, you are unable to teach your dog to do a somersault. He will roll around on the ground, but he refuses to execute the gymnastic move you desire because of
   (A) equipotentiality.
   (B) preparedness.
   (C) instinctive drift.
   (D) chaining.
   (E) shaping.

3. Which of the following is an example of a generalized reinforcer?
   (A) chocolate cake
   (B) water
   (C) money
   (D) applause
   (E) high grades

4. In teaching your cat to jump through a hoop, which reinforcement schedule would facilitate the most rapid learning?
   (A) continuous
   (B) fixed ratio
   (C) variable ratio
   (D) fixed interval
   (E) variable interval

5. The classical conditioning training procedure in which the US is presented before the CS is known as
   (A) backward conditioning.
   (B) aversive conditioning.
   (C) simultaneous conditioning.
   (D) delayed conditioning.
   (E) trace conditioning.

6. Tina likes to play with slugs, but she can find them by the shed only after it rains. On what kind of reinforcement schedule is Tina's slug hunting?
   (A) continuous
   (B) fixed-interval
   (C) fixed-ratio
   (D) variable-interval
   (E) variable-ratio

7. Just before the doors of the elevator close, Lola, a coworker you despise, enters the elevator. You immediately leave, mumbling about having forgotten something. Your behavior results in
   (A) positive reinforcement.
   (B) a secondary reinforcer.
   (C) punishment.
   (D) negative reinforcement.
   (E) omission training.

8. Which of the following phenomena is illustrated by Tolman's study in which rats suddenly evidenced that they had learned to get through a maze once a reward was presented?
   (A) insight learning
   (B) instrumental learning
   (C) latent learning
   (D) spontaneous recovery
   (E) classical conditioning

9. Many psychologists believe that children of parents who beat them are likely to beat their own children. One common explanation for this phenomenon is
   (A) modeling.
   (B) latent learning.
   (C) abstract learning.
   (D) instrumental learning.
   (E) classical conditioning.

10. When Tito was young, his parents decided to give him a quarter every day he made his bed. Tito started to make his siblings' beds also and help with other chores. Behaviorists would say that Tito was experiencing
   (A) internal motivation.
   (B) spontaneous recovery.
   (C) acquisition.
   (D) generalization.
   (E) discrimination.

11. A rat evidencing abstract learning might learn

    (A) to clean and feed itself by watching its mother perform these activities.
    (B) to associate its handler's presence with feeding time.
    (C) to press a bar when a light is on but not when its cage is dark.
    (D) the layout of a maze without hurrying to get to the end.
    (E) to press a lever when he sees pictures of dogs but not cats.

12. With which statement would B. F. Skinner most likely agree?

    (A) Pavlov's dog learned to expect that food would follow the bell.
    (B) Baby Albert thought the white rat meant the loud noise would sound.
    (C) All learning is observable.
    (D) Pigeons peck disks knowing that they will receive food.
    (E) Cognition plays an important role in learning.

13. Before his parents will read him a bedtime story, Charley has to brush his teeth, put on his pajamas, kiss his grandmother good night, and put away his toys. This example illustrates

    (A) shaping.
    (B) acquisition.
    (C) generalization.
    (D) chaining.
    (E) a token economy.

14. Which of the following is an example of positive reinforcement?

    (A) buying a child a video game after she throws a tantrum
    (B) going inside to escape a thunderstorm
    (C) assigning a student detention for fighting
    (D) getting a cavity filled at the dentist to halt a toothache
    (E) depriving a prison inmate of sleep

15. Lily keeps poking Jared in Mr. Clayton's third-grade class. Mr. Clayton tells Jared to ignore Lily. Mr. Clayton is hoping that ignoring Lily's behavior will

    (A) punish her.
    (B) extinguish the behavior.
    (C) negatively reinforce the behavior.
    (D) cause Lily to generalize.
    (E) make the behavior latent.

ANSWER KEY

1. **B**
2. **C**
3. **C**
4. **A**
5. **A**
6. **D**
7. **D**
8. **C**
9. **A**
10. **D**
11. **E**
12. **C**
13. **D**
14. **A**
15. **B**

ANSWERS EXPLAINED

1. **(B)** The music before a scary event in a horror movie serves as a CS. It is something we associate with a fear-inducing event (the US). In this example, preparing to be scared is the CR and the fear caused by the event in the movie is the UR. There is no such thing as a NR.

2. **(C)** Instinctive drift limits your pet's gymnastic abilities. Instinctively, your dog will perform certain behaviors and will drift toward these rather than learning behaviors that go against his nature. Equipotentiality is the opposite position that asserts that any animal can be conditoned to do anything. Preparedness refers to a biological predisposition to learn some things more quickly than others. Preparedness explains why teaching a dog to fetch a stick is easier than teaching it to do a somersault. Chaining is when one has to perform a number of discrete steps in order to secure a reward. Shaping is the process one might use in teaching a dog any new trick. Shaping is when you begin by reinforcing steps preceding the desired response.

3. **(C)** Money is a generalized reinforcer because it can be exchanged for so many things that it is reinforcing to virtually everybody. Chocolate cake (food) and water are examples of primary reinforcers, while applause and high grades are examples of secondary reinforcers.

4. **(A)** In teaching your cat to jump through a hoop, continuous reinforcement would result in the most rapid learning. New behaviors are learned most quickly when they are rewarded every time. However, once the skill has been learned, partial reinforcement will make the behaviors more resistant to extinction.

5. **(A)** The classical conditioning training procedure in which the US is presented first is known as backward conditioning since, in most other procedures, the CS is presented first. The term aversive conditioning does not have anything to do with the order of the presentation of US and CS but rather indicates that the UR and CR are unpleasant. Simultaneous conditioning, as the name suggests, is when the CS and US are presented at the same time. Delayed conditioning is when the CS is presented first and overlaps the presentation of the US. In trace conditioning, the CS is presented first and the CS and US do not overlap. The US is then presented after a short time has elapsed.

6. **(D)** Tina's slug hunting is rewarded on a variable-interval schedule. The passage of time is a key element in when she is reinforced because the slugs appear only after it rains. Since rain does not fall on a fixed schedule (e.g., every third day), she is on a VI schedule. If she were on a continuous schedule, she would find slugs whenever she looked. If the slugs appeared every three days, Tina would be on a fixed-interval schedule. If she needed to turn over three rocks to find a slug, she would be on a fixed-ratio schedule. If the number of rocks she needed to turn over varied, she would be on a variable-ratio schedule.

7. **(D)** Exiting the elevator to avoid Lola is negatively reinforced. Your behavior, leaving the elevator, is reinforced by the removal of an aversive stimulus (Lola). Remember that reinforcement (including negative reinforcement) always increases the likelihood of a behavior as opposed to punishment, which decreases the likelihood of a behavior.

8. **(C)** Tolman is known for his work on latent learning, learning that occurs in the absence of a reward but remains hidden until a reward is made available. Tolman's study involved three groups of rats running a maze under various contingencies of reinforcement.

9. **(A)** Many psychologists believe that children of parents who beat them are likely to beat their own children. One common explanation for this phenomenon is modeling. Modeling, or observational learning, is the idea that people or animals can learn from watching and copying the behavior of others.

10. **(D)** Tito's new bed-making and chore-doing regime indicates that he is generalizing. Just as a rat will press other levers in other cages, Tito is performing more chores in an attempt to maximize his rewards. Behaviorists minimize the role of internal motivation; they believe that the environment motivates. Spontaneous recovery would be if Tito began making his bed again after his parents had stopped rewarding him and he had returned to his slovenly ways. Acquisition occurred when Tito initially learned to make his bed to earn the quarter. By assuming Tito's parents do not reward him for making the rest of the family's beds, he will learn ultimately to discriminate and make only his own bed.

11. **(E)** A rat evidencing abstract learning would learn to press a bar when shown pictures of dogs but not pictures of cats. In this example, the rat has learned the abstract concept of dog. Learning to clean and feed itself by watching its mother would be an example of modeling. Learning to associate a person's presence with food is classical conditioning. Learning to respond only when a light is on is an example of discrimination training. Making a cognitive map of a maze without hurrying through the maze is an example of latent learning.

12. **(C)** B. F. Skinner believed that all learning was observable. He did not believe that learning had a cognitive component but, rather, took a radical behaviorist position that behavior was all there was. All the other choices suggest learning has a cognitive component (expectation, thought, knowing, cognition), and therefore Skinner would disagree with them.

13. **(D)** Charley needs to chain together a series of behaviors in order to get a reward (the bedtime story). Shaping is reinforcing approximations of a desired behavior, usually in an effort to teach it. Acquisition, in operant conditioning, is the learning of a behavior. Generalization is when one performs similar behaviors to those that will result in reinforcement. A token economy uses generalized reinforcers to control people's behavior.

14. **(A)** Buying a child a video game after she throws a tantrum is an example of positively reinforcing a behavior you probably do not want (the tantrum). This example raises an important point: the word *positive* in positive reinforcement refers to the addition of a reinforcer and not to the goodness or badness of the act that is being reinforced. Going inside to escape a thunderstorm and getting a cavity filled at the dentist to halt a toothache are both examples of negative reinforcement (removing something unpleasant). Assigning a student detention for fighting is an example of punishment (adding something unpleasant), depriving someone of sleep is an example of omission training (removing something pleasant).

15. **(B)** Mr. Clayton is hoping that ignoring Lily's behavior will extinguish the behavior. Something that is not reinforced is put onto an extinction schedule.

UNIT 5

Cognitive Psychology

This unit focuses on some of the most important concepts in an introductory psychology class. These concepts are important because they represent a significant number of questions on the AP Psychology test, and because concepts covered in this unit can help you study and learn more effectively (see "Using Psychology to Study Psychology" in the "Introduction: Using this Book" section at the beginning of the book). Most of this unit is devoted to concepts related to memory. Toward the end of the unit, shorter sections are devoted to language and thinking/creativity.

Cognition 7

Key Terms

- Memory
- Three-box/information-processing model
- Levels of processing model
- Sensory memory
- Iconic memory
- Selective attention
- Echoic memory
- Short-term memory (working memory)
- Chunking
- Mnemonic devices
- Rehearsal
- Long-term memory
- Episodic memory
- Semantic memory
- Procedural memory
- Explicit memories (also called declarative memories)
- Implicit memories (also called nondeclarative memories)
- Eidetic, or photographic, memory
- Retrieval
- Recognition
- Recall
- Primacy effect
- Recency effect
- Serial position effect (also called serial position curve)
- Tip-of-the-tongue phenomenon
- Semantic network theory
- Flashbulb memories
- State-dependent memory
- Mood congruent memory
- Constructed (or reconstructed) memory
- Relearning effect
- Retroactive interference
- Proactive interference
- Anterograde amnesia
- Retrograde amnesia
- Long-term potentiation
- Phonemes
- Morphemes
- Syntax
- Language acquisition
- Overgeneralization or overregularization
- Language acquisition device
- Linguistic relativity hypothesis
- Prototypes
- Images
- Algorithm
- Heuristic
- Representativeness heuristic
- Belief bias or belief perseverance
- Functional fixedness
- Confirmation bias
- Convergent thinking
- Divergent thinking
- Availability heuristic

Key People

- George Sperling
- George Miller
- Alexander Luria
- Hermann Ebbinghaus
- Noam Chomsky
- Elizabeth Loftus
- Benjamin Whorf
- Wolfgang Köhler

OVERVIEW

The central question of memory research is: What causes us to remember what we remember and to forget what we forget? Memory is defined by researchers as any indication that learning has persisted over time. You might remember the bully who pushed you into the mud in second grade but forget your appointment with the school counselor. What are the processes that determine which events stick in our memories? Why and how do we lose information from memory? How accurate are our memories? Researchers do not have the final answers to any of these questions. However, models and principles of memory have emerged from the research that give us insight into how we remember.

MODELS OF MEMORY

Several different models, or explanations, of how memory works have emerged from memory research. We will review two of the most important models: the three-box/information-processing model and the levels of processing model. Neither model is perfect. They describe how memory works in different ways and can describe some memory experiences better than others.

TIP

Do not take this memory model too literally. The model describes the process, not physical structures. There is not one spot in the brain that is the long-term memory spot. Memories are distributed around the cortex. Researchers use the model to describe the process rather than define how and where the brain stores memories physically.

Three-Box/Information-Processing Model

The principal model of memory is the three-box model, also called the information-processing model. This model proposes the three stages that information passes through before it is stored (see Fig. 7.1).

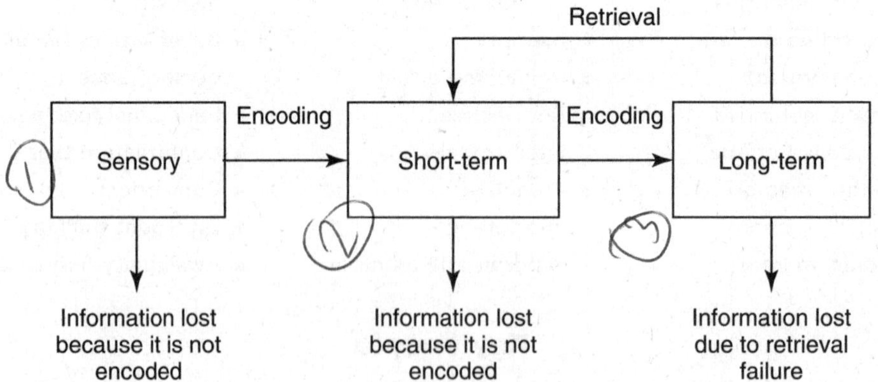

Figure 7.1 Atkinson and Shiffring three-box/information-processing model.

External events are first processed by our sensory memory. Then some information is encoded into our short-term (or working) memory. Some of that information is then encoded into long-term memory.

Sensory Memory

The first stop for external events is **sensory memory**. It is a split-second holding tank for incoming sensory information. All the information your senses are processing right now is held in sensory memory for a very short period of time (less than a second). Researcher **George Sperling** demonstrated this in a series of experiments in which he flashed a grid of nine letters, three rows and three columns, to participants for 1/20th of a second. The participants in the study were directed to recall either the top, middle, or bottom row immediately after the grid was flashed at them. (Sperling used a high, medium, or low tone to indicate which row they should recall.) The participants could recall any of the three rows perfectly. This experiment demonstrated that the entire grid must be held in sensory memory for a split second. This type of sensory memory is called **iconic memory**, a split-second perfect photograph of a scene. Other experiments demonstrate the existence of **echoic memory**, an equally perfect brief (3–4 second) memory for sounds.

Most of the information in sensory memory is not encoded, however. Only some of it is encoded, or stored, in **short-term memory**. Events are encoded as visual codes (a visual image), acoustic codes (a series of sounds), or semantic codes (a sense of the meaning of the event). What determines which sensory messages get encoded? **Selective attention**. We encode what we are attending to or what is important to us. Try the following experiment. Pay attention to how your feet feel in your socks right now. You feel this now because the sensory messages from your feet are encoded from sensory memory into short-term memory. Why did you not feel your feet before? Because the messages entered sensory memory but were not encoded because you were not selectively attending to them. Sometimes selective attention is not as controlled. You have probably had the experience of speaking with one person at a party but then hearing someone say your name across the room. You were selectively attending to the person you were talking to. However, once a sensory message entered sensory memory that you knew was important (like your name or hearing someone shout "Fire!"), you switched your attention to that message, and it was encoded into your short-term memory. (This is also called the **cocktail party effect**, see Chapter 5 for more information about this phenomenon.)

Short-Term/Working Memory

Short-term memory is also called working memory because these are memories we are currently working with and are aware of in our consciousness. Everything you are thinking at the current moment is held in your short-term or working memory. Short-term memories are also temporary. If we do nothing with them, they usually fade in 10 to 30 seconds. Our capacity in short-term memory is limited on average to around seven items (this average was established in a series of famous experiments by **George Miller** titled "The Magical Number Seven, Plus or Minus Two"), but this limit can be expanded through a process called **chunking**. If you want to remember a grocery list with 15 items on it, you should chunk, or group, the items into no more than seven groups. Most **mnemonic devices**, memory aids, are really examples of chunking. If you memorized the names of the planets by remembering the sentence "My Very Educated Mother Just Served Us Nachos," you chunked the names of the planets into the first letters of the words in one sentence.

Another way to retain information in short-term memory is to **rehearse** (or repeat) it. When you look up a phone number and repeat it to yourself on the way to the phone, you are rehearsing that information. Simple repetition can hold information in short-term memory, but other strategies are more effective in ensuring short-term memories are encoded into long-term memory.

Long-Term Memory

Since memories fade from sensory and short-term memory so quickly, we obviously need a more permanent way to remember events. Long-term memory is our permanent storage. As far as we know, the capacity of long-term memory is unlimited. No one reports their memory as being full and unable to encode new information. Studies show that once information reaches long-term memory, we will likely remember it for the rest of our lives. However, memories can decay or fade from long-term memory, so it is not truly permanent (see the section on forgetting). Long-term memories can be stored in three different formats:

Episodic memory	Memories of specific events, stored in a sequential series of events. Example: remembering the last time you went on a date.
Semantic memory	General knowledge of the world, stored as facts, meanings, or categories rather than sequentially. Example: What is the difference between the terms effect and affect?
Procedural memory	Memories of skills and how to perform them. These memories are sequential but might be too complicated to describe in words. Example: How to throw a curveball.

Memories can also be implicit or explicit. **Explicit memories** (also called declarative memories) are what we usually think of first. They are the conscious memories of facts or events we actively tried to remember. When you study this chapter, you try to form explicit memories about the memory theories. **Implicit memories** (also called nondeclarative memories) are unintentional memories that we might not even realize we have. For example, while you are helping your friend clean her house, you might find that you have implicit memories about how to scrub a floor properly after watching your parents do it for so many years.

TIP

Some people say they have a photographic memory when what they mean is very good memory. True eidetic memory occurs very rarely. Most of us could enhance our memories through training with mnemonic devices, context, and visual imagery.

Memory researchers are particularly interested in individuals who demonstrate **eidetic**, or **photographic, memory**. Psychologist **Alexander Luria** studied a patient with eidetic memory who could repeat a list of 70 letters or digits. The patient could even repeat the list backward or recall it up to 15 years later! Luria and other researchers showed that these rare individuals seem to use very powerful and enduring visual images.

Levels of Processing Model

An alternate way to think about memory is the levels of processing model. This theory explains why we remember what we do by examining how deeply the memory was processed or thought about. Memories are neither short- nor long-term. They are **deeply** (or **elaboratively**) **processed** or **shallowly** (or **maintenance**) **processed.** If you simply repeat a fact to yourself several times and then write it on your test as quickly as you can, you have only shallowly processed that fact and you will forget it quickly. However, if you study the context and research the reasons behind the fact, you have deeply processed it and will likely recall it later. According to the levels of processing theory, we remember things we spend more cognitive time and energy processing. This theory explains why we remember stories better than a simple recitation of events and why, in general, we remember questions better than statements. When we get caught up in a story or an intriguing question, we process it deeply and are therefore more likely to remember it.

RETRIEVAL

The last step in any memory model is retrieval, or getting information out of memory so we can use it. There are two different kinds of retrieval: recognition and recall. **Recognition** is the process of matching a current event or fact with one already in memory (e.g., "Have I smelled this smell before?"). **Recall** is retrieving a memory with an external cue (e.g., "What does my Aunt Beki's perfume smell like?"). Studies have identified several factors that influence why we can retrieve some memories and why we forget others.

One factor is the order in which the information is presented. In some of the first psychological experiments, **Hermann Ebbinghaus** (1850–1909) established that the order of items in a list is related to whether or not we will recall them. The **primacy effect** predicts that we are more likely to recall items presented at the beginning of a list. The **recency effect** is demonstrated by our ability to recall the items at the end of a list. Items in the middle are most often forgotten. Together the primacy and recency effect demonstrate the **serial position effect** (also called **serial position curve**). This effect is seen when recall of a list is affected by the order of items in a list.

Context is an important factor in retrieval. Have you ever tried to remember someone's name and start listing things about their appearance or personality until you finally come up with the name? This temporary inability to remember information is sometimes called the **tip-of-the-tongue phenomenon**. One theory that explains why this might work is the **semantic network theory**. This theory states that our brain might form new memories by connecting their meaning and context with meanings already in memory. Thus, our brain creates a web of interconnected memories, each one in context tied to hundreds or thousands of other memories. So, by listing traits, you gradually get closer and closer to the name and you are finally able to retrieve it. Context also explains another powerful memory experience we all have. If you ask someone born in the 1990s or earlier where they were during the September 11, 2001, terrorist attack, they are likely to give you a detailed description of exactly what they were doing in those moments. These **flashbulb memories** are powerful because the importance of the event caused us to encode the context surrounding the event. However, some studies show that flashbulb memories can be inaccurate. Perhaps we tend to construct parts of the memory to fill in gaps in our stories (see "Constructive Memory," below).

The emotional or situational context of a memory can affect retrieval in yet another way. Studies consistently demonstrate the power of **mood-congruent memory** or the greater likelihood of recalling an item when our mood matched the mood we were in when the event happened. We are likely to recall happy events when we are happy and recall negative events when we are feeling pessimistic. **State-dependent memory** refers to the phenomenon of recalling events encoded while in particular states of consciousness. If you suddenly remember an appointment while you are drowsy and about to go to sleep, you need to write it down. Very possibly, you will not remember it again until you are drowsy and in the same state of consciousness. Alcohol and other drugs affect memory in similar ways.

CONSTRUCTIVE MEMORY

Maybe you have seen media coverage of the "**recovered memory**" phenomenon. Individuals claim to suddenly remember events they have repressed for years, often during the process of therapy. Parents have been accused of molesting and even killing children based on these recovered memories. While some of the memories can be corroborated by other means, memory researchers like **Elizabeth Loftus** have shown that many of these memories may be constructed or false recollections of events. A **constructed** (or reconstructed) **memory** can report false details of a real event or might even be a recollection of an event that never occurred. Studies show that leading questions can easily influence us to recall false details, and questioners can create an entirely new memory by repeatedly asking insistent questions. Constructed memories feel like accurate memories to the person recalling them. The only way to differentiate between a false and a real memory is through other types of evidence, such as physical evidence or other validated reports of the event. While some genuine memories may be recalled after being forgotten for years, researchers and therapists are investigating ways to ensure memories are accurate and innocent people are not accused of acts they did not commit.

FORGETTING

Sometimes, despite our best efforts, we forget important events or facts that we try and want to remember. One cause of forgetting is decay, forgetting because we do not use a memory or connections to a memory for a long period of time. For example, you might memorize the state capitals for a civics test but forget many of them soon after the test because you do not need to recall them. However, your studying was not in vain! Even memories that decay do not seem to disappear completely. Many studies show an important **relearning** effect. If you have to memorize the capitals again, it will take you less time than it did the first time you studied them.

Another factor that causes forgetting is **interference**. Sometimes other information in your memory competes with what you are trying to recall. Interference can occur through two processes:

Retroactive interference	**Learning new information interferes with the recall of older information. If you study your psychology at 3:00 and your sociology at 6:00, you might have trouble recalling the psychology information on a test the next day.**
Proactive interference	**Older information learned previously interferes with the recall of information learned more recently. If a researcher reads you a list of items in a certain order, then rereads them differently and asks you to list them in the new order, the old list proactively interferes with recall of the new list.**

HOW MEMORIES ARE PHYSICALLY STORED IN THE BRAIN

Researchers know some of the brain processes and structures involved in memory, but much of this process is still a mystery. By studying patients with specific brain damage, we know that the hippocampus is important in encoding new memories. However, other brain structures are involved. Individuals with damage to the hippocampus might have **anterograde amnesia** (they cannot encode new memories), but they can recall events already in memory. They can learn new skills, although they will not remember learning them. This indicates that the memory for these skills, or procedural memory, is stored elsewhere in the brain (studies on animals indicate procedural memories are stored in the cerebellum).

> **TIP**
>
> **Some students find remembering the difference between retroactive and proactive interference difficult. Focus on which type of information is trying to be recalled. If old information is what you are searching for, retroactive (older) interference most likely applies. If you are searching for newer information, proactive (new) interference might take place.**

At the neurological level, researchers focus on a process called **long-term potentiation**. Studies show that neurons can strengthen connections between each other. Through repeated firings, the connection is strengthened and the receiving neuron becomes more sensitive to the messages from the sending neuron. This strengthened connection might be related to the connections we make in our long-term memory.

LANGUAGE

For us to conceive of thought without language is impossible. Your brain is processing the language you are reading right now. If you stop to think about the previous sentence, you think about it using language. Language is intimately connected to cognition. Some psychologists investigate how language works and how we acquire it in an attempt to understand better how we think and behave.

Elements of Language

All languages can be described with **phonemes** and **morphemes**. Phonemes are the smallest units of sound used in a language. English speakers use approximately 44 phonemes. If you have studied another language or if your primary language is not English, you have experience with other phonemes. Native Spanish speakers find the rolled *R* phoneme natural, but many English speakers have difficulty learning how to produce it since it is not used in English. Speakers of other languages have difficulty learning some English phonemes.

A morpheme is the smallest unit of meaningful sound. Morphemes can be words, such as *a* and *but*, or they can be parts of words, such as the prefixes *an-* and *pre-*. So language consists of phonemes put together to become morphemes, which make up words. These words are then spoken or written in a particular order, called **syntax**. Each language has its own syntax, such as where the verb is usually placed in the sentence. By examining phonemes, morphemes, and syntax (the grammar of a language), psychologists can describe different languages in detail.

Language Acquisition

Many psychologists are particularly interested in how we learn language. Often, developmental psychologists are curious about how our language learning reflects or predicts our cognitive development. These studies show that while babies are learning very different languages, they progress through the same basic stages in order to master the language. First, if you have ever been around babies, you know that babies babble. This is often cute, and it is the first stage of **language acquisition** that occurs about 4 months of age. The babbling stage appears to be innate; even babies born completely deaf go through the babbling stage. A baby's babble represents experimentation with phonemes. They are learning what sounds they are capable of producing. Babies in this stage are capable of producing any phoneme from any language in the world. So while you may not be able to roll your *Rs*, your infant sister can! As language acquisition progresses, we retain the ability to produce phonemes from our primary language (or languages) and lose the ability to make some other phonemes. This is one reason why learning more than one language starting at infancy may be advantageous. Babbling progresses into utterances of words as babies imitate the words they hear caregivers speaking. The time during which babies speak in single words (holophrases) is sometimes called the **holophrastic stage** or **one-word stage**. This usually happens around their first birthday.

The next language acquisition stage occurs at around 18 months and is called **telegraphic speech** or **two-word stage**. Toddlers will combine the words they can say into simple commands. Meaning is usually clear at this stage, but syntax is absent. When your little brother shouts, "No book, movie!" you know that he means, "I do not wish to read a book at this time. I would prefer to watch a movie." Children begin to learn grammar and syntax rules during this stage, sometimes misapplying the rules. For example, they might learn that adding the suffix *-ed* signifies past tense, but they might apply it at inappropriate times, such as, "Marky hitted my head so I throwed the truck at him." Children gradually increase their abilities to combine words in proper syntax if these uses are modeled for them. This misapplication of grammar rules is called **overgeneralization** or **overregularization**.

One important controversy in language acquisition concerns how we acquire language. Behaviorists theorized that language is learned like other learned behaviors: through operant conditioning and shaping. They thought that when children used language correctly, they got rewarded by their parents with a smile or other encouragement, and therefore they would be more likely to use language correctly in the future. More recently, cognitive psychologists challenged this theory. They point out the amazing number of words and language rules learned by children without explicit instruction by parents. Researcher **Noam Chomsky** theorized that humans are born with a **language acquisition device**, the ability to learn a language rapidly as children (this is also called the **nativist theory of language acquisition**). Chomsky pointed to the retarded development of language in cases of children deprived of exposure to language during childhood. He theorized that a critical period (a window of opportunity during which we must learn a skill, or our development will permanently suffer) for learning language may exist. Most psychologists now agree that we acquire language through some combination of conditioning and an inborn propensity to learn language.

Language and Cognition

If language is central to the way we think, how does it influence what we are able to think about? Psychologist **Benjamin Whorf** theorized that the language we use might control, and in some ways limit, our thinking. This theory is called the **linguistic relativity hypothesis**. Many studies demonstrate the effect of labeling on how we think about people, objects, or ideas, but few studies show that the language we speak drastically changes what we can think about.

THINKING AND CREATIVITY

Describing Thought

Trying to describe thought is problematic. Descriptions are thoughts, so we are attempting to describe thought using thought itself. A global, all-inclusive definition of thought is difficult, but psychologists try to define types or categories of thoughts. **Concepts** are similar to the schemata mentioned previously. We each have cognitive rules we apply to stimuli from our environment that allow us to categorize and think about the objects, people, and ideas we encounter. These rules are concepts. Our concept of "mom" is different from our concept of "dad," which is different from our concept of "a soccer game." We may base our concepts on **prototypes** or what we think is the most typical example of a particular concept.

Another type of thought, **images**, are the mental pictures we create in our minds of the outside world. Images can be visual, such as imagining what your cat looks like. However, images can also be auditory, tactile, olfactory, or an image of a taste, such as thinking about what hot chocolate tastes like on a very cold day.

Problem Solving

Many researchers try to study thought by examining the results of thinking. Researchers can ask participants to solve problems and then investigate how the solutions were reached. This research indicates at least two different problem-solving methods we commonly use and some traps to avoid when solving a problem.

Algorithms

One way to solve a problem is to try every possible solution. An **algorithm** is a rule that guarantees the right solution by using a formula or other foolproof method. If you are trying to guess a computer password and you know it is a combination of only two letters, you could use an algorithm and guess pairs of letters in combination until you hit the right one. What if the password is a combination of five letters, not two? Sometimes algorithms are impractical, so a shortcut is needed to solve certain problems.

Heuristics

A **heuristic** is a rule of thumb—a rule that is generally, but not always, true that we can use to make a judgment in a situation. For example, if you are trying to guess the password mentioned previously, you might begin by guessing actual five-letter words rather than random combinations of letters. The password might be a meaningless combination of letters, but you know that passwords are most often actual words. This heuristic limits the possible combinations dramatically. The following shows two specific examples of heuristics.

Availability heuristic	**Judging a situation based on examples of similar situations that come to mind initially. This heuristic might lead to incorrect conclusions due to variability in personal experience. For example, a person may judge his or her neighborhood to be more dangerous than others in the city simply because that person is more familiar with violence in his or her neighborhood than in other neighborhoods.**
Representativeness heuristic	**Judging a situation based on how similar the aspects are to prototypes the person holds in his or her mind. For example, a person might judge a young person more likely to commit suicide because of a prototype of the depressed adolescent when, in fact, suicide rates are not higher in younger populations.**

Use of these heuristics is typically helpful but can lead to specific problems in judgments. Overconfidence is our tendency to overestimate how accurate our judgments are. How confident we are in a judgment is not a good indicator of whether or not we are right. In studies, most people will report extreme confidence in a judgment that turns out to be wrong in a significant number of cases. Two concepts closely related to overconfidence are **belief bias** and **belief perseverance**. Both of these concepts concern our tendency not to change our beliefs in the face of contradictory evidence. Belief bias occurs when we make illogical conclusions in order to confirm our preexisting beliefs. Belief perseverance refers to our tendency to maintain a belief even after the evidence we used to form the belief is contradicted. Overall, these concepts demonstrate that humans are generally more confident in our beliefs than we should be, and we often stick with our beliefs even when presented with evidence that disproves them.

Impediments to Problem Solving

Problem-solving research identifies some common mistakes people make while trying to solve problems. **Rigidity** (also called **mental set**) refers to the tendency to fall into established thought patterns. Most people will use solutions or past experience to try to solve novel problems. Occasionally, this tendency prevents them from seeing a novel solution. One specific example of rigidity is **functional fixedness**, the inability to see a new use for an object. One of my students recently got his car stuck up to the axles in mud. Our attempts to pull him out failed until another student pointed out we could use the car jack to raise the car and put planks under the tires. Most of us thought of the jack only as a tool to help with a flat tire, not getting a car out of the mud. Another common trap in problem solving is not breaking the problem into parts. Studies show that good problem solvers identify subgoals, smaller and more manageable problems they need to solve in order to solve the whole problem. Tackling the problem in these smaller parts helps good problem solvers be more successful.

Another obstacle to successful problem solving is **confirmation bias**. Many studies show that we tend to look for evidence that confirms our beliefs and ignore evidence that contradicts what we think is true. As a consequence, we may miss evidence important to finding the correct solution. For example, when I prepare my students for the AP test, I may emphasize studying techniques or information that I am familiar with and think are very important. What I think is important may be very different than what the designers of the test emphasize. My confirmation bias could hinder the students' success on the test.

Even the way a problem is presented can get in the way of solving it. **Framing** refers to the way a problem is presented. Presentation can drastically change the way we view a problem or an issue. If I tell my students, "The majority of my students have been able to solve this logic problem," they would most likely feel confident and not expect much of a challenge. However, if I tell them, "Almost half of the students in my classes never get the answer to this logic puzzle," they would probably expect a very difficult task. In both cases I am really telling them that 51 percent of the students can solve the logic problem, but the way I frame the task changes their expectation and possibly their ability to solve the problem. Researchers must be careful about unintentionally framing questions in ways that might influence participants in their studies.

Creativity

If you thought defining thought was tough, try defining creativity! The concept itself resists categorization. Again, even though defining this concept is difficult, researchers have investigated definable aspects of creativity. For example, **Wolfgang Köhler** (1887–1967) documented details of the "aha experience" by observing a group of chimpanzees as they generated original solutions to retrieve bananas that were out of reach. Researchers investigating creative thinking find little correlation between intelligence and creativity. Studies show that while we may agree in general about specific examples that demonstrate creativity, individual criteria for creativity vary widely. Most people's criteria do involve both originality and appropriateness. When judging whether or not something is creative, we look at whether it is original or novel and somehow fits the situation. Some researchers are investigating the distinctions between **convergent thinking**, thinking pointed toward one solution, and **divergent thinking**, thinking that searches for multiple possible answers to a question. Divergent thinking is more closely associated with creativity. Creative activities usually involve thinking of new ways to use what we are all familiar with or new ways to express emotions or ideas we share. Painting by the numbers is convergent thinking, but we would probably call painting outside the lines and/or mixing your own hues creative and divergent thinking.

PRACTICE QUESTIONS

Directions: Each of the questions or incomplete statements below is followed by five suggested answers or completions. Select the one that is best in each case.

1. Mr. Krohn, a carpenter, is frustrated because he misplaced his hammer and needs to pound in the last nail in the bookcase he is building. He overlooks the fact that he could use the tennis trophy sitting above the workbench to pound in the nail. Which concept best explains why Mr. Krohn overlooked the trophy?
   (A) representativeness heuristic
   (B) retrieval
   (C) functional fixedness
   (D) belief bias
   (E) divergent thinking

2. Phonemes and morphemes refer to
   (A) elements of telegraphic speech toddlers use.
   (B) elements of language.
   (C) building blocks of concepts.
   (D) basic elements of memories stored in long-term memory.
   (E) two types of influences language has on thought according to the linguistic relativity hypothesis.

3. Which example would be better explained by the levels of processing model than the information-processing model?
   (A) Someone says your name across the room and you switch your attention away from the conversation you are having.
   (B) You forget part of a list you were trying to memorize for a test.
   (C) While visiting with your grandmother, you recall one of your favorite childhood toys.
   (D) You are able to remember verbatim a riddle you worked on for a few days before you figured out the answer.
   (E) You pay less attention to the smell of your neighbor's cologne than to the professor's lecture in your college class.

4. Contrary to what Whorf's linguistic relativity hypothesis originally predicted, what effect does recent research indicate language has on the way we think?
   (A) Since we think in language, the language we understand limits what we have the ability to think about.
   (B) Language is a tool of thought but does not limit our cognition.
   (C) The labels we apply affect our thoughts.
   (D) The words in each language affect our ability to think because we are restricted to the words each language uses.
   (E) The linguistic relativity hypothesis predicts that how quickly we acquire language correlates with our cognitive ability.

5. Which of the following is an example of the use of the representativeness heuristic?
   (A) judging that a young person is more likely to be the instigator of an argument than an older person because you believe younger people are more likely to start fights
   (B) breaking a math story problem down into smaller, representative parts, in order to solve it
   (C) judging a situation by a rule that is usually, but not always, true
   (D) solving a problem with a rule that guarantees the right, more representative, answer
   (E) making a judgment according to past experiences that are most easily recalled, therefore representative of experience

6. Which of the following is the most complete list of elements in the three-box/information-processing model?
   (A) sensory memory, constructive memory, working memory, and long-term memory
   (B) short-term memory, working memory, and long-term memory
   (C) shallow processing, deep processing, and retrieval
   (D) sensory memory, encoding, working memory, and retrieval
   (E) sensory memory, working memory, encoding, long-term memory, and retrieval

7. Which of the following is an effective method for testing whether a memory is actually true or whether it is a constructed memory?
   (A) checking to see whether it was deeply processed or shallowly processed
   (B) testing to see if the memory was encoded from sensory memory into working memory
   (C) using a PET scan to see if the memory is stored in the hippocampus
   (D) using other evidence, such as written records, to substantiate the memory
   (E) there is no way to tell the difference between a true memory and a constructed one

8. One of the ways memories are physically stored in the brain is by what process?
   (A) deep processing, which increases levels of neurotransmitters in the hippocampus
   (B) encoding, which stimulates electric activity in the hippocampus
   (C) long-term potentiation, which strengthens connections between neurons
   (D) selective attention, which increases myelination of memory neurons
   (E) rehearsal, which causes the brain to devote more neurons to what is being rehearsed

9. According to the nativist theory, language is acquired
   (A) by parents reinforcing correct language use.
   (B) using an inborn ability to learn language at a certain developmental stage.
   (C) best in the language and culture native to the child and parents.
   (D) only if formal language instruction is provided in the child's native language.
   (E) best through the phonics instructional method, because children retain how to pronounce all the phonemes required for the language.

10. According to the three-box/information-processing model, stimuli from our outside environment is first stored in
    (A) working memory.
    (B) the hippocampus.
    (C) the thalamus.
    (D) sensory memory.
    (E) selective attention.

11. Which of the following is the best example of the use of the availability heuristic?
    (A) judging a situation by a rule that is usually, but not always, true
    (B) making a judgment according to past experiences that are most easily recalled
    (C) judging that a problem should be solved using a formula that guarantees the right answer
    (D) making a judgment according to what is usually true in your experience
    (E) solving a problem by breaking it into more easily available parts

12. Which sentence most accurately describes sensory memory?
    (A) Sensory memory stores all sensory input perfectly accurately for a short period of time.
    (B) Sensory memory encodes only sensations we are attending to at the time.
    (C) Sensory memory receives memories from the working memory and decides which memories to encode in long-term memory.
    (D) Sensory memory records all incoming sensations and remembers them indefinitely.
    (E) Sensory memory records some sensations accurately, but some are recorded incorrectly, leading to constructive memory.

13. Recall is a more difficult process than recognition because
    (A) memories retrieved by recognition are held in working memory, and recalled memories are in long-term memory.
    (B) memories retrieved by recognition are more deeply processed.
    (C) the process of recall involves cues to the memory that causes interference.
    (D) memories retrieved by recognition are more recent than memories retrieved by recall.
    (E) the process of recognition involves matching a person, event, or object with something already in memory.

14. Which of the following would be the best piece of evidence for the nativist theory of language acquisition?
    (A) a child who acquires language at an extremely early age through intense instruction by her or his parents
    (B) statistical evidence that children in one culture learn language faster than children in another culture
    (C) a child of normal mental ability not being able to learn language due to language deprivation at an early age
    (D) a child skipping the babbling and telegraphic speech stages of language acquisition
    (E) a child deprived of language at an early age successfully learning language later

15. A friend mentions to you that she heard humans never forget anything; we remember everything that ever happens to us. What concept from memory research most directly contradicts this belief?
    (A) sensory memory
    (B) selective attention
    (C) long-term memory
    (D) constructive memory
    (E) recovered memory

ANSWER KEY

1. **C**
2. **B**
3. **D**
4. **C**
5. **A**
6. **E**
7. **D**
8. **C**
9. **B**
10. **D**
11. **B**
12. **A**
13. **E**
14. **C**
15. **B**

ANSWERS EXPLAINED

1. **(C)** Functional fixedness would explain that Mr. Krohn did not think of another use for the trophy, to use it as a hammer. The representativeness heuristic is a rule of thumb for making a judgment that does not apply well to this example, retrieval is a step in the memory process, and divergent thinking is associated with creative thinking. Belief bias is our tendency to stick with a belief even when presented with contrary evidence.

2. **(B)** Phonemes and morphemes are elements of language. They are not used exclusively in telegraphic speech or associated with memory, the linguistic relativity hypothesis, or concepts.

3. **(D)** The levels of processing model would predict that you would remember the riddle because it was deeply processed. Both the levels of processing model and the three-box/information-processing model could explain the other examples, but choice D best fits levels of processing.

4. **(C)** Research demonstrates that the labels we apply to objects, people, and concepts affects how we think and perceive them, but there is little evidence for other ways language influences thoughts. Whorf's hypothesis states that language restricts thought, but our cognition is not strictly limited by our vocabulary (choices A and D). The linguistic relativity hypothesis has nothing to do with language acquisition.

5. **(A)** The representativeness heuristic is judging a situation based on how similar the aspects are to prototypes the person holds in his or her mind. If a person has a prototype of young people as violent, she or he might use the representativeness heuristic to judge the situation. Breaking the problem down into smaller parts is a problem-solving technique. Judging a situation by a rule that is usually, but not always, true is a description of heuristics in general, not specifically the representativeness heuristic. An algorithm is a rule that guarantees the right answer. Making a judgment according to past experiences that are most easily recalled is the availability heuristic, not the representativeness heuristic.

6. **(E)** All five elements listed in this answer are elements in the three-box/information-processing model. Constructive memory mentioned in choice A is not part of this model (although the model can explain this phenomenon). Choice B is less complete than choice E. Choice C describes the levels of processing model. Choice D is missing long-term processing.

7. **(D)** The only way to determine if a memory is accurate or constructed is to look at other evidence for the "remembered" event. Brain scans and memory models cannot differentiate between true and false memories.

8. **(C)** Long-term potentiation strengthens neural connections by allowing them to communicate more efficiently. The other options do not describe brain processes accurately.

9. **(B)** The nativist theory states that we are born with a language acquisition device that enables us to learn language best as children. Choice A reflects a behavioristic view of language acquisition. Nativist theory has nothing to do with native languages or the phonics instructional method.

10. **(D)** Sensory memory is the split-second holding area for sensory information. Some information from sensory memory is encoded into working memory, and this process is controlled by selective attention. The three-box/information-processing model does not refer to specific brain structures like the hippocampus or the thalamus.

11. **(B)** By using the availability heuristic, we draw on examples that are the most readily recalled. Choice A is a good description of heuristics in general but not specifically the availability heuristic. Using a formula or rule that always gets the correct answer is an algorithm. Choice D more accurately describes the representativeness heuristic. Breaking a problem into more easily solved parts is a problem-solving technique, not the availability heuristic.

12. **(A)** Sensory memory holds all sensations accurately for a split second. Selective attention determines which of the memories in sensory memory we will pay attention to. Choice C is incorrect because sensory memory comes before working memory in the three-box/information-processing model. Sensory memory does not last indefinitely and does not record incorrectly, so choices D and E are incorrect.

13. **(E)** Recognition is matching a current experience with one already in memory. Choices A and B are incorrect descriptions of the process. The process of recall does not involve cues, and no difference in recency occurs between recalled and recognized memories.

14. **(C)** The critical-period hypothesis states that children need to learn language during a certain developmental period or their language may be permanently retarded. A child learning language early due to parental instruction is better evidence for the behaviorist view of language acquisition. Language-learning rates between cultures or skipping stages are irrelevant to the critical-period hypothesis. A child deprived of language early on who successfully learns language later would be evidence against the critical-period hypothesis.

15. **(B)** The concept of selective attention contradicts this statement. Selective attention determines what sensations we attend to and encode into short-term memory. Research shows that stimuli not attended to are not remembered, so we do not remember everything that happens to us. Sensory memory, long-term memory, and constructed memories do not obviously contradict the statement. The phenomenon of recovered memories might support the statement. Those who believe in recovered memories believe that we can remember an event for years or decades without being aware of it.

Testing and Individual Differences

8

Key Terms

- Standardized test
- Norms
- Standardization sample
- Psychometrician
- Reliability—split-half, test-retest, equivalent form
- Validity—face, criterion-related (concurrent and predictive), construct
- Aptitude test
- Achievement test
- Intelligence
- Fluid intelligence
- Crystallized intelligence
- Multiple intelligences
- Triarchic theory of intelligence
- Emotional intelligence
- Stanford-Binet IQ test
- Wechsler tests (WAIS, WISC, WPPSI)
- Normal distribution
- Heritability
- Flynn effect

Key People

- Francis Galton
- Charles Spearman
- Howard Gardner
- Daniel Goleman
- Robert Sternberg
- Alfred Binet
- Louis Terman
- David Wechsler

OVERVIEW

We all take many standardized tests and receive scores that tell us how we perform. Given the world in which we have grown up, it is almost unimaginable that there ever could have been a time during which people's mental abilities were not measured and tested. **Francis Galton** was a pioneer in the study of human intelligence and testing, who initiated the use of surveys for collecting data and developed and applied statistics toward its analysis. In this chapter, we will review what makes for a good test, how to interpret your scores on such tests, and what different kinds of tests exist. Then we will focus on one of the most tested characteristics of all, intelligence.

STANDARDIZATION AND NORMS

When we say that a test is **standardized**, we mean that the test items have been piloted on a similar population of people as those who are meant to take the test and that achievement **norms** have been established. For instance, consider the scholastic achievement test (SAT), a test with which many of you are probably all too familiar. When you take the SAT, you take an experimental section, a group of questions on which you will not be evaluated.

In this case, you are helping the Educational Testing Service (ETS) to standardize its future examinations. Those people taking the SAT on a particular testing date are fairly representative of the population of people taking the SAT in general. Such a group of people is known as the **standardization sample**. The **psychometricians** (people who make tests) at ETS use the performance of the standardization sample on the experimental sections to choose items for future tests.

The purpose of tests is to distinguish between people. Therefore, test questions that virtually everyone answers correctly as well as questions that almost no one can answer are discarded. Such items do not provide information that differentiates between the people taking the test. As you are probably aware, questions on the SAT are arranged, within a given section, in order of difficulty. The difficulty level of the questions has been predetermined by the performance of the standardization sample. Ideally, this process of standardization yields equivalent exams, allowing a fair comparison between one person's score on the November 2018 SAT with another's on the May 2019 SAT.

RELIABILITY AND VALIDITY

In order for us to have any faith in the meaning of a test score, we must believe the test is both reliable and valid. **Reliability** refers to the repeatability or consistency of the test as a means of measurement. For instance, if you were to take a test three times that purportedly determined what career you should pursue, and on each occasion you received radically different recommendations, you might question the reliability of the test. Similarly, if you scored 115, 92, and 133 on three different administrations of the same IQ (intelligence quotient) test, you would have little reason to believe your intelligence had been accurately measured.

The reliability of a test can be measured in several different ways. **Split-half reliability** involves randomly dividing a test into two different sections and then correlating people's performances on the two halves. The closer the correlation coefficient is to +1, the greater the split-half reliability of the test. Many tests are available in several equivalent forms. The correlation between performance on the different forms of the test is known as **equivalent-form reliability**. Finally, **test-retest reliability** refers to the correlation between a person's score on one administration of the test with the same person's score on a subsequent administration of the test.

A test is **valid** when it measures what it is supposed to measure. Validity is often referred to as the accuracy of a test. A personality test is valid if it truly measures an individual's personality, and the career inventory described above is valid only if it actually measures for what jobs a person is best suited. The latter example should serve to highlight an important point: a test cannot be valid if it is not reliable. If subsequent administrations of the career inventory yield grossly disparate results for the same person, it clearly does not accurately reflect a person's vocational strengths or interests. However, a test may be reliable without being valid. Even if someone's performance on the test repeatedly indicates that he or she should be a chef and thus is reliable, if the person hates to cook, the test is not a valid measure of his or her interest.

Just as several different kinds of reliability exist, a number of different kinds of validity exist. **Face validity** refers to a superficial measure of accuracy. A test of cake-baking ability has high face validity if you are looking for a chef but low face validity if you are in the market for a doctor. Face validity is a type of **content validity**. Content validity refers to how well a measure reflects the entire range of material it is supposed to be testing. If one really wanted to design a test to find a good chef, a test that required someone to create an entrée and whip up a salad dressing in addition to baking a cake would have greater content validity.

> **TIP**
> Reliability and validity are important terms for you to know. The psychological meaning ascribed to these two terms may differ somewhat from how they are used by the general population. Reliability refers to a test's consistency, and validity refers to a test's accuracy.

Another kind of validity is **criterion-related validity**. Tests may have two kinds of criterion-related validity, concurrent and predictive. **Concurrent validity** measures how much of a characteristic a person has now; is a person a good chef now? **Predictive validity** is a measure of future performance; does a person have the qualities that would enable him or her to become a good chef?

Finally, **construct validity** is thought to be the most meaningful kind of validity. If an independent measure already exists that has been established to identify those who will make fine chefs and love their work, we can correlate prospective chefs' performance on this measure with their performance on any new measure. The higher the correlation, the more construct validity the new measure has. The limitation, of course, is the difficulty in creating any measure that we believe is perfectly valid in the first place.

Table 8.1 Reliability Versus Validity in Archery

Neither reliable nor valid	An archer always misses the target, sometimes shooting too high, sometimes too low, sometimes too far to the left, sometimes too far to the right.
Reliable, but not valid	An archer always misses the target, but the arrows consistently go just over the right side of the top of the target.
Reliable and valid	An archer always puts the arrow in or near the bull's-eye.

TYPES OF TESTS

Two common types of tests are aptitude tests and achievement tests. **Aptitude tests** measure ability or potential, while **achievement tests** measure what one has learned or accomplished. For instance, any intelligence test is supposed to be an aptitude test. These tests are made to express someone's potential, not his or her current level of achievement. Conversely, most, if not all, the tests you take in school are supposed to be achievement tests. They are meant to indicate how much you have learned in a given subject. However, making a test that exclusively measures one of these qualities is virtually impossible. Whatever one's aptitude for a particular field or skill, one's experience affects it. Someone who has had a lot of schooling will score better on a test of mathematics aptitude than someone who might have an equally great potential to be a mathematician but who has never had any formal training in math. Similarly, two people who have achieved equally in learning biology will not necessarily score the same on an achievement test. If one has far greater test-taking aptitude, she or he will likely outscore the other.

TIP

Even though it is essentially impossible to create a pure aptitude or pure achievement test, tests that purport to measure aptitude seek to measure someone's ability or potential, whereas achievement tests seek to measure how much of a body of material someone has learned.

Distinguishing between speed and power tests is also possible. **Speed tests** generally consist of a large number of questions asked in a short amount of time. The goal of a speed test is to see how quickly a person can solve problems. Therefore, the amount of time allotted should be insufficient to complete the problems. The goal of a **power test** is to gauge the difficulty level of problems an individual can solve. Power tests consist of items of increasing difficulty levels. Examinees are given sufficient time to work through as many problems as they can since the goal is to determine the ceiling difficulty level, not their problem-solving speed.

Finally, some tests are **group tests** while others are **individual tests**. Group tests are administered to a large number of people at a time. Interaction between the examiner and the people taking the test is minimal. Generally, instructions are provided to the group, and then people are given a certain amount of time to complete the various sections of the test. Group tests are less expensive to administer and are thought to be more objective than individual tests. Individual tests involve greater interaction between the examiner and examinee. Several of the IQ tests that will be discussed later in this chapter are individual tests. The Rorschach inkblot test, discussed in Chapter 11, "Personality," is also an individual test. The examiner attends not only to what the person says about the inkblots but also to the process by which he or she analyzes the stimuli.

THEORIES OF INTELLIGENCE

While **intelligence** is a commonly used term, it is an extremely difficult concept to define. Typically, intelligence is defined as the ability to gather and use information in productive ways. However, we will not present any one correct definition of intelligence because nothing that approaches a consensus has been achieved. Rather, we will present brief summaries of some of the most widely known theories of intelligence.

Many psychologists differentiate between **fluid intelligence** and **crystallized intelligence**. Fluid intelligence refers to our ability to solve abstract problems and pick up new information and skills, while crystallized intelligence involves using knowledge accumulated over time. While fluid intelligence seems to decrease as adults age, research shows that crystallized intelligence holds steady or may even increase. For instance, a 20-year-old may be able to learn a computer language more quickly than a 60-year-old, whereas the older person may well have the advantage on a vocabulary test or an exercise dependent upon wisdom.

Charles Spearman

One fundamental issue of debate is whether intelligence refers to a single ability, a small group of abilities, or a wide variety of abilities. **Charles Spearman** argued that intelligence could be expressed by a single factor. He used factor analysis, a statistical technique that measures the correlations between different items, to conclude that underlying the many different specific abilities *s* that people regard as types of intelligence is a single factor that he named *g* for general.

Howard Gardner

Howard Gardner also subscribes to the idea of **multiple intelligences**. Unlike many other researchers, however, the kinds of intelligences that this contemporary researcher has named thus far encompass a large range of human behavior. Three of Gardner's multiple intelligences—linguistic, logical-mathematical, and spatial—fall within the bounds of qualities traditionally labeled as intelligences. To that list Gardner has added musical, bodily-kinesthetic, intrapersonal, interpersonal, and naturalist intelligence. He is working on naming others. Musical intelligence, as one might suspect, includes the ability to play an instrument or compose a symphony. A dancer or athlete would have a lot of bodily-kinesthetic intelligence as would a hunter. Intrapersonal intelligence refers to one's ability to understand oneself. People who are able to persevere without becoming discouraged or who can differentiate between situations in which they will be successful and those that may simply frustrate them have int*ra*personal intelligence. Int*er*personal intelligence, on the other hand, corresponds to a person's ability to get along with and be sensitive to others. Successful psychologists, teachers, and salespeople would have a lot of interpersonal intelligence. Finally, naturalist intelligence is found in people gifted at recognizing and organizing the things they encounter in the natural environment. Such people would be successful in fields such as biology and ecology.

Daniel Goleman

Recently there has been a lot of discussion of **EQ**, which is also known as **emotional intelligence**. One of the main proponents of EQ is **Daniel Goleman**. EQ roughly corresponds to Gardner's notions of interpersonal and intrapersonal intelligence. Researchers who argue for the importance of EQ point out that the people with the highest IQs are not always the most successful people. They contend that both EQ and IQ are needed to succeed.

Table 8.2 Theories of Intelligence

Spearman	Intelligence can be measured by a single, general ability (*g*)
Gardner	Theory of multiple intelligences—the term "intelligence" should be applied to a wide variety of abilities including kinesthetic, musical, interpersonal, intrapersonal, naturalistic, verbal, spatial, and mathematical
Sternberg	Triarchic theory of intelligence—people can be intelligent in different ways; they can evidence analytic, practical, and creative intelligence

Robert Sternberg

Robert Sternberg is another contemporary researcher who has offered a somewhat nontraditional definition of intelligence. **Sternberg's triarchic theory** holds that three types of intelligence exist. Componential or analytic intelligence involves the skills traditionally thought of as reflecting intelligence. Most of what we are asked to do in school involves this type of intelligence: the ability to compare and contrast, explain, and analyze. The second type, experiential or creative intelligence, focuses on people's ability to use their knowledge and experiences in new and innovative ways. Rather than comparing the different definitions of intelligence that others have offered, someone with this type of intelligence might prefer to come up with his or her own theory of what constitutes intelligence. The third kind of intelligence Sternberg discusses is contextual or practical intelligence. People with this type of intelligence are what we consider street-smart, they are able to apply what they know to real-world situations.

This last aspect of Sternberg's theory, the idea of practical intelligence, raises another important and unresolved issue in the study of intelligence: does intelligence depend upon context? The other theories of intelligence discussed above essentially posit that intelligence is an ability, some thing or collection of things that one has or does not have. Sternberg, on the other hand, asserts that what is intelligent behavior depends on the context or situation in which it occurs. If intelligence does, indeed, depend upon context, devising an intelligence test becomes a particularly difficult task. The most common intelligence tests used (described in the next section) are based on the view of intelligence as ability-based.

INTELLIGENCE TESTS

Not surprisingly, the ongoing debate over what constitutes intelligence makes constructing an assessment particularly difficult. Two widely used individual tests of intelligence are the Stanford-Binet and the Wechsler.

Alfred Binet was a Frenchman who wanted to design a test that would identify which children needed special attention in schools. His purpose was not to rank or track children but, rather, to improve the children's education by finding a way to tailor it better to their specific needs. Binet came up with the concept of **mental age**, an idea that presupposes that intelligence increases as one gets older. The average 10-year-old child has a mental age of 10. When this average child grows to age 12, she or he will seem more intelligent and will have a mental age of 12. By using this method, Binet created a test that would identify children who lagged behind most of their peers, were in step with their peer group, and were ahead of their peers. Binet created a standardized test using the method described earlier in this chapter. He administered questions to a standardization sample and constructed a test that would differentiate between children functioning at different levels.

Louis Terman, a Stanford professor, used this system to create the measure we know as IQ and the test known as the **Stanford-Binet IQ** test. **IQ** stands for intelligence quotient. A person's IQ score on this test is computed by dividing the person's mental age by his or her chronological age and multiplying by 100. Thus, the child described above has an IQ of 100 because $10/10 \times 100 = 100$. A child who has a mental age of 15 at age 10 would have an IQ of 150, $15/10 \times 100 = 150$. A commonly asked question about this system is how it deals with adults. While talking about a mental age of 8 or 11 or 17 makes sense, what does having a mental age of 25 or 33 or 58 mean? To address this problem, Terman assigned all adults an arbitrary age of 20.

David Wechsler used a different way to measure intelligence. Although it does not involve finding a quotient, it is still known as an IQ test. Three different Wechsler tests actually exist. The **Wechsler Adult Intelligence Scale (WAIS)** is used in testing adults, the **Wechsler Intelligence Scale for Children (WISC)** is given to children between the ages of 6 and 16, and the **Wechsler Preschool and Primary Scale of Intelligence (WPPSI)** can be administered to children as young as 4. The Wechsler tests yield IQ scores based on what is known as **deviation IQ**. The tests are standardized so that the mean is 100, the standard deviation is 15, and the scores form a normal distribution. Remember that in a normal distribution, the percentages of scores that fall under each part of the normal curve are predetermined (see Fig. 8.1).

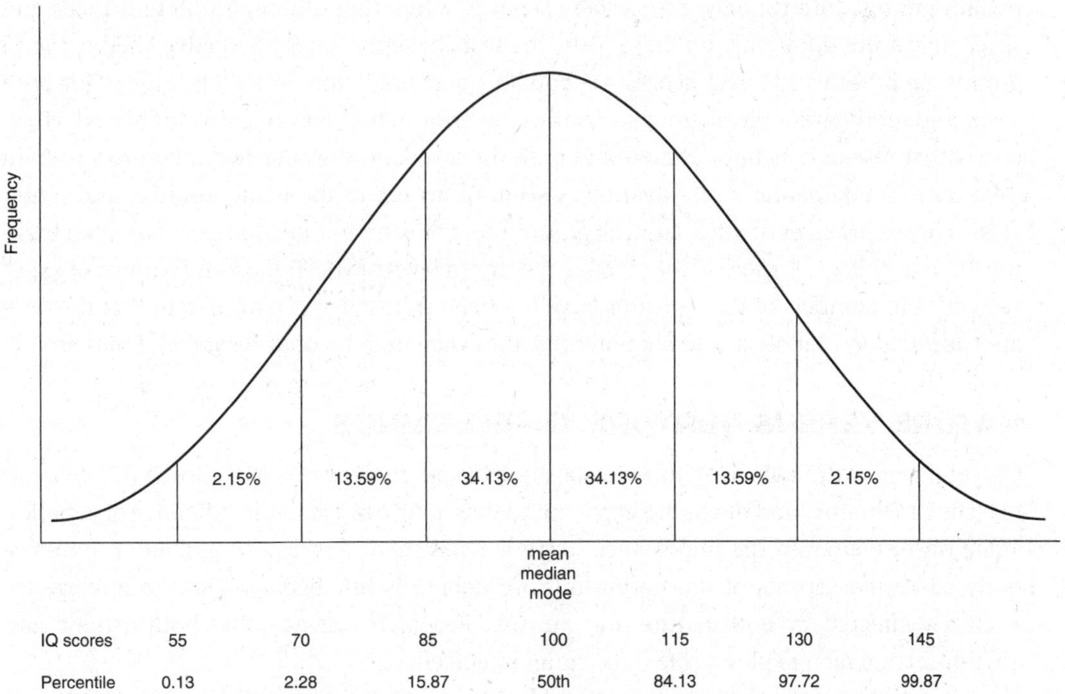

Figure 8.1 The normal distribution on an IQ test.

For instance, approximately 68 percent of scores fall within one standard deviation of the mean, approximately 95 percent fall within two standard deviations of the mean, and 98 to 99 percent of scores fall within three standard deviations of the mean. People's scores are determined by how many standard deviations they fall away from the mean. Thus, Peter who scores at the 15.87th percentile falls at one standard deviation below the mean and is assigned a score of 85, while Juanita who scores at the 97.72nd percentile has scored two standard deviations above the mean and has scored 130. Of course, most people do not fall exactly one or two standard deviations above the mean. However, using such an example would necessitate less obvious mathematical calculations. For more information on the normal curve, you might want to refer to the "Statistics" section in Chapter 2.

Whereas the Stanford-Binet IQ test utilizes a variety of different kinds of questions to yield a single IQ score, the Wechsler tests result in scores on a number of subscales as well as a total IQ score. For instance, the WAIS has 11 subscales. Six of them are combined to produce a verbal IQ score. Five are used to indicate performance IQ. The kinds of questions used to measure verbal IQ ask people to define words, solve mathematical word problems, and explain ways in which different items are similar. The items on the performance section involve tasks like duplicating a pattern with blocks, correctly ordering pictures so they tell a story, and identifying missing elements in pictures. Differences between a person's score on the verbal and performance sections of this exam can be used to identify learning disabilities.

BIAS IN TESTING

Much discussion has centered on whether widely used IQ tests or the SAT are biased against certain groups. Interestingly, researchers seem to agree that although different races and sexes may score differently on these tests, the tests have the same predictive validity for all groups. In other words, SAT scores are equally good predictors of college grades for both sexes and for different racial groups and thus, in a sense, the test is clearly not biased. However, other researchers have argued that both the tests and the college grades are biased in a far more fundamental way. Advantages seem to accrue to the white, middle, and upper class. The experiences of other cultural groups seem to work to their detriment both on these tests and in college. Writers of the test may assume a level of vocabulary and a range of experiences that members of these groups have not been exposed to. To the extent that the tests are supposed to identify academic potential, they may then be both flawed and biased.

NATURE VERSUS NURTURE: INTELLIGENCE

One of the most difficult and controversial issues in psychology involves sorting out the relative effects of nature and nurture. Keep in mind that nature refers to the influence of genetics, while nurture stresses the importance of the environment and learning. One of the more hotly contested aspects of the nature-nurture debate is intelligence. Human intelligence is clearly affected by both nature and nurture. Research suggests that both genetic and environmental factors play a role in molding intelligence.

An important term that researchers use in discussing the effects of nature and nurture is **heritability**. Heritability is a measure of how much of a trait's variation is explained by genetic factors. Heritability can range from 0 to 1, where 0 indicates that the environment is totally responsible for differences in the trait and 1 means that all of the variation in the trait can be accounted for genetically. Thus, the question is how heritable is intelligence? That heritability does not apply to an individual but rather to a population is important to point out. Whatever the heritability ratio for intelligence, it will not tell us how much of any particular person's intelligence was determined by nature or nurture.

Solving this controversy once and for all is essentially impossible because we cannot ethically set up the kind of controlled experiment necessary to provide definitive answers to this question. However, many researchers have studied this issue, and some of their findings are presented below:

- Performance on intelligence tests has been increasing steadily throughout the century, a finding known as the **Flynn effect**. Since the gene pool has remained relatively stable, this finding suggests that environmental factors such as nutrition, education, and, perhaps, television and video games play a role in intelligence.
- Monozygotic (identical) twins, who share 100 percent of their genetic material, score much more similarly on intelligence tests than do dizygotic (fraternal) twins, who have, on average, only 50 percent of their genes in common. Nonetheless, some researchers have suggested that monozygotic twins tend to be treated more similarly than dizygotic twins, thus confounding the effects of nature with those of nurture.
- Research on identical twins separated at birth has found strong correlations in intelligence scores. However, researchers advocating more of an environmental influence point out that usually the twins are placed into similar environments, again making it difficult to sift out the relative effects of nature and nurture. For instance, if each of

the twins is placed into a white, middle-class, suburban home, concluding that all their similarities are genetically based does not make sense.

- Some researchers have argued that racial differences in IQ scores provide evidence that intelligence is largely genetically determined. The majority of psychologists disagree, arguing that these racial differences are more likely explained by differences in environments, particularly by socioeconomic factors. For example, African Americans, as a group, tend to score 10–15 points lower on IQ tests than do whites. Many researchers argue that the greater poverty level in many minority populations, an environmental factor, is the main cause of the disparity in test scores and not a difference in genetics. Test bias is an additional factor that may contribute to the gap in test scores.
- Participation in government programs such as Head Start, meant to redress some of the disadvantages faced by impoverished groups, has been shown to correlate with higher scores on intelligence tests. However, opponents of such programs assert that these gains are limited and of short duration. Advocates of such interventions respond that expecting the gains to outlast the programs is unreasonable.

After putting the issue of cause aside, when comparing groups of people on any characteristic, keep in mind that differences within groups generally dwarf differences between groups. In other words, within any one group will be more diversity than between any two groups. Practically speaking, if we find that boys perform better on a certain test than girls do, more of a difference will exist between the highest scoring boy and the lowest scoring boy than between the average boy and the average girl. Furthermore, knowing that boys generally outperform girls on this test tells us nothing about the performance of any particular girl compared with the performance of any particular boy. Therefore, we need to be careful about how we use information about differences between groups. Essentially, we should not use it. We should ignore it and evaluate each person, regardless of group membership, as an individual.

Within-group differences are typically larger than between-group differences.

A CAUTIONARY NOTE

It is often said that we live in a testing society. We like to be able to measure things and assign them a number. Therefore, keeping in mind the limitations and extraordinary labeling power of these instruments is particularly important. As we have discussed, the definition of intelligence (and many other concepts) remains hotly debated and many factors affect people's performances on tests. Thus, we need to take care not to ascribe too great a meaning to a test score. Many schools that used to measure all their students' IQs periodically have abandoned that practice. Schools that used to base admission to programs for exceptional children solely on these tests now frequently gather information in other ways as well. When IQ tests are given, the results remain confidential so as not to create expectations about how people ought to perform (see the information on self-fulfilling prophecy in Chapter 14). While well-designed tests can be extremely useful, we must recognize their limitations.

PRACTICE QUESTIONS

Directions: Each of the questions or incomplete statements below is followed by five suggested answers or completions. Select the one that is best in each case.

1. Paul takes a test in the army to see if he would make a good pilot. Such a test is a (an)
   (A) standardized test.
   (B) aptitude test.
   (C) intelligence test.
   (D) achievement test.
   (E) biased test.

2. If a test is reliable, it means that it
   (A) is given in the same way every time.
   (B) tests what it is supposed to test.
   (C) is a fair assessment.
   (D) yields consistent results.
   (E) is also valid.

3. The standardization sample is
   (A) the group of people who take the test.
   (B) a random sample of the test takers used to evaluate the performance of others.
   (C) the people used to represent the population for whom the test was intended.
   (D) all the people who might ever take the test.
   (E) the top 15 percent of scores on the test.

4. Which of the following is not one of Howard Gardner's multiple intelligences?
   (A) practical
   (B) musical
   (C) interpersonal
   (D) spatial
   (E) linguistic

5. Mrs. Cho is careful to make sure that she fairly represents the whole year's work on the final exam for her American literature class. If Mrs. Cho achieves this goal, her test will have
   (A) test-retest reliability.
   (B) construct validity.
   (C) content validity.
   (D) split-half reliability.
   (E) criterion validity.

6. Astor scores at the 84th percentile on the WISC. Which number most closely expresses his IQ?
   (A) 85
   (B) 110
   (C) 115
   (D) 120
   (E) 130

7. Spearman argued that intelligence could be boiled down to one ability known as
   (A) *s*.
   (B) *i*.
   (C) *g*.
   (D) *a*.
   (E) *x*.

8. Which of the following would provide the strongest evidence for the idea that intelligence is highly heritable?
   (A) The IQ scores of parents are positively correlated with the scores of their children.
   (B) Monozygotic twins separated at birth have extremely similar IQ scores.
   (C) Dizygotic twins score more similarly on IQ tests than do other siblings.
   (D) Adopted children's IQ scores are positively correlated with their adopted parents' scores.
   (E) Different ethnic groups have different average IQ scores.

9. Which is the best example of crystallized intelligence?
   (A) Tino uses his exceptional vocabulary to excel at Scrabble.
   (B) Susan quickly learns to use a computerized statistics program for her class.
   (C) Gina is always the first to finish class math tests.
   (D) Arjun changes jobs and adapts to the demands of the new environment.
   (E) Kevin is able to perform complex mathematical calculations in his head.

10. Which statement is true of power tests?
    (A) They are administered in a short amount of time.
    (B) They are an example of an individual test.
    (C) They are a pure measure of achievement.
    (D) They consist of items of varying difficulty levels.
    (E) They yield IQ scores.

11. People with high EQs would be likely to
    (A) pursue high-paying occupations.
    (B) complete college.
    (C) find jobs well suited to their individual strengths.
    (D) be creative problem solvers.
    (E) have a lot of close friends.

12. Although her score on the personality test indicated that Mary was devoid of social grace, painfully shy, and frightened of other people, she is extremely popular and outgoing. This personality test lacks

(A) reliablity.
(B) standardization.
(C) consistency.
(D) validity.
(E) practical worth.

13. Santos is 8 years old and, according to the Stanford-Binet, he has a mental age of 10. What is his IQ?

(A) 80
(B) 100
(C) 120
(D) 125
(E) 150

14. The Flynn effect is the finding that

(A) intelligence seems to increase with every generation.
(B) television has decreased intellectual performance.
(C) linguistic skills decline with age.
(D) within-group differences are larger than between-group differences.
(E) the more times people take a test, the better they tend to score.

15. Desmond believes that nature is far more important in shaping personality than nurture. Desmond probably believes in the strong influence of

(A) environment.
(B) learning.
(C) reinforcement.
(D) genetics.
(E) culture.

ANSWER KEY

1. **B**
2. **D**
3. **C**
4. **A**
5. **C**
6. **C**
7. **C**
8. **B**
9. **A**
10. **D**
11. **C**
12. **D**
13. **D**
14. **A**
15. **D**

ANSWERS EXPLAINED

1. **(B)** Aptitude tests aim to measure someone's ability or potential. In this case, the test is supposed to show whether Paul has the ability to be a pilot. The test may or may not be standardized or biased. The test is not attempting to measure Paul's intelligence. Since Paul has not yet been trained as a pilot, the test is not an achievement test.

2. **(D)** If a test is reliable, it yields consistent results. Standardized tests are generally given in the same way every time. A test is valid if it measures what it is supposed to measure. While valid tests are reliable, reliable tests are not necessarily valid. Whether a test is fair or biased can be evaluated in several ways as explained in the chapter. However, the fairness of a test is not synonymous with its consistency.

3. **(C)** The standardization sample represents the population for whom the test was intended and is used to construct the test. None of the other choices are referred to by any specific terminology.

4. **(A)** Practical intelligence is part of Sternberg's triarchic theory of intelligence. Gardner's multiple intelligences include linguistic, spatial, logical-mathematical, musical, bodily-kinesthetic, interpersonal, intrapersonal, and naturalist.

5. **(C)** Mrs. Cho is concerned about the content validity of her test. A test that fairly represents all the material taught in her class has content validity. Validity, in general, measures how well a test measures what it is supposed to measure. In order for Mrs. Cho's test to have construct validity, we would need to know that the test was successful in differentiating between varying levels of achievement in her class. If the test has criterion validity, we would have to know that the test successfully identified either those students who had excelled in their study of American literature (concurrent validity) or those students who would excel in the future (predictive validity). Reliability is a measure of how consistent the scores are on a test. Test-retest reliability involves giving the same test to the same population on at least two different occasions and measuring the correlation between the sets of scores. Split-half reliability is when one test is divided into two parts and the correlation between people's scores on the two halves is measured.

6. **(C)** The WISC (Wechsler Intelligence Scale for Children) yields a deviation IQ score. The mean on the WISC is set at 100. Therefore, someone who scores 100 has scored at the 50th percentile on the test. The standard deviation on the WISC is set at 15. Since approximately 34 percent of the scores in a normal distribution fall between the mean and one standard deviation above the mean, Astor's score at the 84th percentile

indicates that he scored almost exactly one standard deviation above the mean. Therefore, to compute Astor's score, we simply have to add the mean (100) to one standard deviation (15).

7. **(C)** Spearman argued that intelligence could be boiled down to one ability known as *g*. The *g* stands for general intelligence. Spearman also discussed *s*, which stands for specific intelligences. The other letters are all simply distractors.

8. **(B)** The strongest evidence presented for intelligence to be highly heritable is that monozygotic twins separated at birth have extremely similar IQ scores. Monozygotic twins share 100 percent of their genetic material. If they are separated at birth and therefore raised in different environments, similarity in their IQ scores argues for the influence of nature or heritability. Parents' IQ scores do tend to correlate positively with those of their children, but this similarity could be explained by either genetic or environmental factors. Dizygotic twins and other siblings share the same amount of genetic material on average (50 percent). Therefore, if the former score more similarly on IQ tests, an environmental influence is suggested. For instance, dizygotic twins may be treated more similarly than other siblings and grow up during the same time period. Since adopted children do not share any genetic material with the parents who adopted them, similarities must be due to environmental factors. Differences in average IQ scores between ethnic groups could be explained by either genetic or environmental factors.

9. **(A)** Vocabulary tends to increase with age and does not depend on speed; such attributes characterize crystallized intelligence. Choices B, C, and D are more typically associated with fluid intelligence because they involve speed and learning new things. Choice E is also more likely to be associated with fluid intelligence because the ability to perform complex mathematical calculations in one's head is linked to working memory that tends to decline with age.

10. **(D)** Power tests consist of items of varying levels of difficulty because their purpose is to identify the upper limit of a person's ability. Speed tests are given in a small amount of time since they seek to test how quickly someone can solve problems. Power tests could be given individually or in a group. Having a pure measure of achievement is impossible. IQ tests yield IQ scores.

11. **(C)** People with high EQs would be likely to find jobs well suited to their individual strengths. Emotional intelligence is thought to help people achieve what they want to achieve. Someone who has a high EQ will not necessarily want a high-paying job, go to college, be a creative problem solver, or have many close friends.

12. **(D)** Since the personality test does not seem to have resulted in an accurate depiction of Mary's personality, the test lacks validity. If repeated administrations of the test yielded similar results, the test could still be reliable. The test may or may not have been standardized. Consistency is generally equated with reliability. If the test lacks validity, it will not have practical worth, but the latter is not a psychological term.

13. **(D)** Scores on the Stanford-Binet IQ test are computed by dividing mental age by chronological age and multiplying by 100. Since 10 divided by 8 equals 1.25, Santos has an IQ of 125.

14. **(A)** The Flynn effect is the finding that intelligence seems to be increasing with every generation. Although television is often cast as a great social evil that rots the minds of our nation's youth, one hypothesized contribution to the Flynn effect is the exposure to the complex and rapid visual stimuli that appear on television. Linguistic skills do not decline with age. The statements in choices D and E are true but are not known as the Flynn effect.

15. **(D)** Adherents to a nature perspective often emphasize the effect of genetic makeup in shaping personality. All the other factors (environment, learning, reinforcement, and culture) are associated with a nurture perspective.

UNIT 6

Developmental Psychology

The developmental psychology unit is an example of "applied" psychology, meaning that researchers use psychological research to apply it to questions about how humans develop. Developmental psychologists use some unique research methods and study the entire lifespan, from before we are born to old age. Issues related to parenting, cognitive, moral other specific developmental topics are addressed. You will find content in this unit in the Development chapter in the textbook you use in your AP Psychology class.

Developmental Psychology 9

Key Terms

- Developmental psychologist
- Nature versus nurture
- Cross-sectional research
- Longitudinal research
- Teratogens
- Fetal alcohol syndrome (FAS)
- Newborn reflexes
- Attachment
- Harry Harlow's attachment research
- Mary Ainsworth's strange situation
- Secure attachments
- Avoidant attachments
- Anxious/ambivalent attachments
- Authoritarian parents
- Permissive parents
- Authoritative parents
- Oral stage
- Anal stage
- Phallic stage
- Genital stage
- Erik Erikson's psycho-social developmental theory
- Trust versus mistrust
- Autonomy versus shame and doubt
- Initiative versus guilt
- Industry versus inferiority
- Identity versus role confusion
- Intimacy versus isolation
- Generativity versus stagnation
- Integrity versus despair
- Jean Piaget's cognitive developmental theory
- Schemata
- Assimilation
- Accommodation
- Sensorimotor stage
- Object permanence
- Preoperational stage
- Egocentric
- Concrete operations
- Concepts of conservation
- Formal operations
- Metacognition
- Lawrence Kohlberg's moral developmental theory
- Preconventional stage
- Conventional stage
- Postconventional stage

Key People

- Konrad Lorenz
- Harry Harlow
- Mary Ainsworth
- Diana Baumrind
- Lev Vygotsky
- Sigmund Freud
- Erik Erikson
- Jean Piaget
- Alfred Binet
- Lawrence Kohlberg
- Carol Gilligan

OVERVIEW

In a way, developmental psychology is the most comprehensive topic psychologists attempt to research. Developmental psychologists study how our behaviors and thoughts change over the course of our entire lives, from birth to death (or conception to cremation). Consequently, developmental psychology involves many concepts traditionally included in other areas of psychology. For example, both personality researchers and developmental psychologists closely examine identical twins for personality similarities and differences. Some psychologists consider developmental psychology to be an applied research topic because developmental psychologists apply research from other areas of psychology to topics involving maturation.

One way to organize the information included in the developmental psychology section is to think about one of the basic controversies: nature versus nurture. This chapter discusses influences on development from **nature** (genetic factors) first and then moves on to theories about **nurture** (environmental factors).

RESEARCH METHODS

Studies in developmental psychology are usually either **cross-sectional** or **longitudinal**. Cross-sectional research uses participants of different ages to compare how certain variables may change over the life span. For example, a developmental researcher might be interested in how our ability to recall nonsense words changes as we age. The researcher might choose participants from different age groups, say 5–10, 10–20, 20–30, 30–40, and test the recall of a list of nonsense words in each group. Cross-sectional research can produce quick results, but researchers must be careful to avoid the effects of historical events and cultural trends. For example, the 30–40-year-old participant group described in the study above might have had a very different experience in school than the 5–10-year-olds are having. Perhaps memorization was emphasized in school for one group and not another. When the researcher examines the results, she or he might not know if the differences in recall between groups are due to age or different styles of education.

Longitudinal research takes place over a long period of time. Instead of sampling from various age groups as in cross-sectional research, a longitudinal study examines one group of participants over time. For example, a developmental researcher might study how a group of mentally challenged children progress in their ability to learn skills. The researcher would gather the participants and test them at various intervals of their lives (e.g., every three years). Longitudinal studies have the advantage of precisely measuring the effects of development on a specific group. However, they are obviously time consuming, and the results can take years or decades to develop.

PRENATAL INFLUENCES ON DEVELOPMENT

Genetics

In Chapter 3, you reviewed basic information about how hereditary traits are passed on from parents to their children. Many developmental psychologists investigate how our genes influence our development. Specifically, researchers might look at identical twins in order to determine which traits are most influenced by genetic factors (e.g., the Bouchard twin study). Our genes also help determine what abilities we are born with, such as our reflexes and our process of developing motor skills.

Teratogens

Most prenatal influences on our development are strictly genetic (nature) in origin. However, the environment can also have profound influences on us before we are born. Certain chemicals or agents (called **teratogens**) can cause harm if ingested or contracted by the mother. The placenta can filter out many potentially harmful substances, but teratogens pass through this barrier and can affect the fetus in profound ways. One of the most common teratogens is alcohol. Even small amounts of alcohol can change the way the fetal brain develops. Children of alcoholic mothers who drink heavily during pregnancy are at high risk for **fetal alcohol syndrome (FAS)**. Children born with FAS have small, malformed skulls and intellectual disability. Researchers are also investigating a less severe effect of moderate drinking during pregnancy, **fetal alcohol effect**. These children typically do not show all the symptoms of FAS but may have specific developmental problems later in life, such as learning disabilities or behavioral problems.

Alcohol is certainly not the only teratogen. Unlike alcohol, other psychoactive drugs, like cocaine and heroin, can cause newborns to share their parent's physical drug addiction. The serious withdrawal symptoms associated with these addictions can kill an infant. Some polluting chemicals in the environment can cause abnormal infant development. Certain bacteria and viruses are not screened by the placenta and may be contracted by the fetus.

MOTOR/SENSORY DEVELOPMENT

Reflexes

In the past, some philosophers and early psychologists believed that humans are born as blank slates—helpless and without any skills or reflexes. In fact, they believed this lack of reflexes or instinctual behavior was one of the factors that separated humans from animals. Researchers now know that humans are far from blank slates when we are born. All babies exhibit a set of specific **reflexes**, which are specific, inborn, automatic responses to certain specific stimuli. Some important reflexes humans are born with are listed below:

Rooting reflex	When touched on the cheek, a baby will turn his or her head to the side where he or she felt the touch and seek to put the object into his or her mouth.
Sucking reflex	When an object is placed into the baby's mouth, the infant will suck on it. (The combination of the rooting and sucking reflexes obviously helps babies eat.)
Grasping reflex	If an object is placed into a baby's palm or foot pad, the baby will try to grasp the object with his or her fingers or toes.
Moro reflex	When startled, a baby will fling his or her limbs out and then quickly retract them, making himself or herself as small as possible.
Babinski reflex	When a baby's foot is stroked, he or she will spread the toes.

TIP

These are the reflexes we are born with and lose later in life. Humans have other reflexes (for example, eye blinking in response to a puff of air to the eye) that remain with us throughout our life. Humans lose the reflexes listed in this table as our brain grows and develops.

The Newborn's Senses

In addition to inborn reflexes, humans are also born equipped with our sensory apparatus. Some of the ways that babies sense the world are identical to the way you do, but some differ greatly. Researchers know that babies can hear even before birth. Minutes after birth, a baby will try to turn his or her head toward the mother's voice. Babies have the same basic preferences in taste and smell as we do. Babies love the taste of sugar and respond to a higher concentration of sugar in foods. Preferences in tastes and smells will change as we develop (we might learn to like the smell of fish or hate it), but babies are born with the basic preferences in place. Babies' vision is different than ours in important ways, however. Sight becomes our dominant sense as we age, but when we are born, hearing is the dominant sense due to babies' poor vision. Babies are born almost legally blind. They can see well 8–12 inches in front of them, but everything beyond that range is a blur. Their vision improves quickly as they age, improving to normal vision (barring any vision problems) by the time they are about 12 months old. In addition, babies are born with certain visual preferences. Babies like to look at faces and facelike objects (symmetrical objects and shapes organized in an imitation of a face) more than any other objects. This preference and their ability to focus about 12 inches in front of them make babies well equipped to see their mother as soon as they are born.

Motor Development

Barring developmental difficulties, all humans develop the same basic motor skills in the same sequence, although the age we develop them may differ from person to person. Our motor control develops as neurons in our brain connect with one another and become **myelinated** (see Chapter 3 for a review of neural anatomy). Research shows that most babies can roll over when they are about 5-1/2 months old, stand at about 8–9 months, and walk by themselves after about 15 months. These ages are very approximate and apply to babies all over the world. While environment and parental encouragement may have some effect on motor skills, the effect is slight.

PARENTING

Attachment Theory

The influences discussed so far in this chapter have mostly been genetic or prenatal in nature. After birth, uncountable environmental influences begin to affect how we develop. Some species respond in very predictable ways to environmental stimuli: biologist **Konrad Lorenz** established that some infant animals (such as geese) become attached ("imprint") on individuals or even objects they see during a critical period after birth. Certainly one of the most important aspects of babies' early environment is the relationship between parent(s) and child. Some researchers focus on how **attachment**, or the reciprocal relationship between caregiver and child, affects development. Two significant researchers in this area demonstrate some of the basic findings regarding attachment.

Harry Harlow

In the 1950s, researcher **Harry Harlow** raised baby monkeys with two artificial wire frame figures made to resemble mother monkeys. One mother figure was fitted with a bottle the infant could eat from, and the other was wrapped in a soft material. Harlow found that infant monkeys when frightened preferred the soft mother figure even over the figure that they fed from.

When the infants were surprised or stressed, they fled to the soft mother for comfort and protection. Harlow's studies demonstrated the importance of physical comfort in the formation of attachment with parents. As Harlow's infant monkeys developed, he noticed that the monkeys raised by the wire frame mothers became more stressed and frightened than monkeys raised with real mothers when put into new situations. The deprivation of an attachment with a real mother had long-term effects on these monkeys' behavior.

Mary Ainsworth

Mary Ainsworth researched the idea of attachment by placing human infants into novel situations. Ainsworth observed infants' reactions when placed into a **strange situation**: their parents left them alone for a short period of time and then returned. She divided the reactions into three broad categories:

1. Infants with **secure attachments** (about 66 percent of the participants) confidently explore the novel environment while the parents are present, are distressed when they leave, and come to the parents when they return.
2. Infants with **avoidant attachments** (about 21 percent of the participants) may resist being held by the parents and will explore the novel environment. They do not go to the parents for comfort when they return after an absence.
3. Infants with **anxious/ambivalent attachments** (also called **resistant attachments**, about 12 percent of the participants) have ambivalent reactions to the parents. They may show extreme stress when the parents leave but resist being comforted by them when they return.

Parenting Styles

So far, the developmental research and categories described focus on the behaviors of children. Parents' interaction with their children definitely has an influence on the way we develop and can be categorized in similar ways. Developmental psychologist **Diana Baumrind** researched parent-child interactions and described three overall categories of parenting styles.

Authoritarian parents set strict standards for their children's behavior and apply punishments for violations of these rules. Obedient attitudes are valued more than discussions about the rationale behind the standards. Punishment for undesired behavior is more often used than reinforcement for desired behavior. If your parents were authoritarian and you came in 15 minutes after your curfew, you might be grounded from going out again the rest of the month without explanation or discussion.

Permissive parents do not set clear guidelines for their children. The rules that do exist in the family are constantly changed or are not enforced consistently. Family members may perceive that they can get away with anything at home. If your parents were permissive and you came in 15 minutes after your curfew, your parents' reaction would be unpredictable. They may not notice, not seem to mind, or threaten you with a punishment that they never follow through on.

Authoritative parents have set, consistent standards for their children's behavior, but the standards are reasonable and explained. The rationale for family rules are discussed with children old enough to understand them. Authoritative parents encourage their children's independence but not past the point of violating rules. They praise as often as they punish.

In general, explanations are encouraged in an authoritative house, and the rules are reasonable and consistent. If your parents were authoritative and you came in 15 minutes after your curfew, you would already know the consequences of your action. You would know what the family rule was for breaking curfew, why the rule existed, what the consequences were, and your parents would make sure you suffered the consequences!

> **TIP**
>
> Some students confuse the terms **authoritative** and **authoritarian.** Remember that the authoritarian style involves very strict rules without much explanation, while authoritative parents set strict rules but make sure they are reasonable and explained.

Studies show that the authoritative style produces the most desirable and beneficial home environment. Children from authoritative homes are more socially capable and perform better academically, on average. The children of permissive parents are more likely to have emotional control problems and are more dependent. Authoritarian parents' children are more likely to distrust others and be withdrawn from peers. These studies indicate another way in which our upbringing influences our development. Researchers agree that parenting style is certainly not the whole or final answer to why we develop the way we do (and the research is correlational, not causational). However, it is a key influence along with genetic makeup, peer relationships, and other environmental influences on thought and behavior.

STAGE THEORIES

Besides nature versus nurture, one of the other major controversies in developmental psychology is the argument about **continuity** versus **discontinuity**. Do we develop continually, at a steady rate from birth to death, or is our development discontinuous, happening in fits and starts with some periods of rapid development and some of relatively little change? Biologically, we know our development is somewhat discontinuous. We grow more as an infant and during our adolescent growth spurt than at other times in our lives. However, what about psychologically? Do we develop in our thought and behavior continuously or discontinuously?

Psychologist **Lev Vygotsky's** concept of "zone of proximal development" is one answer to this question of continuity versus discontinuity: a child's zone of proximal development is the range of tasks the child can perform independently and those tasks the child needs assistance with. Teachers/parents can provide "scaffolds" for students to help them accomplish tasks at the upper end of their zone of proximal development, encouraging further cognitive development. Several theorists concluded that we pass through certain stages in the development of certain psychological traits, and their theories attempt to explain these stages. Stage theories are, by definition, discontinuous theories of development. You may notice that the first two stage theorists, **Sigmund Freud** and **Erik Erikson**, base their stages on psychoanalytic theories and are therefore less scientifically verifiable than the other stage theories. They are included because their stages are still often used to describe how we develop in specific areas and are of historic importance.

> **TIP**
> Each stage theory describes how different aspects of thought and behavior develop. One stage theory does not necessarily contradict another even though they may say different things about a child of the same age. Be careful when you are contrasting stage theories. Comparing one against another may be like comparing apples with oranges.

Sigmund Freud

Freud was the first to theorize that we pass though different stages in childhood. Freud said we develop through five **psychosexual** stages. Sexual to Freud meant not the act of intercourse but how we get sensual pleasure from the world. If we fail to resolve a significant conflict in our lives during one of these stages, Freud said we could become **fixated** in the stage, meaning we might remain preoccupied with the behaviors associated with that stage. (See Chapter 11, "Personality," for a further review of this theory.) Freud described five psychosexual stages:

Oral stage	In this stage, infants seek pleasure through their mouths. You might notice that babies tend to put everything they can grab into their mouths if they can get away with it. Freud thought that people fixated at this stage might overeat, smoke, and in general have a childlike dependence on things and people.
Anal stage	This stage develops during toilet training. If conflict around toilet training arises, a person might fixate in the stage and be overly controlling (retentive) or out of control (expulsive).
Phallic stage	During this stage, babies realize their gender and this causes conflict in the family. Freud described the process boys go through in this stage as the Oedipus complex: a time when a boy resents his father's relationship with his mother. The process for girls is called the Electra complex. Freud thought that conflict in this stage could cause later problems in relationships.
Latency stage	After the phallic stage, Freud thought children go through a short latency stage, or period of calm, and between the ages of six and puberty of low psychosexual anxiety that most psychologists don't regard as a separate stage.
Genital stage	They then enter the genital stage where they remain for the rest of their lives. The focus of sexual pleasure is the genitals, and fixation in this stage is what Freud considers normal.

Erik Erikson

Erik Erikson was a **neo-Freudian**, a theorist who believed in the basics of Freud's theory but adapted it to fit his own observations. Through his own life experiences of identity formation and his study in psychoanalysis with Anna Freud (Sigmund Freud's daughter), Erikson developed his own stage theory of development. He thought that our personality was profoundly influenced by our experiences with others, so he created the **psychosocial stage theory**. It consists of eight stages, each stage centering on a specific social conflict.

Trust versus mistrust	Babies' first social experience of the world centers on need fulfillment. Babies learn whether or not they can trust that the world provides for their needs. Erikson thought that babies need to learn that they can trust their caregivers and that their requests (crying, at first) are effective. This sense of trust or mistrust will carry throughout the rest of our lives, according to Erikson.
Autonomy versus shame and doubt	In this next stage, toddlers begin to exert their will over their shame and doubt own bodies for the first time. Autonomy is our control over our own body, and Erikson thought that potty training was an early effort at gaining this control. Toddlers should also learn to control temper tantrums during this stage. Childrens' most popular word during this stage might be "No!," demonstrating their attempt to control themselves and others. If we learn how to control ourselves and our environment in reasonable ways, we develop a healthy will. Erikson believes we can then control our own body and emotional reactions during the rest of the social challenges we will face.
Initiative versus guilt	In this stage, childrens' favorite word changes from "No!" to "Why?" If we trust those around us and feel in control of our bodies, we feel a natural curiosity about our surroundings. Children in this stage want to understand the world. We take the initiative in problem solving and ask many (many!) questions. If this initiative is encouraged, we will feel comfortable about expressing our curiosity through the rest of the stages. If those around us scold us for our curiosity, we might learn to feel guilty about asking questions and avoid doing so in the future.
Industry versus inferiority	This stage is the beginning of our formal education. Preschool inferiority and kindergarten were mostly about play and entertainment. In the first grade, for the first time we are asked to produce work that is evaluated. We expect to perform as well as our peers at games and school work. If we feel that we are as good at kick ball (or math problems, or singing, and so on) as the child in the next desk, we feel competent. If we realize that we are behind or cannot do as well as our peers, having an **inferiority complex**, we may feel anxious about our performance in that area throughout the rest of the stages.

Identity versus role confusion	In adolescence, Erikson felt our main social task is to discover what social identity we are most comfortable with. He thought that a person might naturally try out different roles before he or she found the one that best fit his or her internal sense of self. Adolescents try to fit into groups in order to feel confident in their identities. An adolescent should figure out a stable sense of self before moving on to the next stage or risk having an identity crisis later in life.
Intimacy versus isolation	Young adults who established stable identities then must figure out how to balance their ties and efforts between work (including careers, school, or self-improvement) and relationships with other people. How much time should we spend on ourselves and how much time with our families? What is the difference between a platonic and a romantic relationship? Again, the patterns established in this stage will influence the effort spent on self and others in the future.
Generativity versus stagnation	Erikson felt that by the time we reach this age, we are starting to look critically at our life path. We want to make sure that we are creating the type of life that we want for ourselves and family. We might try to seize control of our lives at this point to ensure that things go as we plan. In this stage, we try to ensure that our lives are going the way we want them to go. If they are not, we may try to change our identities or control those around us to change our lives.
Integrity versus despair	Toward the end of life, we look back at our accomplishments and decide if we are satisfied with them or not. Erikson thought that if we can see that our lives were meaningful, we can "step outside" the stress and pressures of society and offer wisdom and insight. If, however, we feel serious regret over how we lived our lives, we may fall into despair over lost opportunities.

TIP

If Freud's psychosexual stages sound out of date to you, you are not alone. Many developmental psychologists would say that Freud's stage theory might have only historical importance and it is not likely to be used in scientific research.

COGNITIVE DEVELOPMENT

Parents often focus intently on the intellectual development of their children. Intelligence is a notoriously difficult trait to assess (see Chapter 8 for more information). However, developmental researchers try to describe how children think about and evaluate the world. **Jean Piaget's** cognitive-development theory is the most famous theory of this type. However, some researchers now criticize parts of his theory and offer alternative explanations for the same behaviors.

Jean Piaget

Jean Piaget was working for **Alfred Binet**, creator of the first intelligence test, when he started to notice interesting behaviors in the children he was interviewing. Piaget noted that children of roughly the same age almost always gave similar answers to some of the questions on the intelligence test, even if the answers were wrong. He hypothesized that this was because they were all thinking in similar ways and these ways of thinking differed from the ways adults think. This hypothesis led to Piaget's theory of cognitive development. Piaget described how children viewed the world through schemata, cognitive rules we use to interpret the world. Normally, we incorporate our experiences into these existing schemata in a process called **assimilation**. Sometimes, information does not fit into or violates our schemata, so we must accommodate and change our schemata. For example, a four-year-old boy named Daniel gets a pair of cowboy boots from his parents for his birthday. He wears his cowboy boots constantly and does not see anyone else wearing them. Daniel develops a schema for cowboy boots: only little boys wear boots. Most of his experiences do not violate this schema. He sees other little boys wearing boots and assimilates this information into his schema. Then Daniel's family takes a trip to Arizona. When he gets off the plane, he sees a huge (huge to a four-year-old, at least) man wearing cowboy boots. Daniel points at the man and starts to laugh hysterically. Why is Daniel causing this scene? His schema has been violated. To Daniel, the large man is dressing like a little boy! After he stops laughing, Daniel will have to accommodate this new information and change his schema to include the fact that adults can wear cowboy boots, too. By the way, this process may repeat itself the first time Daniel sees a woman in boots!

Piaget thinks humans go through this process of schema creation, assimilation, and accommodation as we develop cognitively. His cognitive development theory describes how our thinking progresses through four stages:

Sensorimotor stage (birth to approximately two years old)

Babies start experiencing and exploring the world strictly through their senses. At the beginning of life, Piaget noted that behavior is governed by the reflexes we are born with. Soon, we start to develop our first cognitive schemata that explain the world we experience through our senses. One of the major challenges of this stage is to develop **object permanence**. Babies at first do not realize that objects continue to exist even when they are out of sensory range. When babies start to look for or somehow acknowledge that objects do exist when they cannot see them, they have object permanence.

Preoperational stage (two to approximately seven years old)

Acquiring the scheme of object permanence prepares a child to start to use symbols to represent real-world objects. This ability is the beginning of language, the most important cognitive development of this stage. We start speaking our first words and gradually learn to represent the world more completely through language. While we can refer to the world through symbols during the preoperational stage, we are still limited in the ways we can think about the relationships between objects and the characteristics of objects. Children in this stage are also **egocentric** in their thinking, since they cannot look at the world from anyone's perspective but their own.

Concrete operations (eight to approximately 12 years old)

During the concrete-operations stage, children learn to think more logically about complex relationships between different characteristics of objects. Piaget categorized children in the concrete-operations stage when they demonstrated knowledge of **concepts of conservation**, the realization that properties of objects remain the same even when their shapes change. These concepts demonstrate how the different aspects of objects are conserved even when their arrangment changes. See Table 9.1 for examples of the concepts.

Table 9.1 Concepts of Conservation

Concept	Description	How to Test
Volume	The volume of a material is conserved even if the material's container or shape changes.	Pour water into differently shaped glasses and ask if the volume of the water increased, decreased, or stayed the same.
Area	Area is conserved even if objects within that area are rearranged. Do these 2 squares have the same amount of shaded area? Do the squares ***still*** have the same amount of shaded area?	Ask a child to examine two different squares of equal area, and rearrange objects within the area in order to determine if children realize the area was conserved.
Number	The number of objects stays the same when the objects are rearranged. Does each row have the same number of circles? Now does each row have the same number of circles?	Take a few objects, let the child count them, rearrange the objects, and ask the child how many there are now. If the child counts them again, he or she does not understand conservation of number.

Formal operations (12 through adulthood)

This final stage of Piaget describes adult reasoning. Piaget theorized that not all of us reach formal operations in all areas of thought. Formal operational reasoning is abstract reasoning. We can manipulate objects and contrast ideas in our mind without physically seeing them or having real-world correlates. One example of abstract reasoning is **hypothesis testing**.

A person in Piaget's formal-operations stage can reason from a hypothesis. To test for formal-operational thought, you might ask a child, "How would you be different if you were born on a planet that had no light?" A child in the preoperational or concrete-operational stage would have trouble answering the question because no real-world model exists to fall back on. Someone in the formal-operations stage would be able to extrapolate from this hypothesis and reason that the beings on that planet might not have eyes, would have no words for color, and might exclusively rely on other senses. Also in the formal-operations stage, we gain the ability to think about the way we think; this is called metacognition. We can trace our thought processes and evaluate the effectiveness of how we solved a problem.

Criticisms of Piaget: Information-Processing Model

Many developmental psychologists still value Piaget's insights about the order in which our cognitive skills develop, but most agree that he underestimated children. Many children go through the stages faster and enter them earlier than Piaget predicted. Piaget's error may be due to the way he tested children. Some psychologists wonder if some of his tests relied too heavily on language use, thus biasing the results in favor of older children with more language skills. Other theorists wonder if development does not occur more continuously than Piaget described. Perhaps our cognitive skills develop more continuously and not in discrete stages.

The **information-processing model** is a more continuous alternative to Piaget's stage theory. Information processing points out that our abilities to memorize, interpret, and perceive gradually develop as we age rather than developing in distinct stages. For example, research shows that our attention span gradually increases as we get older. This one continuous change could explain some apparent cognitive differences Piaget attributed to different cognitive stages. Maybe children's inability to understand conservation of number has more to do with their ability to focus for long periods of time than any developing reasoning ability. Developmental researchers agree that no one has the perfect model to describe cognitive development. Future research will refine our current ideas and create models that more closely describe how our thinking changes as we mature.

MORAL DEVELOPMENT

Lawrence Kohlberg

Lawrence Kohlberg's stage theory studied a completely different aspect of human development: morality. Kohlberg wanted to describe how our ability to reason about ethical situations changed over the course of our lives. In order to do this, he asked a subject group of children to think about specific moral situations. One situation Kohlberg used is the Heinz dilemma, which describes a man named Heinz making a moral choice about whether to steal a drug he cannot afford in order to save his wife's life.

Kohlberg collected all the participants' responses and catgorized them into three levels:

Preconventional

The youngest children in Kohlberg's sample focus on making the decison most likely to avoid punishment. Their moral reasoning is limited to how the choice affects themselves. Children in the preconventional level might say that Heinz should not steal the drug because he might get caught and put into prison.

Conventional

During the next level of moral reasoning, children are able to move past personal gain or loss and look at the moral choice through others' eyes. Children in this stage make a moral choice based on how others will view them. Children learn conventional standards of what is right and wrong from their parents, peers, media, and so on. They may try to follow these standards so that other people will see them as good. Children in the conventional level might say that Heinz should steal the drug because then he could save his wife and people would think of him as a hero.

Postconventional

The last level Kohlberg describes is what we usually mean by moral reasoning. A person evaluating a moral choice using postconventional reasoning examines the rights and values involved in the choice. Kohlberg described how **self-defined ethical principles**, such as a personal conviction to uphold justice, might be involved in the reasoning in this stage. Those doing the reasoning might weigh the merit of altruism or limiting certain rights for the good of the group. For the first time, the morality of societal rules are examined rather than blindly accepted. Persons in the postconventional stage might say that Heinz should steal the drug because his wife's right to life outweighs the store owner's right to personal property.

Criticisms of Kohlberg

Some developmental psychologists challenge Kohlberg's conclusions. One researcher, **Carol Gilligan**, pointed out that Kohlberg developed the model based on the responses of boys. When girls were later tested, she continued, Kohlberg placed their responses into lower categories. Gilligan theorized that Kohlberg's assumption that boys and girls (and men and women) come to moral conclusions in the same way is incorrect. Perhaps some gender-based developmental difference occurs in how we develop our morals and ethics. According to Gilligan's research, boys have a more absolute view of what is moral while girls pay more attention to the situational factors. Boys might have moral rules that apply in every context, while girls might want to know more about the situation and relationships of the people involved before making a moral decision. Gilligan's insights about Kohlberg's theory demonstrate the importance of studying possible gender differences and how they might change as we develop. However, recent research does not support Gilligan's theory of gender differences in moral development.

GENDER AND DEVELOPMENT

Another area of developmental research focuses on gender issues. Specifically, researchers are interested in how we develop our ideas about what it means to be male and female and in developmental differences between genders.

Different cultures encourage different gender roles, which are behaviors that a culture associates with a gender. Gender roles vary widely between cultures. A behavior considered feminine in one culture, such as holding hands with a friend, might be considered masculine or not gender specific in another. Different psychological perspectives provide different theories that try to explain how gender roles develop.

Biopsychological (neuropsychological) theory

Biopsychogical psychologists concentrate on the nature element in the nature/nurture combination that produces our gender role. Children learn (and are often very curious about!) the obvious biological differences between the sexes. However, biopsychologists look for more subtle biological gender differences. For the purposes of this book, going into extensive detail about all the differences between male and female brains is unnecessary. For the AP test, you should know that studies demonstrate that these differences do exist. One of the most significant findings is that, on average, women have larger corpus callosums (see Fig. 3.3, Chapter 3) than men. Theoretically, this difference may affect how the right and left hemispheres communicate and coordinate tasks.

Freud's Psychosexual Stages	Erikson's Psychosocial Stages	Piaget's Cognitive Development Stages	Kohlberg's Moral Development Stages
Oral stage (approximately birth to 1.5 years old)	Trust versus mistrust (approximately birth to 1 year old)	Sensorimotor (approximately birth to 2 years old)	Preconventional (approximately birth to 9 years old)
Anal stage (approximately 1.5 to 3 years old)	Autonomy versus shame/doubt (approximately 1 to 3 years old)	Preoperational (approximately 2 to 7 years old)	
Phallic stage (approximately 3 to 6 years old)	Initiative versus guilt (approximately 3 to 6 years old)		
Latency stage (approximately 6 years old to puberty)	Industry versus inferiority (approximately 6 years old to early adolescents)	Concrete operations (approximately 7 to 12 years old)	Conventional (approximately 10 years old through early adolesence)
Genital stage (approximately puberty and older)	Identity versus role confusion (approximately late adolescents into the 20s)	Formal operations (approximately 12 through adulthood)	Postconventional (approximately late adolesence through adulthood)
	Intimacy versus isolation (approximately the 20s through early 40s)		
	Generativity versus stagnation (approximately 40s through 60s)		
	Integrity versus despair (approximately 60s and older)		

Psychoanalytic theory

As noted in Chapter 1 in the section about psychological perspectives, many of Freud's psychodynamic ideas are difficult to verify with research. However, his ideas are widely known and often referenced in popular media, so they are worth being familiar with.

For example, Freud thought that boys and girls develop their gender identities because they realize, unconsciously, that they can't compete with their same-sex parent for the affections of the opposite sex parent. This is a compelling idea, and the Oedipus and Electra complex have been used in many movies and novels, but they are impossible to study experimentally. As they work with patients, modern clinical psychologists aren't likely to use these and other ideas from Freud.

Social-cognitive theory

Social and cognitive psychologists concentrate on the effects society and our own thoughts about gender have on role development. Social psychologists look at how we react to boys and girls differently. For example, boys are more often encouraged in rough physical play than are girls. Cognitive psychologists focus on the internal interpretations we make about the gender message we get from our environment. **Gender schema** theory explains that we internalize messages about gender into cognitive rules about how each gender should behave. If a girl sees that her little brother is encouraged to wrestle with their father, she creates a rule governing how boys and girls should play.

PRACTICE QUESTIONS

Directions: Each of the questions or incomplete statements below is followed by five suggested answers or completions. Select the one that is best in each case.

1. Some researchers consider developmental psychology an applied research topic because
   (A) it is more easily applied to people's lives than research such as behaviorism.
   (B) researchers apply findings and theories from other areas of psychology to the specific topic of human development.
   (C) it is more commonly studied by a graduate student rather than an undergraduate because of the applications for other research.
   (D) doing original research in this area is difficult, so most of the research is about application.
   (E) pure research is difficult to gain support for, especially when a researcher needs to recruit children as participants.

2. You read in your philosophy class textbook that humans are born "tabula rasa" or "blank slates." As a student of psychology, which of the following responses would you have?
   (A) The statement is incorrect. Humans may be born without reflexes and instincts, but we are born with the ability to learn them.
   (B) The statement is correct. Humans are born without instincts or other mechanisms in place to help us survive.
   (C) The statement is correct. Humans are born with a certain number of neurons, but most develop later as we learn.
   (D) The statement is incorrect. Humans are born with a set of reflexes that help us survive.
   (E) The statement is impossible to prove since we cannot infer what babies know or do not know due to their lack of language.

3. Which of the following statements is most true about how a newborn's senses function?
   (A) A newborn's senses function the same as an adult's since the sensory apparatus develops in the womb.
   (B) All of our senses function normally when we are newborns except taste due to lack of stimulation in the womb.
   (C) All of our senses function normally when we are newborns except touch due to lack of stimulation in the womb.
   (D) A newborn's senses function at a very low level but develop very quickly with experience.
   (E) Most senses function normally, but sight develops slowly with experience.

4. Most prenatal influences on humans are genetic or hormonal in origin except for
   (A) teratogens.
   (B) stress on the mother.
   (C) parents' level of education about fetal development.
   (D) family history of mental illness.
   (E) operant conditioning occurring before birth.

5. Parental involvement can have dramatic effects on all the following human traits except
   (A) intelligence.
   (B) reading ability.
   (C) self-esteem.
   (D) motor development.
   (E) emotional development.

6. A principal difference between a longitudinal study and a cross-sectional study is the
   (A) number of participants involved.
   (B) developmental stage of the participants.
   (C) time span of the study.
   (D) statistical methods employed to evaluate the data.
   (E) sampling method used to choose participants.

7. Harlow's experiments with substitute mothers made of wire demonstrated the importance of what aspect of nurturing?
   (A) feeding
   (B) responsiveness to needs
   (C) imprinting
   (D) touch
   (E) stranger anxiety

8. According to research, the most advantageous parenting style for children's development is
   (A) authoritarian, because children learn boundaries quickly and appreciate consistency.
   (B) permissive, because young children need to explore the environment more than they need guidelines for behavior.
   (C) authoritarian, because it combines the best elements of the permissive and authoritative styles.
   (D) securely attached, because children are confident parents will meet their needs.
   (E) authoritative, because children have boundaries that are reasonable and justified.

9. A major difference between the psychoanalytic stage theories (Freud and Erikson) and the more cognitive or experiential stage theories (Piaget and Kohlberg) is
   (A) the psychoanalytic theories are less empirical.
   (B) the psychoanalytic theories were based exclusively on data from children with developmental disorders.
   (C) Freud and Erikson studied only young children, while Piaget and Kohlberg studied the full range of development.
   (D) only the psychoanalytic theories take parental effects into account.
   (E) the psychoanalytic theories are continuous, the others are discontinuous.

10. You have a cousin named Holden who flunked out of three expensive private schools and was arrested for wandering the streets of New York using his parents' credit card. Holden is intelligent but cannot seem to get motivated toward any career. What conflict would Erikson say Holden is struggling with?
   (A) autonomy versus authority
   (B) identity versus role confusion
   (C) integrity versus despair
   (D) industry versus inferiority
   (E) trust versus isolation

11. In which stage of cognitive development do infants learn object permanence?
   (A) preoperational
   (B) formal-operations
   (C) autonomy
   (D) sensorimotor
   (E) conventional

12. According to Erikson's theory, adolescents are most primarily concerned in a search for
   (A) career.
   (B) identity.
   (C) affection.
   (D) autonomy.
   (E) archetypes.

13. The ability to generate several alternate hypotheses in order to explain a phenomenon demonstrates cognition in which of the following Piagetian stages?
   (A) operational
   (B) hypothetical-operations
   (C) syllogistic
   (D) formal-operations
   (E) abstract reasoning

14. Which of the following attachment styles did Mary Ainsworth find most often in her research (in about 66 percent of the cases she studied)?

    (A) avoidant
    (B) authoritarian
    (C) secure
    (D) anxious/ambivalent
    (E) authoritative

15. Which of the following is the correct term for a mental rule Piaget said we use to interpret our environment?

    (A) schema
    (B) syllogism
    (C) assimilation
    (D) accommodation
    (E) hypothesis

ANSWER KEY

1. **B**
2. **D**
3. **E**
4. **A**
5. **D**
6. **C**
7. **D**
8. **E**
9. **A**
10. **B**
11. **D**
12. **B**
13. **D**
14. **C**
15. **A**

ANSWERS EXPLAINED

1. **(B)** Developmental psychology can be called an applied topic because many findings from other areas are applied to the topic of maturation. Many topics such as behaviorism are easily applied to our lives. It is studied at both the graduate and undergraduate levels, many original research studies are done, and pure research is still well supported even when it involves children.

2. **(D)** Humans are born with reflexes that help us nurse and find our mother. We are born with all the neurons we will ever have, and we can observe babies' behavior and infer what reflexes and abilities babies have.

3. **(E)** Most of our senses function at birth, except for sight, which develops quickly as we mature. Lack of stimulation seems to have little effect on touch and taste, and most senses function at a normal level, not a low one.

4. **(A)** Teratogens are chemicals that the mother is exposed to in the environment, making them environmental influences. The rest of the answers either are not environmental in origin or do not have proven effects on a fetus.

5. **(D)** Motor development is not dramatically affected by parental involvement or encouragement since the rate of development is controlled mostly by development of the neurons in the cerebellum. The other answers are traits that might be greatly affected by parental involvement.

6. **(C)** Longitudinal studies take place over a number of years, while cross-sectional studies do not. The rest of the answers are not necessarily differences between the two types of studies.

7. **(D)** The monkeys in Harlow's experiment ran to the soft mother when frightened, demonstrating the importance of a mother's touch in attachment. The soft mothers did not feed the infant monkeys or (obviously) respond more to their needs. Stranger anxiety was present in the experiment but is not an important aspect of nurturing.

8. **(E)** The authoritative parenting style has been shown as the most advantageous in studies. The rest of the answers are incorrect because they identify the incorrect parenting style. Secure attachment is not a parenting style.

9. **(A)** The psychoanalytic theories are based on anecdotal evidence and personal inference rather than empirical research methods.

10. **(B)** Holden's inability to stay in school and decide about goals indicates a search for identity, according to Erikson.

11. **(D)** Infants learn object permanence during the sensorimotor stage, not the preoperational or formal-operations stages. Choices C and E are not stages in Piaget's theory of cognitive development.

12. **(B)** Erikson's theory places adolescents into the identity versus role confusion stage. Adolescents would very possibly be concerned with the other factors listed in the choices, but Erikson's theory identifies identity as the area of primary concern.

13. **(D)** Creating hypotheses demonstrates formal operational thought. The other choices are not stages in Piaget's theory.

14. **(C)** Most of the infants Ainsworth studied demonstrated secure attachments, rather than anxious/ambivalent or avoidant attachments. The terms authoritarian and authoritative refer to parenting styles, not attachment theory.

15. **(A)** A schema is a mental rule we use to interpret our environment. Assimilation and accommodation are steps in the process of learning described by Piaget. We first try to assimilate new information into an existing schema, then accommodate the new information by changing the schema if we need to. A syllogism is a type of logical argument, and a hypothesis is an explanation for an environmental event.

UNIT 7

Motivation, Emotion, and Personality

This unit combines several chapters in the textbook you use in your AP Psychology class, even though the connections between those chapters may not be immediately obvious. The unit starts with an overview of several theories about what motivates humans to do what we do. Specific examples of motivation are discussed, then the focus shifts to theories about emotion and the impacts of stress. Finally, personality theories are discussed, which is one of the historically oldest and most comprehensive research topic in psychology. You will most likely find the content in this unit represented covered in several chapters: motivation, emotion, and personality.

10 Motivation and Emotion

Key Terms

- Motivations
- Instincts
- Drive reduction theory
- Need
- Drive
- Primary drives
- Secondary drives
- Homeostasis
- Arousal theory
- Yerkes-Dodson law
- Opponent-process theory of motivation
- Incentives
- Maslow's hierarchy of needs
- Self-actualization
- Lateral hypothalamus
- Ventromedial hypothalamus
- Set-point theory
- Bulimia
- Anorexia
- Obesity
- Achievement motivation
- Extrinsic motivators
- Intrinsic motivators
- Management theory
- Approach-approach conflict
- Avoidance-avoidance conflict
- Approach-avoidance conflict
- James-Lange theory of emotion
- Cannon-Bard theory of emotion
- Two-factor theory
- General adaptation syndrome (GAS)

Key People

- Charles Darwin
- Abraham Maslow
- William Masters
- Virginia Johnson
- Alfred Kinsey
- William James
- Carl Lange
- Walter Cannon
- Philip Bard
- Stanley Schachter
- Thomas Holmes
- Richard Rahe
- Hans Selye

OVERVIEW

I often ask students at the beginning of my psychology class why they wanted to take this course. One of the most common replies is "Because I wanted to figure out why people do what they do." Motivation theories address this question directly. Motivations are feelings or ideas that cause us to act toward a goal. Some motivations are obvious and conscious, but others are more subtle. In this chapter, we will review the connections between physiology and motivation, general motivation theories, and specific examples of motivation in hunger and sex. Finally, we will review the psychological research and theories about emotion and stress that are closely related to motivation theory.

THEORIES OF MOTIVATION

If you have pets, you know that different animals are born with instincts, which are automatic behaviors performed in response to specific stimuli. Your cat did not have to learn how to clean itself, it was born with this instinct. When **Charles Darwin's** theory of natural selection was published, many psychologists unsuccessfully tried to explain all human behaviors through instincts. Many ethologists, researchers who study animal behavior in a natural environment, examine the role evolution plays in human thought and behavior. They look for the evolutionary advantages of persistent human behaviors. While psychologists debate whether humans are born with any instincts, they agree that our behavior is also motivated by other biological and psychological factors.

Drive Reduction Theory

One early theory about how our physiology motivates us was drive reduction theory, the theory that our behavior is motivated by biological needs. A need is one of our requirements for survival, such as food, water, or shelter. A drive is our impulse to act in a way that satisfies this need. If, for example, you wake up late and skip breakfast, your body has a need for food that is not satisfied. This need creates a drive, hunger, and this drive causes you to get a candy bar from the vending machines in order to satisfy the need. Our body seeks **homeostasis**, a balanced internal state. When we are out of homeostasis, we have a need that creates a drive. Drives can be categorized in two ways: primary drives and secondary drives. **Primary drives** are biological needs, like thirst. **Secondary drives** are learned drives. For instance, we learn that resources like money can get us food and water to satisfy our primary drives. However, **drive reduction theory** cannot explain all our motivations. Sometimes, we are motivated to perform behaviors that do not seem connected with any need or drive, primary or secondary. One of my cousins has always been motivated by speed and excitement. He made sure his first car was faster than anyone else's, he went into the Air Force for the opportunity to fly the fastest planes in the world, and he liked to drag race motorcycles in amateur races. These activities can be risky and seem to violate biological explanations for motivation. Why does anyone go skydiving or ride a roller coaster? Where do these motivations come from?

Arousal Theory

Some motivations that seem to violate biological theories of motivation can be explained by arousal theory, which states that we seek an optimum level of excitement or arousal. This arousal level can be measured by different physiological tests. Each of us has a different need for excitement or arousal, and we are motivated by activities that will help us achieve this level. People with high optimum levels of arousal might be drawn to high-excitement behaviors, while the rest of us are satisfied with less exciting and less risky activities. In general, most of us perform best with an optimum level of arousal, although this varies with different activities. We might perform well at an easy task with a very high level of arousal, but the same high level of arousal would prevent us from performing well on a difficult task (this concept is similar to **social facilitation**, see Chapter 14). This relationship is called the **Yerkes-Dodson law** after the researchers who first investigated the concept in animals, and is graphed in Figure 10.1.

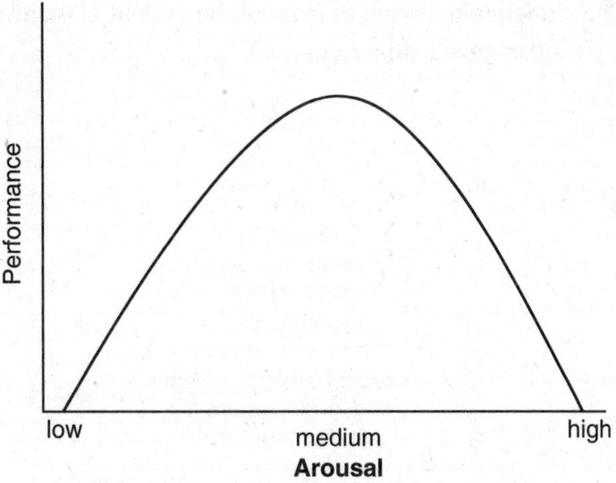

Figure 10.1 The Yerkes-Dodson law.

Another theory of motivation, which is similar in some ways to the arousal theory, is the opponent-process theory of motivation. This theory is often used to explain addictive behaviors. The theory states that people are usually at a normal, or **baseline**, state. We might perform an act that moves us from the baseline state, such as smoking a cigarette. These acts may be initially pleasurable (because nicotine is a stimulant and it makes us feel a good "buzz"), but the theory states that we eventually feel an **opponent process**, meaning a motivation to return to our baseline, neutral state. Smokers may tire of the jittery feeling they get when smoking and try to reduce the number of cigarettes they smoke. But with physically addictive substances, we also experience **withdrawal** (see Chaper 4, "States of Consciousness"), and the discomfort of the withdrawal state moves us away from our neutral baseline. A smoker might feel uncomfortable without nicotine in her or his system. So this state creates a motivation to return to the baseline state of feeling all right, creating a desire to smoke more cigarettes to return to a state of feeling normal.

Incentive Theory

Sometimes, behavior is not pushed by a need, it is pulled by a desire. **Incentives** are stimuli that we are drawn to due to learning. We learn to associate some stimuli with rewards and others with punishment, and we are motivated to seek the rewards. For example, you may learn that studying with friends is fun but does not produce the desired results around test time, so you are motivated to study alone to get the reward of a good test score.

Maslow's Hierarchy of Needs

Psychologist **Abraham Maslow** pointed out that not all needs are created equal. He described a hierarchy of needs (see Fig. 10.2) that predicts which needs we will be motivated to satisfy first. Maslow predicted that we will act to satisfy biological needs like survival and safety. Then we will act to satisfy our emotional needs like love and self-esteem. Finally, once the previous goals have been met, we will want to attain our life goals like satisfaction and **self-actualization**, a need to fulfill our unique potential as a person. The more basic needs must be met before moving on to the next level. Maslow's theory makes intuitive sense, but some common human behaviors seem to violate the theory. How would the hierarchy of needs explain a student going without heat or a phone in her or his apartment in order to pay for books for school? The student who stood in front of the tank in Tiananmen Square was definitely motivated to put other needs above survival.

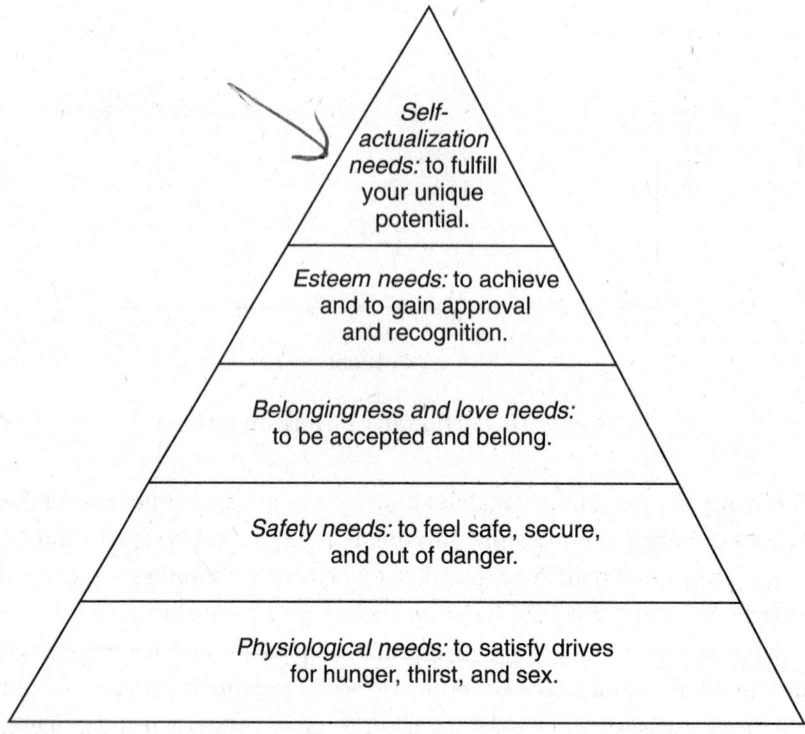

Figure 10.2 Maslow's hierarchy of needs.

HUNGER MOTIVATION

Some human behaviors appear to be deceptively simple. Why do we become hungry? Our bodies need food! However, we know the relationship is not that simple. Some people eat even when their body has enough food, and some people do not eat when their body needs nourishment. Even a seemingly simple motivation such as hunger involves several biological, psychological, and social factors.

Biological Basis of Hunger

Several biological cues create a feeling of hunger. Researchers inserted balloons into participants' stomachs. By inflating and deflating the balloons, they were able to determine that we report feeling hungry when our stomach is empty and contracts and full when our stomach feels full.

Our brain also plays a role in the feeling of hunger. The hypothalamus (see Fig. 3.3, page 66) monitors and helps to control body chemistry (including the ratio of glucose and insulin) and makes us feel hungry when we need to eat. Electric stimulation of animals' brains indicates that different parts of the hypothalamus act in opposition to controlling hunger. The **lateral** hypothalamus (hunger center), when stimulated, causes the animal to eat. Destruction of this area destroys hunger, and the animal will starve to death unless forced to eat. Another part of the hypothalamus, the **ventromedial** hypothalamus (satiety center), causes the animal to stop eating when it is stimulated. If this area is destroyed, the animal will eat and gain more and more weight unless it is deprived of food. If the hypothalamus functions normally, these two areas oppose each other and signal impulses to eat and stop eating at appropriate times.

Set-point theory describes how the hypothalamus might decide what impulse to send. This theory states that the hypothalamus wants to maintain a certain optimum body weight. When we drop below that weight, the hypothalamus tells us we should eat and lowers our **metabolic rate**—how quickly our body uses energy. The hypothalamus tells us to stop eating when that set point is reached and raises our metabolic rate to burn any excess food. Not all researchers agree that we have a set point for weight, however. They might point to psychological factors and believe that weight maintenance has more to do with learning and cognition than with the hypothalamus. In addition, the brain monitors the levels of insulin (released by the liver) and glucose, and this balance also influences our perception of hunger.

Psychological Factors in Hunger Motivation

So far, our drive to eat appears to be governed strictly by our physiology. However, some of the reasons we get hungry have little to do with our brain and body chemistry. For example, research indicates that some of us (called **externals**) are more motivated to eat by external food cues, such as attractiveness or availability of food. Others, **internals**, are less affected by the presence and presentation of food and respond more often to internal hunger cues. Everyone responds to both types of cues but to greater or lesser extents. These and other factors in eating might be learned. The **Garcia effect**, in particular, can drastically affect what foods make us hungry. You can probably think of a particular food that brings back unpleasant memories of being sick. If you eat hot dogs and then happen to get nauseous, hot dogs will probably be unappetizing to you even if you know the hot dogs did not cause your sickness. This is caused by the Garcia effect and occurs whenever nausea is paired with either food or drink. (See Chapter 6 for more information about learned taste aversions and other examples of classical conditioning.)

Culture and background affect our food preferences. The foods we are raised with are most likely the foods we find most appetizing, although new preferences are acquired. Where I live in Nebraska, we eat a traditional Czechoslovakian sandwich called a *runza*, which is spiced beef and cabbage inside a bread pocket. Some of my friends who now live in other parts of the country have cravings for *runza*, but I am willing to bet that it sounds quite unappetizing to some of you reading this. We usually prefer foods our family, region, and culture prefer because those are the foods we learned to like.

Eating Disorders

Research into hunger motivations has at least one very important practical application—eating disorders. Many researchers seek to apply what we know about hunger and eating to treat individuals with harmful eating patterns.

The following lists the three most common eating disorders:

Bulimia	**Bulimics eat large amounts of food in a short period of time (binging) and then get rid of the food (purging) by vomiting, excessive exercise, or the use of laxatives. Bulimics are obsessed with food and their weight. The majority of bulimics are women.**
Anorexia nervosa	**Anorexics starve themselves to below 85 percent of their normal body weight and refuse to eat due to their obsession with weight. The vast majority of anorexics are women.**

TIP

The key difference between an anorexic and a bulimic is their weight. People who suffer from both disorders tend to be obsessed with food, and some anorexics even binge and purge. However, while anorexics are at least 15 percent below the typical weight of someone their age and size, bulimics' weight tends to be average or even slightly above.

Many researchers are investigating the causes of eating disorders. Different cultures have drastically different rates of eating disorders, possibly due to the emphasis on body weight emphasized in the culture. Eating disorder rates are highest in the United States, possibly for this reason. Research also identifies a family history of eating disorders as a risk actor, indicating a potential genetic component. Researchers agree that eating disorders are influenced by a complex set of factors, and are not merely a lack of willpower about food.

SEXUAL MOTIVATION

Sexual motivations are vital for the continuation of any species. One of the primary tasks for most living organisms is reproduction. Since humans are one of the most complex living organisms, our sexual motivations are correspondingly complex. Like hunger, sex is motivated by both biological and psychological factors.

Sexual Response Cycle

The famous lab studies done by **William Masters** and **Virginia Johnson** documented the sexual response cycle in men and women. Our sexual response progresses through four stages:

Initial excitement	Genital areas become engorged with blood, penis becomes erect, clitoris swells, respiration and heart rate increase.
Plateau phase	Respiration and heart rate continue at an elevated level, genitals secrete fluids in preparation for coitus.
Orgasm	Rhythmic genital contractions that may help conception, respiration, and heart rate increase further, males ejaculate, often accompanied by a pleasurable euphoria.
Resolution phase	Respiration and heart rate return to normal resting states, men experience a refractory period—a time period that must elapse before another orgasm. However, women do not have a similar refractory period and can repeat the cycle immediately.

Psychological Factors in Sexual Motivation

Unlike many animals, our sexual desire is not motivated strictly by hormones. Many studies demonstrate that sexual motivation is controlled to a great extent by psychological rather than biological sources. Sexual desire can be present even when the capability to have sex is lost. Accident victims who lose the ability to have sex still have sexual desires. Erotic material can inspire sexual feelings and physiological responses in men and women, including elevated levels of hormones. The interaction between our physiology and psychology creates the myriad of sexual desires we see in society and ourselves.

Sexual Orientation

As attention and controversy about sexual-orientation issues increase, so does research about homosexuality. Researchers (like **Alfred Kinsey**, who documented the variety of human sexual behaviors in the famous Kinsey Reports) have been able to dispel some common myths about homosexuality. Studies show that homosexuality is not related to traumatic childhood experiences, parenting styles, the quality of relationships with parents, masculinity or femininity, or whether we are raised by heterosexual or homosexual parents. Although some researchers believe environmental influences probably affect sexual orientation, these factors have not yet been identified.

Researchers have identified possible biological influences, however. Some studies indicate that specific brain structures might differ in size in brains of homosexuals when compared with the same structures in heterosexuals. Twin studies indicate a genetic influence on sexual orientation since a twin is much more likely to be gay if his or her identical twin is gay. Some researchers theorize that hormones in the womb might change brain structure and influence sexual orientation. Since 3 to 10 percent (estimates vary) of the population worldwide is homosexual, research in this area will certainly continue, and the causes of sexual orientations will become more clear.

SOCIAL MOTIVATION

So far, we have described the research regarding the motivations behind some relatively simple human behaviors such as eating and sex. What motivates the more complicated behaviors, such as taking the AP psychology exam? Your attitudes and goals, the society you live in, and the people you surround yourself with also affect what you are motivated to do.

Achievement Motivation

Achievement motivation is one theory that tries to explain the motivations behind these more complex behaviors. Achievement motivation examines our desires to master complex tasks and knowledge and to reach personal goals. Humans (and some other animals) seem to be motivated to figure out our world and master skills, sometimes regardless of the benefits of the skills or knowledge.

Studies in achievement motivation find that some people have high achievement motivation and consistently feel motivated to challenge themselves more than do other people. They always set the bar a little higher and seek greater challenges. Obviously, this varies not only from person to person but from activity to activity. Not many people are motivated to achieve in every aspect of life, which is fortunate because we don't have time to pursue every possible interest. However, studies that measure achievement motivation do indicate a higher-than-average achievement motivation in some people.

TIP

Achievement motivation is different than optimum arousal. Achievement motivation involves meeting personal goals and acquiring new knowledge or skills. Optimum arousal indicates the general level of arousal a person is motivated to seek, whether or not the arousal is productive in meeting a goal. The concepts might overlap in a person. (For example, a person with high achievement motivation might also have a high optimum level of arousal.) However, the concepts refer to different aspects of motivation.

Extrinsic/Intrinsic Motivation

Another way to think about the social factors that influence motivation is by dividing them into extrinsic and intrinsic motivations. **Extrinsic motivators** are rewards that we get for accomplishments from outside ourselves (for example, grades, salary, and so on). **Intrinsic motivators** are rewards we get internally, such as enjoyment or satisfaction. Think about your own motives regarding the AP psychology exam. Are you internally or externally motivated or both? Are you taking the test to get the grade and possible college credit (external) or are you internally motivated to gain the knowledge and challenge yourself by taking a difficult test? Knowing what type of motivation an individual responds best to can give managers and other leaders insight into what strategies will be most effective. Psychologists working with people managing work groups (in government, business, or other areas) might test or evaluate group members for intrinsic or extrinsic motivation and try to alter group policies accordingly. Studies show that if we want an advantageous behavior to continue, intrinsic motivation is most effective. Extrinsic motivations are very effective for a short period of time. Inevitably, though, the extrinsic motivations end and so will the desired behavior unless some intrinsic motivation continues to motivate the behavior.

Management Theory

Some research into how managers behave is closely related to extrinsic/intrinsic motivation. Studies of management styles show two basic attitudes that affect how managers do their jobs:

Theory X	Managers believe that employees will work only if rewarded with benefits or threatened with punishment.
Theory Y	Managers believe that employees are internally motivated to do good work and policies should encourage this internal motive.

Cross-cultural studies show the benefits of moving from a theory X attitude about employees to a theory Y attitude. Some companies hire consultants from other countries to teach their managers how to promote intrinsic motivation in employees.

When Motives Conflict

Sometimes what you want to do in a situation is clear to you, but at other times you no doubt find yourself conflicted about what choice to make. Psychologists discuss four major types of motivational conflicts. The first, named an **approach-approach conflict**, occurs when you must choose between two desirable outcomes. For instance, imagine that for Spring Break one of your friends invites you to spend the week in Puerto Rico and another asks you to go to San Francisco. Assuming that both choices appeal to you, you have a conflict because you can only do one. Another type of conflict, an **avoidance-avoidance conflict**, occurs when you must choose between two unattractive outcomes. If, one weekend, your parents were to give you a choice between staying home and cleaning out the garage or going on a family trip to visit some distant relatives, you might experience an avoidance-avoidance conflict. An **approach-avoidance conflict** exists when one event or goal has both attractive and unattractive features. If you were lactose-intolerant, an ice-cream cone would present such a conflict; the taste of the ice cream is appealing but its effects on you are not. Finally, people experience **multiple approach-avoidance conflicts**. In these, you must choose between two or more things, each of which has both desirable and undesirable features. You may well face such a conflict in choosing which college to attend. Of the schools at which you have been accepted, University A is the best academically, but you do not like its location. University B is close to your family and boyfriend or girlfriend but you would like to go someplace with better weather. University C has the best psychology department (hopefully one of your favorite subjects!), but you visit the campus and find it less than attractive.

THEORIES ABOUT EMOTION

Our emotional state is closely related to our motivation. In fact, imagining one without the other is difficult. Can you imagine wanting to do a behavior without an accompanying feeling about the action? Emotion influences motivation, and motivation influences emotion. Psychologists investigate emotional states and create theories that try to explain our emotional experiences.

James-Lange Versus Cannon-Bard

One of the earliest theories about emotion was put forth by **William James** and **Carl Lange**. They theorized that we feel emotion because of biological changes caused by stress. So when the big bad wolf jumps out of the woods, Little Red Riding Hood's heart races, and this physiological change causes her to feel afraid.

Walter Cannon and **Philip Bard** doubted this order of events. They demonstrated that similar physiological changes correspond with drastically different emotional states. When Little Red Riding Hood's heart races, how does she know if she feels afraid, in love, embarrassed, or merely joyful? They theorized that the biological change and the cognitive awareness of the emotional state occur simultaneously. Cannon thought the thalamus is responsible for both the biological change and the cognitive awareness of emotions. Cannon believed that when the thalamus receives information about our environment, it sends signals simultaneously to our cortex and to our autonomic nervous system, creating the awareness of emotion and the physiological change at the same time. Recent research shows Cannon overestimated the role of the thalamus in this process. Many other brain structures, such as the amygdala, are also involved.

TIP

The James-Lange theory is mentioned for historical purposes. Current theories about emotion demonstrate that while biological changes are involved in emotions, they are not the sole cause of them.

Two-Factor Theory

Stanley Schachter's two-factor theory explains emotional experiences in a more complete way than either the James-Lange or Cannon-Bard theories do. Schachter pointed out that both our physical responses and our cognitive labels (our mental interpretations) combine to cause any particular emotional response. So, to continue the previous example, Little Red Riding Hood's emotional response depends on both her heart racing and her cognitive label of the event as being scary. Schachter showed that people who are already physiologically aroused experience more intense emotions than unaroused people when both groups are exposed to the same stimuli. For example, if your heart rate is already elevated after a quick jog, you will report being more frightened by a sudden surprise than you would if you got a surprise in a resting state. Two-factor theory demonstrates that emotion depends on the interaction between two factors, biology and cognition.

NONVERBAL EXPRESSIONS OF EMOTION

Many psychologists researching emotions find that the ways we express emotion nonverbally (through facial expressions, etc.) are universal. No matter what culture we grew up in, we are likely to use the same facial expressions for basic emotions like happiness, sadness, anger, disgust, surprise, and fear. Researchers establish this by showing pictures of people experiencing these emotions to people from different cultures and asking them to label the emotions. Most people from cultures around the world are able to label these facial expressions very accurately. This area of research (sometimes called sociobiology) indicates that the facial expressions we make for basic emotions may be an innate part of our physiological makeup.

STRESS

You may have noticed that many of the examples used to describe emotional theories involved stressful experiences. Stress and emotion are intimately connected concepts. Psychologists study stress not only to further our understanding of motivation and emotion but also to help us with problems caused by stress. The term stress can refer to either certain life events (**stressors**) or how we react to these changes in the environment (**stress reactions**). Studies try to describe our reactions to stress and identify factors that influence how we react to stressors.

Measuring Stress

Psychologists **Thomas Holmes** and **Richard Rahe** designed one of the first instruments to measure stress. Their social readjustment rating scale (SRRS) measured stress using life-change units (LCUs). A person taking the SRRS reported changes in her or his life, such as selling a home or changing jobs. Different changes in life were assigned different LCUs; making a career change would be counted as more LCUs than moving to a new apartment. Any major life change increases the score on the SRRS. An event usually considered to be positive, like getting married, counts for as many or more LCUs as a negative event like being fired. A person who scored very high on the SRRS is more likely to have stress-related diseases than a person with a low score. Other researchers have designed more sophisticated measures of stress that take into account individual perceptions of how stressful events are and whether the stresses are pleasant or unpleasant. These more precise measures of stress show an even higher correlation with disease than the original stress measures did.

Selye's General Adaptation Syndrome

Hans Selye's general adaptation syndrome (GAS) describes the general response humans and other animals have to a stressful event. Our response pattern to many different physical and emotional stresses is very consistent. Selye's GAS theory describes the following stages:

Alarm reaction	Heart rate increases, blood is diverted away from other body functions to muscles needed to react. The organism readies itself to meet the challenge through activation of the sympathetic nervous system.
Resistance	The body remains physiologically ready (high heart rate, and so on). Hormones are released to maintain this state of readiness. If the resistance stage lasts too long, the body can deplete its resources.
Exhaustion	The parasympathetic nervous system returns our physiological state to normal. We can be more vulnerable to disease in this stage especially if our resources were depleted by an extended resistance stage.

Selye's model explains some of the documented problems associated with extended periods of stress. Excessive stress can contribute to both physical diseases, such as some forms of ulcers and heart conditions, and emotional difficulties, such as depression. Our bodies can remain ready for a challenge only so long before our resources are depleted and we are vulnerable to disease due to exhaustion.

Perceived Control

Various studies show that a perceived lack of control over events exacerbates the harmful effects of stress. Rats given control over the duration of electric shocks are less likely to get ulcers than rats without this control even if both groups of rats receive the same amount of shock overall. A patient given control over the flow of morphine will report better pain control than a patient given mandated levels of morphine, even though both patients get the same amount of morphine overall. Control over events tends to lessen stress, while a perceived lack of control generally makes the event more stressful.

PRACTICE QUESTIONS

Directions: Each of the questions or incomplete statements below is followed by five suggested answers or completions. Select the one that is best in each case.

1. How would drive reduction theory explain a person accepting a new job with a higher salary but that requires more work and responsibility?
   (A) Money is a more powerful incentive for this individual than free time.
   (B) This person seeks a higher activity level and takes the job in order to satisfy this drive.
   (C) For this person, money is a higher-level need than free time.
   (D) The person takes the job to satisfy the secondary drive of increased salary.
   (E) Humans instinctively seek greater resources and control over their environment.

2. Which aspects of hunger are controlled by the lateral and ventromedial hypothalamus?
   (A) contraction and expansion of the stomach, indicating too much or too little food
   (B) body temperature and desire to eat
   (C) desire to eat and physiological processes needed for eating and digestion (such as salivation)
   (D) the binge and purge cycle in bulimics
   (E) the desire to eat and the feeling of satiety, or fullness, that makes us stop eating

3. All of the following are identified by researchers as important factors in the causes of eating disorders EXCEPT
   (A) cultural attitude toward weight.
   (B) lack of willpower.
   (C) genetic tendencies.
   (D) family history of eating disorders.
   (E) food obsessions.

4. The Yerkes-Dodson law predicts that most people would perform an easy task best if they are at a
   (A) high level of arousal.
   (B) low level of arousal.
   (C) baseline state.
   (D) level of self-actualization.
   (E) state of homeostasis.

5. What is the principal difference between how achievement motivation theory and arousal theory explain human motivation?
   (A) Achievement motivation is a specific example of arousal motivation.
   (B) Arousal theory describes the optimum level of general arousal an individual seeks, while achievement motivation describes what type of goals the individual is motivated to achieve.
   (C) Arousal theory describes motivation by referring to stages in our responses to stress (the general adaptation syndrome), while achievement motivation is not used to describe motivation due to stress.
   (D) A person with a low optimum level of arousal according to arousal theory would have a high achievement motivation.
   (E) Arousal theory is an older, outdated precursor to achievement motivation theory.

6. Which of the following are reasons why intrinsic motivation might be more advantageous than extrinsic motivation?
   (A) Intrinsic motivation might be more enduring since extrinsic motivations are usually temporary.
   (B) Intrinsic motivations are easier and more convenient to provide.
   (C) Intrinsic motivations are higher on Maslow's hierarchy of needs, so we are motivated to meet them before extrinsic needs.
   (D) Intrinsic motivations are more likely to be primary drives. Extrinsic motivations are secondary drives.
   (E) Intrinsic motivations are more effective with a wider range of individuals.

7. Which sentence most closely describes the difference between theory X and theory Y types of management?
   (A) Theory X managers are more active in work groups. Theory Y managers are more hands-off, letting groups work out problems on their own.
   (B) The management theories differ in regard to what tasks they delegate to workers.
   (C) Theory Y managers regard employees as intrinsically motivated. Theory X managers see them as extrinsically motivated.
   (D) Management theory X is dominant in collectivist cultures. Theory Y is more prevalent in individualist cultures.
   (E) Theory Y is used with workers who have high optimum levels of arousal. Theory X is used with those whose arousal levels are low.

8. What does Schachter's two-factor theory state about the relationship between emotion and physiological reaction?
   (A) Emotions are caused by physiological reactions. For example, we feel excited because our heart begins to race.
   (B) Physiological reactions are caused by emotions. For example, our experience of fear causes our breathing rate to increase.
   (C) A combination of physiological reactions and our cognitive interpretation of an event produces emotion.
   (D) Physiological reactions and emotional response occur simultaneously.
   (E) Cognitive emotions occur independently of physiological states and are unrelated.

9. Excessive time spent in the resistance phase of Selye's general adaptation syndrome can contribute to

   (A) increased time needed to adapt to new emotional situations.
   (B) decreased motivation to perform novel tasks.
   (C) stress-related diseases like ulcers or heart conditions.
   (D) a reduction in the drive to achieve goals.
   (E) resistance to learning skills needed for novel tasks.

10. Perceived control over a stressful event tends to result in

   (A) less reported stress.
   (B) more frustration regarding the stressful event.
   (C) more motivation to solve the stressful problem.
   (D) increased arousal.
   (E) higher heart and respiration rates.

11. The balanced physiological state we are driven to attain by satisfying our needs is called

   (A) equilibrium.
   (B) homeostasis.
   (C) self-actualization.
   (D) primary satisfaction.
   (E) secondary satisfaction.

12. The Garcia effect describes

   (A) the increased motivation felt by individuals with high levels of arousal.
   (B) the increased susceptibility to illness experienced in the exhaustion phase of the stress response.
   (C) classical conditioning associating nausea with food or drink.
   (D) the effect of a theory Y management style.
   (E) the effect the hypothalamus has on perceiving hunger.

13. Which of the following factors does research indicate may influence sexual orientation?

   (A) parenting styles
   (B) degree of masculinity or femininity expressed in childhood
   (C) traumatic childhood experiences
   (D) genetic influences
   (E) being raised by homosexual parents

14. Selye's general adaptation syndrome describes
    (A) how the central nervous system processes emotions.
    (B) the effect of low levels of arousal on emotion.
    (C) our reactions to stress.
    (D) our reactions to the different levels of Maslow's hierarchy of needs.
    (E) the sexual response cycle in humans.

15. A high score on Holmes and Rahe's social readjustment rating scale correlates with
    (A) high optimum levels of arousal.
    (B) level of need reduction.
    (C) incidence of eating disorders.
    (D) incidence of stress-related illness.
    (E) levels of perceived control.

ANSWER KEY

1. **D**
2. **E**
3. **B**
4. **A**
5. **B**
6. **A**
7. **C**
8. **C**
9. **C**
10. **A**
11. **B**
12. **C**
13. **D**
14. **C**
15. **D**

ANSWERS EXPLAINED

1. **(D)** Money is a secondary drive people learn to associate with primary drives. Choice A refers to incentive theory, choice B refers to arousal theory, and choice C refers to the hierarchy of needs. Not all psychologists agree that humans are born with instincts, so choice E is incorrect.

2. **(E)** The lateral part of the hypothalamus causes animals to eat when stimulated. The ventromedial hypothalamus causes animals to stop eating. The aspects described in the other answers are not controlled by these parts of the hypothalamus.

3. **(B)** All the other factors can be risk factors for the development of eating disorders, except for lack of willpower. As with most psychological disorders, the behaviors associated with eating disorders cannot be controlled by a sufferer through an act of will or by just trying harder. Most people suffering from an eating disorder need therapy, psychological help, and possible medication in order to stop their harmful behaviors.

4. **(A)** The Yerkes-Dodson law predicts that most people perform easy tasks best at high levels of arousal and difficult tasks best at low levels of arousal. The term baseline state applies best to the opponent-process theory of motivation. *Self-actualization* is a term used in Maslow's hierarchy of needs, and homeostasis is a term that describes a state of equilibrium in drive-reduction theory.

5. **(B)** Arousal theory says humans are motivated to seek a certain level of arousal. Achievement motivation theory describes how we are motivated to meet goals and master our environment. The rest of the choices describe the theories incorrectly.

6. **(A)** An intrinsically motivated person motivates himself or herself with internal rewards like satisfaction. Extrinsic motivators like money are usually temporary, and the individual may lose motivation for the task when the motivator stops or does not increase. Intrinsic motivations are not easier to provide. In fact, inspiring people to become intrinsically motivated may be more difficult. Intrinsic/extrinsic motivation does not relate to Maslow's hierarchy or primary and secondary drives. Both types of motivation are effective with a wide range of individuals.

7. **(C)** Theory Y managers believe workers are internally motivated. Theory X managers think workers must have external rewards in order to motivate work. Both types of managers might be equally active in work groups and might ask workers to do similar tasks. The theories might relate to types of cultures, but not the way described in choice D. Theory X and Y do not relate to optimum levels of arousal.

8. **(C)** Schachter said the cognitive label we apply to an event combined with our body's reaction creates emotion. James-Lange said biological changes cause emotion, and Cannon-Bard states that emotional reactions occur at the same time as physiological changes. No theory maintains that emotions are unrelated to biological changes.

9. **(C)** If individuals spend an excessive amount of time in the resistance phase, it may deplete their bodies' resources. They become more vulnerable to diseases in the exhaustion phase. The other answers do not relate to Selye's general adaptation syndrome.

10. **(A)** Studies show that if people think they are in control of an event, they report the event is less stressful. Frustration might decrease, but perceived control would not increase the feeling of frustration (choice B). Perceived control does not necessarily relate to motivation, arousal, or our heart/respiration rates.

11. **(B)** Homeostasis is a balanced internal state we seek by satisfying our drives. The word equilibrium does indicate balance but is not the most correct term in this context. Self-actualization is the highest need in Maslow's hierarchy. Primary and secondary refer to drives, but the terms primary and secondary satisfaction are made-up distractions.

12. **(C)** The Garcia effect occurs when an organism associates nausea with food or drink through classical conditioning. This is a powerful form of learning that takes only one trial to establish. Pairing illness with food and drink is an adaptive response that may be hardwired in order to create a survival advantage. The other choices incorrectly describe the Garcia effect.

13. **(D)** Twin studies indicate a possible genetic influence on sexual orientation. A person whose identical twin is homosexual is more likely to be homosexual than is a member of the general population. Research indicates the other factors mentioned are not environmental factors correlated with homosexuality.

14. **(C)** The GAS describes different stages in reactions to stress. The other choices do not relate to Selye's general adaptation syndrome.

15. **(D)** The social readjustment rating scale is designed to measure stress. A high score on this instrument indicates the test taker experiences a high amount of stress, and this correlates with stress-related illnesses. The factors described in the other choices are not correlated with this test.

11 Personality

Key Terms

- Personality
- Type A
- Type B
- Stage theory
- Freud's psychosexual stage theory
- Oedipus crisis
- Unconscious
- Id
- Ego
- Superego
- Defense mechanisms
- Womb envy
- Personal unconscious
- Collective unconscious
- Complexes
- Archetypes
- Trait theorist
- Big five traits
- Factor analysis
- Heritability
- Temperament
- Somatotype theory
- Triadic reciprocality or reciprocal determinism
- Self-efficacy
- Locus of control—internal and external
- Self-concept
- Self-esteem
- Self-actualization
- Unconditional positive regard
- Projective tests—Rorschach inkblot test, thematic apperception test (TAT)
- Self-report inventories—MMPI
- Reliability
- Validity
- Barnum effect

Key People

- Sigmund Freud
- Karen Horney
- Nancy Chodorow
- Carl Jung
- Alfred Adler
- Hans Eyesenck
- Raymond Cattell
- Paul Costa
- Robert McCrae
- Gordon Allport
- Hippocrates
- William Sheldon
- B. F. Skinner
- Albert Bandura
- George Kelly
- Julian Rotter
- Abraham Maslow
- Carl Rogers

OVERVIEW

Personality is a term we use all the time. When we describe people to others, we try to convey a sense of what their personalities are like. Psychologists define personality as the unique attitudes, behaviors, and emotions that characterize a person. As you might expect, psychologists from each of the different perspectives have different ideas about how an individual's personality is created. However, some ideas about personality do not fit neatly into one school of thought. An example is the concept of **Type A** and **Type B** personalities. Type A people tend to feel a sense of time pressure and are easily angered. They are competitive and ambitious; they work hard and play hard. Interestingly, research has shown that Type A people are at a higher risk for heart disease than the general population. Type B individuals, on the other hand, tend to be relaxed and easygoing. But these types do not fall on opposite ends of a continuum; some people fit into neither type.

PSYCHOANALYTIC THEORY

Freudian Theory

Sigmund Freud believed that one's personality was essentially set in early childhood. He proposed a psychosexual stage theory of personality. **Stage theories** are ones in which development is thought to be discontinuous. In other words, the stages are qualitatively different from one another and recognizable, and people move between them in a stepwise fashion. Stage theories also posit that all people go through all the stages in the same order. Freud's theory has four stages: the oral stage, the anal stage, the phallic stage, and the adult genital stage. Between the phallic stage and the adult genital stage is a latency period that some people refer to as a stage. Freud believed that sexual urges were an important determinant of people's personality development. Each of the stages is named for the part of the body from which people derive sexual pleasure during the stage.

During the **oral stage** (birth to one year), Freud proposed that children enjoy sucking and biting because it gives them a form of sexual pleasure. During the **anal stage** (one to three years), children are sexually gratified by the act of elimination.

During the **phallic stage** (three to five years), sexual gratification moves to the genitalia. The **Oedipus crisis**, in which boys sexually desire their mothers and view their fathers as rivals for their mothers' love, occurs in this stage. Some theorists have suggested that girls have a similar experience, the **Electra crisis**, in which they desire their fathers and see their mothers as competition for his love. Both the Oedipus and Electra crises are named after figures in Greek mythology who lived out these conflicts. In the phallic stage, Freud suggests that boys and girls notice their physical differences. As a result, girls come to evidence **penis envy**, the desire for a penis, and boys suffer from **castration anxiety**, the fear that if they misbehave, they will be castrated. Boys specifically fear that their fathers will castrate them to eliminate them as rivals for their mothers. To protect them against this threatening realization, Freud believed that the boys used the defense mechanism of **identification**. The purpose of defense mechanisms, in general, is to protect the conscious mind from thoughts that are too painful. Identification is when people emulate and attach themselves to an individual who they believe threatens them. Identification, according to Freud, serves a dual purpose. It prevents boys from fearing their fathers. It also encourages boys to break away from their attachment to their mothers (usually their primary caregivers) and learn to act like men.

After the phallic stage, children enter **latency** (six years to puberty), during which they push all their sexual feelings out of conscious awareness (repression). During latency, children turn their attention to other issues. They start school, where they learn both how to interact with others and a myriad of academic skills.

At puberty, children enter the last of Freud's stages, the **adult genital stage**. People remain in this stage for the rest of their lives and seek sexual pleasure through sexual relationships with others.

Freud suggested that children could get fixated in any one of the stages. A **fixation** could result from being either undergratified or overgratified. For instance, a child who was not fed regularly or who was overly indulged might develop an **oral fixation**. Such people, as adults, might evidence a tendency to overeat, a propensity to chew gum, an addiction to smoking, or another similar mouth-related behavior. Freud described two kinds of personalities resulting from an anal fixation due to a traumatic toilet training. Someone with an **anal expulsive personality** tends to be messy and disorganized. The term **anal retentive** is used to describe people who are meticulously neat, hyperorganized, and a bit compulsive. Fixation in the phallic stage can result in people who appear excessively sexually assured and aggressive or, alternatively, who are consumed with their perceived sexual inadequacies. These fixations result from psychic energy, the **libido**, getting stuck in one of the psychosexual stages.

Freud believed that much of people's behavior is controlled by a region of the mind he called the **unconscious**. We do not have access to the thoughts in our unconscious. In fact, Freud asserted that we spend tremendous amounts of psychic energy to keep threatening thoughts in the unconscious. Freud contrasted the unconscious mind with the **preconscious** and the **conscious**. The conscious mind contains everything we are thinking about at any one moment, while the preconscious contains everything that we could potentially summon to conscious awareness with ease. For instance, as you read these words, I hope you are not thinking about your plans for the upcoming weekend; these thoughts were in your preconscious. However, now that I have mentioned these plans, you have brought them into your conscious mind.

Students frequently confuse the terms subconscious and unconscious. Freud wrote about the unconscious.

Freud posited that the personality consists of three parts: the **id**, the **ego**, and the **superego**. The id is in the unconscious and contains instincts and psychic energy. Freud believed two types of instincts exist: **Eros** (the life instincts) and **Thanatos** (the death instincts). **Libido** is the energy that directs the life instincts. Eros is most often evidenced as a desire for sex, while Thanatos is seen in aggression.

Table 11.1 Freud's Parts of the Mind

Id	Follows the pleasure principle	Exists from birth
Ego	Follows the reality principle	Emerges around ages 2 or 3
Superego	Acts as a conscience	Develops around age 5

The id is propelled by the **pleasure principle**; it wants immediate gratification. The id exists entirely in the unconscious mind. Babies are propelled solely by their ids. They cry whenever they desire something without regard to the external world around them. The next part of the personality to develop is the ego. The ego follows the **reality principle**, which means its job is to negotiate between the desires of the id and the limitations of the environment. The ego is partly in the conscious mind and partly in the unconscious mind. The last part of the personality to develop is the superego. Like the ego, the superego operates on both the conscious and unconscious level. Around the age of five, children begin to develop a conscience and to think about what is right and wrong. This sense of conscience, according to Freud, is their superego. Oftentimes, the ego acts as a mediator between the id and the superego. As you cram for that midterm, the id tells you to go to sleep because you are tired or to go to that party because it will be fun. The superego tells you to study because it is the right thing to do. The ego makes some kind of a compromise. You will study for two hours, drop by the party, and then go to sleep.

> **TIP**
>
> Students sometimes confuse the terms **conscious and conscience.** Freudian theory puts great emphasis on the contents of the unconscious as opposed to the conscious. We are aware of what is in our conscious mind but unaware of what is in our unconscious. The conscience, on the other hand, is our sense of right and wrong and is typically associated with the superego in Freudian theory.

Part of the ego's job is to protect the conscious mind from the threatening thoughts buried in the unconscious. The ego uses defense mechanisms to help protect the conscious mind. Assume that Muffy, captain of the high school cheerleading squad, decides to leave her boyfriend of two years, Biff, the star wide receiver of the football team, for Alvin, the star of the school's chess team. Needless to say, Biff is devastated, but his ego can choose from a great variety of defense mechanisms with which to protect him. Some of these defense mechanisms are as follows:

REPRESSION

- Blocking thoughts out from conscious awareness.
- When asked how he feels about the breakup with Muffy, Biff replies, "Who? Oh, yeah, I haven't thought about her in a while."

DENIAL

- Not accepting the ego-threatening truth.
- Biff continues to act as if he and Muffy are still together. He waits by her locker, calls her every night, and plans their future dates.

DISPLACEMENT

- Redirecting one's feeling toward another person or object. When people displace negative emotions like anger, they often displace them onto people who are less threatening than the source of the emotion. For instance, a child who is angry at his or her teacher would be more likely to displace the anger onto a classmate than onto the teacher.
- Biff could displace his feelings of anger and resentment onto his little brother, pet hamster, or football.

PROJECTION

- Believing that the feelings one has toward someone else are actually held by the other person and directed at oneself.
- Biff insists that Muffy still cares for him.

REACTION FORMATION

- Expressing the opposite of how one truly feels.
- Biff claims he loathes Muffy.

REGRESSION

- Returning to an earlier, comforting form of behavior.
- Biff begins to sleep with his favorite childhood stuffed animal, Fuzzy Kitten.

RATIONALIZATION

- Coming up with a beneficial result of an undesirable occurrence.
- Biff believes that he can now find a better girlfriend. Muffy is not really all that pretty, smart, and fun to be with.

> **TIP**
>
> **Students frequently confuse displacement and projection. In displacement, person A has feelings about person B but redirects these feelings onto a third person or an object. In projection, person A has feelings toward person B but believes, instead, that person B has those feelings toward him or her (person A).**

INTELLECTUALIZATION

- Undertaking an academic, unemotional study of a topic.
- Biff embarks on an in-depth research project about failed teen romances.

SUBLIMATION

- Channeling one's frustration toward a different goal. Sublimation is viewed as a particularly healthy defense mechanism.
- Biff devotes himself to writing poetry and publishes a small volume before he graduates high school.

Criticisms of Freud

One common criticism of Freudian theory is that little empirical evidence supports it. For example, verifying the existence of many of Freud's constructs such as the unconscious, the Oedipus complex, or Thanatos is extremely difficult, if not impossible. Furthermore, psychoanalytic theory is able to interpret both positive and negative reactions to the theory as support. For instance, both the man who is convinced by his analyst's suggestion that his difficulties stem from an unresolved attraction to his mother, and the man who vociferously protests this idea can be accommodated by psychoanalytic theory, could be said to provide evidence for the theory. The former is compelled by the logic of the argument, while the latter's very resistance to the idea is evidence of the threatening nature of a repressed desire.

In addition, Freudian theory has little predictive power. While analysts can use the theory to create logical and often compelling explanations of why an individual acted in a certain way or developed a certain problem after the fact, psychoanalytic theory does not allow us to predict ahead of time what problems an individual will develop.

Psychoanalytic theory is also criticized for overestimating the importance of early childhood and of sex. Much contemporary research contradicts the idea that personality is essentially set by the age of five. Similarly, Freud's almost exclusive focus on sexual motivation led some psychologists to try to broaden the theory.

Finally, feminists find much of Freudian theory to be objectionable. One example is the concept of penis envy. Feminists such as **Karen Horney** and **Nancy Chodorow** believe that this idea grew out of Freud's assumption that men were superior to women rather than from any empirical observations. They suggested that if women were envious of men, it was probably due to all the advantages men enjoyed in society. Horney posited that men may suffer from **womb envy**, jealousy of women's reproductive capabilities. Feminists also take issue with Freud's assertion that men have stronger superegos than women.

Impact of Freudian Theory

Despite its shortcomings, Freudian theory has profoundly affected the world. Many people accept the idea that children are sexual creatures and that our behavior is shaped by unconscious thoughts. Freud's impact on culture is arguably greater than its impact on contemporary psychology. Many of the terms originally invented by Freud have crept into laypeople's language (e.g., ego, unconsious, penis envy, denial). Many of Freud's ideas play a prominent role in the arts. Salvador Dali's surrealist paintings are said to depict the unconscious, and Woody Allen's films frequently feature a character undergoing psychoanalysis and playing out a Freudian drama.

PSYCHODYNAMIC THEORIES

A number of Freud's early followers developed offshoots of psychoanalytic theory. These approaches are now usually referred to as **psychodynamic** or **neo-Freudian** approaches. Two of the best-known creators of psychodynamic theories are **Carl Jung** and **Alfred Adler**. Jung proposed that the unconscious consists of two different parts: the **personal unconscious** and the **collective unconscious.** The personal unconscious is similar to Freud's view of the unconscious. Jung believed that an individual's personal unconscious contains the painful or threatening memories and thoughts the person does not wish to confront; he termed these **complexes**. Jung contrasted the personal unconscious with the **collective unconscious**. The collective unconscious is passed down through the species and, according to Jung, explains certain similarities we see between cultures. The collective unconscious contains **archetypes** that Jung defined as universal concepts we all share as part of the human species. For example, the **shadow** represents the evil side of personality and the **persona** is people's creation of a public image. Jung suggested that the widespread existence of certain fears, such as fear of the dark, and the importance of the circle in many cultures, provides evidence for archetypes.

Adler is called an ego psychologist because he downplayed the importance of the unconscious and focused on the conscious role of the ego. Adler believed that people are motivated by the fear of failure, which he termed **inferiority**, and the desire to achieve, which he called **superiority**. Adler is also known for his work about the importance of birth order in shaping personality.

TRAIT THEORIES

Trait theorists believe that we can describe people's personalities by specifying their main characteristics, or traits. These characteristics (for example, honesty, laziness, ambition) are thought to be stable and to motivate behavior in keeping with the trait. In other words, when we describe someone as friendly, we mean that the person acts in a friendly manner across different situations and times.

Some trait theorists believe that the same basic set of traits can be used to describe all people's personalities. Such a belief characterizes a **nomothetic** approach. For instance, **Hans Eysenck** believed that by classifying all people along an introversion-extraversion scale and a stable-unstable scale, we could describe their personalities. **Raymond Cattell** developed the 16 PF (personality factor) test to measure what he believed were the 16 basic traits present in all people, albeit to different degrees.

More recently, **Paul Costa** and **Robert McCrae** have proposed that personality can be described using the **big five** personality traits: extraversion, agreeableness, conscientiousness, openness to experience, and emotional stability (or neuroticism). Extraversion refers to how outgoing or shy someone is. Agreeableness has to do with how easy to get along with someone is. People high on the conscientiousness dimension tend to be hardworking, responsible, and organized. Openness to new experiences is related to one's creativity, curiosity, and willingness to try new things. Finally, emotional stability has to do with how consistent one's mood is.

TIP

Today, the most popular trait theory contends that personality can be described with the big five traits of extraversion, agreeableness, conscientiousness, openness, and emotional stability.

One might wonder how psychologists can reduce the vast number of different terms we use to describe people to 16 or 5 basic traits. **Factor analysis** is a statistical technique used to accomplish this feat. Factor analysis allows researchers to use correlations between traits in order to see which traits cluster together as factors. If a strong correlation is found between punctuality, diligence, and neatness, for example, one could argue that these traits represent a common factor that we could name conscientiousness.

Other trait theorists, called **idiographic** theorists, assert that using the same set of terms to classify all people is impossible. Rather, they argue, each person needs to be seen in terms of what few traits best characterize his or her unique self. For example, while honesty may be a very important trait in describing one person, it may not be at all important in describing someone else.

Gordon Allport believed that although there were common traits useful in describing all people, a full understanding of someone's personality was impossible without looking at his or her personal traits. Allport differentiated between three different types of personal traits. He suggested that a small number of people are so profoundly influenced by one trait that it plays a pivotal role in virtually everything they do. He referred to such traits as **cardinal dispositions.** Allport posited that there are two other types of dispositions, central and secondary, that can be used to describe personality. As their names indicate, **central dispositions** have a larger influence on personality than **secondary dispositions**. Central dispositions are more often apparent and describe more significant aspects of personality.

The main criticism of trait theories is that they underestimate the importance of the situation. Nobody is always conscientious or unfailingly friendly. Therefore, critics assert, to describe someone's personality, we need to take the context into consideration.

BIOLOGICAL THEORIES

Biological theories of personality view genes, chemicals, and body types as the central determinants of who a person is. A growing body of evidence supports the idea that human personality is shaped, in part, by genetics. Although many people associate traits with genetics, traits are not necessarily inherited. Thus far, little evidence exists for the **heritability** of specific personality traits. Heritability is a measure of the amount of variation in a trait in a given population that is due to genetics. For instance, some traits, like height, are highly heritable; over 90 percent of the variation in Americans' height is thought to be due to genetic factors. Other traits, like intelligence, seem less strongly linked to genetic factors; estimates are that the heritability of intelligence is in the 50–70 percent range.

Conversely, much evidence suggests that genes play a role in people's **temperaments**, typically defined as their emotional style and characteristic way of dealing with the world. Psychologists and laypeople alike have long noticed that infants seem to differ immediately at birth. Some welcome new stimuli whereas others seem more fearful. Some seem extremely active and emotional while others are calmer. Psychologists believe that babies are born with different temperaments. A child's temperament, then, is thought to influence the development of his or her personality.

One of the earliest theories of personality was biological. **Hippocrates** believed that personality was determined by the relative levels of four humors (fluids) in the body. The four humors were blood, yellow bile, black bile, and phlegm. A cheerful person, for example, was said to have an excess of blood. While Hippocrates' theory has obviously turned out to be untrue, he is thought to be one of the first people to recognize that biological factors impact personality.

Another relatively early biological theory of personality was **William Sheldon's somatotype theory**. Sheldon identified three body types: endomorphs (fat), mesomorphs (muscular), and ectomorphs (thin). Sheldon argued that certain personality traits were associated with each of the body types. For instance, ectomorphs were shy and secretive, mesomorphs were confident and assertive, and endomorphs were friendly and outgoing. Sheldon's findings have not been replicated, and his methodology has been questioned. In addition, his research shows only a correlation and therefore, even if it were found to be reliable and valid, it does not show that biology shapes personality.

BEHAVIORIST THEORIES

Radical behaviorists like **B. F. Skinner** take a very different approach to personality. In fact, these theorists argue that behavior is personality and that the way most people think of the term personality is meaningless. According to this view, personality is determined by the environment. The reinforcement contingencies to which one is exposed creates one's personality. Therefore, by changing people's environments, behaviorists believe we can alter their personalities. Radical behaviorists are criticized for failing to recognize the importance of cognition. Today, many psychologists call themselves cognitive-behavioral or social-cognitive theorists. Their ideas about personality are described below.

SOCIAL-COGNITIVE THEORIES

Many models of personality meld together behaviorists' emphasis on the importance of the environment with cognitive psychologists' focus on patterns of thought. Such models are referred to as social-cognitive or cognitive-behavioral models.

Albert Bandura suggested that personality is created by an interaction between the person (traits), the environment, and the person's behavior. His model is based on the idea of **triadic reciprocality**, also known as **reciprocal determinism**. These terms essentially mean that each of these three factors influence both of the other two in a constant looplike fashion. Look at an example. Brad is a friendly person. This personality trait influences Brad's behavior in that he talks to a lot of people. It influences the environments into which he puts himself in that he goes to a lot of parties. Brad's loquacious behavior affects his environment in that it makes the parties even more partylike. In addition, Brad's talkativeness reinforces his friendliness; the more he talks, the more friendly he thinks he is. Finally, the environment of the party reinforces Brad's outgoing nature and encourages him to strike up conversations with many people.

Bandura also posited that personality is affected by people's sense of **self-efficacy**. People with high self-efficacy are optimistic about their own ability to get things done, whereas people with low self-efficacy feel a sense of powerlessness. Bandura theorized that people's sense of self-efficacy has a powerful effect on their actions. For example, assume two students of equal abilities and knowledge are taking a test. The one with higher self-efficacy would expect to do better and therefore might act in ways to make that true (e.g., spend more time on the test questions).

George Kelly proposed the **personal-construct theory** of personality. Kelly argued that people, in their attempts to understand their world, develop their own, individual systems of personal constructs. Such constructs consist of pairs of opposites such as fair-unfair, smart-dumb, and exciting-dull. People then use these constructs to evaluate their worlds. Kelly believed that people's behavior is determined by how they interpret the world. His theory is based on a **fundamental postulate** that essentially states that people's behavior is influenced by their cognitions and that by knowing how people have behaved in the past, we can predict how they will act in the future.

Some of the ideas put forth by social-cognitive theorists, including Bandura's concept of self-efficacy, are almost like traits that describe an individual's characteristic way of thinking. A final example is **Julian Rotter's** concept of **locus of control**. A person can be described as having either an internal or an external locus of control. People with an **internal locus of control** feel as if they are responsible for what happens to them. For instance, they tend to believe that hard work will lead to success. Conversely, people with an **external locus of control** generally believe that luck and other forces outside of their own control determine their destinies. A person's locus of control can have a large effect on how a person thinks and acts, thus impacting his or her personality.

A number of positive outcomes has been found to be associated with having an internal locus of control. As compared with externals, internals tend to be healthier, to be more politically active, and to do better in school. Of course, these findings are based on correlational research, so we can't conclude that locus of control causes such differences.

HUMANISTIC THEORIES

Many of the models of personality already discussed are deterministic. **Determinism** is the belief that what happens is dictated by what has happened in the past. According to psychoanalysts, personality is determined by what happened to an individual in his or her early childhood (largely during the psychosexual stages). Behaviorists assert that personality is similarly determined by the environment in which one has been raised. Neither theory supports the existence of **free will**, an individual's ability to choose his or her own destiny. Free will is an idea that has been embraced by humanistic psychology. This perspective is often referred to as the **third force** because it arose in opposition to the determinism so central to both psychoanalytic and behaviorist models.

Humanistic theories of personality view people as innately good and able to determine their own destinies through the exercise of free will. These psychologists stress the importance of people's subjective experience and feelings. They focus on the importance of a person's **self-concept** and **self-esteem**. Self-concept is a person's global feeling about himself or herself. Self-concept develops through a person's involvement with others, especially parents. Someone with a positive self-concept is likely to have high self-esteem.

Two of the most influential humanistic psychologists were **Abraham Maslow** and **Carl Rogers**. Both of these men believed that people are motivated to reach their full potential or **self-actualize**. Maslow developed the hierarchy of needs that you read about in the motivation chapter. Self-actualization sits atop this hierarchy. Rogers created self-theory. He believed that although people are innately good, they require certain things from their interactions with others, most importantly, **unconditional positive regard**, in order to self-actualize. Unconditional positive regard is a kind of blanket acceptance. Parents that make their children feel as if they are loved no matter what provide unconditional positive regard. However, parents who make their children feel as if they will be loved only if they earn high grades or have the right kind of friends, send their children the message that their love is conditional. Just as Maslow believes one needs to satisfy the needs lower on the hierarchy in order to move upward, Rogers believes that people must feel accepted in order to make strides toward self-actualization. Humanistic theories of personality are criticized for putting forth an overly optimistic theory of human nature. If people are innately good and striving to do their best, it is difficult to explain the number and range of truly terrible acts that people commit.

Table 11.2 Summary of Major Theories of Personality

Perspective	Major Theorists	Key Concepts	Roots of Personality
Psychoanalytic	Freud	Psychosexual stages	Unconscious
Humanistic	Rogers, Maslow	Free will, self-actualization	Subjective feelings about self
Trait	Costa and McCrae	Big five, factor analysis	Established patterns of behavior
Sociocognitive	Bandura	Triadic reciprocality	Ways of thinking

ASSESSMENT TECHNIQUES

As with any other kind of testing, **reliability** and **validity** are a concern in personality assessment. Reliability is often likened to consistency; reliable measures yield consistent, similar results even if the results are not accurate. Validity, on the other hand, means accuracy; a valid test measures what it purports to measure. See Chapter 8, "Testing and Individual Differences," for a more detailed discussion of these issues.

Not surprisingly, psychologists' methods of assessing people's personalities differ depending upon their theoretical orientation. Some of the most common ways of measuring personality are described below along with the types of psychologists most likely to use them.

Projective tests are often used by psychoanalysts. They involve asking people to interpret ambiguous stimuli. For instance, the **Rorschach inkblot test** involves showing people a series of inkblots and asking them to describe what they see. The **thematic apperception test (TAT)** consists of a number of cards, each of which contains a picture of a person or people in an ambiguous situation. People are asked to describe what is happening in the pictures. Since both the inkblots and TAT cards are ambiguous, psychoanalysts reason that people's interpretations reflect their unconscious thoughts. People are thought to project their unconscious thoughts onto the ambiguous stimuli. For instance, someone who is struggling with his or her unconscious aggressive impulses may be more likely to describe violent themes. Scoring projective tests, however, is a complicated process. For instance, the Rorschach test looks not only at the content people describe but also the way they hold and turn the card and whether they focus on the whole inkblot or just a portion of it. Many people believe that projective tests are particularly unreliable given that they rely so extensively on the therapists' interpretations.

A far simpler and more widespread method of personality assessment is to use **self-report inventories**. Self-report inventories are essentially questionnaires that ask people to provide information about themselves. Many different kinds of psychologists, such as humanistic psychologists, trait theorists, and cognitive-behavioral psychologists, might use self-report inventories as one means by which to gather data about someone. These kinds of tests are often referred to as objective personality tests since people's scores are determined simply by their answers and are thus unlikely to be affected by evaluator bias. An interview, on the other hand, is a subjective assessment. Although such subjectivity decreases reliability and opens the door to bias, some believe that subjective measures yield richer and more valid data.

The **Minnesota Multiphasic Personality Inventory (MMPI-2)** is one of the most widely used self-report instruments. A potential problem with such inventories is that people may not be completely honest in answering the questions. Some tests have "lie scales" built in to try to detect when people are not being honest.

Radical behaviorists would reject all the above methods, arguing instead that the only way to measure people's personality is to observe their behavior. Again, a number of other kinds of psychologists, particularly cognitive-behavioral ones, would utilize observations of a person's behavior as one way to gather data.

People are naturally curious about what various personality assessments will say about them. Unfortunately, this curiosity makes people susceptible to being deceived. Research has demonstrated that people have the tendency to see themselves in vague, stock descriptions of personality. This phenomenon, the **Barnum effect**, is named after the famous circus owner P. T. Barnum, who once said "There's a sucker born every minute." Astrologers, psychics, and fortune-tellers take advantage of the Barnum effect in their work. Personality has proved difficult to define, much less measure, so be skeptical when confronted with people who offer you quick, pat descriptions of your life or future.

PRACTICE QUESTIONS

Directions: Each of the questions or incomplete statements below is followed by five suggested answers or completions. Select the one that is best in each case.

1. According to Freud, which part of the mind acts as a person's conscience?
   (A) Eros
   (B) ego
   (C) libido
   (D) superego
   (E) id

2. Cettina fills out a personality inventory several times over the course of one year. The results of each administration of the test are extremely different. Cettina's situation suggests that this personality inventory may not be
   (A) reliable.
   (B) standardized.
   (C) normed.
   (D) projective.
   (E) fair.

3. Which approach toward personality is the least deterministic?
   (A) psychoanalytic
   (B) humanistic
   (C) trait
   (D) behaviorist
   (E) biological

4. One of your classmates remarks that "Mary is all id." What does she likely mean?
   (A) Mary uses a lot of defense mechanisms.
   (B) Mary is a highly ethical person.
   (C) Mary is a perfectionist.
   (D) Mary frequently pursues immediate gratification.
   (E) Mary is in constant conflict over the proper course of action to take.

5. The belief that personality is created by the interaction between a person, his or her behavior, and the environment is known as
   (A) combination theory.
   (B) interactionist perspective.
   (C) reciprocal determinism.
   (D) mutuality.
   (E) circular creation.

6. Juan has a huge crush on Sally, but he never admits it. Instead, he tells all who will listen that Sally is really "into him." Psychoanalysts would see Juan's bragging as an example of

   (A) displacement.
   (B) reaction formation.
   (C) sublimation.
   (D) denial.
   (E) projection.

7. Dr. Li asks her clients to interpret ambiguous pictures of people in various settings. The method she is using is called

   (A) the Rorschach test.
   (B) the MMPI.
   (C) the TAT.
   (D) factor analysis.
   (E) the WISC.

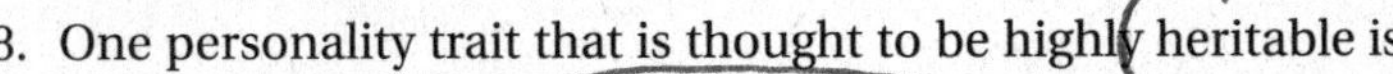

8. One personality trait that is thought to be highly heritable is

   (A) generosity.
   (B) sense of humor.
   (C) neatness.
   (D) introversion.
   (E) diligence.

9. Humanistic psychologists assert that people are motivated to self-actualize. Which of the following statements best describes the meaning of this term?

   (A) accepting themselves the way they are
   (B) encouraging others to pursue their dreams
   (C) identifying core principles by which to live
   (D) trying to achieve their full potential
   (E) bringing their actions into line with their desires

10. Which is NOT one of the big five personality traits?

   (A) extraversion
   (B) openness
   (C) agreeableness
   (D) honesty
   (E) conscientiousness

11. Feminist psychoanalytic critics of Freud most commonly argue that

   (A) there is no proof that the unconscious exists.
   (B) Freud devoted too much attention to childhood.
   (C) women's superegos are just as strong as men's.
   (D) men and women use different defense mechanisms.
   (E) while women all suffer from penis envy, men all suffer from womb envy.

12. Jamal sucked his thumb until age eight. As an adult, he smokes, chews gum, and thinks constantly of food. Psychoanalysts would describe Jamal as having a (an)

    (A) obsession.
    (B) orally controlled libido.
    (C) Oedipus complex.
    (D) oral fixation.
    (E) mother complex.

13. Someone who has an external locus of control is likely to have a

    (A) positive self-concept.
    (B) high sense of self-efficacy.
    (C) strong libido.
    (D) belief in luck.
    (E) high IQ.

14. What kind of psychologist would be most likely to use a projective personality assessment?

    (A) social cognitive
    (B) trait
    (C) behaviorist
    (D) humanistic
    (E) psychoanalytic

15. Redirecting one's unacceptable urges into more socially acceptable pursuits best defines which of the following defense mechanisms?

    (A) intellectualization
    (B) denial
    (C) sublimation
    (D) rationalization
    (E) regression

ANSWER KEY

1. **D**	6. **E**	11. **C**
2. **A**	7. **C**	12. **D**
3. **B**	8. **D**	13. **D**
4. **D**	9. **D**	14. **E**
5. **C**	10. **D**	15. **C**

ANSWERS EXPLAINED

1. **(D)** Freud described the superego as the part of the mind that acts as a conscience. The other two parts of the mind are the id and ego. The id acts according to the pleasure principle, while the ego acts as a buffer between the id and the demands of the external world. Eros is the life instinct, and the libido is the energy that drives Eros.

2. **(A)** A test that does not yield consistent results is not reliable. Such a test may still have been standardized and normed, both of which mean that it has been pretested on a large population and structured so that certain percentages of people answer each question in certain ways. Projective tests are used by psychoanalysts to try to see what is in a person's unconscious. Fair is not a scientific term; tests may be perceived as unfair for a variety of reasons.

3. **(B)** The humanistic model of personality arose in opposition to the determinism of earlier models. One of the fundamental precepts of humanistic psychology is that people have free will, that their behavior is not predetermined. Conversely, all of the other models listed suggest that behavior is determined, at least to an extent, rather than freely chosen.

4. **(D)** Because the id follows the pleasure principle, it pursues immediate gratification. If Mary were all id, she would be unlikely to need many defense mechanisms; she would just do what she wanted. Similarly, such a person would rarely be in conflict over what to do and would have little interest in the proper course of action to take. A highly ethical person would be guided by her superego. A perfectionist might also have a strong superego or, alternatively, might have an anal retentive personality.

5. **(C)** Reciprocal determinism, also known as triadic reciprocality, is Bandura's theory that personality arises out of the interaction of a person's traits, environment, and behavior. All of the remaining choices are made-up distractors.

6. **(E)** Juan is projecting. Instead of acknowledging the feelings he has toward Sally, he views Sally as having those feelings toward him. Were Juan to displace his feelings, he would express love for someone else or something else. If Juan were to use reaction formation, he would claim to hate Sally. Juan could sublimate by directing his energies toward honing his ice hockey skills or writing poetry. Finally, were Juan to deny his crush, when asked about it, he would continue to deny it.

7. **(C)** Dr. Li is using the TAT (thematic apperception test). The Rorschach test asks people to look at inkblots, not people. The MMPI is a personality inventory and therefore simply involves answering questions about oneself. Factor analysis is a statistical technique, not a personality assessment. The WISC is an intelligence test.

8. **(D)** A lot of research suggests that shyness or inhibition is inherited. Relatively little evidence exists that suggests generosity, sense of humor, neatness, or diligence is genetically predisposed. However, many psychologists persevere in looking for this evidence.

9. **(D)** Self-actualization is typically defined as achieving one's full potential; very few people ever truly self-actualize. Rather than accepting oneself as is, self-actualization is a drive to grow and improve. It is self-focused, not other-focused, and does not necessarily involve the identification of core principles or bringing one's actions into line with one's desires.

10. **(D)** Honesty is not considered one of the big five personality traits. The big five are extraversion, openness, agreeableness, conscientiousness, and emotional stability.

11. **(C)** Feminist critics of Freud most commonly argue that, contrary to Freud's assertion, women's superegos are as strong as men's. Psychoanalysts, feminist or not, generally believe in the unconscious. Feminists would be no more likely than any other group of people to argue that Freud overstressed the importance of childhood. Men and women do not seem to use categorically different defense mechanisms. While Karen Horney did suggest that men might suffer from womb envy, most feminists, including Horney, make the point that women are probably more envious of the advantages that men enjoy in society than they are of men's penises.

12. **(D)** Psychoanalysts would say that Jamal has an oral fixation. They would argue that some traumatic event during the oral stage (birth to one year) caused some of his libidinal energy to become fixated in that stage. Orally controlled libido is a made-up distractor, Oedipus complex refers to boys' supposed sexual desires for their mothers, and mother complex is a term that Jung might use.

13. **(D)** Rotter's concept of locus of control has to do with how much power one feels over his or her life. Someone who has an external locus of control feels as if she or he cannot control what happens. Externals often believe their futures are in the hands of fate or luck. Someone with a positive self-concept feels good about himself or herself. Someone with a high sense of self-efficacy believes in his or her own ability to accomplish things. When we say someone has a strong libido, we usually mean she or he has a strong sex drive. Someone with a high IQ is thought to be intelligent, at least in terms of traditional measures of intelligence.

14. **(E)** A psychoanalyst would be most likely to use a projective test since such measures supposedly allow the person taking the test to project his or her unconscious thoughts onto the stimuli. Trait theorists might ask the person to fill out a personality inventory such as Cattell's 16 PF. Behaviorists would monitor the person's behavior. Social-cognitive theorists might use both self-report inventories and behavioral measures. A humanistic psychologist would also use self-report techniques and watch someone's behavior. However, this psychologist might also want to talk to the person using an unstructured interview approach in order to get a fuller sense of the person.

15. **(C)** Sublimation is when one redirects unacceptable urges into a more socially acceptable pursuit. An example would be channeling your sexual frustration over your attraction to your opposite-sex parent to becoming a marathon runner. Intellectualization involves distancing oneself from the threatening issue by making it into an intellectual matter. Denial is when one denies the existence of the thought or feeling. Rationalization is when one explains away a behavior or feeling by making up a plausible excuse for it. Regression is when one returns to a behavior that was common and usually comforting at an earlier stage of life.

UNIT 8

Clinical Psychology

This unit addresses psychological disorders and treatment of these mental health issues. Professional psychologists often describe themselves as "clinical psychologists" or "academic psychologists." Clinical psychologists are concerned with how psychological disorders are defined and diagnosed, and what treatments are recommended for these disorders. You will find content from this unit in two chapters in the textbook you use for your AP Psychology class: "Psychological Disorders" and "Treatment."

12 Psychological Disorders

Key Terms

- Insane
- DSM
- Anxiety disorders
- Specific phobia
- Agoraphobia
- Social anxiety disorder
- Generalized anxiety disorder
- Panic disorder
- Somatic symptom disorders
- Conversion disorder
- Dissociative disorders
- Psychogenic amnesia
- Dissociative identity disorder
- Depressive disorders
- Major depressive disorder
- Seasonal affective disorder
- Bipolar disorder
- Cognitive triad
- Learned helplessness
- Schizophrenic disorders
- Delusions of persecution
- Delusions of grandeur
- Hallucinations
- Disorganized language—neologisms, clang associations
- Inappropriate or flat affect
- Catatonia
- Waxy flexibility
- Dopamine hypothesis
- Tardive dyskinesia
- Double bind
- Diathesis-stress model
- Personality disorders
- Antisocial personality disorder
- Dependent personality disorder
- Paranoid personality disorder
- Narcissistic personality disorder
- Histrionic personality disorder
- Obsessive-compulsive personality disorder
- Post-traumatic stress disorder
- Paraphilia or psychosexual disorder
- Anorexia nervosa
- Bulimia
- Autism spectrum disorder
- Attention-deficit/hyperactivity disorder
- Dementia

Key People

- Aaron Beck
- Martin Seligman
- David Rosenhan

OVERVIEW

Abnormal psychology is the study of people who suffer from psychological disorders. These disorders may be manifested in a person's behavior and/or thoughts. Abnormal psychology encompasses the study of relatively common problems such as depression, substance abuse, and learning difficulties, as well as the study of fairly rare, and particularly severe, disorders such as bipolar disorder and schizophrenia.

DEFINING PSYCHOLOGICAL DISORDERS

In order to identify a psychological disorder, we must first define it. This task is surprisingly difficult. Common characteristics of disorders include:

1. It is maladaptive (harmful) and/or disturbing to the individual. For instance, someone who has agoraphobia, fear of open spaces, and is thus unable to leave his or her home experiences something maladaptive and disturbing.
2. It is disturbing to others. Zoophilia, being sexually aroused by animals, for example, disturbs others.
3. It is unusual—that is, not shared by many members of the population. In the United States, having visions is atypical, whereas in some other cultures it occurs more commonly. Thus, in the United States, having visions is likely to be seen as a symptom of a psychological disorder.
4. It is irrational; it does not make sense to the average person. Feeling depressed when your family first moves away from all your friends is not seen as irrational, whereas prolonged depression due to virtually any situation is.

Note that people may be diagnosed with a psychological disorder even if they are not experiencing all, or even most, of the above symptoms. Another important point is that the term **insane**, often used by laypeople to describe psychological disorders in general, is not a medical term. Rather, **insanity** is a legal term. The reason behind the legal definition of insanity is to differentiate between those people who can be held entirely responsible for their crimes (the sane) and those people who, because of a psychological disorder, cannot be held fully responsible for their actions. When defendants plead not guilty by reason of insanity (NGRI), they are asking that the court acquit them due to psychological factors.

An important question is how psychologists determine whether or not someone has a psychological disorder. To do so, psychologists use a book called the ***Diagnostic and Statistical Manual of Mental Disorders*** **(DSM)**. The DSM, as its name suggests, provides a way for psychologists to diagnose their patients. The DSM contains the symptoms of everything currently considered to be a psychological disorder.

The DSM does not include much discussion of the causes (also called etiology) or treatments of the various disorders, because adherents to each of the psychological perspectives disagree. Psychoanalytic theorists locate the cause of psychological disturbances in unconscious conflicts often caused by traumatic events that occurred during the psychosexual stages (see Chapter 9). Behaviorists assert that psychological problems result from the person's history of reinforcement. Cognitive theorists locate the source of psychological disorders in maladaptive ways of thinking. Humanistic psychologists view the root of such disorders in a person's feelings, self-esteem, and self-concept. One of the most recent perspectives, the sociocultural perspective, holds that social ills such as racism, sexism, and poverty lie at the heart of psychological disorders. Finally, the biomedical model sees psychological disorders as caused by biological factors such as hormonal or neurotransmitter imbalances or differences in brain structure. Biomedical psychologists believe that many psychological disorders are associated with genetic abnormalities that may lead to the physiological abnormalities described above. However, the differences do not have to occur at the genetic level.

Most clinical psychologists do not subscribe strictly to one perspective or another. Rather, most psychologists are eclectic, which means that they accept and use ideas from a number of different perspectives (see Table 12.1).

Table 12.1 Different Perspectives on the Causes of Psychological Disorders

Perspective	Cause of Disorder
Psychoanalytic/psychodynamic	Internal, unconscious conflicts
Humanistic	Failure to strive toward one's potential or being out of touch with one's feelings
Behavioral	Reinforcement history, the environment
Cognitive	Irrational, dysfunctional thoughts or ways of thinking
Sociocultural	Dysfunctional society
Biomedical	Organic problems, biochemical imbalances, genetic predispositions

Periodically, the DSM is revised. The book's revisions have resulted in astronomical growth in the number and kinds of disorders included since the original DSM. However, sometimes behaviors classified as disorders in earlier editions, for instance homosexuality, have been removed from the definition of abnormality.

In 2013, the American Psychiatric Association published its first major revision to the DSM in approximately 20 years—the DSM-5. Given that high schools tend to use textbooks over multiple years, it is possible that your classroom text is not in line with the most recent version of the **DSM**. The most up-to-date information about what students are expected to know can always be found in the College Board AP Psychology Description.

CATEGORIES OF DISORDERS

The DSM-5 lists hundreds of different psychological disorders, most of which lie beyond the scope of your introductory course. We will deal with the disorders you are most likely to encounter on the AP Psychology exam.

After a short explanation of each type of disorder, we will briefly discuss how psychologists from a few of the various perspectives might view the cause of some of the disorders within the category. Keep in mind that many psychologists do not strictly adhere to any one perspective.

Anxiety Disorders

Anxiety disorders, as their name suggests, share a common symptom of anxiety. We will discuss three anxiety disorders: phobias, generalized anxiety disorder, and panic disorder.

A simple or **specific phobia** is an intense unwarranted fear of a situation or object such as **claustrophobia** (fear of enclosed spaces) or **arachnophobia** (fear of spiders). Another common type of phobia is **agoraphobia**. Agoraphobia is a fear of open, public spaces. People with severe agoraphobia may be afraid to venture out of their homes at all. Phobias are classified as anxiety disorders because contact with the feared object or situation results in anxiety. Social anxiety disorder, formerly known as social phobia, is a fear of a situation in which one could embarrass oneself in public, such as when eating in a restaurant or giving a lecture.

A person who suffers from **generalized anxiety disorder**, often referred to as GAD, experiences constant, low-level anxiety. Such a person constantly feels nervous and out of sorts. On the other hand, someone with **panic disorder** suffers from acute episodes of intense anxiety without any apparent provocation. Panic attacks tend to increase in frequency, and people often suffer additional anxiety due to anticipating the attacks.

Theories About the Cause of Anxiety Disorders

We will follow the discussion of the psychological disorders with a brief description of how adherents from several perspectives view the etiology of such disorders. Because many introductory psychology texts do not deal with the etiology of specific disorders, we will be selective and focus on the information most likely to appear on the AP exam.

Psychoanalytic theorists see psychological disorders as caused by unresolved, unconscious conflicts. Anxiety is viewed as the result of conflicts among the desires of the id, ego, and superego. For instance, a young woman's repressed sexual attraction to her father may cause a conflict between her id, which desires the father, and her superego, which forbids such a relationship. Anxiety disorders could be the outward manifestation of this internal conflict.

Behaviorists believe all behaviors are learned. Therefore, they assert that anxiety disorders are learned. Consider acrophobia, the fear of heights, as an example. Behaviorists would say that someone who has acrophobia learned the fear response. This learning could happen through classical conditioning, operant conditioning, or some type of cognitive learning. (See Chapter 6 for more information about basic learning principles.) Suppose three-year-old Pablo went with his family to visit the Space Needle in Seattle, Washington. While on the observation deck, Pablo got separated from his family and was found hours later crying hysterically in the gift shop. Ever since then, Pablo has been terrified of heights. In this example, behaviorists would say that Pablo learned through classical conditioning to associate heights with the fear that resulted from losing his family.

Cognitive theorists believe that disorders result from dysfunctional ways of thinking. Therefore, they would attribute an anxiety disorder to an unhealthy and irrational way of thinking and/or specific irrational thoughts. For instance, someone with GAD may have an unrealistically high standard for his or her own behavior. Because the person believes, irrationally, that he or she must always excel at everything he or she does, the person feels constant anxiety stemming from the impossibility of meeting this goal.

Somatic Symptom and Related Disorders

The DSM-5 renamed **somatoform disorders** as somatic symptom and related disorders. The number of these disorders included in the DSM-5 has been reduced and reflects a growing sense that an absence of an identified medical cause is not necessarily indicative of a psychological problem.

Somatic symptom disorders occur when a person manifests a psychological problem through a physiological symptom. In other words, such a person experiences a physical problem in the absence of any identifiable physical cause. An example of such a disorder is **conversion disorder**. People who have conversion disorder report the existence of a severe physical problem such as paralysis or blindness, and they will, in fact, be unable to move their arms or see. However, again, no biological reason for such problems can be identified. Prior to the latest revision of the DSM, hypochondriasis (complaining frequently about physical problems for which doctors are unable to find a cause) was also diagnosed as a type of somatoform disorder. Under the DSM-5, these symptoms are diagnosed as somatic symptom disorder. Hypochondriasis fits under somatic symptom disorder if the person reports concern with symptoms. If the person is very focused on fears of disease and not so much on symptoms, the diagnosis would be illness anxiety disorder.

Theories About the Cause of Somatic Symptom Disorders

Psychodynamic theorists would assert that somatic symptom disorders are merely outward manifestations of unresolved unconscious conflicts. Behaviorists would say that people with somatic symptom disorders are being reinforced for their behavior. For instance, someone experiencing blindness due to conversion disorder may avoid unpleasant tasks like working.

Dissociative Disorders

Dissociative disorders involve a disruption in conscious processes. Dissociative amnesia and dissociative identity disorder (DID) are classified as dissociative disorders. **Dissociative amnesia** is when a person cannot remember things and no physiological basis for the disruption in memory can be identified. Biologically induced amnesia is called **organic amnesia**.

Dissociative identity disorder, formerly known as multiple personality disorder, is when a person has several personalities rather than one integrated personality. Someone with DID can have any number of personalities. The different personalities can represent many different ages and both sexes. Often, two of the personalities will be the opposite of each other. People with DID commonly have a history of sexual abuse or some other terrible childhood trauma.

Theories About the Cause of Dissociative Disorders

Psychoanalytic theorists believe that dissociative disorders result when an extremely traumatic event has been so thoroughly repressed that a split in consciousness results. Behaviorists posit that people who have experienced trauma simply find not thinking about it to be rewarding, thus producing amnesia or, in extreme cases, DID.

Interestingly, cases of DID are rare outside of the United States, where the number increased dramatically in the last century as cases became more publicized. Coupled with the growing belief on the part of many psychologists that people do not engage in repression, these facts have led many to question whether DID is a legitimate psychological disorder. Critics suggest that some people diagnosed with DID may have been led to role-play the disorder inadvertently as a result of their therapists' questions (e.g., "Is there a part of you that feels differently?") and media portrayals.

Depressive Disorders

Someone with a **mood** or **affective disorder** experiences extreme or inappropriate emotions. **Major depressive disorder**, also known as unipolar depression, is the most common mood disorder and is often referred to as the common cold of all psychological disorders. While we all feel unhappy now and again, most of us do not suffer from major depressive disorder. The DSM-5 outlines the symptoms that must be present for such a diagnosis. One key factor is the length of the depressive episode. People who are clinically depressed remain unhappy for more than two weeks in the absence of a clear reason. Other common symptoms of depression include loss of appetite, fatigue, change in sleeping patterns, lack of interest in normally enjoyable activities, and feelings of worthlessness. Some people experience depression but only during certain times of the year, usually winter, when there is less sunlight. **Seasonal affective disorder (SAD)** is the resulting diagnosis. SAD is often treated with light therapy.

Theories About the Cause of Depressive Disorders

Psychoanalysts commonly view depression as the product of anger directed inward, loss during the early psychosexual stages, or an overly punitive superego. Learning theorists view the mood disorder as bringing about some kind of reinforcement such as attention or sympathy.

Aaron Beck, a cognitive theorist, believed that depression results from unreasonably negative ideas that people have about themselves, their world, and their futures. Beck calls these three components the **cognitive triad**. Another way that cognitive psychologists look at the cause of depression is by exploring the kind of attributions that people make about their experiences. An attribution is an explanation of cause. For instance, if Jonas fails a math test, he may attribute his failure to lack of studying, stupidity, his teacher, or a host of other causes. Pessimistic attributional styles seem more likely to promote depression. Jonas may attribute his failure to an internal (I am bad at math) or an external (The class is difficult) cause. He may attribute his failure to a global (I am bad at all subjects) or a specific (I have trouble with trigonometry) cause. Finally, Jonas may attribute his failure to a stable (I will always be bad at math) or to an unstable (I had a bad day) cause. People who tend to make internal, global, and stable attributions for bad events are more likely to be depressed. Often, these same people tend to make external, specific, and unstable attributions when good things happen to them.

Many theories about the cause of depression combine a cognitive and a behavioral component. An example of these social cognitive or cognitive-behavioral theories is **Martin Seligman's** idea of **learned helplessness**. Seligman conducted an experiment in which dogs received electric shocks. One group of dogs was able to terminate the shock by pressing a button with their noses, whereas the helpless group had no way to stop the shocks. In a second phase of the experiment, both groups of dogs were put in a situation in which they could easily escape electric shocks by moving to another part of the experimental chamber. While the dogs that were able to stop the shock in the first phase of the experiment quickly learned to move to the area where they would not be shocked, the other group of dogs just hunkered down and endured the shocks. Seligman suggested that due to their lack of ability to control their fate in the first phase of the experiment, these dogs had learned to act helpless.

Seligman further posited that humans, too, might suffer from learned helplessness. Depression has been found to correlate positively with feelings of learned helplessness. Learned helplessness is when one's prior experiences have caused that person to view him- or herself as unable to control aspects of the future that are controllable. This belief, then, may result in passivity and depression. When undesirable things occur, that individual feels unable to improve the situation and therefore becomes depressed.

A growing body of evidence suggests that a biological component to affective disorders exists. Low levels of serotonin, a neurotransmitter, have been linked with major depressive disorder. People who suffer from bipolar disorder have more receptors for acetylcholine, also a neurotransmitter, in their brains and skin. Other researchers have suggested that low levels of norepinephrine are associated with depression. Both unipolar depression and bipolar disorder often respond to somatic therapies (see Chapter 13, "Treatment of Psychological Disorders"). This suggests that these disorders are caused, at least partially, by biological factors. In addition, both major depressive disorder and bipolar disorder seem to run in families, a finding that can also be interpreted as indicative of a genetic component to their etiology.

Bipolar and Related Disorders

Unlike unipolar depression, **bipolar disorder**, formerly known as **manic depression**, usually involves both depressed and manic episodes. The depressed episodes involve all of the symptoms discussed above. People experience manic episodes in different ways but they usually involve feelings of high energy. While some sufferers will feel a heightened sense of confidence and power, others simply feel anxious and irritable. Even though some people feel an inflated sense of well-being during the manic period, they usually engage in excessively risky and poorly thought-out behavior that ultimately has negative consequences for them. A small number of people appear to experience **mania** without depression.

Schizophrenic Disorders

Schizophrenia is probably the most severe and debilitating of the psychological disorders. It tends to strike people as they enter young adulthood. The fundamental symptom of schizophrenia is disordered, distorted thinking often demonstrated through delusions, hallucinations, disorganized language, and/or unusual affect and motor behavior.

Delusions are beliefs that have no basis in reality. If I believed that I was going to win a Nobel Prize in literature for writing this book, I would be experiencing a delusion. Common delusions include:

- **Delusions of persecution**—the belief that people are out to get you.
- **Delusions of grandeur**—the belief that you enjoy greater power and influence than you do, that you are the president of the United States or a Nobel Prize–winning author.

Hallucinations are perceptions in the absence of any sensory stimulation. If I keep thinking I see newspaper headlines, "Weseley Wins Nobel," and hordes of autograph seekers outside my window, then I am suffering from hallucinations.

Schizophrenics often evidence some odd uses of language. They may make up their own words (**neologisms**) or string together a series of nonsense words that rhyme (**clang associations**). In addition, people with schizophrenia often evidence **inappropriate affect**. For instance, they might laugh in response to hearing someone has died. Alternatively, they may consistently have essentially no emotional response at all (**flat affect**).

TIP

People often confuse schizophrenia with DID. Schizophrenics *do not* have split personalities. Schism does mean break, but the break referred to in the term **schizophrenia** is a break from reality and not a break within a person's consciousness.

Some schizophrenics suffer from **catatonia**, a motor problem. They may remain motionless in strange postures for hours at a time, move jerkily and quickly for no apparent reason, or alternate between the two. When motionless, catatonic schizophrenics usually evidence **waxy flexibility**. That is, they allow their body to be moved into any alternative shape and will then hold that new pose.

Schizophrenic symptoms are often divided into two types: positive and negative. **Positive symptoms** refer to excesses in behavior, thought, or mood such as neologisms and hallucinations, whereas **negative symptoms** correspond to deficits such as flat affect or catatonia.

The DSM-IV-TR distinguished among several different subtypes of schizophrenia. The new edition eliminates these subtypes due to concerns about the reliability and validity of these more specific diagnoses.

Theories About the Cause of Schizophrenic Disorders

One of the most popular ideas about the cause of schizophrenia is biological and is called the **dopamine hypothesis**. The basic idea behind the dopamine hypothesis is that high levels of dopamine seem to be associated with schizophrenia. The evidence for this link includes the findings detailed below:

- Antipsychotic drugs used to treat schizophrenia result in lower dopamine levels and a decrease in the disordered thought and behavior that is the hallmark of schizophrenia. However, extensive use of these drugs may also cause negative side effects: muscle tremors and stiffness, a problem known as **tardive dyskinesia**.
- Parkinson's disease, characterized by muscle stiffness and tremors not unlike tardive dyskinesia, is treated with a drug called l-dopa that acts to increase dopamine levels. When given in excess, l-dopa causes schizophrenic-like distortions in thought.

More evidence suggests a biological basis for schizophrenia as well. Enlarged brain ventricles are associated with schizophrenia, as are brain asymmetries. Furthermore, a genetic predisposition seems to exist for schizophrenia. People who are related to schizophrenics suffer from the disorder at an increased rate, and the closer the relationship, the higher the incidence of the disorder. The incidence of schizophrenia in the general population is 1 in 100, but it rises to nearly 1 in 2 among identical twins whose co-twins are schizophrenic. As is the case with most disorders, a number of genes have been identified that seem to play a role in predisposing people to schizophrenia. Some research has suggested that negative symptoms are linked to genetic factors, whereas positive symptoms tend to be related to abnormalities in dopamine levels.

Not surprisingly, not all psychologists agree that schizophrenia has a biological basis. Some people believe that certain kinds of environments may cause or increase the likelihood of developing schizophrenia. One commonly suggested cognitive-behavioral cause is the existence of **double binds**. A double bind is when a person is given contradictory messages. If when growing up, Sally is continually cautioned by her parents against acting promiscuously while they give her revealing, provocative outfits as gifts, Sally would be experiencing a double bind. People who live in environments full of such conflicting messages may develop distorted ways of thinking due to the impossibility of rationally resolving their experiences.

TIP

Do not confuse double binds, a hypothesized cause of schizophrenia, with double blinds, a way of eliminating experimenter bias.

Another theorized cause of schizophrenia comes from the **diathesis-stress model**. The diathesis-stress model is often applied to schizophrenia but can be more widely applied to many psychological and physical disorders. According to this model, environmental stressors can provide the circumstances under which a biological predisposition for illness can express itself. This theory helps explain why even people with identical genetic makeups (e.g., monozygotic twins) do not always suffer from the same disorders.

Personality Disorders

Personality disorders are well-established, maladaptive ways of behaving that negatively affect people's ability to function. The most important personality disorder with which you should be familiar is **antisocial personality disorder**. People with antisocial personality disorder have little regard for other people's feelings. They view the world as a hostile place where people need to look out for themselves. Not surprisingly, criminals seem to manifest a high incidence of antisocial personality disorder.

TIP

Although your vocabulary will generally help you figure out what psychological terms mean, sometimes it will mislead you. For instance, many students incorrectly assume that people who suffer from antisocial personality disorder are merely unfriendly. In reality, as explained above, people with antisocial personality disorder are insensitive to others and thus often act in ways that bring pain to others.

The characteristics of many other personality disorders are deducible from the names of the disorders. For instance, people with **dependent personality disorder** rely too much on the attention and help of others, and those with **paranoid personality disorder** feel persecuted. Similarly, but based on words more difficult to define, **narcissistic personality disorder** involves seeing oneself as the center of the universe (**narcissism** means "self-love"), and **histrionic personality disorder** connotes overly dramatic behavior (histrionics). Keep in mind that a personality disorder is a more minor form of disorder than the others we have discussed. Therefore, people with paranoid personality disorder may believe they are being persecuted, but they will not experience the distortion of thought and delusions that some schizophrenics do. Likewise, people with **obsessive-compulsive personality disorder** may be overly concerned with certain thoughts and performing certain behaviors, but they will not be debilitated to the same extent that someone with obsessive-compulsive disorder would.

Other Examples of Psychological Disorders

The DSM describes a wide variety of disorders. Although this chapter certainly cannot be comprehensive, some additional problems will be briefly discussed.

Table 12.2 Summary of Categories of Psychological Disorders

Category of Disorder	Major Symptoms	Examples
Anxiety disorders	Anxiety—autonomic arousal, nervousness	Phobias, GAD, panic disorder
Somatic sympton disorders	Physical complaints without any organic cause	Conversion disorder
Dissociative disorders	Disruption in consciousness	DID, psychogenic amnesia
Mood disorders	Disturbances in mood	Major depressive disorder, bipolar disorder
Schizophrenia	Delusions, hallucinations	Prior to the latest revision of the DSM, schizophrenics were categorized as disorganized, paranoid, catatonic, undifferentiated
Personality disorders	Maladaptive ways of behaving	Antisocial, narcissistic, obsessive

Obsessive-compulsive disorder, known as **OCD**, is when persistent, unwanted thoughts (obsessions) cause someone to feel the need (compulsion) to engage in a particular action. For instance, a common obsession concerns cleanliness. A man experiencing this obsession might be plagued with constant worries that his environment is dirty and full of germs. These thoughts might drive him to wash his hands and shower repeatedly, even to the extent that he is able to do virtually nothing else. Obsessions result in anxiety, and this anxiety is reduced when the person performs the compulsive behavior. For this reason, OCD used to be classified as an anxiety disorder. However, the DSM-5 has created a separate classification for OCD and related disorders including hoarding and body dysmorphic disorder (an obsession with perceived defects related to one's appearance).

Post-traumatic stress disorder (PTSD) usually involves flashbacks or nightmares following a person's involvement in or observation of an extremely troubling event such as a war or natural disaster. Memories of the event cause anxiety. Like OCD, PTSD used to be classified as an anxiety disorder, but the DSM-5 moves it to a group of trauma and stressor-related disorders.

Paraphilias or **psychosexual disorders** are marked by the sexual attraction to an object, person, or activity not usually seen as sexual. For instance, attraction to children is called **pedophilia**, to animals is called **zoophilia**, and to objects, such as shoes, is called **fetishism**. Someone who becomes sexually aroused by watching others engage in some kind of sexual behavior is a **voyeur**, someone who is aroused by having pain inflicted upon him or her is a **masochist**, and someone who is aroused by inflicting pain on someone else is a **sadist**. Interestingly, the incidence of paraphilias is much higher in men than in women.

Feeding and eating disorders are another kind of psychological problem classified in the DSM-5. The relevant disorders we most often hear about include **anorexia nervosa**, **bulimia**, and **binge-eating disorder**. The basic symptoms that result in a diagnosis of anorexia nervosa are being at significantly low weight for one's age and size, an intense fear of fat and food, and a distorted body image. Anorexia nervosa, which predominates in girls and young women, is essentially a form of self-starvation. Bulimia shares similar features with anorexia nervosa such as a fear of food and fat and a distorted body image. However, bulimics do not lose as much of their body weight. Bulimia commonly involves a binge-purge cycle in which sufferers eat large quantities of food and then attempt to purge the food from their bodies by throwing up or using laxatives. Binge-eating disorder is thought to be the most commonly occurring eating disorder in the United States. It involves eating very large quantities of food in a short time while experiencing feelings of loss of control.

Another category of psychological disorders involves the use of substances such as alcohol and drugs. Use of such substances does not automatically mean one would be classified as having a disorder. **Substance-related and addictive disorders** is a diagnosis made when the use of such substances or behaviors like gambling regularly negatively affects a person's life.

One final example of the kinds of disorders in the DSM-5 is neurodevelopmental disorders. Some developmental disorders deal with deviations from typical social development. Children with **autism spectrum disorder** seek out less social and emotional contact than do other children and are less likely to seek out parental support when distressed. In addition, people with autism spectrum disorder tend to be hypersensitive to sensory stimulation and often exhibit intense interest in objects not viewed as interesting by most people (e.g., rubber bands) and often engage in simple, repetitive behaviors (e.g., flipping things).

Other developmental disorders involve difficulties in terms of developing skills. **Attention-deficit/hyperactivity disorder (ADHD)** is one example. A child with ADHD may have difficulty paying attention or sitting still. This disorder occurs much more commonly in boys. Critics suggest that the kind of behavior typical of young boys (regardless of whether its cause is biological, environmental, or a combination of the two) results in an overdiagnosis of this problem.

Finally, the DSM-5 discusses neurocognitive disorders, the most famous of which may be Alzheimer's disease. Alzheimer's is a form of dementia, a deterioration of cognitive abilities, often seen most dramatically in memory. The DSM-5 includes a diagnosis for both a major and mild form of neurocognitive disorders.

A CAUTIONARY NOTE

The DSM provides psychologists with an invaluable tool by enabling them to diagnose their clients. However, keep in mind that diagnostic labels are not always correct and have a tendency to outlast their usefulness.

THE ROSENHAN STUDY: THE INFLUENCE OF LABELS

In 1978, **David Rosenhan** conducted a study in which he and a number of associates sought admission to a number of mental hospitals. All claimed that they had been hearing voices; that was the sole symptom they reported. All were admitted to the institutions as suffering from schizophrenia. At that time, they ceased reporting any unusual symptoms and behaved as they normally did. None of the researchers were exposed as imposters, and all ultimately left the institutions with the diagnosis of schizophrenia in remission. While in the institutions, the researchers' every behavior was interpreted as a sign of their disorder. The Rosenhan study, while flawed and widely critiqued, raises several important issues:

1. Should people who were once diagnosed with a psychological problem carry that diagnosis for the rest of their lives?
2. To what extent are disorders the product of a particular environment, and to what extent do they inhere in the individual?
3. What is the level of institutional care available if the imposters could go undetected for a period of days and, in some cases, weeks?

Now that we have discussed various psychological disorders, the next chapter will discuss treatment methods.

Table 12.3 Major Changes in the DSM-V

Disorder	DSM-IV-TR	DSM-5
OCD	Classified as a type of anxiety disorder	Classified under "OCD and related disorders"
PTSD	Classified as an anxiety disorder	Classified under "trauma and stressor-related disorders"
Schizophrenia	Divided into disorganized, paranoid, catatonic, and undifferentiated	Subcategories eliminated
Autism, Asperger's	Four separate but related diagnoses, including autistic disorder and Asperger's	Autism spectrum disorder replace the four
Hypochondriasis	Diagnosed when many seemingly typical physical sensations were interpreted as signs of catastrophic illness	Now diagnosed as somatic symptom disorder

PRACTICE QUESTIONS

Directions: Each of the questions or incomplete statements below is followed by five suggested answers or completions. Select the one that is best in each case.

1. According to the DSM-5, which of the following is an anxiety disorder?
   (A) obsessive-compulsive disorder
   (B) conversion disorder
   (C) mania
   (D) post-traumatic stress disorder
   (E) panic disorder

2. All schizophrenics suffer from
   (A) depression.
   (B) multiple personalities.
   (C) flat affect.
   (D) distorted thinking.
   (E) delusions of persecution.

3. Juan hears voices that tell him to kill people. Juan is experiencing
   (A) delusions.
   (B) obsessions.
   (C) anxiety.
   (D) hallucinations.
   (E) compulsions.

4. Linda's neighbors describe her as typically shy and mild mannered. She seems to be a devoted wife and mother to her husband and three children. Unbeknown to these neighbors, Linda sometimes dresses up in flashy, revealing clothing and goes to bars to pick up strange men. At such times, she is boisterous and overbearing. She tells everyone she meets that her name is Jen. At other times, when she is upset, Linda slips into childlike behavior and responds only to the name Sally. Linda is suffering from a
   (A) schizophrenic disorder.
   (B) mood disorder.
   (C) dissociative disorder.
   (D) somatic symptom disorder.
   (E) psychosexual disorder.

5. The DSM contains

   I. a description of the symptoms of mental disorders.
   II. a description of the likely causes of all mental disorders.
   III. recommended methods of treatment for mental disorders.

   (A) I only
   (B) II only
   (C) III only
   (D) I and II
   (E) I, II, and III

6. All of the following are biomedical explanations for schizophrenia EXCEPT

   (A) double binds.
   (B) brain asymmetries.
   (C) the dopamine hypothesis.
   (D) a genetic predisposition.
   (E) enlarged brain ventricles.

7. Psychologists who draw from several different theoretical perspectives rather than strictly following one are known as

   (A) open-minded.
   (B) mixed.
   (C) flexible.
   (D) eclectic.
   (E) broad.

8. Depression is associated with low levels of

   (A) acetylcholine.
   (B) epinephrine.
   (C) serotonin.
   (D) dopamine.
   (E) GABA.

9. "I am the most important person in the world" is a statement that might characterize the views of someone with which of the following personality disorders?

   (A) schizoid
   (B) antisocial
   (C) histrionic
   (D) dependent
   (E) narcissistic

10. What kind of psychologist would be most likely to describe depression as the result of an unconscious process in which anger is turned inward?

   (A) biomedical
   (B) psychoanalytic
   (C) cognitive
   (D) behavioral
   (E) sociocultural

11. Women in the United States have a higher rate of depression than do men. Which kind of psychologist would be most likely to explain this higher incidence in terms of the pressures and prejudices that women suffer?
   (A) humanistic
   (B) psychoanalytic
   (C) cognitive
   (D) behavioral
   (E) sociocultural

12. The relationship between schizophrenia and Parkinson's disease is that
   (A) both are caused by too little dopamine.
   (B) both are treated by antipsychotic drugs.
   (C) both can be caused by excessive use of amphetamines.
   (D) schizophrenia is associated with too much dopamine and Parkinson's with too little.
   (E) Parkinson's is associated with too much dopamine and schizophrenia with too little.

13. Anand is unable to move his right arm. He has been to scores of physicians seeking a cure, but none have been able to find any physiological reason for his paralysis. Anand may be suffering from
   (A) conversion disorder.
   (B) dissociative amnesia.
   (C) GAD.
   (D) SAD.
   (E) OCD.

14. Reni is sexually aroused by shoes. Reni might be diagnosed as having
   (A) pedophilia.
   (B) masochism.
   (C) sadism.
   (D) exhibitionism.
   (E) fetishism.

15. Which statement about bulimia is true?
   (A) Only women suffer from this disorder.
   (B) All bulimics use vomiting to rid their bodies of unwanted calories.
   (C) Bulimics lose in excess of 15 percent of the normal body weight for their age and size.
   (D) The sole cause of bulimia is society's emphasis on thinness.
   (E) Bulimics tend to be overly concerned with their weight and body image.

ANSWER KEY

1. **E**
2. **D**
3. **D**
4. **C**
5. **A**
6. **A**
7. **D**
8. **C**
9. **E**
10. **B**
11. **E**
12. **D**
13. **A**
14. **E**
15. **E**

ANSWERS EXPLAINED

1. **(E)** Panic disorder is an anxiety disorder. Although both obsessive-compulsive disorder and post-traumatic stress disorder were considered anxiety disorders under the DSM-IV-TR, both have been recategorized. Conversion disorder is a somatic symptom disorder, and mania is a mood disorder.

2. **(D)** Distortion of thought is the fundamental characteristic of schizophrenia. Schizophrenia is distinct from both depression and dissociative identity disorder, although, as discussed in the chapter, it is often confused with the latter. Although some schizophrenics manifest flat affect, it is not a symptom shared by all schizophrenics. Only some schizophrenics experience delusions of persecution.

3. **(D)** Perceiving sensory stimulation when none exists defines a hallucination. Delusions are irrational thoughts but do not involve a belief in the existence of sensory stimulation. Obsessions are persistent, unwanted thoughts. Compulsions are unwanted, repetitive actions that people engage in to reduce anxiety.

4. **(C)** Linda is suffering from dissociative identity disorder, a type of dissociative disorder.

5. **(A)** The DSM mainly contains the symptoms of the various disorders. For many disorders, neither causes nor treatments are addressed in the DSM because beliefs about both causes and treatments often depend on the theoretical model to which one subscribes.

6. **(A)** A double bind is when someone is told to do something and then punished for doing it. While some researchers theorize that double binds cause schizophrenia, they would be an environmental cause, not a physical or medical cause. All the other choices are biological factors that theoretically play a role in schizophrenia.

7. **(D)** Psychologists who draw on various perspectives in their work are known as eclectic. The other terms have no specific psychological meaning.

8. **(C)** Depression is associated with low levels of serotonin.

9. **(E)** Narcissism is the love of oneself. People who view themselves as the focus of the world would most likely be classified as having narcissistic personality disorder.

10. **(B)** Psychoanalysts view depression as the result of anger turned inward. Biomedical psychologists would see depression as the result of some biological cause. Cognitive psychologists would locate the cause in the person's style of thinking. Behaviorists believe depression is caused by one's reinforcement history. Psychologists adhering to the sociocultural model would fault aspects of society such as racism or poverty.

11. **(E)** Sociocultural psychologists believe that mental illness is mainly caused by certain negative aspects of society such as sexism.

12. **(D)** Schizophrenia is associated with high levels of dopamine and Parkinson's disease with low levels of dopamine. Schizophrenia is often treated with antipsychotic drugs. Excessive use of amphetamines is associated with both high levels of dopamine and schizophrenic-like symptoms.

13. **(A)** Anand's symptoms suggest he has conversion disorder, a type of somatoform or somatic symptom disorder in which no physical cause can be found for a physical complaint. The hallmark of dissociative amnesia is difficulty remembering things that are potentially disturbing and which cannot be explained by a physical trauma. GAD is generalized anxiety disorder, a constant, low-level sense of nervous tension. SAD, seasonal affective disorder, is a type of mood disorder in which people become depressed during prolonged periods of bad weather. OCD, obsessive-compulsive disorder, is unwanted, persistent thoughts that push people to perform unwanted, repetitive actions to reduce anxiety.

14. **(E)** Paraphilias involve sexual arousal and interest in people, objects, or situations not generally considered arousing. More specifically, Reni has a fetish since he is aroused by an object. Pedophilia is a sexual attraction to children. Masochism is when one needs to be hurt in order to be sexually aroused, and sadism is when one is aroused by inflicting pain on others. Exhibitionism is when one is aroused by exposing him- or herself to others.

15. **(E)** Bulimics tend to be overly concerned with their weight and body image. These concerns lead them to engage in the binge-purge cycle that typifies bulimia. A growing number of men suffer from bulimia. Not all bulimics use vomiting to purge unwanted calories. Other methods include using laxatives, diuretics, and excessive exercise. Anorexics, not bulimics, lose more than 15 percent of their normal body weight. As is true of most, if not all, disorders, the cause of bulimia is a matter of some debate.

Treatment of Psychological Disorders

13

Key Terms

- Trephining
- Deinstitutionalization
- Prevention
- Psychotherapy
- Psychoanalysis
- Free association
- Dream analysis
- Manifest content
- Latent content
- Resistance
- Transference
- Insight therapies
- Humanistic therapies
- Client or person-centered therapy
- Unconditional positive regard
- Active or reflective listening
- Gestalt therapy
- Existential therapies
- Behaviorist therapies
- Counterconditioning
- Systematic desensitization
- Anxiety hierarchy
- Flooding
- Aversive conditioning
- Token economy
- Cognitive therapies
- Attributional style
- Cognitive therapy
- Cognitive behavioral therapy (CBT)
- Rational emotive behavior therapy (REBT)
- Group therapies
- Somatic therapies
- Psychopharmacology
- Antipsychotic drugs
- Antidepressants
- Antianxiety drugs
- Electroconvulsive therapy (ECT)
- Psychosurgery
- Psychiatrists
- Clinical psychologists
- Counseling psychologists
- Psychoanalysts

Key People

- Sigmund Freud
- Carl Rogers
- Fritz (Friedrich, Frederick) Perls
- Mary Cover Jones
- Joseph Wolpe
- B. F. Skinner
- Aaron Beck
- Albert Ellis

OVERVIEW

Just as there are many different views about the cause of mental disorders, many different beliefs exist about the appropriate way to treat psychological illness. All the methods of treatment, however, share a common purpose: to alter the client's behavior, thoughts, and/or feelings.

HISTORY

People have always suffered from psychological problems, but the attitudes toward and treatment of these people have changed dramatically. In many early societies, the mentally ill were seen as possessed by evil spirits. Archaeologists have unearthed human skulls with regularly shaped holes that seem to have been purposefully made. Researchers theorize that the making of the holes, a process called **trephining** was an early form of treatment that was supposed to let the harmful spirits escape.

Although both Hippocrates, who lived in Ancient Greece circa 500 B.C., and Galen, who lived in Rome circa 200 A.D., posited that psychological illnesses were influenced by biological factors and could therefore be treated, Europeans during the Middle Ages returned to the belief that demons and spirits were the cause. Persecution, rather than treatment, usually resulted.

The Enlightenment led to a more sympathetic view. Leading the call to treat victims of mental illness more humanely at the turn of the nineteenth century were Philippe Pinel in France and Dorothea Dix in the United States. These reformers railed against a system that treated the mentally ill as if they were criminals, even caging and beating them. These two helped bring about the development of separate and kinder institutions for people with severe psychological disorders.

Several recent trends in the field of mental health in the United States must also be mentioned. Following the development of drugs in the 1950s that could moderate the effects of severe disorders, many people were released from mental institutions. This phenomenon, called **deinstitutionalization**, was intended to save money as well as benefit the former inpatients. Unfortunately, deinstitutionalization was far less successful than initially hoped. Once released, many of the former patients were unable to care for themselves. Their psychological needs were supposed to be met by local clinics on an outpatient basis. Many of the people released, however, were schizophrenics who ended up homeless and delusional, unable to secure the psychological or the financial care they needed.

Recently, in the United States, a growing emphasis has been placed on **preventative efforts**. If psychological problems can be treated proactively, or before they become severe, the suffering of the client as well as the cost of providing care can be reduced. Preventative efforts can be described as primary, secondary, or tertiary. **Primary prevention** efforts attempt to reduce the incidence of societal problems, such as joblessness or homelessness, that can give rise to mental health issues. **Secondary prevention** involves working with people at-risk for developing specific problems. One example would be counseling people who live in an area that has experienced a trauma such as a natural disaster or terrorist attack. Finally, **tertiary prevention** efforts aim to keep people's mental health issues from becoming more severe, for instance, working with earthquake survivors who are already suffering from an anxiety disorder in the hopes of preventing the disorder from becoming more severe.

TYPES OF THERAPY

Clearly, people's beliefs about effective treatment are grounded in their ideas about the cause of the problem. Psychoanalytic, humanistic, behavioral, and cognitive psychologists share a belief in the power of **psychotherapy** to treat mental disorders. On the other hand, psychologists who subscribe to a biomedical model assert that such problems require **somatic treatments** such as drugs. Psychotherapies, except for behavioral treatments, largely consist of talking to a psychologist. Behaviorists, as you know, believe that psychological problems result from the contingencies of reinforcement to which a person has been exposed. Therefore, behavioral therapy focuses on changing these contingencies.

> **TIP**
> Some students confuse psychotherapy, a general term used to describe any kind of therapy that treats the mind and not the body, with psychoanalysis, a specific kind of psychotherapy pioneered by Sigmund Freud.

Both psychologists with a biomedical orientation and psychoanalysts generally refer to the people who come to them for help as **patients**. Other therapists, humanistic therapists in particular, prefer the term **clients**. In discussing the various types of therapy, we will follow these conventions.

Psychoanalytic Therapy

Psychoanalysis is a therapeutic technique developed by **Sigmund Freud**. A patient undergoing traditional psychoanalysis will usually lie on a couch while the therapist sits in a chair out of the patient's line of vision.

Psychoanalytic theorists view the cause of disorders as unconscious conflicts. As a result, their focus is on identifying the underlying cause of the problem. Psychoanalysts believe that other methods of therapy may succeed in ridding a client of a particular symptom but do not address the true problem. As a result, psychoanalysts assert that patients will suffer from **symptom substitution**. Symptom substitution is when, after a person is successfully treated for one psychological disorder, that person begins to experience a new psychological problem. Psychoanalytic therapists argue that a person's symptoms are the outward manifestations of deeper problems that can be cured only through analysis. Often, this approach entails a lengthy, and therefore expensive, course of therapy.

To delve into the unconscious minds of his patients, Freud developed a number of techniques including hypnosis, free association, and dream analysis. **Hypnosis**, as described in Chapter 4, "States of Consciousness," is an altered state of consciousness. When in this state, psychoanalysts believe that people are less likely to repress troubling thoughts. More commonly, psychoanalysts ask patients to **free associate**—to say whatever comes to mind without thinking. This technique is based on the idea that we all constantly censor what we say, thereby allowing us to hide some of our thoughts from ourselves. If we force ourselves to say whatever pops into our minds, we are more likely to reveal clues about what is really bothering us by eluding the ego's defenses. When psychoanalysts use **dream analysis**, discussed further in Chapter 4, they ask their patients to describe their dreams. Again, since the ego's defenses are relaxed during sleep, they hope the dreams will help the therapist see what is at the root of the patient's problem.

All three of these techniques rely heavily on the **interpretations** of the therapists and are criticized for their inherent subjectivity. In dream analysis, what the patient reports is called the **manifest content** of the dream. What is really of interest to the analyst is the **latent** or hidden content. The latent content of the dream is revealed only as a result of the therapist's interpretive work.

Sometimes patients may disagree with their therapists' interpretations. Psychoanalysts may see such objections as signs of **resistance**. Since psychoanalysis can be a painful process of coming to terms with deeply repressed, troubling thoughts, people are thought to try to protect themselves through resistance. In fact, a particularly strongly voiced disagreement to an analyst's suggestion is often viewed as an indication that the analyst is closing in on the source of the problem.

One final aspect of psychoanalysis involves **transference**. Transference is when, in the course of therapy, patients begin to have strong feelings toward their therapists. Patients may think they are in love with their therapists, may view their therapists as parental figures, or may seethe with hatred toward them. Psychoanalysts believe that, in the process of therapy, patients often redirect strong emotions felt toward people with whom they have had troubling relationships (often their parents) onto their therapists. Analysts try to interpret their patients' transference as a further technique to reveal the source of the problem.

As discussed earlier in this book, while strict adherents to Freudian theory are still known as psychoanalysts, many other psychologists have been influenced by Freud's work but have significantly modified his original theory. Such psychologists are known as **psychodynamic** theorists. While psychodynamic psychologists generally still see the unconscious as an important element in understanding a person's difficulties, they will be more likely to use a variety of techniques associated with other perspectives.

Psychoanalytic/psychodynamic treatments and the humanistic therapies that will be discussed in the next section are sometimes referred to as insight therapies. **Insight therapies** highlight the importance of the patients/clients gaining an understanding of their problems.

Humanistic Therapies

Humanistic therapies focus on helping people to understand and accept themselves, and strive to **self-actualize**. Self-actualization means to reach one's highest potential. Humanistic psychologists view it as a powerful motivational goal. Humanistic therapists operate from the belief that people are innately good and also possess **free will**. A belief that people have free will means that they are capable of controlling their own destinies. **Determinism** is the opposite belief. It holds that people have no influence over what happens to them and that their choices are predetermined by forces outside of their control. Humanistic psychologists' belief in human goodness and free will leads these psychologists to assert that if people are supported and helped to recognize their goals, they will move toward self-fulfillment.

One of the best known of humanistic therapists is **Carl Rogers**. Rogers created **client-centered therapy**, also known as **person-centered therapy**. This therapeutic method hinges on the therapist providing the client with what Rogers termed **unconditional positive regard**. Unconditional positive regard is blanket acceptance and support of a person regardless of what the person says or does. Rogers believes that unconditional positive regard is essential to healthy development. People who have not experienced it may come to see themselves in the negative ways that others have made them feel. By providing unconditional positive regard, humanistic therapists seek to help their clients accept and take responsibility for themselves.

In stark contrast to the cognitive therapies to be discussed later, client-centered therapy, and humanistic therapies in general, are **non-directive**. In other words, Rogerian therapists would not tell their clients what to do but, rather, would seek to help the clients choose a course of action for themselves. Often, client-centered therapists say very little. They encourage the clients to talk a lot about how they feel and sometimes mirror back those feelings ("So what I'm hearing you say is . . .") to help clarify the feelings for the client. This technique is known as **active listening**.

Another type of humanistic therapy is **Gestalt therapy**, developed by **Fritz Perls**. As we have discussed, Gestalt psychologists emphasize the importance of the whole. These therapists encourage their clients to get in touch with their whole selves. For example, Gestalt therapists encourage their clients to explore feelings of which they may not be aware and emphasize the importance of body position and seemingly minute actions. These therapists want their clients to integrate all of their actions, feelings, and thoughts into a harmonious whole. Gestalt therapists also stress the importance of the present because one can best appreciate the totality of an experience as it occurs.

Existential therapies are humanistic therapies that focus on helping clients achieve a subjectively meaningful perception of their lives. Existential therapists see clients' difficulties as caused by the clients having lost or failed to develop a sense of their lives' purpose. Therefore, these therapists seek to support clients and help them formulate a vision of their lives as worthwhile.

Behavioral Therapies

Behaviorists believe that all behavior is learned. In Chapter 6, we discussed various ways that people learn including classical conditioning, operant conditioning, and modeling. Behaviorists base their therapies upon these same learning principles.

One such technique is **counterconditioning**, a kind of classical conditioning developed by **Mary Cover Jones** in which an unpleasant conditioned response is replaced with a pleasant one. For instance, suppose Charley is afraid of going to the doctor and cries hysterically as soon as he enters the doctor's office. His mother might attempt to replace the conditioned response of crying with contentment by bringing Charley's favorite snacks and toys with them every time they go to the office.

One behaviorist method of treatment involving counterconditioning has had considerable success in helping people with anxiety disorders, especially phobias. It was developed by **Joseph Wolpe** and is called **systematic desensitization**. This process involves teaching the client to replace the feelings of anxiety with **relaxation**. The first step in systematic desensitization is teaching the client to relax. A variety of techniques can be used such as breathing exercises and meditation. Next the therapist and client work together to construct what is called an anxiety hierarchy. An **anxiety hierarchy** is a rank-ordered list of what the client fears, starting with the least frightening and ending with the most frightening. In the process of **in vivo desensitization**, the client confronts the actual feared objects or situations, while in **covert desensitization**, the client imagines the fear-inducing stimuli.

Imagine that Penelope has gone to a therapist for help with her arachnophobia (fear of spiders) and that she elects to try covert desensitization. At the bottom of Penelope's anxiety hierarchy is looking at a photograph of a small spider in a magazine while at the top is thinking of a number of harmless spiders crawling all over her. Other possible steps in the anxiety hierarchy include imagining engaging in behaviors such as looking at a live spider in a tank, touching a live spider while wearing gloves, and allowing one small spider to crawl on her leg. Once Penelope has learned some relaxation techniques and constructed an anxiety hierarchy with the therapist, she can begin to use **counterconditioning** to replace her fear of spiders with relaxation.

The therapist will ask Penelope to relax and then will ask her to imagine the first step on the anxiety hierarchy. In this case, she imagines looking at a picture of a small spider in a magazine. When Penelope can accomplish this task without feeling fear, the therapist will ask her to imagine the second step on the anxiety hierarchy. Penelope will continue to climb up the hierarchy until she feels anxious. As soon as she experiences anxiety, the therapist will tell her to take a step back down on the hierarchy until she feels calm again. This process will continue throughout Penelope's sessions with the therapist until she feels no anxiety, even when reaching the top of the hierarchy. This process is effective because learning through classical conditioning is strengthened by repeated pairings. Thus, the more times relaxation is paired with the feared stimuli, the stronger the relaxation response becomes.

Table 13.1 Penelope's Anxiety Hierarchy

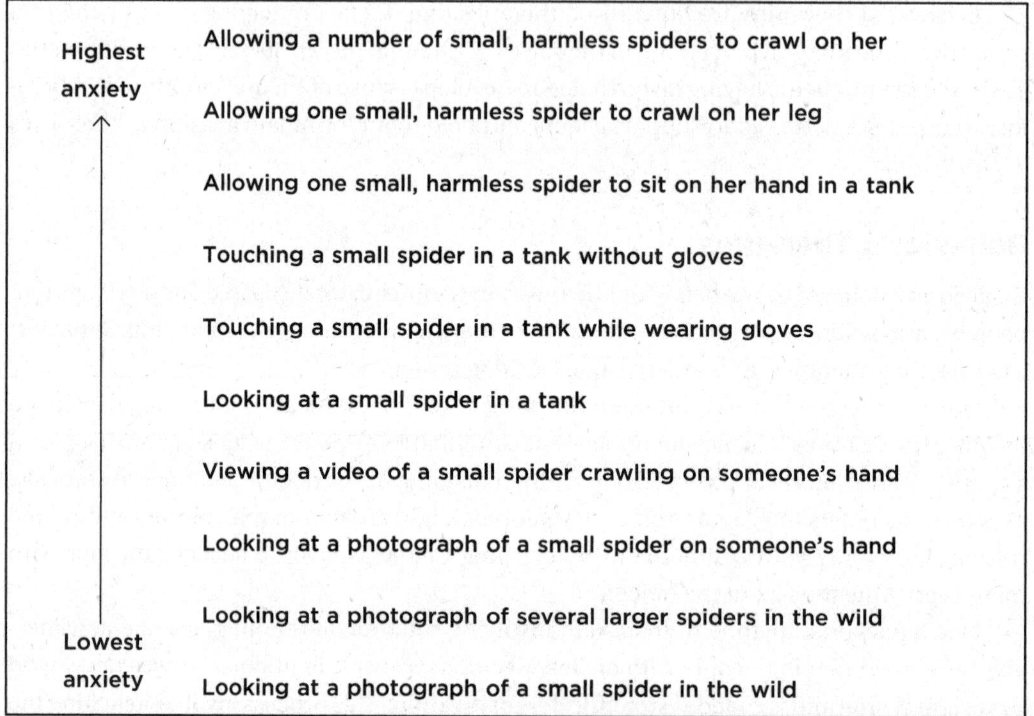

Highest anxiety ↑	Allowing a number of small, harmless spiders to crawl on her
	Allowing one small, harmless spider to crawl on her leg
	Allowing one small, harmless spider to sit on her hand in a tank
	Touching a small spider in a tank without gloves
	Touching a small spider in a tank while wearing gloves
	Looking at a small spider in a tank
	Viewing a video of a small spider crawling on someone's hand
	Looking at a photograph of a small spider on someone's hand
	Looking at a photograph of several larger spiders in the wild
Lowest anxiety	Looking at a photograph of a small spider in the wild

Another method of treating anxiety disorders that uses classical conditioning techniques is called **flooding**. Flooding, like systematic desensitization, can be in vivo or covert. Unlike the gradual process of systematic desensitization, flooding involves having the client address the most frightening scenario first. As one might expect, this technique produces tremendous anxiety. The idea, however, is that if clients face their fears and do not back down, they will soon realize that their fears are, in fact, irrational. In Penelope's case, if she were to begin by imagining that large spiders were crawling on her but that nothing bad was happening as a result, her fear would soon be **extinguished**.

Alternatively, Penelope's therapist could try to cure the phobia by using modeling. Modeling, as you will recall from Chapter 6, is a process through which one person learns by observing and then imitating the behavior of another. Unlike the other techniques described in this section, modeling is a melding of cognitive and behavioral ideas, but it makes sense to discuss it with systematic desensitization and flooding because all three are exposures therapies; all involve some degree of contact with the feared stimuli. Modeling could be used to treat Penelope's phobia by having her watch someone else interact calmly and without ill effect with various spiders and then asking her to reenact what she had witnessed. Modeling can also be used to help people with a host of other difficulties, as well.

Another way that classical conditioning techniques can be used to treat people is called **aversive conditioning**. This process involves pairing a habit a person wishes to break such as smoking or bedwetting with an unpleasant stimulus such as electric shock or nausea.

Operant conditioning can also be used as a method of treatment. This process involves using the principles developed by **B. F. Skinner** such as reinforcement and punishment to modify a person's behavior. One form of instrumental conditioning used in mental institutions, schools, and even in some people's homes is called a **token economy**. In a token economy, desired behaviors are identified and rewarded with tokens. The tokens can then be exchanged for various objects or privileges.

Cognitive Therapies

As cognitive therapists locate the cause of psychological problems in the way people think, their methods of therapy concentrate on changing these unhealthy thought patterns. Cognitive therapy is often quite combative as therapists challenge the irrational thinking patterns of their clients. An example of an unhealthy way of thinking is to attribute all failures to internal, global, and permanent aspects of the self. Assume Josephine fails a psychology test. She can explain this failure in many ways. A pessimistic and unhealthy **attributional style** would involve thinking that she is an idiot who will fail all tests in all subjects all the time. A healthier attributional style would view the cause of the failure as external (the test was difficult), specific (this topic was particularly difficult), and temporary (she will do better next time).

Aaron Beck created **cognitive therapy**, a process most often employed in the treatment of depression. This method involves trying to get clients to engage in pursuits that will bring them success. This will alleviate the depression while also identifying and challenging the irrational ideas that cause their unhappiness. Beck explains depression using the **cognitive triad**, people's beliefs about themselves, their worlds, and their futures. People suffering from depression often have irrationally negative beliefs about all three of these areas. Cognitive therapy aims to make these beliefs more positive.

Cognitive Behavioral Therapies

One popular group of therapies combines the ideas and techniques of cognitive and behavioral psychologists. This approach to therapy is known as **cognitive behavioral therapy** or **CBT**.

An example of a specific type of CBT is **rational emotive behavior therapy** (also known as REBT and sometimes referred to as RET). REBT was developed by **Albert Ellis**. Therapists employing REBT look to expose and confront the dysfunctional thoughts of their clients. For instance, someone suffering from a social phobia might voice concern over being publicly embarrassed when giving a class presentation. By using REBT, a therapist would question both the likelihood of such embarrassment occurring and the impact that would result. The therapist's goal would be to show the client that not only is his or her failure an unlikely occurrence but that, even if it did occur, it would not be such a big deal. REBT focuses not just on how and what clients think but also on what they do. Often, clients are given homework assignments in which they are asked to engage in the behaviors they fear, thus demonstrating that the cataclysmic outcome they expect does not actually occur.

Group Therapy

Psychotherapy can involve groups of people in addition to one-on-one client-therapist interactions. Therapists running groups can have any of the orientations described above or can be eclectic, as described in the last chapter. One common use of group therapy is in treating families. This form of treatment is known as **family therapy**. Since a client's problems do not occur in a vacuum, many therapists find meeting with the whole family helpful in revealing the patterns of interaction between family members and altering the behavior of the whole family rather than just one member.

Sometimes group therapy involves meeting with a number of people experiencing similar difficulties. Such an approach is less expensive for the clients and offers them the insight and feedback of their peers in addition to that of the therapist. **Self-help groups** such as Alcoholics Anonymous (AA) are a form of group therapy that does not involve a therapist at all.

Somatic Therapies

Psychologists with a biomedical (biological) orientation, as mentioned earlier, see the cause of psychological disorders in organic causes. These include imbalances in neurotransmitters or hormones, structural abnormalities in the brain, or genetic predispositions that might underlie the other two. Therefore, these psychologists advocate the use of somatic therapies—therapies that produce bodily changes.

Table 13.2 Summary of Types of Psychotherapy

Perspective	Specific Example	Key Concepts/Techniques	Founder
Psychoanalytic	Psychoanalysis	Free association, dream analysis	Sigmund Freud
Humanistic	Client-centered therapy	Unconditional positive regard	Carl Rogers
Behaviorist	Systematic desensitization	Relaxation, anxiety hierarchy, counterconditioning	Joseph Wolpe
Cognitive	Cognitive	Challenging negative beliefs about the cognitive triad	Aaron Beck
Cognitive-behavioral	Rational emotive behavior therapy	Challenging illogical ways of thinking and assigning behavioral homework	Albert Ellis

The most common type of somatic therapy is drug therapy or **psychopharmacology**, also known as **chemotherapy**. Drugs treat many kinds of psychological problems, ranging from anxiety disorders to mood disorders to schizophrenia. The more severe a disorder, the more likely that drugs will be used to treat it. Schizophrenia, for example, is almost always treated with drugs. A shortcoming of most kinds of psychotherapy is its limited use in dealing with patients unable to express themselves coherently. Since disordered thought is the primary symptom of schizophrenia, people suffering from this disorder overwhelmingly have difficulty communicating with others, thus rendering psychotherapy of limited use.

Schizophrenia is generally treated with **antipsychotic** drugs such as **Thorazine** or **Haldol**. These drugs generally function by blocking the receptor sites for dopamine. Their effectiveness therefore provides support for the dopamine hypothesis described in Chapter 12.

An unfortunate side effect of antipsychotic medication is **tardive dyskinesia**, Parkinsonian-like, chronic muscle tremors.

Mood disorders often respond well to chemotherapy. The three most common kinds of drugs used to treat unipolar depression are **tricyclic antidepressants**, **monoamine oxidase (MAO) inhibitors**, and **serotonin-reuptake-inhibitor drugs** (most notably **Prozac**). All tend to increase the activity of serotonin, although tricyclics and MAO inhibitors seem to have wider effects. **Lithium**, a metal, is often used to treat the manic phase of bipolar disorder.

Anxiety disorders are also often treated with drugs. Essentially, these drugs act by depressing the activity of the central nervous system, thus making people feel more relaxed. Two main types of antianxiety drugs are **barbiturates**, such as **Miltown**, and **benzodiazepines**, including **Xanax** and **Valium**.

Table 13.3 lists the most common kinds of drugs used to treat many of the disorders discussed in Chapter 12.

Table 13.3 Chemotherapy

Type of Disorder	Type of Drug(s)
Anxiety disorders	Barbiturates, benzodiazepines
Unipolar depression	Monoamine oxidase (MAO) inhibitors, tricyclic antidepressants, serotonin-reuptake-inhibitors
Bipolar disorder	Lithium
Schizophrenia	Antipsychotics (neuroleptics)

Another kind of somatic therapy is **electroconvulsive therapy (ECT)**. In bilateral ECT, electric current is passed through both hemispheres of the brain. Unilateral ECT involves running current through only one hemisphere. Bilateral ECT, although generally more effective, also has more significant negative side effects, most notably loss of memory. The electric shock causes patients to experience a brief seizure. Prior to administering ECT, patients are given a muscle relaxant to reduce the effects of the seizure. Usually, following the seizure, patients briefly lose consciousness. ECT is a less common treatment than chemotherapy. It is used, most often, for severe cases of depression after other methods have failed. Although the means by which ECT works is not completely understood, one theory suggests that the benefits are the result of a change in the brain's blood flow patterns.

The most intrusive and rarest form of somatic therapy is **psychosurgery**. Psychosurgery involves the purposeful destruction of part of the brain to alter a person's behavior. Clearly, such a procedure is used only as a last resort and only on people suffering to a great extent. An early, and unfortunately widespread, form of psychosurgery was the **prefrontal lobotomy**. This operation involved cutting the main neurons leading to the frontal lobe of the brain. Although this procedure often calmed the behavior of patients, it reduced their level of functioning and awareness to a vegetative state. Even today, when surgical procedures have grown much more precise, debate remains over the risks of psychosurgery, and such procedures are done as a last resort.

Eclectic Therapies

If you asked a therapist which of the preceeding orientations they use, you might hear something like: "It depends. I use what works." Many therapists do not exclusively use one type of therapy. Therapeutic orientations can be combined in effective ways. For example, cognitive behavioral therapies combine some of the techniques you read about in the cognitive and behavioral therapies sections. Research indicates that cognitive behavioral therapies can be particularly effective for some anxiety and some mood disorders. For example, to treat an anxiety disorder a therapist might combine a behavioral intervention, such as a systematic desensitization, with talk therapy that helps the client understand his or her unrealistic cognitions about the source of the anxiety.

Somatic cognitive therapy is another very common combination eclectic therapy. Many therapists combine drug therapy along with cognitive talk therapy for mood and other disorders. For example, a person diagnosed with unipolar depression might receive a prescription for one of the serotonin-reuptake inhibitor (SSRI) drugs, such as Prozac or Zoloft, while going through cognitive talk therapy to explore negative cognitions that might be contributing to his or her depression.

KINDS OF THERAPISTS

In addition to the different orientations discussed above, therapists have various levels and kinds of training.

- Psychiatrists are medical doctors and are therefore the only therapists permitted to prescribe medication in most U.S. states. Not surprisingly, because of their backgrounds, psychiatrists often favor a biomedical model of mental illness and are often less extensively trained in psychotherapy.
- Clinical psychologists earn doctoral degrees (PhDs) that require four or more years of study. Part of their training involves an internship during which they are overseen by a more experienced professional. Clinical psychologists usually deal with people who are suffering from problems more severe than everyday difficulties with work or family.
- Counseling therapists or counseling psychotherapists typically have some kind of graduate degree in psychology. Their training also includes an internship overseen by a more experienced professional. Examples of counseling therapists include school psychologists and marriage and family therapists. Counseling therapists generally help people whose problems are less severe than those that bring people to clinical psychologists.
- Psychoanalysts are people specifically trained in Freudian methods. They may or may not hold medical degrees.

HOW EFFECTIVE IS THERAPY?

Although therapy is clearly not always successful and many people recover from a variety of disorders without any intervention, a number of studies have documented that therapy is generally effective. The success of the treatment process is also clearly affected by the relationship between client and therapist. Therefore, a person who has a bad experience with therapy with one therapist at one time might respond more positively to another practitioner in another situation.

PRACTICE QUESTIONS

Directions: Each of the questions or incomplete statements below is followed by five suggested answers or completions. Select the one that is best in each case.

1. Which kind of therapist is most likely to analyze a client's dreams?
   (A) behaviorist
   (B) cognitive
   (C) humanistic
   (D) psychoanalytic
   (E) biomedical

2. Coretta's therapist says little during their sessions and never makes any recommendations about what Coretta ought to do. What kind of therapy does Coretta's therapist most likely practice?
   (A) psychodynamic
   (B) behavioral
   (C) cognitive
   (D) biomedical
   (E) humanistic

3. Craig saw a behaviorist to treat his crippling test anxiety. After a few months, Craig no longer experiences any fear when taking tests; however, he has developed an obsessive-compulsive disorder. According to psychoanalysts, Craig is experiencing
   (A) free association.
   (B) symptom substitution.
   (C) an anxiety hierarchy.
   (D) problem transference.
   (E) interpretation.

4. Systematic desensitization is to in vivo desensitization as
   (A) flooding is to aversion therapy.
   (B) modeling is to implosive therapy.
   (C) aversion therapy is to modeling.
   (D) implosive therapy is to flooding.
   (E) implosive therapy is to in vivo implosive therapy.

5. At his last appointment with his therapist, Ivan explained that since he lost his job he has felt completely worthless and depressed. Which of the following statements would a strictly cognitive therapist be most likely to say?

   (A) "Tell me about your recent dreams."
   (B) "I'm going to give you a homework assignment to do three things that you used to enjoy."
   (C) "That's ridiculous; no one is completely worthless."
   (D) "So, you're feeling very down."
   (E) "What is your earliest childhood memory?"

6. Which process involves counterconditioning?

   (A) REBT
   (B) ECT
   (C) transference
   (D) somatic therapy
   (E) systematic desensitization

7. Which of the following is used as a somatic therapy for depression?

   (A) MAO inhibitors
   (B) client-centered therapy
   (C) cognitive therapy
   (D) dream analysis
   (E) free association

8. All of the following methods of treatment are or may be based on classical conditioning principles EXCEPT

   (A) token economy.
   (B) implosive therapy.
   (C) flooding.
   (D) systematic desensitization.
   (E) aversion therapy.

9. Maria has been in analysis for over a year. Recently, she has begun to suspect that she has fallen in love with Dr. Chin, her analyst. When she confesses her feelings, Dr. Chin is likely to tell Maria that she is experiencing

   (A) resistance.
   (B) transference.
   (C) a breakthrough.
   (D) irrational expectations.
   (E) unconditional positive regard.

10. Jeb has been working for the same company for three years. While his responsibilities have increased, his salary has not. Every time he resolves to talk with his supervisor about a raise, he loses his nerve. In therapy, Dr. Flores and her assistant demonstrate how Jeb might go about asking for a raise. Then the assistant pretends to be Jeb's boss, and Jeb practices asking for a raise. This process most closely resembles

    (A) REBT.
    (B) existential therapy.
    (C) modeling.
    (D) free association.
    (E) aversion therapy.

11. One difference between psychoanalytic and cognitive modes of treatment is that cognitive therapists

    (A) say little during sessions.
    (B) emphasize the primacy of behavior.
    (C) focus on the present.
    (D) view repressed thoughts about one's childhood as the root of most problems.
    (E) do not face their clients.

12. Which method of therapy is most eclectic?

    (A) psychodynamic
    (B) client-centered
    (C) aversive conditioning
    (D) psychoanalytic
    (E) token economy

13. Schizophrenia is most likely to be treated with

    (A) Prozac.
    (B) lithium.
    (C) Miltown.
    (D) Haldol.
    (E) Valium.

14. A common side effect of ECT is

    (A) tardive dyskinesia.
    (B) memory loss.
    (C) hallucinations.
    (D) hysteria.
    (E) violent episodes.

15. An unanticipated result of the deinstitutionalization movement was a (an)

    (A) increase in the homeless population.
    (B) increase in drug-related crime.
    (C) increase in the incidence of catatonic schizophrenia.
    (D) decrease in the availability of antipsychotic drugs.
    (E) decrease in the population of mental institutions.

ANSWER KEY

1. **D**
2. **E**
3. **B**
4. **D**
5. **C**
6. **E**
7. **A**
8. **A**
9. **B**
10. **C**
11. **C**
12. **A**
13. **D**
14. **B**
15. **A**

ANSWERS EXPLAINED

1. **(D)** Psychoanalysts see the root of disorders in unconscious conflicts. Therefore, their initial focus is to bring the conflict into conscious awareness. Due to patients' defenses, psychoanalysts need to employ special techniques to reveal the contents of the unconscious. Dream analysis is one such technique. Behaviorists are interested only in the clients' behavior. Cognitive therapists are more likely to explore the clients' waking thoughts. Humanistic psychologists will try to help clients clarify their own thoughts and feel positively about themselves. Therapists with a biomedical orientation will be most likely to recommend somatic therapies, like drugs.

2. **(E)** Coretta's therapist is nondirective and therefore is most likely to have a humanistic orientation. An example of such a therapy is Carl Rogers' client-centered therapy.

3. **(B)** Psychoanalysts believe that disorders are caused by unconscious conflicts that are not immediately apparent. Treating the symptom is essentially pointless since it may disappear but a new one will take its place, a phenomenon known as symptom substitution. Therefore, when Craig went to a behaviorist and was cured of his test anxiety in a few months, psychoanalysts would predict the development of a new symptom. Free association is a technique used by psychoanalysts to uncover the contents of the unconscious. An anxiety hierarchy is part of systematic desensitization, a behaviorist treatment for anxiety disorders. While no such thing as problem transference exists, transference occurs when patients put feelings about significant people in their lives onto the analyst. Analysts necessarily engage in interpretation to figure out the source of their patients' difficulties.

4. **(D)** Both systematic desensitization and in vivo desensitization are treatments for phobias and other anxiety disorders. In systematic desensitization, clients imagine the different levels of the anxiety hierarchy. However, in vivo densensitization involves experiencing the anxiety-provoking situations. Similarly, implosive therapy involves imagining an intensely feared situation until the fear is extinguished, while flooding consists of experiencing the highly anxiety-provoking situation until the fear is extinguished.

5. **(C)** Cognitive therapy is often somewhat confrontational as cognitive psychologists attempt to change the irrational ways their clients think. A common problem that cognitive psychologists fight is depressed people's tendency to globalize and internalize negative thoughts as evidenced by Ivan's assertion that he is completely worthless. The statements in choices A and E would more likely be made by a psychoanalytic or psychodynamic theorist as they suggest that the roots of many problems are laid in childhood and they stress the importance of the unconscious mind to which dreams are clues.

The statement in choice B would most likely be made by a behaviorist as it stresses the importance of behavior, and the statement in D reflects humanistic psychologists' belief in being nondirective and reflecting back what their clients say.

6. **(E)** Counterconditioning involves replacing a CR with a new CR. In systematic desensitization, clients are taught to replace fear with relaxation. None of the other therapies listed are based on learning principles.

7. **(A)** Somatic therapies, as opposed to psychotherapies, view the cause of the problem in biology and therefore involve medical treatments. MAO inhibitors are drugs sometimes prescribed to treat depression. All the other choices are types or aspects of psychotherapy.

8. **(A)** Classical conditioning is a kind of learning that results from associating two things, one of which is an unconditioned stimulus, together. In operant conditioning, the consequences of one's actions lead to learning. Token economies are based on the principles of operant conditioning; people will act in certain ways to attain rewards. Implosive therapy, flooding, and systematic desensitization are all based on classical conditioning methods. Aversion therapy is a broader term that includes both classical and operant conditioning methods.

9. **(B)** Transference is when patients misdirect feelings toward important people in their lives onto the therapist. Resistance also commonly occurs in psychoanalysis but is when a patient rejects the analyst's interpretations or otherwise seeks to thwart the therapeutic process.

10. **(C)** Modeling consists of observation and imitation. Jeb watches someone model how to ask for a raise, and then he practices that skill himself.

11. **(C)** Psychoanalysis stresses the importance of early childhood experience. Psychoanalysts spend a lot of time exploring patients' early lives. Cognitive therapists focus on helping their clients deal with the present. Neither type of therapist is particularly reticent; humanistic therapists are. Neither psychoanalysts nor cognitive therapists emphasize the importance of behavior; that focus characterizes behaviorists. Psychoanalysts, not cognitive psychologists, do see repressed thoughts from childhood as the root of most adult problems and do not face their patients.

12. **(A)** Eclectic therapies incorporate aspects of several different models rather than strictly adhere to one theoretical orientation. Psychodynamic therapy, while based on psychoanalysis, tends to incorporate aspects of other models as well. Client-centered therapy is humanistic. Aversive conditioning and token economies are behavioral. Psychoanalytic therapy is, of course, psychoanalytic.

13. **(D)** Haldol is an antipsychotic drug. Prozac is used to treat depression, lithium to treat mania, and Miltown and Valium to treat anxiety disorders.

14. **(B)** Memory loss, although often temporary, is a common side effect of ECT. Tardive dyskinesia is a side effect of the antipsychotic medications used to treat schizophrenia.

15. **(A)** The deinstitutionalization movement occurred when many patients were released from mental hospitals in the 1960s and 1970s. Many were schizophrenics who, unable to find jobs and adequate care outside of the hospital setting, became homeless.

UNIT 9

Social Psychology

This social psychology unit addresses several important theories that influence how human beings behave in groups, and how group membership impacts our thinking and behavior. Some of the most well-known and influential psychological research studies are described and discussed in this unit. You will find content from this unit in the "Social Psychology" chapter in the textbook you use for your AP Psychology class.

14 Social Psychology

Key Terms

- Attitude
- Mere exposure effect
- Central versus peripheral route to persuasion
- Cognitive dissonance
- Foot-in-the-door
- Door-in-the-face
- Norms of reciprocity
- Attribution theory
- Self-fulfilling prophecy
- Fundamental attribution error
- Collectivist versus individualistic cultures
- False-consensus effect
- Self-serving bias
- Just-world bias
- Stereotype
- Prejudice
- Ethnocentrism
- Discrimination
- Out-group homogeneity
- In-group bias
- Superordinate goals
- Frustration-aggression hypothesis
- Bystander effect
- Diffusion of responsibility
- Pluralistic ignorance
- Attraction research
- Social facilitation
- Social impairment
- Conformity
- Obedience
- Group norms
- Social loafing
- Group polarization
- Groupthink
- Deindividuation

Key People

- Richard LaPiere
- Leon Festinger
- James Carlsmith
- Harold Kelley
- Robert Rosenthal
- Lenore Jacobson
- Muzafer Sherif
- John Darley
- Bibb Latane
- Solomon Asch
- Stanley Milgram
- Irving Janis
- Philip Zimbardo

OVERVIEW

Social psychology is a broad field devoted to studying the way that people relate to others. Our discussion will focus on the development and expression of attitudes, people's attributions about their own behavior and that of others, the reasons why people engage in both antisocial and prosocial behavior, and how the presence and actions of others influence the way people behave.

A major influence on the first two areas we will discuss, attitude formation and attribution theory, is **social cognition**. This field applies many of the concepts you learned about in the field of cognition, such as memory and biases, to help explain how people think about themselves and others. The basic idea behind social cognition is that, as people go through their daily lives, they act like scientists, constantly gathering data and making predictions about what will happen next so that they can act accordingly.

ATTITUDE FORMATION AND CHANGE

One main focus of social psychology is attitude formation and change. An **attitude** is a set of beliefs and feelings. We have attitudes about many different aspects of our environment such as groups of people, particular events, and places. Attitudes are evaluative, meaning that our feelings toward such things are necessarily positive or negative.

A great deal of research focuses on ways to affect people's attitudes. In fact, the entire field of advertising is devoted to just this purpose. How can people be encouraged to develop a favorable attitude toward a particular brand of potato chips? Having been the target audience for many such attempts, you are no doubt familiar with a plethora of strategies used to promote favorable opinions toward a product.

The **mere exposure effect** states that the more one is exposed to something, the more one will come to like it. Therefore, in the world of advertising, more is better. When you walk into the supermarket, you will be more likely to buy the brand of potato chips you have seen advertised thousands of times rather than one that you have never heard of before.

Persuasive messages can be processed through the **central route** or the **peripheral route**. The central route to persuasion involves deeply processing the content of the message; what about this potato chip is so much better than all the others? The peripheral route, on the other hand, involves other aspects of the message including the characteristics of the person imparting the message (the communicator).

Certain characteristics of the communicator, have been found to influence the effectiveness of a message. Attractive people, famous people, and experts are among the most persuasive communicators. As a result, professional athletes and movie stars often have second careers making commercials. Certain characteristics of the audience also affect how effective a message will be. Some research suggests that more educated people are less likely to be persuaded by advertisements. Finally, the way the message is presented can also influence how persuasive it is. Research has found that when dealing with a relatively uninformed audience, presenting a one-sided message is best. However, when attempting to influence a more sophisticated audience, a communication that acknowledges and then refutes opposing arguments will be more effective. Some research suggests that messages that arouse fear are effective. However, too much fear can cause people to react negatively to the message itself.

THE RELATIONSHIP BETWEEN ATTITUDES AND BEHAVIOR

TIP

Attitudes do not perfectly predict behaviors. What people say they would do and what they actually would do often differ.

Although you might think that knowing people's attitudes would tell you a great deal about their behavior, research has found that the relationship between attitudes and behaviors is far from perfect. In 1934, **Richard LaPiere** conducted an early study that illustrated this difference. In the United States in the 1930s, prejudice and discrimination against Asians was pervasive. LaPiere traveled throughout the West Coast visiting many hotels and restaurants with an Asian couple to see how they would be treated. On only one occasion were they treated poorly due to their race. A short time later, LaPiere contacted all of the establishments they had visited and asked about their attitudes toward Asian patrons. Over 90 percent of the respondents said that they would not serve Asians. This finding illustrates that attitudes do not perfectly predict behaviors.

Sometimes if you can change people's behavior, you can change their attitudes. **Cognitive dissonance theory** is based on the idea that people are motivated to have consistent attitudes and behaviors. When they do not, they experience unpleasant mental tension or dissonance. For example, suppose Amira thinks that studying is only for geeks. If she then studies for 10 hours for her chemistry test, she will experience cognitive dissonance. Since she cannot, at this point, alter her behavior (she has already studied for 10 hours), the only way to reduce this dissonance is to change her attitude and decide that studying does not necessarily make someone a geek. Note that this change in attitude happens without conscious awareness.

Leon Festinger and **James Carlsmith** conducted the classic experiment about cognitive dissonance in the late 1950s. Their participants performed a boring task and were then asked to lie and tell the next subject (actually a confederate[1] of the experimenter) that they had enjoyed the task. In one condition, subjects were paid $1 to lie, and in the other condition they were paid $20. Afterward, the participants' attitudes toward the task were measured. Contrary to what reinforcement theory would predict, those subjects who had been paid $1 were found to have significantly more positive attitudes toward the experiment than those who were paid $20. According to Festinger and Carlsmith, having already said that the boring task was interesting, the subjects were experiencing dissonance. However, those subjects who had been paid $20 experienced relatively little dissonance; they had lied because they had been paid $20. On the other hand, those subjects who were paid only $1 lacked sufficient external motivation to lie. Therefore, to reduce the dissonance, they changed their attitudes and said that they actually did enjoy the experiment.

COMPLIANCE STRATEGIES

Often people use certain strategies to get others to comply with their wishes. Such **compliance strategies** have also been the focus of much psychological research. Suppose you need to borrow $20 from a friend. Would you be better off asking him or her for $20 right away, asking the friend first for $5 and then following up this request with another for the additional $15, or asking him or her for $100 and, after the friend refuses, asking for $20? The **foot-in-the-door** phenomenon suggests that if you can get people to agree to a small request, they will become more likely to agree to a follow-up request that is larger. Thus, once your friend agrees to lend you $5, he or she becomes more likely to lend you the additional funds. After all, the friend is clearly willing to lend you money. The **door-in-the-face** strategy argues that after people refuse a large request, they will look more favorably upon a follow-up request that seems, in comparison, much more reasonable. After flat-out refusing to lend you $100, your friend might feel bad. The least he or she could do is lend you $20.

Another common strategy involves using **norms of reciprocity**. People tend to think that when someone does something nice for them, they ought to do something nice in return. Norms of reciprocity is at work when you feel compelled to send money to the charity that sent you free return address labels or when you cast your vote in the student election for the candidate that handed out those delicious chocolate chip cookies.

[1] Many social psychology experiments use confederates to deceive participants. Confederates are people who, unbeknownst to the participants in the experiment, work with the experimenter.

ATTRIBUTION THEORY

Attribution theory is another area of study within the field of social cognition. Attribution theory tries to explain how people determine the cause of what they observe. For instance, if your friend Charley told you he got a perfect score on his math test, you might find yourself thinking that Charley is very good at math. In that case, you have made a **dispositional** or **person attribution.** Alternatively, you might attribute Charley's success to a situational factor, such as an easy test; in that case you make a **situation attribution.** Attributions can also be stable or unstable. If you infer that Charley has always been a math whiz, you have made both a person attribution and a **stable attribution**, also called a **person-stable attribution**. On the other hand, if you think that Charley studied a lot for this one test you have made a **person-unstable attribution**. Similarly, if you believe that Ms. Mahoney, Charley's math teacher, is an easy teacher, you have made a **situation-stable attribution.** If you think that Ms. Mahoney is a tough teacher who happened to give one easy test, you have made a **situation-unstable attribution.**

Table 14.1 How to Use Compliance Strategies to Get Your Teacher to Postpone a Test by One Day

Compliance Strategy	Definition	Example
Foot-in-the-door	A small request is followed by a larger request.	First ask for a little time to review by asking questions in class. After your teacher says yes, ask if the test could be postponed by one day.
Door-in-the-face	An unrealistically large request is followed by a smaller request.	First ask if the test could be postponed by one week. After your teacher says no, ask if the test could be postponed by one day.
Norms of reciprocity	People have the tendency to feel obligated to reciprocate kind behavior.	First bring your teacher his or her favorite snack. Then ask if the test could be postponed by one day.

Harold Kelley put forth a theory that explains the kind of attributions people make based on three kinds of information: **consistency**, **distinctiveness**, and **consensus**. Consistency refers to how similarly the individual acts in the same situation over time. How does Charley usually do on his math tests? Distinctiveness refers to how similar this situation is to other situations in which we have watched Charley. Does Charley do well on all tests? Has he evidenced an aptitude for math in other ways? Consensus asks us to consider how others in the same situation have responded. Did many people get a perfect score on the math test?

Consensus is a particularly important piece of information to use when determining whether to make a person or situation attribution. If Charley is the only one to earn such a good score on the math test, we seem to have learned something about Charley. Conversely, if everyone earned a high score on the test, we would suspect that something in the situation contributed to that outcome. Consistency, on the other hand, is extremely useful when determining whether to make a stable or unstable attribution. If Charley always aces his math tests, then it seems more likely that Charley is particularly skilled at math than that he happened to study hard for this one test. Similarly, if everyone always does well on Ms. Mahoney's tests, we would be likely to make the situation-stable attribution that she is an easy teacher.

However, if Charley usually scores low in Ms. Mahoney's class, we will be more likely to make a situation-unstable attribution such as this particular test was easy.

People often have certain ideas or prejudices about other people before they even meet them. These preconceived ideas can obviously affect the way someone acts toward another person. Even more interesting is the idea that the expectations we have about others can influence the way those others behave. Such a phenomenon is called a **self-fulfilling prophecy**. For instance, if Jon is repeatedly told that Chet, whom he has never met, is really funny, when Jon does finally meet Chet, he may treat Chet in such a way as to elicit the humorous behavior he expected.

A classic study involving self-fulfilling prophecies was **Robert Rosenthal** and **Lenore Jacobson's** (1968) "Pygmalion in the Classroom" experiment. They administered a test to elementary school children that supposedly would identify those children who were on the verge of significant academic growth. In reality, the test was a standard IQ test. These researchers then randomly selected a group of children from the population who took the test, and they informed their teachers that these students were ripe for such intellectual progress. Of course, since the children were selected randomly, they did not differ from any other group of children in the school. At the end of the year, the researchers returned to take another measure of the students' IQ and found that the scores of the identified children had increased more than the scores of their classmates. In some way, the teachers' expectations that these students would bloom intellectually over the year actually caused the students to outperform their peers.

Attributional Biases

Although people are quite good at sifting through all the data that bombards them and then making attributions, you will probably not be surprised to learn that errors are not uncommon. Moreover, people tend to make the same kinds of errors. A few typical biases are the fundamental attribution error, false-consensus effect, self-serving bias, and the just-world belief.

When looking at the behavior of others, people tend to overestimate the importance of dispositional factors and underestimate the role of situational factors. This tendency is known as the **fundamental attribution error**. Say that you go to a party where you are introduced to Claude, a young man you have never met before. Although you attempt to engage Claude in conversation, he is unresponsive. He looks past you and, soon after, seizes upon an excuse to leave. Most people would conclude that Claude is an unfriendly person. Few consider that something in the situation may have contributed to Claude's behavior. Perhaps Claude just had a terrible fight with his girlfriend, Isabelle. Maybe on the way to the party he had a minor car accident. The point is that people systematically seem to overestimate the role of dispositional factors in influencing another person's actions.

Interestingly, people do not evidence this same tendency in explaining their own behaviors. Claude knows that he is sometimes extremely outgoing and warm. Since people get to view themselves in countless situations, they are more likely to make situational attributions about themselves than about others. Everyone has been shy and aloof at times, and everyone has been friendly. Thus, people are more likely to say that their own behavior depends upon the situation.

TIP

Students often confuse self-serving bias and self-fulfilling prophecies, ostensibly because they both contain the word *self*. Self-serving bias is the tendency to overstate one's role in a positive venture and underestimate it in a failure. Thus, people serve themselves by making themselves look good. Self-fulfilling prophecies, on the other hand, explain how people's ideas about others can shape the behavior of those others.

One caveat must be added to our discussion of the fundamental attribution error. The fundamental attribution was named **fundamental** because it was believed to be so widespread. However, many cross-cultural psychologists have argued that the fundamental attribution error is far less likely to occur in **collectivist cultures** than in **individualistic cultures**. In an individualistic culture, like the American culture, the importance and uniqueness of the individual is stressed. In more collectivist cultures, like Japanese culture, a person's link to various groups such as family or company is stressed. Cross-cultural research suggests that people in collectivist cultures are less likely to commit the fundamental attribution error, perhaps because they are more attuned to the ways that different situations influence their own behavior.

The tendency for people to overestimate the number of people who agree with them is called the **false-consensus effect**. For instance, if Jamal dislikes horror movies, he is likely to think that most other people share his aversion. Conversely, Sabrina, who loves a good horror flick, overestimates the number of people who share her passion.

Self-serving bias is the tendency to take more credit for good outcomes than for bad ones. For instance, a basketball coach would be more likely to emphasize her or his role in the team's championship win than in their heartbreaking first-round tournament loss.

Researchers have found that people evidence a bias toward thinking that bad things happen to bad people. This belief in a just world, known simply as the **just-world bias**, in which misfortunes befall people who deserve them, can be seen in the tendency to blame victims. For example, the woman was raped because she was stupidly walking alone in a dangerous neighborhood. People are unemployed because they are lazy. If the world is just in this manner, then, assuming we view ourselves as good people, we need not fear bad things happening to ourselves.

STEREOTYPES, PREJUDICE, AND DISCRIMINATION

We all have ideas about what members of different groups are like, and these expectations may influence the way we interact with members of these groups. We call these ideas **stereotypes**. Stereotypes may be either negative or positive and can be applied to virtually any group of people (e.g., racial, ethnic, geographic). For instance, people often stereotype New Yorkers as pushy, unfriendly, and rude and Californians as easygoing and attractive. Some cognitive psychologists have suggested that stereotypes are basically schemata about groups. People who distinguish between stereotypes and group schemata argue that the former are more rigid and more difficult to change than the latter.

Prejudice is an undeserved, usually negative, attitude toward a group of people. Stereotyping can lead to prejudice when negative stereotypes (those rude New Yorkers) are applied uncritically to all members of a group (she is from New York, therefore she must be rude) and a negative attitude results.

Ethnocentrism, the belief that one's culture (e.g., ethnic, racial) is superior to others, is a specific kind of prejudice. People become so used to their own cultures that they see them as the norm and use them as the standard by which to judge other cultures. Many people look down upon others who don't dress the same, eat the same foods, or worship the same God in the same way that they do.

While prejudice is an attitude, **discrimination** involves an action. When one discriminates, one acts on one's prejudices. If I dislike New Yorkers, I am prejudiced, but if I refuse to hire New Yorkers to work in my company, I am engaging in discrimination. Unfortunately, stereotypes, prejudice, and discrimination all reinforce one another. People's beliefs and attitudes influence each other and guide people's behavior. In addition, when people act in discriminatory ways, they are motivated to strengthen their prejudices and stereotypes to justify their behavior.

Table 14.2 The Vicious Cycle of Stereotyping, Prejudice, and Discrimination

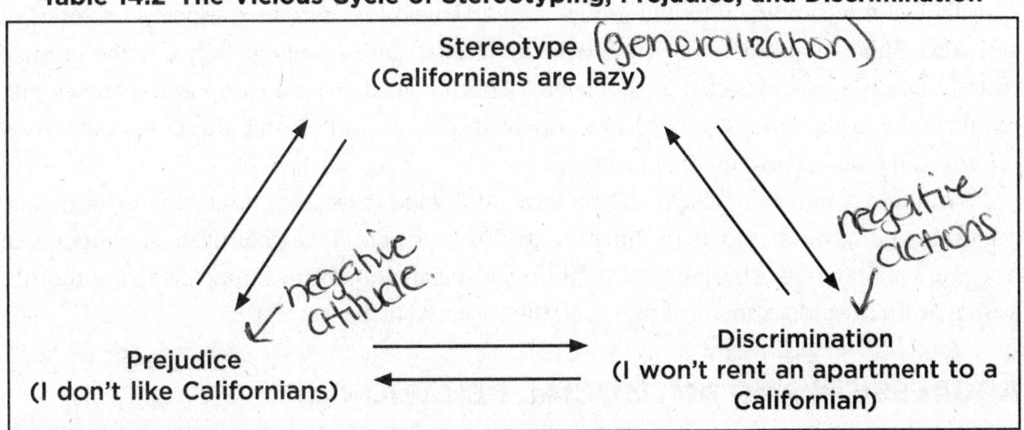

People tend to see members of their own group, the *in-group*, as more diverse than members of other groups, **out-groups**. This phenomenon is often referred to as **out-group homogeneity**. For example, as a New Yorker myself, I know that while some New Yorkers are indeed pushy and rude, most are not. I know many well-mannered and deferential New Yorkers as well as short New Yorkers, tall New Yorkers, honest New Yorkers, and dishonest New Yorkers. While we all have extensive experience with the members of our own groups, we lack that degree of familiarity with other groups and therefore tend to see them as more similar. In addition, researchers have documented a preference for members of one's own group, a kind of **in-group bias**. In-group bias is thought to stem from people's belief that they themselves are good people. Therefore, the people with whom they share group membership are thought to be good as well.

TIP

Students have difficulty distinguishing between prejudice and discrimination. Remember, the former is an attitude and the latter is a behavior.

Origin of Stereotypes and Prejudice

Many different theories attempt to explain how people become prejudiced. Some psychologists have suggested that people naturally and inevitably magnify differences between their own group and others as a function of the cognitive process of categorization. By taking into account the in-group bias discussed above, this idea suggests that people cannot avoid forming stereotypes.

Social learning theorists stress that stereotypes and prejudice are often learned through modeling. Children raised by parents who express prejudices may be more likely to embrace such prejudices themselves. Conversely, this theory suggests that prejudices could be unlearned by exposure to different models.

Combating Prejudice

One theory about how to reduce prejudice is known as the **contact theory**. The contact theory, as its name suggests, states that contact between hostile groups will reduce animosity, but only if the groups are made to work toward a goal that benefits all and necessitates the participation of all. Such a goal is called a **superordinate goal**.

Muzafer Sherif's (1966) camp study (also known as the Robbers Cave study) illustrates both how easily out-group bias can be created and how superordinate goals can be used to unite formerly antagonistic groups. He conducted a series of studies at a summer camp. He first divided the campers into two groups and arranged for them to compete in a series of activities. This competition was sufficient to create negative feelings between the groups. Once such prejudices had been established, Sherif staged several camp emergencies that required the groups to cooperate. The superordinate goal of solving the crises effectively improved relations between the groups.

A number of educational researchers have attempted to use the contact theory to reduce prejudices between members of different groups in school. One goal of most cooperative learning activities is to bring members of different social groups into contact with one another as they work toward a superordinate goal, the assigned task.

AGGRESSION AND ANTISOCIAL BEHAVIOR

Another major area of study for social psychologists is aggression and antisocial behavior. Psychologists distinguish between two types of aggression: **instrumental aggression** and **hostile aggression**. Instrumental aggression is when the aggressive act is intended to secure a particular end. For example, if Bobby wants to hold the doll that Carol is holding and he kicks her and grabs the doll, Bobby has engaged in instrumental aggression. Hostile aggression, on the other hand, has no such clear purpose. If Bobby is simply angry or upset and therefore kicks Carol, his aggression is hostile aggression.

Many theories exist about the cause of human aggression. Freud linked aggression to Thanatos, the death instinct. Sociobiologists suggest that the expression of aggression is adaptive under certain circumstances. One of the most influential theories, however, is known as the **frustration-aggression hypothesis**. This hypothesis holds that the feeling of frustration makes aggression more likely. Considerable experimental evidence supports it. Another common theory is that the exposure to aggressive models makes people aggressive as illustrated by Bandura, Ross, and Ross's (1963) classic Bobo doll experiment (see the modeling section in Chapter 6 for more information).

PROSOCIAL BEHAVIOR

While social psychologists have devoted a lot of time and effort to studying antisocial behavior, they have also studied the factors that make people more likely to help one another. Such helping behavior is termed **prosocial behavior**. Much of the research in this area has focused on **bystander intervention**, the conditions under which people nearby are more and less likely to help someone in trouble.

The vicious murder of Kitty Genovese in Kew Gardens, New York, committed within view of at least 38 witnesses, none of whom intervened, led **John Darley** and **Bibb Latane** to explore how people decided whether or not to help others in distress. Counterintuitively, the larger the number of people who witness an emergency situation, the less likely any one is to intervene. This finding is known as the **bystander effect**. One explanation for this phenomenon is called **diffusion of responsibility**. The larger the group of people who witness a problem, the less responsible any one individual feels to help. People tend to assume that someone else will take action so they need not do so. Another factor contributing to the bystander effect is known as **pluralistic ignorance**. People seem to decide what constitutes appropriate behavior in a situation by looking to others. Thus, if no one in a classroom seems worried by the black smoke coming through the vent, each individual concludes that taking no action is the proper thing to do.

ATTRACTION

Social psychologists also study what factors increase the chance that people will like one another. A significant body of research indicates that we like others who are similar to us, with whom we come into frequent contact, and who return our positive feelings. These three factors are often referred to as **similarity**, **proximity**, and **reciprocal liking**. Although conventional wisdom holds that opposites attract, psychological research indicates that we are drawn to people who are similar to us, those who share our attitudes, backgrounds, and interests. Proximity means nearness. As is suggested by the mere-exposure effect, the greater the exposure one has to another person, the more one generally comes to like that person. In addition, only by talking to someone can one identify the similarities that will draw the pair closer together. Finally, every reader has probably had the misfortune to experience that liking someone who scorns you is not enjoyable. Thus, the more someone likes you, the more you will probably like that person.

Not surprisingly, people are also attracted to others who are physically attractive. In fact, the benefits of being nice-looking extend well beyond the realm of attraction. Research has demonstrated that good-looking people are perceived as having all sorts of positive attributes including better personalities and greater job competence.

Psychologists have also devoted tremendous time and attention to the concept of love. While research seems to indicate that the emotion of love qualitatively differs from liking and a number of theories about love have been proposed, the subject has proven difficult to explain adequately.

A term often employed as part of liking and loving studies is **self-disclosure**. One self-discloses when one shares a piece of personal information with another. Close relationships with friends and lovers are often built through a process of self-disclosure. On the path to intimacy, one person shares a detail of his or her life and the other reciprocates by exposing a facet of his or her own.

THE INFLUENCE OF OTHERS ON AN INDIVIDUAL'S BEHAVIOR

A major area of research in social psychology is how an individual's behavior can be affected by another's actions or even merely by another person's presence. A number of studies have illustrated that people perform tasks better in front of an audience than they do when they are alone. They yell louder, run faster, and reel in a fishing rod more quickly. This phenomenon, that the presence of others improves task performance, is known as **social facilitation**.

Later studies, however, found that when the task being observed was a difficult one rather than a simple, well-practiced skill, being watched by others actually hurt performance, a finding known as **social impairment**.

Conformity has been an area of much research as well. Conformity is the tendency of people to go along with the views or actions of others. **Solomon Asch** (1951) conducted one of the most interesting conformity experiments. He brought participants into a room of confederates and asked them to make a series of simple perceptual judgments. Asch showed the participants three vertical lines of varying sizes and asked them to indicate which one was the same length as a different target line. All members of the group gave their answers aloud, and the participant was always the last person to speak. All of the trials had a clear, correct answer. However, on some of them, all of the confederates gave the same, obviously incorrect judgment. Asch was interested in what the participants would do. Would they conform to a judgment they knew to be wrong or would they differ from the group? Asch found that in approximately one-third of the cases when the confederates gave an incorrect answer, the participants conformed. Furthermore, approximately 70 percent of the participants conformed on at least one of the trials. In general, studies have suggested that conformity is most likely to occur when a group's opinion is unanimous. Although it would seem that the larger the group, the greater conformity that would be expressed, studies have shown that groups larger than three (in addition to the participant) do not significantly increase the tendency to conform.

While conformity involves following a group without being explicitly told to do so, **obedience studies** have focused on participants' willingness to do what another asks them to do. **Stanley Milgram** (1974) conducted the classic obedience studies. His participants were told that they were taking part in a study about teaching and learning, and they were assigned to play the part of teacher. The learner, of course, was a confederate. As teacher, each participant's job was to give the learner an electric shock for every incorrect response. The participant sat behind a panel of buttons each labeled with the number of volts, beginning at 15 and increasing by increments of 15 up to 450. The levels of shock were also described in words ranging from *mild* up to *XXX* - severe shock. In reality, no shocks were delivered; the confederate pretended to be shocked. As the level of the shocks increased, the confederate screamed in pain, said he suffered from a heart condition, and eventually fell silent. Milgram was interested in how far participants would go before refusing to deliver any more shocks. The experimenter watched the participant and, if questioned, gave only a few stock answers, such as "Please continue." Contrary to the predictions of psychologists who Milgram polled prior to the experiment, over 60 percent of the participants obeyed the experimenter and delivered all the possible shocks.

Milgram replicated his study with a number of interesting twists. He found that he could decrease participants' compliance by bringing them into closer contact with the confederates. Participants who could see the learners gave fewer shocks than participants who could only hear the learners. The lowest shock rates of all were administered by participants who had to force the learner's hand onto the shock plate. However, even in that last condition, approximately 30 percent delivered all of the shocks. When the experimenter left in the middle of the experiment and was replaced by an assistant, obedience also decreased. Finally, when other confederates were present in the room and they objected to the shocks, the percentage of participants who quit in the middle of the experiment skyrocketed.

One final note about the Milgram experiment bears mentioning. It has been severely criticized on ethical grounds, and such an experiment would surely not receive the approval of an institutional review board (IRB) today. When debriefed, many participants learned that had the shocks been real, they would have killed the learner. Understandably, some people were profoundly disturbed by this insight.

Table 14.3 Famous Social Psychology Experiments

Experimenter	Topic	Major Finding
LaPiere	Attitudes	Attitudes don't always predict behavior; establishments that served a Chinese couple later reported they would refuse such a couple service.
Festinger and Carlsmith	Cognitive dissonance	Changing one's behavior can lead to a change in attitudes; people who described a boring task as interesting for $1 in compensation later reported liking the task more than people who were paid $20.
Rosenthal and Jacobson	Self-fulfilling prophecy	One person's attitudes can elicit a change in another person's behavior; teachers' positive expectations led to increases in students' IQ scores.
Sherif	Superordinate goals	Intergroup prejudice can be reduced through working toward superordinate goals; campers in unfriendly, competing groups came to have more positive feelings about one another after working together to solve several camp-wide problems.
Darley and Latane	Bystander effect	The more people that witness an emergency, the less likely any one person is to help; in one study, college students who thought they were the only person to overhear a peer have a seizure were more likely to help than students who thought others heard the seizure, too.
Asch	Conformity	People are loathe to contradict the opinions of a group; 70 percent of people reported at least one obviously incorrect answer.
Milgram	Obedience	People tend to obey authority figures; 60 percent of participants thought they delivered the maximum possible level of shock.
Zimbardo	Roles, deindividuation	Roles are powerful and can lead to deindividuation; college students role-playing prisoners and guards acted in surprisingly negative and hostile ways.

GROUP DYNAMICS

We are all members of many different groups. The students in your school are a group, a baseball team is a group, and the lawyers at a particular firm are a group. Some groups are more cohesive than others and exert more pressure on their members. All groups have **norms**, rules about how group members should act. For example, the lawyers at the firm mentioned above may have rules governing appropriate work dress. Within groups is often a set of specific **roles**. On a baseball team, for instance, the players have different, well-defined roles such as pitcher, shortstop, and center fielder.

Sometimes people take advantage of being part of a group by **social loafing**. Social loafing is the phenomenon when individuals do not put in as much effort when acting as part of a group as they do when acting alone. One explanation for this effect is that when alone, an individual's efforts are more easily discernible than when in a group. Thus, as part of a group, a person may be less motivated to put in an impressive performance. In addition, being part of a group may encourage members to take advantage of the opportunity to reap the rewards of the group effort without taxing themselves unnecessarily.

Group polarization is the tendency of a group to make more extreme decisions than the group members would make individually. Studies about group polarization usually have participants give their opinions individually, then group them to discuss their decisions, and then have the group make a decision. Explanations for group polarization include the idea that in a group, individuals may be exposed to new, persuasive arguments they had not thought of themselves and that the responsibility for an extreme decision in a group is diffused across the group's many members.

Groupthink, a term coined by **Irving Janis**, describes the tendency for some groups to make bad decisions. Groupthink occurs when group members suppress their reservations about the ideas supported by the group. As a result, a kind of false unanimity is encouraged, and flaws in the group's decisions may be overlooked. Highly cohesive groups involved in making risky decisions seem to be at particular risk for groupthink.

Sometimes people get swept up by a group and do things they never would have done if on their own, such as looting or rioting. This loss of self-restraint occurs when group members feel anonymous and aroused, and this phenomenon is known as **deindividuation**.

One famous experiment that showed not only how such conditions can cause people to deindividuate but also the effect of roles and the situation in general, is **Philip Zimbardo's** prison experiment. Zimbardo assigned a group of Stanford students to either play the role of prison guard or prisoner. All were dressed in uniforms and the prisoners were assigned numbers. The prisoners were locked up in the basement of the psychology building, and the guards were put in charge of their treatment. The students took to their assigned roles perhaps too well, and the experiment had to be ended early because of the cruel treatment the guards were inflicting on the prisoners.

PRACTICE QUESTIONS

Directions: Each of the questions or incomplete statements below is followed by five suggested answers or completions. Select the one that is best in each case.

1. Which of the following suggestions is most likely to reduce the hostility felt between antagonistic groups?

   (A) force the groups to spend a lot of time together
   (B) encourage the groups to avoid each other as much as possible
   (C) give the groups a task that cannot be solved unless they work together
   (D) set up a program in which speakers attempt to persuade the groups to get along
   (E) punish the groups whenever they treat each other badly

2. On Monday, Tanya asked her teacher to postpone Tuesday's test until Friday. After her teacher flatly refused, Tanya asked the teacher to push the test back one day, to Wednesday. Tanya is using the compliance strategy known as

   (A) foot-in-the-door.
   (B) norms of reciprocity.
   (C) compromise.
   (D) strategic bargaining.
   (E) door-in-the-face.

3. In the Milgram studies, the dependent measure was the

   (A) highest level of shock supposedly administered.
   (B) location of the learner.
   (C) length of the line.
   (D) number of people in the group.
   (E) instructions given by the experimenter.

4. The tendency of people to look toward others for cues about the appropriate way to behave when confronted by an emergency is known as

   (A) bystander intervention.
   (B) pluralistic ignorance.
   (C) modeling.
   (D) diffusion of responsibility.
   (E) conformity.

5. Advertisements are made more effective when the communicators are

   I. attractive.
   II. famous.
   III. perceived as experts.

   (A) II only
   (B) III only
   (C) I and II
   (D) II and III
   (E) I, II, and III

6. Your new neighbor seems to know everything about ancient Greece that your social studies teacher says during the first week of school. You conclude that she is brilliant. You do not consider that she might already have learned about ancient Greece in her old school. You are evidencing

   (A) the self-fulfilling prophecy effect.
   (B) pluralistic ignorance.
   (C) confirmation bias.
   (D) the fundamental attribution error.
   (E) cognitive dissonance.

7. In Asch's conformity study, approximately what percentage of participants gave at least one incorrect response?

   (A) 30
   (B) 40
   (C) 50
   (D) 60
   (E) 70

8. Janine has always hated the color orange. However, once she became a student at Princeton, she began to wear a lot of orange Princeton Tiger clothing. The discomfort caused by her long-standing dislike of the color orange and her current ownership of so much orange-and-black-striped clothing is known as

   (A) cognitive dissonance.
   (B) contradictory concepts.
   (C) conflicting motives.
   (D) opposing cognitions.
   (E) inconsistent ideas.

9. When Pasquale had his first oboe solo in the orchestra concert, his performance was far worse than it was when he rehearsed at home. A phenomenon that helps explain Pasquale's poor performance is known as

(A) social loafing.
(B) groupthink.
(C) deindividuation.
(D) social impairment.
(E) diffusion of responsibility.

10. Kelley's attribution theory says that people use which of the following kinds of information in explaining events?

(A) conformity, reliability, and validity
(B) consensus, consistency, and distinctiveness
(C) uniqueness, explanatory power, and logic
(D) salience, importance, and reason
(E) distinctiveness, conformity, and salience

11. After your school's football team has a big win, students in the halls can be heard saying "We are awesome." The next week, after the team loses to the last-place team in the league, the same students lament that "They were terrible." The difference in these comments illustrates

(A) the fundamental attribution error.
(B) self-serving bias.
(C) the self-fulfilling prophecy effect.
(D) the false consensus effect.
(E) conformity.

12. Which of the following is the best example of prejudice?

(A) Billy will not let girls play on his hockey team.
(B) Santiago dislikes cheerleaders.
(C) Athena says she can run faster than anybody on the playground.
(D) Mr. Tamp calls on boys more often than girls.
(E) Ginny thinks all Asians are smart.

13. On their second date, Megan confides in Francisco that she still loves to watch *Aladdin.* He, in turn, tells her that he still cries when he watches *Bambi.* These two young lovers will be brought closer together through this process of

(A) self-disclosure.
(B) deindividuation.
(C) in-group bias.
(D) dual sharing.
(E) open communication.

14. On the first day of class, Mr. Simpson divides his class into four competing groups. On the fifth day of school, Jody is sent to the principal for kicking members of the other groups. Mr. Simpson can be faulted for encouraging the creation of

(A) group polarization.
(B) deindividuation.
(C) out-group bias.
(D) superordinate goals.
(E) groupthink.

15. Rosenthal and Jacobson's "Pygmalion in the Classroom" study showed that

(A) people's expectations of others can influence the behavior of those others.
(B) attitudes are not always good predictors of behavior.
(C) contact is not sufficient to break down prejudices.
(D) people like to think that others get what they deserve.
(E) cohesive groups often make bad decisions.

ANSWER KEY

1. **C**
2. **E**
3. **A**
4. **B**
5. **E**
6. **D**
7. **E**
8. **A**
9. **D**
10. **B**
11. **B**
12. **B**
13. **A**
14. **C**
15. **A**

ANSWERS EXPLAINED

1. **(C)** A task that requires groups to cooperate is an example of a superordinate goal. Such superordinate goals are effective in breaking down hostility between groups. Contact between antagonistic groups without superordinate goals is less successful, and simply avoiding members of the other group is unlikely to decrease the intergroup hostility. While guest speakers may be able to influence the group members' attitudes, they will be less effective than the use of superordinate goals. Punishing the groups may actually increase the antagonism between them.

2. **(E)** Tanya made a large request and, when refused, came back with a smaller, more reasonable sounding request. This compliance strategy is known as door-in-the-face. Foot-in-the-door is when one makes a small request and, once that request is agreed to, follows up with a larger request. Had Tanya brought her teacher an apple and then made her request she would have been attempting to capitalize on norms of reciprocity, the idea that one good turn deserves another. Although Tanya is, in fact, attempting to broker a compromise and engage in some bargaining, the strategy she used has a more specific, psychological name.

3. **(A)** The dependent measure in the Milgram experiment was the level of shock the participants thought they were administering. While Milgram manipulated a number of independent variables including the location of the learner relative to the teacher, the dependent variable he measured was always how far the participants would go in shocking the learners. The length of the line is a reference to the Asch conformity experiment. No groups were involved in the Milgram experiment. The experimenter's instructions did not vary between conditions.

4. **(B)** Pluralistic ignorance is defined as the tendency of people to look toward others for cues about how to act, particularly in emergency situations. Pluralistic ignorance is often tested in bystander intervention studies. Pluralistic ignorance can be seen as a kind of modeling or conformity that occurs in emergencies. However, pluralistic ignorance is a superior answer due to its clear relationship to emergency situations. Diffusion of responsibility is the finding that the more people who witness an emergency, the less likely any one is to intervene.

5. **(E)** Communications are made more effective when communicators are attractive, famous, and/or perceived as experts. All of these factors enhance the persuasiveness of an appeal.

6. **(D)** Your failure to consider the role of situational factors in explaining your new neighbor's knowledge of ancient Greece is known as the fundamental attribution error. The self-fulfilling prophecy effect is when one person's expectations affect another person's behavior. Pluralistic ignorance is the tendency to look to others for hints about how one is supposed to act in certain situations. Confirmation bias is the tendency to focus on information that supports one's initial ideas. Cognitive dissonance is the tension felt when one holds two contradictory ideas.
7. **(E)** In Asch's conformity study, approximately 70 percent of participants gave at least one incorrect answer.
8. **(A)** Janine is experiencing cognitive dissonance. The combination of her hatred of the color orange and her ownership of a lot of orange clothing results in a tension called cognitive dissonance. It will motivate her to reduce the tension by either changing her opinion of orange or radically altering her wardrobe. All of the other terms are made up.
9. **(D)** When the presence of other people inhibits someone's performance, social impairment, the opposite of social facilitation, has occurred. Social loafing is the tendency of people to exert less effort in a group than they would if they were alone. Groupthink is the idea that because group members are often loathe to express opinions different from those of the majority, some groups fall prey to poor decisions. Deindividuation is when people in a group lose their self-restraint due to arousal and anonymity. Diffusion of responsibility is one way to explain the inverse relationship between group size and the expression of prosocial behavior.
10. **(B)** According to Kelley, people use information about consensus, consistency, and distinctiveness when analyzing the cause of people's actions. The other terms, while related to psychology, are not generally important in attribution theory.
11. **(B)** The students in the school are evidencing self-serving bias, the tendency to take more credit for good outcomes than bad ones. When the football team wins, they want to identify with them and therefore say "We are awesome." When that same team loses, the students distance themselves from the players, explaining that "They were terrible." Fundamental attribution error is a different attributional bias. It explains that people overestimate the role of personal factors when explaining other people's behavior. The self-fulfilling prophecy effect is the finding that people's expectations about others can influence the behavior of those others. The false consensus effect is another example of an attributional bias. It says that people overestimate the number of people who share their beliefs. Finally, conformity is the tendency for people to go along with a group.
12. **(B)** A prejudice is an attitude, while discrimination involves an action. Santiago has a negative attitude or prejudice toward cheerleaders. Billy and Mr. Tamp are engaging in discrimination by acting differently toward different groups of people. Athena may be really fast or overconfident, but she is not evidencing a prejudice. Ginny's belief that all Asians are smart is a stereotype that may or may not lead her to have some kind of prejudice against Asians.

13. **(A)** Self-disclosure is the process by which two people become closer by sharing intimate details about themselves. Deindividuation is when people in a group lose their self-restraint due to arousal and anonymity. In-group bias is the preference that people show for members of their own groups. Dual sharing is a made-up term, and open communication, while healthy in a relationship, does not describe this specific exchange.

14. **(C)** By dividing his students into groups, Mr. Simpson fostered the development of in-group and out-group bias, the belief that members of one's own group are superior to members of other groups. While Jody's aggressive behavior cannot be fully explained by Mr. Simpson's grouping, the fact that he attacks only members of other groups suggests that out-group bias may play a role. Group polarization is the tendency of groups to take more extreme positions than those taken by their individual members. Since Jody acts alone and not as part of a group, his aggression cannot be seen as an example of deindividuation. Superordinate goals are helpful in reducing conflict between groups by making their success contingent upon their cooperation. Groupthink is the idea that because group members often avoid expressing opinions different from those of the majority, some groups fall prey to poor decisions.

15. **(A)** Rosenthal and Jacobson's "Pygmalion in the Classroom" study illustrated the self-fulfilling prophecy effect, the ability for people's expectations about others to influence how those others behave. Attitudes do not always predict behavior well, as LaPiere's study evidenced. Contact is not usually sufficient to break down prejudice. The just-world belief tells us that people like to think that others get what they deserve. Cohesive groups sometimes engage in groupthink, resulting in bad decisions.

Multiple-Choice Test-Taking Tips

15

OVERVIEW

Two-thirds of your test grade depends upon your performance on the multiple-choice questions. You will take the multiple-choice section of the test first. It is comprised of 100 questions, and you will be allotted 70 minutes to answer them. This section of the test includes a mix of easier and more difficult multiple choice questions. Therefore, don't be alarmed if you have more trouble answering some of the questions: do your best and move on! If you have time after finishing all the questions, you can look back at the items you had trouble with and think about them a bit more. Below, we summarized a few test-taking strategies we think will help you with the exam.

TEST-TAKING STRATEGIES

Sometimes You Don't Even Need the Answer Choices!

Once you've prepared for this test you'll see that in order to answer many of the questions on the test, you don't even need to look at the answer choices. In fact, it's a good test-taking strategy to try to answer multiple-choice questions before you look at the choices. That way, once you do look at the answer choices, you have a good sense of what you are looking for.

For example, consider the following question:

EXAMPLE

Tiger is extremely concerned about doing the right thing. He feels very guilty when he even thinks about doing something immoral or illegal. According to Freud, Tiger has a strong

If you are familiar with Freud's theory of personality, you could probably guess that the answer would be "superego" without checking the answer choices. In this case, you would then have a very easy job as the choices are:

(A) id.
(B) ego.
(C) libido.
(D) superego.
(E) unconscious.

Here's another example:

EXAMPLE

A psychologist who subscribes to the biomedical perspective would be most likely to emphasize the importance of

In this case, the answer is slightly less obvious. You probably realize that it will have to do with concepts such as genetics, nature, and/or neurochemicals. Once you identify these potential answers, selecting the answer is, again, fairly simple. The choices are:

(A) the environment.
(B) hormones and neurotransmitters.
(C) repressed impulses.
(D) self-esteem.
(E) attributional style.

The correct answer is B, as hormones and neurotransmitters are examples of the kind of neurochemicals the biomedical psychologists believe influence thought and behavior.

Read All the Answer Choices

Always read all the answer choices before making your final selection. Even though it is helpful to imagine what the answer might be without reading the answer choices, it is essential that you read and carefully consider all the choices presented. Occasionally, particularly on the more difficult questions, one of the answer choices will be appealing, but another answer is superior. Remember that on a multiple-choice test you are supposed to identify the BEST possible answer.

Narrow Down the Possible Answers

Sometimes the questions on the exam are more difficult than the examples above and you will not be able to identify the correct answer before reading the answer choices. That is the beauty of the multiple-choice format: even if you are not sure you completely understand the concept in the question, you should be able to narrow down the possible answers by using what you do know about psychology. As mentioned above, you should always carefully read each of the answer choices. When you decide a choice is incorrect, cross it out, and eliminate it from consideration. You will be able to use this method often to identify the correct answer.

When I Don't Know the Answer, Should I Guess?

Some tests include a "guessing penalty" to discourage students from guessing on multiple-choice items (past versions of the AP Psychology exam included a guessing penalty). Beginning with the 2011 administration of the AP Psychology exam, the score for the multiple-choice section of the AP test is based on the number of questions answered correctly, and no points are deducted for questions answered incorrectly or left blank. Since there is no penalty for guessing on the exam, you should answer each multiple-choice question, even if you feel like you are guessing.

Don't Get Bogged Down

If you come to a question you find difficult, do not spend an inordinate amount of time on it. Remember, this is a timed test, and there's no sense in spending a long time worrying about one question if it's going to impede you from getting to the last five questions! After you read a question and look at the answer choices, make your best guess and move on. If you doubt your answer, mark the question in your test booklet so that if you have time at the end of the section, you can come back and think more about it.

In addition, don't let any thoughts about having missed a question get in the way of your doing well on subsequent questions. Rather than dwell on negative thoughts about a few difficult questions, focus on all the information you know. Don't "psych" yourself out!

Guess Smart

When you are not sure of the answer to a question and therefore are trying to eliminate incorrect choices, a few other suggestions about how to make good guesses on multiple-choice tests may help you.

1. **USE YOUR COMMON SENSE**. Don't get so caught up thinking about what you learned that you forget to use your common sense. For instance, consider the following question:

   What is the likely correlation between the amount of time students spend studying psychology and their scores on the AP Psychology exam?

   (A) −.80
   (B) −.25
   (C) −.18
   (D) .62
   (E) .97

   Assuming you know that "0" represents no correlation and that "1" is indicative of a perfect, direct relationship between the variables, your common sense can help you choose the answer. Since one would suspect that the relationship between these variables is a positive one, you are choosing between choices D and E. As an answer, .97 seems too strong; clearly some of the variation in how people do on the test is related to factors other than time spent studying (for example, prior knowledge, how rested they are, and test anxiety). Therefore, common sense dictates that .62 is the best of these choices.

2. **USE YOUR KNOWLEDGE OF THE PSYCHOLOGICAL PERSPECTIVES**. Sometimes language used in the stem of the question can give you a clue about the right answer. Each perspective uses certain terms, and the correct answer will frequently use language from the perspective indicated in the stem of the question. For example, consider the following question:

   How would a behaviorist like B. F. Skinner explain how people learn table manners?

   (A) Table manners are learned by interpreting events we have observed.
   (B) Table manners are learned as a result of reinforcement and punishment.
   (C) Table manners are a product of repressed childhood events in the unconscious.
   (D) Table manners are controlled by brain chemistry and evolutionary forces.
   (E) Table manners are learned by remembering and thinking about past social events we have experienced.

The stem of the question tells you that the correct answer must be one that a behaviorist would agree with, so you know you're looking for an answer that uses behaviorist terms and concepts. Options A and E use cognitive psychological terms (interpreting, thinking, remembering). Option C uses psychoanalytic language (repressed, unconscious), and Option D uses bio-psychological language (brain chemistry and evolutionary forces). Only Option B uses terms from the behavioral perspective (reinforcement and punishment), so it must be the right answer.

3. **AVOID EXTREME ANSWER CHOICES.** Choices that contain words like *all* or *never* or *everyone* are rarely (notice we don't say *never*) correct.
4. **BE WARY OF ANSWER CHOICES THAT ARE VERY SIMILAR TO ONE ANOTHER.** Remember, you're looking for the best answer. If some of the choices are so similar that one cannot be better than the other, neither can be the correct answer.

Budget Your Time

While most students find that they have enough time on the multiple-choice section of the exam, you should make sure not to spend an undue amount of time on any of the questions. Wear a watch to the exam and make sure to note the time the section begins and when it is scheduled to end. Since you have 70 minutes to answer 100 questions, you have just over two-thirds of a minute for each question. Read each question and use the techniques we have suggested. If you find yourself confused, skip the question and plan to come back to it once you have completed the section. If you are debating among several answer choices, choose one temporarily, but mark the question so that you will remember to review it once you have finished the other questions.

All These Tips Are Interesting, but How Many Questions Do I Need to Get Right to Pass?

Each exam is different. Assuming your essays are average (keep in mind that they will determine one-third of your grade), you need to earn approximately 60 points on the multiple-choice section to earn a "3," 70 points to earn a "4," and 80 points to earn a "5."

Finally, Remember to Apply Some of What You've Learned About Psychology to How You Study

- It's better to space out your studying over many days than to cram for the same amount of time right before the exam.
- Studying is important, but so is sleep. You'll think better if you're well rested.
- According to the **Yerkes-Dodson law** (Chapter 10), a moderate level of arousal will help you perform well on the test. Although you do not want to be so anxious that you can't focus, you will want to "psych" yourself up for the test.
- In cognitive psychology research (see Chapter 7), **retrieval practice** is one of the most effective study methods. Made sure you quiz yourself after you study content. Use the practice questions at the end of each chapter to test yourself and use the results to go back and review concepts as needed. In addition, you can use the "blank paper" technique: after you read about a group of concepts, close the book, get out a blank sheet of paper and write down everything you can remember. This technique helps you realize what you actually learned from the reading and what

you need to review. Another effective technique is to try to answer the practice questions at the end of the chapter *before* you read the chapter. You may not get many of the questions right, but thinking about those questions and answers will provide context that you will use to encode the new information you'll read in the chapter.

Skills

Starting with the 2020 AP Psychology test, the College Board began "keying" multiple choice items to one of 3 skills, in addition to the specific content area the item is addressing. Each multiple choice item assesses content from one or more of the 9 units (14 chapters), as well as one of the following skills:

Skill 1 - Concept Understanding: applying concepts, theories, and perspectives in context.
Skill 2 - Data Analysis: understanding and making inferences based on numerical data.
Skill 3 - Scientific Investigation: analyzing and explaining examples of research studies.

Notice that Skill 1, Concept Understanding, is different than the other two skills. Every multiple choice item on the AP Psychology exam is an example of "concept understanding" because every item requires you to understand and use psychological concepts in a scenario or other context. Answering AP Psychology multiple choice items always require you to know psychological concepts well enough to define, apply, compare, or evaluate that concept in order to identify the correct answer.

Skills 2 and 3 (Data Analysis and Scientific Investigation) are different than Skill 1. These are more specific skills and apply to only a subset of the multiple choice items on the test. Most of the content relevant to these two skills are explained in Chapter 2: "Methods." In that chapter you will learn about the research methods psychologists use to investigate research questions and hypotheses, as well as the kinds of statistical analyses researchers use to analyze research results. We also use **Tips** to highlight information relevant to research methods and data analysis in other chapters.

THE FABULOUS 15

Although the official AP Psychology course description includes the names of many famous psychologists (all described within this book!), we want to highlight the individuals you are most likely to be asked about on the AP exam. They are listed in the table below, along with the chapter(s) in which you can find more information about them and their major contributions to the field.

Psychologist	Chapter	Major Contributions to Psychology
Solomon Asch	Social Psychology (14)	Conformity and impression formation experiments
Albert Bandura	Learning (6), Personality (11)	Social-learning theory (modeling); reciprocal determinism; self-efficacy
Albert Ellis	Treatment of Psychological Disorders (13)	Rational emotive behavior therapy (REBT)
Erik Erikson	Developmental Psychology (9)	Psychosocial stage theory of development
Sigmund Freud	Personality (11), Developmental Psychology (9), States of Consciousness (4)	Psychosexual stage theory of personality; stressed importance of unconscious and sexual drive; psychoanalysis; theory of dreaming
Harry Harlow	Developmental Psychology (9)	Attachment studies with infant monkeys
Lawrence Kohlberg	Developmental Psychology (9)	Stage theory of moral development
Abraham Maslow	Motivation and Emotion (10), Treatment of Psychological Disorders (13)	Hierarchy of needs; self-actualization
Stanley Milgram	Social Psychology (14)	Obedience studies
Ivan Pavlov	Learning (6)	Classical conditioning—studies of dogs and salivation
Jean Piaget	Developmental Psychology (9)	Stage theory of cognitive development
Carl Rogers	Treatment of Psychological Disorders (13), Personality (11)	Person-(client-)centered therapy; unconditional positive regard
B. F. Skinner	Learning (6)	Operant conditioning—reinforcement; invented Skinner box
John B. Watson	Learning (6)	Father of behaviorism; Baby Albert experiment—classically conditioned fear
Wilhelm Wundt	History and Approaches (1)	Set up first psychological laboratory; theory of structuralism

Answering Free-Response Questions 16

HOW TO WRITE THE AP PSYCHOLOGY FREE-RESPONSE ANSWER

Every year around the beginning of June, high school and college psychology teachers gather at a university for one purpose: to grade AP Psychology free-response question answers. These readers are assigned to one of the two essay questions and go through careful training to ensure they grade your writing fairly and consistently. Readers go through several reliability checks during the reading to make sure each free-response answer is read fairly. This is a unique grading experience for many of the readers, just as writing the AP Psychology free-response answer might be a unique writing experience for you.

Writing an effective free-response answer on the AP Psychology test may require you to modify the way you usually answer a normal essay question. These essays are graded in a very specific way, and your writing should take this difference into account. Free-response graders strive to be very consistent and objective, so the tests are graded in a systematic way. The entire grading system is set up to ensure that every student's response is given a fair reading. Understanding how the tests are graded should give you insight as to how to best use your writing time.

This chapter begins with general suggestions about answering the free-response questions. These suggestions and hints apply specifically to AP Psychology free-response questions and are based on how the items are designed and graded. Then a sample AP-style free-response question and rubric are provided. AP readers use rubrics similar to this one to score student responses. Finally, a fictional student response is provided with a complete explanation of how this student response would be scored. Carefully examining this question, rubric, and scored sample student response will give you a complete picture of how the items are structured and scored.

GENERAL HINTS AND TIPS FOR THE FREE-RESPONSE PORTION OF THE EXAM

Style/Organization Hints

1. **Remember to think before you start writing and feel free to jot down a few notes.** You should have timed some practice responses before the test in order to get an idea about how much time you need to answer the questions. Use two to three minutes to organize your thoughts about each response, but be careful not to spend so much time that you feel rushed later.
2. **Do *not* write your answer in outline form.** While readers do not give points for the use of full sentences, proper paragraph form, and so on, they are not allowed to give

any points for a response written as an outline. Write your response in sentences and paragraphs. Do not label parts of your response with letters; use paragraphs to show where you move from one point to the next.

3. **Make sure you cover everything in the question.** If possible, try to answer the different parts of the question in order. Picture the likely rubric in your mind, and answer each part of the question in a clear, organized way.
4. **Structure your answer so that it clearly shows you answered all parts of the question.** Each paragraph should begin with a topic sentence that indicates which part of the question you are answering.
5. **Do not worry about an introduction and conclusion.** Remember, you get points for accurate information, not the style or aesthetic considerations of your response. Do not waste time repeating the question; the reader knows it well enough by now!
6. **Try to write as legibly as you can in the time you have.** Readers become experts in reading difficult handwriting, but undecipherable handwriting certainly will not help you get a better score. If you have time at the end of the test, look back through your response and rewrite any particularly messy words. If you need to add text in the middle of your response, clearly indicate where the additional text should go. Some students find leaving a little space between paragraphs for this purpose effective.
7. **Use all your time.** If you have extra time, use it to go back and make sure you said what you wanted to, add more examples for clarification, and rewrite any confusing sections.

Content Hints

1. **Keep it simple.** When asked to describe several methods of experimental control, for example, the graders will want the best and therefore most common ones. Do not waste time and energy explaining unnecessarily complicated techniques. For instance, write about random assignment, not group matching.
2. **Use psychological terms.** Readers are looking for your psychological knowledge, not what these terms mean in other contexts. In all cases, use the term, define it clearly, and give an example if possible.
3. **If asked to define a term, make sure not to use the word itself in your definition.** For instance, the sentence "*Modeling* is when someone *models* another person's behavior," is unlikely to score a point, because the writer is not demonstrating any knowledge about the concept.
4. **Make sure your context is clear.** Sometimes whether you get the point or not is determined by whether you use an example in the right context. For instance, you might give a great example of retroactive interference. However, if you place it into a paragraph discussing state-dependent memory, you may not get the point if the reader is not sure you know which concept the example applies to.
5. **If you feel clueless about part of a question, do not despair.** Do your best—write something, if at all possible. You might hit on what the rubric asks for. If not, you will not be penalized for trying. Do not worry—missing one part of the question will not ruin your score.
6. **When asked about a psychological term, define and give an example of the term in your response.** Although most free-response questions ask for applications or examples rather than definitions of terms, defining and giving an example of the term

gives you an additional opportunity to demonstrate your knowledge to the reader. It is possible that either your definition or the example you provide may fit the scoring rubric. But make sure you pay attention to the question: If it specifically asks for an example, make *sure* you provide a clear example in context because the scoring guide will focus on examples.

SAMPLE FREE-RESPONSE QUESTION

Professor Reiman places participants in a room with three confederates who are all asked to compare the size of geometric figures. The participants are randomly assigned to one of two conditions: In the first condition, the three confederates are introduced as introductory psychology students. In the second condition, one confederate is identified as a graduate student in perception research. During both conditions, the confederates all give the same wrong answers to the size-comparison questions. Professor Reiman tracks how many times participants conform to the incorrect answers. For this experiment, identify:

- the independent variable
- the dependent variable
- the operational definition of the dependent variable
- one confounding variable controlled for by this research design
- the principal difference between Professor Reiman's study and Asch's original conformity research
- your prediction about the level of conformity in the first condition
- your prediction about the level of conformity in the second condition

After reading the question, stop and think about what it is asking you. You are allowed to make notes on the question sheet, and many students find making a simple outline at this point and organizing their thoughts helpful. All free-response questions imply a certain organization for your answer. *Use* this implied organization; *do not ignore it.* You might be tempted to create a unique organization for your answer. However, your reader is not giving you points based on organization, so the time you spend planning this unique organization is wasted. In addition, if you answer a question out of order, you increase the chances the reader might misunderstand what you are trying to say. In this case, the format of the question indicates that you organize your essay based on the seven bulleted elements. Do *not* write your answer as an outline (this is specifically prohibited in the instructions in the test booklet), but you *should* organize your answer in the same order as the elements in the question. Writing one paragraph per bullet in the implied order will help AP readers score your response (and you want to help your reader!).

Also, notice that this question does not ask you to review the Asch study in detail. Knowing the basic findings of Asch's conformity study will help you with the last two bullets, but a detailed description of Asch's study does not directly answer this question. Always do what is asked of you in the free-response question: adding information that the question does not ask for (even if it is accurate information) will not help your score.

In addition, remember not to spend your precious time writing an introduction or conclusion. Grading rubrics (as you will see) are focused on measuring your psychological knowledge, not general writing skills like introductions, conclusions, writing mechanics, and so on. Answer the elements of the question clearly and in order rather than spending time with introductions, conclusions, or creative ways to organize your response.

At this point, you may want to write *your* response to this free-response question before looking at the scoring rubric provided below. After you write your response, you can use the scoring rubric to score your answer.

RUBRIC FOR SAMPLE QUESTION

This is a seven-point question.

Point 1

Independent variable

The answer should identify the different introductions of the confederates as the independent variable. In the first condition, all the confederates were introduced as psychology students. In the second condition, one of them was identified as a graduate student in perception. This was the only designed difference between the groups and is thus the variable the experimenter is trying to manipulate, the independent variable.

Point 2

Dependent variable

You should identify conformity as the dependent variable. Professor Reiman manipulates the independent variable to see how it affects conformity, the dependent variable.

Point 3

Operational definition

Professor Reiman operationally defines conformity as the participant agreeing with the wrong answers of the confederates. Do *not* award a point if you identified the operational definition as conformity. Conformity is the dependent variable.

Point 4

Confounding variable

The main element of the experimental design mentioned that would control for potential confounding variables is the random assignment. Randomly assigning participants to the two conditions would control for many possible subject- (participant-)relevant confounding variables (you do not need to use this term, examples are enough). You might say "random assignment would control for the possibility that participants might misunderstand the directions" or "might be in a bad mood at the time of the study" or "might have hostile reactions to psychology students," and so on. Any example of a subject-relevant confounding variable is correct.

Point 5

Difference

The main difference between Professor Reiman's and Asch's study is the inclusion of this particular independent variable. In one of the conditions, Professor Reiman identifies one of the confederates as a graduate student in perception.

Point 6

Level of conformity in the first group

You receive one point for demonstrating your understanding that most of the participants in the first condition would conform to the group's wrong answers some of the time. This condition is similar to Asch's original study, so the results would be similar.

Point 7

Level of conformity in the second group

You receive another point for predicting the level of conformity in the second group, with one confederate identified as the expert. You should predict a higher level of conformity in this group due to the addition of the authority figure.

INTERPRETING THE RUBRIC

Notice how the rubric directs the readers to look for points that correspond to correct answers, not mistakes you make. You might be relieved to know that you will not be penalized for saying something incorrectly or even making a factual error. Readers look for points and ignore incorrect information. This rule has one exception: Do not directly contradict yourself. Readers will not give you a point if you directly contradict something you wrote earlier.

The rubric shows you how you should write your response; it is organized in the way the question implies. If you organize your answer in this way, the reader can go through your response and look for the points in order. This is not just to be kind to the reader (although that is a nice thing to do). It increases your chances of communicating effectively with the reader. The more clearly you communicate to the reader, the better your chances of getting points.

AP Psychology readers often use "grids" as they grade responses to keep track of how many points a response earns. The grid is based on the organization of the question and mirrors the rubric. If it helps you think about how to organize your answer, you can imagine or even sketch out what you think the grid for a question might look like (but don't spend much of your precious writing time drawing a grid!). The grid for this example free-response question might look like the one in Table 16.1. Readers would use the column on the right to check off when a student essay earned a point.

Point 1	IV
Point 2	DV
Point 3	Op. Def. DV
Point 4	Conf. Var.
Point 5	Difference
Point 6	Predict Group 1
Point 7	Predict Group 2

Use the sample free-response question and rubric to grade the following fictional student essay.

FICTIONAL STUDENT RESPONSE

Professor Reiman picked a valuable psychological topic to study. Her experimental design includes many valuable elements but also includes several problems. In this essay, I will critically examine Professor Reiman's experiment to determine the most likely results.

The independent variable in this experiment is prestige. In one condition, all the confederates are introduced as psychology students. In the other situation, one of the confederates is a graduate student in perception. This change is the independent variable. The dependent variable is whether the people change their answers or not. This is also the operational definition. One of the confounding variables in the study is the presence of the confederates. For an accurate study, Professor Reiman should not use confederates in the research, she should use a random sampling of people not familiar with her research.

The only major difference between Professor Reiman's study and Asch's research is the fact that she had one of the people in one of the groups pretend to be a graduate student in research. That is the principal difference.

I think people would conform in both groups but more in the second one than the first. Most of the people in the first group would conform to the wrong answers because speaking out against the group is hard. However, more people would conform in the second group because not only is the majority saying the wrong answer, the graduate student in psychology is saying the wrong answer, too. The participants in the study would consider that person to know what he or she is talking about.

In conclusion, Professor Reiman's study is a valuable addition to the world of psychology. She proves that people are too easily swayed by experts. This can become dangerous if those experts do not know what they are talking about.

Grading the Fictional Response

You may want to use the rubric explained earlier to grade this sample response (and/or the response you wrote for this question) on your own. Before we begin discussing individual points, notice the introduction and conclusion to this sample response. The student does not write anything in those two sections that directly addresses the question. These two sections did not help this response. The student could have used his or her time more effectively by just starting the response in the second paragraph where he or she starts answering the question directly.

Grading this response using the rubric would result in the following:

Point 1

Awarded

The student correctly identifies the difference in the two groups as the independent variable:

> "In one condition, all the confederates are introduced as psychology students. In the other situation, one of the confederates is a graduate student in perception. This change is the independent variable."

Point 2

Not awarded

This student is unclear about the difference between an operational definition and the dependent variable.

Point 3

Awarded

The student identifies "whether people change their answers or not" as the operational definition. The student incorrectly says this is also the dependent variable, but the point is awarded for this correct identification.

Point 4

Not awarded

The student misunderstood that the use of confederates in this study is not a confounding variable. Researchers can and often do use confederates in research. It is not in and of itself a confounding variable.

Point 5

Awarded

The student correctly explains that the difference between this study and Asch's research is the inclusion of the graduate student in perception.

Point 6

Awarded

The student states, "Most of the people in the first group would conform to the wrong answers," which corresponds with the findings in Asch's study.

Point 7

Awarded

The student predicts more of the participants exposed to the second condition would conform than those in the first condition.

So, overall, this essay would get 5 out of 7 possible points.

Practice Tests

ANSWER SHEET
Practice Test 1

1. Ⓐ Ⓑ Ⓒ Ⓓ Ⓔ	26. Ⓐ Ⓑ Ⓒ Ⓓ Ⓔ	51. Ⓐ Ⓑ Ⓒ Ⓓ Ⓔ	76. Ⓐ Ⓑ Ⓒ Ⓓ Ⓔ
2. Ⓐ Ⓑ Ⓒ Ⓓ Ⓔ	27. Ⓐ Ⓑ Ⓒ Ⓓ Ⓔ	52. Ⓐ Ⓑ Ⓒ Ⓓ Ⓔ	77. Ⓐ Ⓑ Ⓒ Ⓓ Ⓔ
3. Ⓐ Ⓑ Ⓒ Ⓓ Ⓔ	28. Ⓐ Ⓑ Ⓒ Ⓓ Ⓔ	53. Ⓐ Ⓑ Ⓒ Ⓓ Ⓔ	78. Ⓐ Ⓑ Ⓒ Ⓓ Ⓔ
4. Ⓐ Ⓑ Ⓒ Ⓓ Ⓔ	29. Ⓐ Ⓑ Ⓒ Ⓓ Ⓔ	54. Ⓐ Ⓑ Ⓒ Ⓓ Ⓔ	79. Ⓐ Ⓑ Ⓒ Ⓓ Ⓔ
5. Ⓐ Ⓑ Ⓒ Ⓓ Ⓔ	30. Ⓐ Ⓑ Ⓒ Ⓓ Ⓔ	55. Ⓐ Ⓑ Ⓒ Ⓓ Ⓔ	80. Ⓐ Ⓑ Ⓒ Ⓓ Ⓔ
6. Ⓐ Ⓑ Ⓒ Ⓓ Ⓔ	31. Ⓐ Ⓑ Ⓒ Ⓓ Ⓔ	56. Ⓐ Ⓑ Ⓒ Ⓓ Ⓔ	81. Ⓐ Ⓑ Ⓒ Ⓓ Ⓔ
7. Ⓐ Ⓑ Ⓒ Ⓓ Ⓔ	32. Ⓐ Ⓑ Ⓒ Ⓓ Ⓔ	57. Ⓐ Ⓑ Ⓒ Ⓓ Ⓔ	82. Ⓐ Ⓑ Ⓒ Ⓓ Ⓔ
8. Ⓐ Ⓑ Ⓒ Ⓓ Ⓔ	33. Ⓐ Ⓑ Ⓒ Ⓓ Ⓔ	58. Ⓐ Ⓑ Ⓒ Ⓓ Ⓔ	83. Ⓐ Ⓑ Ⓒ Ⓓ Ⓔ
9. Ⓐ Ⓑ Ⓒ Ⓓ Ⓔ	34. Ⓐ Ⓑ Ⓒ Ⓓ Ⓔ	59. Ⓐ Ⓑ Ⓒ Ⓓ Ⓔ	84. Ⓐ Ⓑ Ⓒ Ⓓ Ⓔ
10. Ⓐ Ⓑ Ⓒ Ⓓ Ⓔ	35. Ⓐ Ⓑ Ⓒ Ⓓ Ⓔ	60. Ⓐ Ⓑ Ⓒ Ⓓ Ⓔ	85. Ⓐ Ⓑ Ⓒ Ⓓ Ⓔ
11. Ⓐ Ⓑ Ⓒ Ⓓ Ⓔ	36. Ⓐ Ⓑ Ⓒ Ⓓ Ⓔ	61. Ⓐ Ⓑ Ⓒ Ⓓ Ⓔ	86. Ⓐ Ⓑ Ⓒ Ⓓ Ⓔ
12. Ⓐ Ⓑ Ⓒ Ⓓ Ⓔ	37. Ⓐ Ⓑ Ⓒ Ⓓ Ⓔ	62. Ⓐ Ⓑ Ⓒ Ⓓ Ⓔ	87. Ⓐ Ⓑ Ⓒ Ⓓ Ⓔ
13. Ⓐ Ⓑ Ⓒ Ⓓ Ⓔ	38. Ⓐ Ⓑ Ⓒ Ⓓ Ⓔ	63. Ⓐ Ⓑ Ⓒ Ⓓ Ⓔ	88. Ⓐ Ⓑ Ⓒ Ⓓ Ⓔ
14. Ⓐ Ⓑ Ⓒ Ⓓ Ⓔ	39. Ⓐ Ⓑ Ⓒ Ⓓ Ⓔ	64. Ⓐ Ⓑ Ⓒ Ⓓ Ⓔ	89. Ⓐ Ⓑ Ⓒ Ⓓ Ⓔ
15. Ⓐ Ⓑ Ⓒ Ⓓ Ⓔ	40. Ⓐ Ⓑ Ⓒ Ⓓ Ⓔ	65. Ⓐ Ⓑ Ⓒ Ⓓ Ⓔ	90. Ⓐ Ⓑ Ⓒ Ⓓ Ⓔ
16. Ⓐ Ⓑ Ⓒ Ⓓ Ⓔ	41. Ⓐ Ⓑ Ⓒ Ⓓ Ⓔ	66. Ⓐ Ⓑ Ⓒ Ⓓ Ⓔ	91. Ⓐ Ⓑ Ⓒ Ⓓ Ⓔ
17. Ⓐ Ⓑ Ⓒ Ⓓ Ⓔ	42. Ⓐ Ⓑ Ⓒ Ⓓ Ⓔ	67. Ⓐ Ⓑ Ⓒ Ⓓ Ⓔ	92. Ⓐ Ⓑ Ⓒ Ⓓ Ⓔ
18. Ⓐ Ⓑ Ⓒ Ⓓ Ⓔ	43. Ⓐ Ⓑ Ⓒ Ⓓ Ⓔ	68. Ⓐ Ⓑ Ⓒ Ⓓ Ⓔ	93. Ⓐ Ⓑ Ⓒ Ⓓ Ⓔ
19. Ⓐ Ⓑ Ⓒ Ⓓ Ⓔ	44. Ⓐ Ⓑ Ⓒ Ⓓ Ⓔ	69. Ⓐ Ⓑ Ⓒ Ⓓ Ⓔ	94. Ⓐ Ⓑ Ⓒ Ⓓ Ⓔ
20. Ⓐ Ⓑ Ⓒ Ⓓ Ⓔ	45. Ⓐ Ⓑ Ⓒ Ⓓ Ⓔ	70. Ⓐ Ⓑ Ⓒ Ⓓ Ⓔ	95. Ⓐ Ⓑ Ⓒ Ⓓ Ⓔ
21. Ⓐ Ⓑ Ⓒ Ⓓ Ⓔ	46. Ⓐ Ⓑ Ⓒ Ⓓ Ⓔ	71. Ⓐ Ⓑ Ⓒ Ⓓ Ⓔ	96. Ⓐ Ⓑ Ⓒ Ⓓ Ⓔ
22. Ⓐ Ⓑ Ⓒ Ⓓ Ⓔ	47. Ⓐ Ⓑ Ⓒ Ⓓ Ⓔ	72. Ⓐ Ⓑ Ⓒ Ⓓ Ⓔ	97. Ⓐ Ⓑ Ⓒ Ⓓ Ⓔ
23. Ⓐ Ⓑ Ⓒ Ⓓ Ⓔ	48. Ⓐ Ⓑ Ⓒ Ⓓ Ⓔ	73. Ⓐ Ⓑ Ⓒ Ⓓ Ⓔ	98. Ⓐ Ⓑ Ⓒ Ⓓ Ⓔ
24. Ⓐ Ⓑ Ⓒ Ⓓ Ⓔ	49. Ⓐ Ⓑ Ⓒ Ⓓ Ⓔ	74. Ⓐ Ⓑ Ⓒ Ⓓ Ⓔ	99. Ⓐ Ⓑ Ⓒ Ⓓ Ⓔ
25. Ⓐ Ⓑ Ⓒ Ⓓ Ⓔ	50. Ⓐ Ⓑ Ⓒ Ⓓ Ⓔ	75. Ⓐ Ⓑ Ⓒ Ⓓ Ⓔ	100. Ⓐ Ⓑ Ⓒ Ⓓ Ⓔ

Practice Test 1

PART I: MULTIPLE-CHOICE QUESTIONS

1 Hour and 10 Minutes

DIRECTIONS: Each of the questions or incomplete statements below is followed by five suggested answers or completions. Select the one that is best in each case.

1. Neural transmission is often described as an electrochemical process. Which of the following is most directly involved in the electrical aspect?
   (A) the synapse
   (B) terminal buttons
   (C) hormones
   (D) myelin
   (E) neurotransmitters

2. The sound made by the "c" in the word *cat* is best described as a
   (A) phoneme.
   (B) morpheme.
   (C) holophrase.
   (D) syllable.
   (E) grapheme.

3. When first born, humans' dominant sense is
   (A) taste.
   (B) smell.
   (C) touch.
   (D) seeing.
   (E) hearing.

4. Ryan suffers from nearly constant, low-level arousal of his autonomic nervous system. Ryan is most likely to be classified as suffering from
   (A) GAD.
   (B) major depressive disorder.
   (C) somatic symptom disorder.
   (D) obsessive-compulsive personality disorder.
   (E) PTSD.

5. Which psychological perspective was most popular at the turn of the 20th century in Western Europe?
   (A) neuroscience
   (B) evolutionary
   (C) behaviorist
   (D) cognitive
   (E) psychoanalytic

6. Pascale is interested in the processing strategies children use to learn new information. Pascale would best be classified as what type of psychologist?
   (A) sociocultural
   (B) clinical
   (C) cognitive
   (D) behaviorist
   (E) personality

7. Cyan has come up with a test to identify people with the potential to be great civil rights lawyers. Such a test would be classified as a (an)
   (A) speed test.
   (B) achievement test.
   (C) EQ test.
   (D) IQ test.
   (E) aptitude test.

Use the following information to answer questions 8 and 9.

Whenever Marva has a difficult day at work, she slams her car door and screams at her children as soon as she enters her house. The children now cringe whenever they hear the sound of a car door.

8. The learning process described would best be labeled
   (A) classical conditioning.
   (B) instrumental learning.
   (C) observational learning.
   (D) operant conditioning.
   (E) latent learning.

9. The fact that the children now cringe when they hear any car door slam is an example of
   (A) acquisition.
   (B) generalization.
   (C) spontaneous recovery.
   (D) discrimination.
   (E) extinction.

10. Your girlfriend dumps you. "I knew you shouldn't have gone out with her," says your best friend, who has never uttered this sentiment before. Your friend's comment best illustrates
    (A) overconfidence.
    (B) a theory.
    (C) hindsight bias.
    (D) response bias.
    (E) a hypothesis.

11. A low level of glucose in Sam's bloodstream is most likely to make him want to
    (A) engage in risky behavior.
    (B) pursue a romantic interest.
    (C) eat a meal.
    (D) study to improve his grades.
    (E) make new friends.

12. What kind of personality theorist would be most interested in the results of the MMPI?
    (A) psychoanalytic
    (B) humanistic
    (C) behaviorist
    (D) biological
    (E) trait

13. Light enters the eye through an opening in the
    (A) lens.
    (B) retina.
    (C) iris.
    (D) blind spot.
    (E) fovea.

14. In people, rods, unlike cones,
    (A) are located in the center of the retina.
    (B) synapse with bipolar cells.
    (C) respond more quickly to bright colors.
    (D) have a low absolute threshold for light.
    (E) are unable to detect motion.

15. Which term describes the phenomenon of like-minded groups taking more extreme positions than the individuals that comprise the group?

(A) social facilitation
(B) deindividuation
(C) groupthink
(D) group polarization
(E) conformity

16. Julie is more alert in the morning and her brother Jack is more alert in the afternoon. This difference stems from a difference in the siblings'

(A) sleep cycles.
(B) circadian rhythms.
(C) daily activities.
(D) personalities.
(E) ultradian rhythms.

17. To treat Zoe's anorexia nervosa, her doctors put her on intravenous feeding tubes, tried to change her irrational belief that she was too fat, and discussed how her early family relationships may have contributed to her current problems. This approach would best be classified as

(A) cognitive behavioral.
(B) biological.
(C) psychodynamic.
(D) eclectic.
(E) humanistic.

18. Counterconditioning lies at the heart of which therapeutic approach?

(A) flooding
(B) systematic desensitization
(C) REBT
(D) token economies
(E) stress inoculation

19. Which personality theory is criticized for having an unrealistically optimistic view of human nature?

(A) cognitive
(B) biological
(C) humanistic
(D) trait
(E) psychoanalytic

20. Which of the following is LEAST likely to contribute to prejudice?

(A) stereotyping
(B) scapegoating
(C) out-group homogeneity
(D) superordinate goals
(E) discrimination

21. Which of the following is a key difference between the experimental method and naturalistic observation?

(A) Experiments yield qualitative data, whereas naturalistic observation yields quantitative data.
(B) Naturalistic observation involves surveys, whereas experiments measure behavior.
(C) Naturalistic observation takes place in the field, whereas experiments take place in a lab.
(D) Researchers can exercise greater control over experiments than in naturalistic observation.
(E) Experiments can yield statistically significant results and naturalistic observation cannot.

22. According to humanistic psychologists, psychological disorders are most likely caused by

(A) neurochemical imbalances.
(B) unhealthy attributional styles.
(C) learned associations.
(D) unfulfilled needs.
(E) genetic predispositions.

23. A fetus with the genotype XXY will most likely
(A) result in a miscarriage.
(B) suffer from sterility as an adult.
(C) be color blind.
(D) grow into a depressed adult.
(E) develop into a passive, withdrawn woman.

24. Of the following, most children will develop which skill first?
(A) write with a pencil
(B) cut with a knife
(C) say a sentence
(D) turn pages of a book
(E) clap their hands

25. Antonia has a cat. The first time she sees a rabbit, she calls it a cat. Her mistake is due to the process of
(A) discrimination.
(B) generalization.
(C) accommodation.
(D) assimilation.
(E) habituation.

26. Which of the following terms is most closely associated with creativity?
(A) hypothesis testing
(B) contextual intelligence
(C) divergent thinking
(D) habituation
(E) echoic memory

27. The somatic nervous system is part of the
(A) central nervous system.
(B) peripheral nervous system.
(C) autonomic nervous system.
(D) parasympathetic nervous system.
(E) sympathetic nervous system.

28. Which part of the brain is the newest in an evolutionary sense?
(A) pons
(B) cerebral cortex
(C) forebrain
(D) reticular formation
(E) hypothalamus

29. Which of the following disorders responds best to cognitive behavioral therapy?
(A) schizophrenia
(B) bipolar disorder
(C) dissociative identity disorder
(D) Alzheimer's disease
(E) major depressive disorder

30. Which structure is found in the inner ear?
(A) hammer
(B) basilar membrane
(C) tympanic membrane
(D) pinna
(E) auditory canal

31. What type of psychologist would assert that a key motivation for people is the desire to spread their genetic material?
(A) cognitive
(B) evolutionary
(C) humanistic
(D) psychodynamic
(E) behavioral

32. After Suzy decided to go to the prom with Dylan, Max was unconsciously furious. Max then channeled all his energies into his artwork. Which defense mechanism is Max using?
(A) displacement
(B) sublimation
(C) rationalization
(D) repression
(E) projection

33. Which of the following graphs best represents the relationship between arousal and performance?

(A)

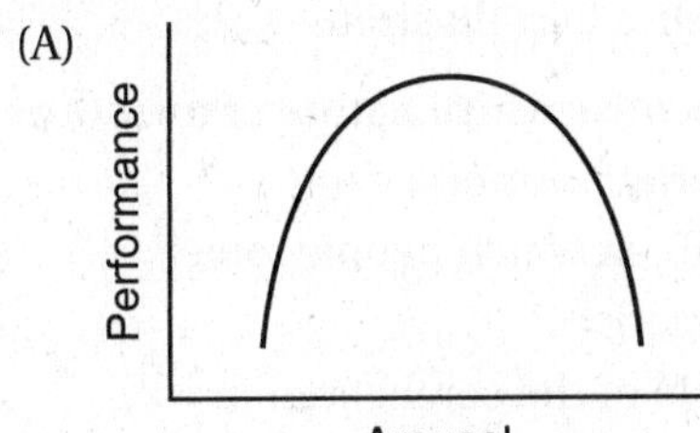

(B)

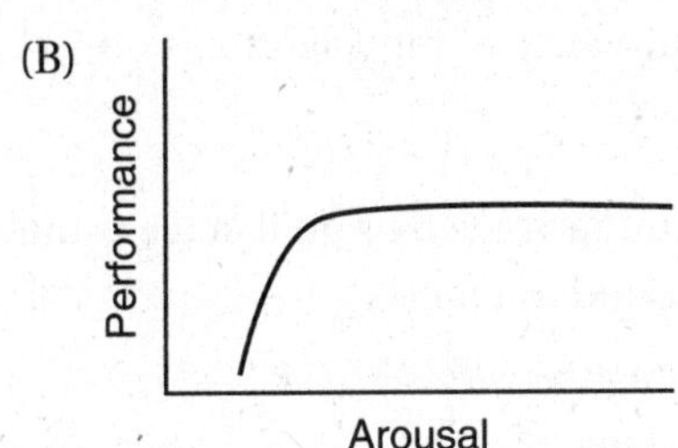

(C)

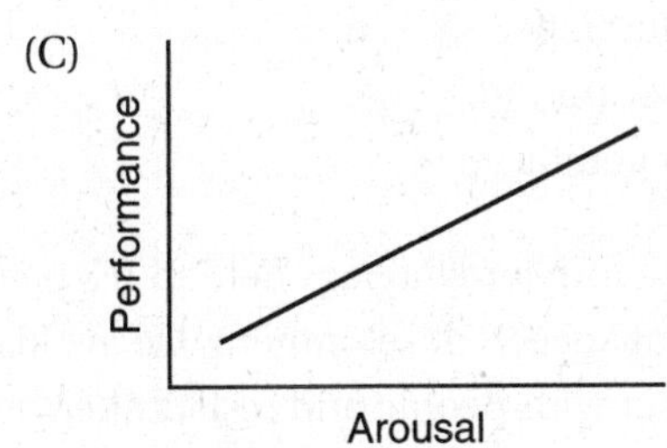

(D)

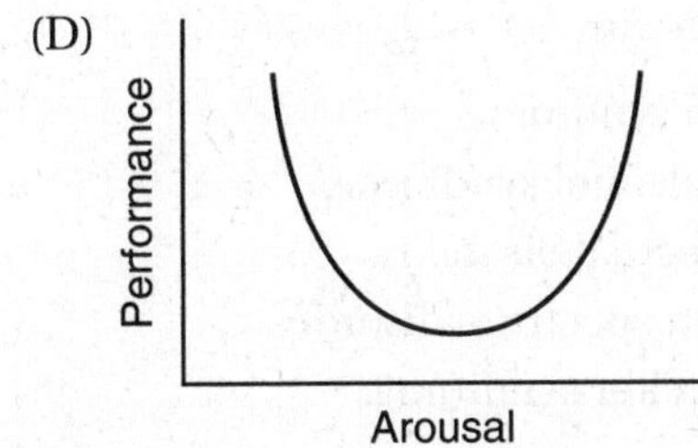

(E)

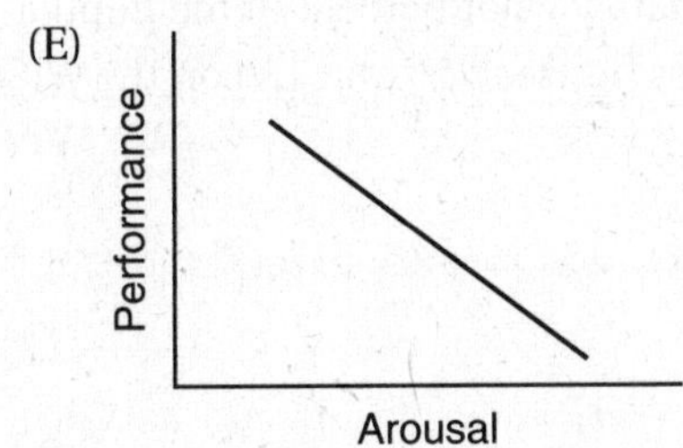

34. Which of the following statistics provides the most information about how spread out a distribution of scores is?

(A) variance
(B) mean
(C) range
(D) median
(E) mode

35. Because Jake, the team's starting, star center, is late to basketball practice, Coach Peterson sits him out for the first quarter of the next game. Jake is on time for the rest of the season. Coach Peterson has used

(A) positive punishment.
(B) negative reinforcement.
(C) modeling.
(D) positive reinforcement.
(E) omission training.

36. Some contemporary intelligence researchers like Howard Gardner and Robert Sternberg complain that schools focus too much on

(A) nonessential subjects like art and music.
(B) encouraging creative thought.
(C) the environmental factors that influence the expression of intelligence.
(D) traditional subjects and methods.
(E) meeting the needs of students with disabilities.

37. Delusions of grandeur are most characteristic of

(A) OCD.
(B) schizophrenia.
(C) conversion disorder.
(D) antisocial personality disorder.
(E) dissociative identity disorder.

38. Faye believes that victims of natural disasters are foolish because they should have developed better advance detection and warning systems. Faye is manifesting the

(A) false consensus effect.
(B) self-fulfilling prophecy effect.
(C) self-serving bias.
(D) just-world bias.
(E) Barnum effect.

39. Four-year-old Kate positions herself squarely in front of all the other kids to watch a magician. Piaget would attribute this to Kate's

(A) egocentrism.
(B) lack of object permanence.
(C) inability to conserve.
(D) animism.
(E) artificialism.

40. Someone who is unable to encode new memories is said to suffer from

(A) overgeneralization.
(B) belief bias.
(C) state-dependent memory.
(D) retroactive interference.
(E) anterograde amnesia.

41. The brainstem is comprised of the

(A) forebrain and RAS.
(B) hindbrain and midbrain.
(C) cerebellum and cerebrum.
(D) right and left hemispheres.
(E) cortex and the limbic system.

42. The limbic system plays an important role in

(A) maintaining balance.
(B) regulating emotion.
(C) monitoring arousal.
(D) processing sensory information.
(E) planning for the future.

43. In a number of experiments, Elizabeth Loftus has shown that the wording of a question can affect participants' recall of an incident. These studies best illustrate

(A) the reconstructive nature of memory.
(B) the serial position effect.
(C) the rate at which people forget information.
(D) the role of the cerebellum in memory.
(E) the influence of hindsight bias on memory.

44. Erikson's initiative versus guilt stage is most closely related to Freud's

(A) oral stage.
(B) anal stage.
(C) phallic stage.
(D) latency period.
(E) adult genital stage.

45. Daniel is a toddler who lags behind his peers in terms of speech development. He avoids eye contact with people and resists alterations to routine. Daniel is most likely to be diagnosed with

(A) Down syndrome.
(B) fetal alcohol syndrome.
(C) intellectual disability.
(D) autism spectrum disorder.
(E) Klinefelter syndrome.

46. Approximately what percent of the population scores between 70 and 130 on the WISC?

(A) 34
(B) 50
(C) 68
(D) 84
(E) 95

Use the following information to answer questions 47 and 48.

The school librarian wants to encourage children to read over the summer. Therefore, she sets up a system where students get a prize for every five books they read over the summer.

47. The librarian is using
    (A) continuous reinforcement.
    (B) a fixed ratio schedule.
    (C) a variable ratio schedule.
    (D) a fixed interval schedule.
    (E) a variable interval schedule.

48. The librarian is pleased to find that students report reading more books over the summer than ever before. However, the number of books borrowed from the library decreases in the fall. Psychologists would likely explain these findings with
    (A) the overjustification effect.
    (B) social learning theory.
    (C) the Premack principle.
    (D) the law of effect.
    (E) latent learning.

---

49. In order to prove a psychological theory,
    (A) you need to run an experiment.
    (B) you need to find statistically significant results.
    (C) you must replicate your findings.
    (D) you have to first prove your hypotheses.
    (E) it is impossible to prove a theory.

50. Lupe has been dating Craig for a few months. She's attracted to him and has fun with him, but she can't stand his friends or his family. Lupe's conflict would best be classified as
    (A) an approach-approach conflict.
    (B) an approach-avoidance conflict.
    (C) an avoidance-avoidance conflict.
    (D) a multiple approach-avoidance conflict.
    (E) Lupe does not have a conflict.

51. Ani believes that her attitudes and behavior play a central role in what happens to her. Such a belief is likely to be associated with
    (A) a strong superego.
    (B) low self-esteem.
    (C) low self-efficacy.
    (D) an internal locus of control.
    (E) an extraverted personality.

52. The fact that people's ears are located on opposite sides of their heads is most adaptive because it helps us
    (A) sense a greater range of frequencies.
    (B) gauge the intensity of a stimulus.
    (C) identify the origin of a sound.
    (D) respond to noises behind us.
    (E) figure out what sounds to ignore.

53. Young Tina had never seen the space shuttle until her parents pointed out a picture of it ready to launch. When she next saw a picture of it flying, she had difficulty recognizing it. Which concept best explains this problem?
    (A) autokinetic effect
    (B) dishabituation
    (C) summation
    (D) shape constancy
    (E) egocentrism

54. Sal meets Petunia for the first time. She is outgoing and funny. He walks away with the opinion that Petunia is a fun person, whereas in actuality Petunia is temporarily gleeful because she just won the lottery. Sal's opinion that Petunia is funny is best explained by
    (A) the mere-exposure effect.
    (B) self-serving bias.
    (C) equipotentiality.
    (D) the fundamental attribution error.
    (E) cognitive dissonance.

55. As part of her campaign for school president, Edy personally gives out cookies that say "Vote for Edy" on them. Which of the following is one reason that this approach might improve Edy's chances in the election?

(A) foot-in-the-door
(B) mere-exposure effect
(C) central route of persuasion
(D) pluralistic ignorance
(E) deindividuation

56. Alyssa presents one group of shoppers with an advertisement for milk that is 99 percent fat free and another group of shoppers with an advertisement for milk that is 1 percent fat. What is Alyssa most likely testing?

(A) representativeness heuristic
(B) confirmation bias
(C) schema
(D) mere-exposure effect
(E) framing

57. Eli is just beginning to sit up. Assuming he is developing at a typical pace, how old is Eli?

(A) 1 month
(B) 3 months
(C) 6 months
(D) 9 months
(E) 12 months

58. Harlow's monkey experiment illustrated

(A) the importance of physical contact to development.
(B) that language is a uniquely human skill.
(C) that primates can make and use tools.
(D) the danger of separating babies from their natural parents.
(E) that shyness is highly heritable.

59. Disorganized language like clang associations or neologisms is associated with

(A) autism spectrum disorder.
(B) schizophrenia.
(C) dissociative identity disorder.
(D) bipolar disorder.
(E) obsessive-compulsive disorder.

60. Jupiter pilots his newly created perfectionism scale on a high school psychology class. He returns one month later to administer the same test to the same students, and then he correlates the two sets of results. What is Jupiter probably doing?

(A) checking for outliers
(B) standardizing the test
(C) looking to see if the mean level of perfectionism has changed
(D) assessing the test's validity
(E) measuring the test's reliability

61. Albert Bandura's work evidenced that children who witnessed aggressive behavior on the part of adults would be likely to imitate the aggressive behavior later on. This phenomenon is known as

(A) instrumental learning.
(B) modeling.
(C) the copycat effect.
(D) thanatos.
(E) sublimation.

62. Coach Perry is training Lana to be the kindergarten soccer team's goalie. Coach Perry starts by rolling the ball to Lana slowly so she can stop it; he gradually begins to roll the ball faster and to different parts of the goal, all the while praising her successful attempts. The technique Coach Perry is using is called

(A) the law of effect.
(B) the partial reinforcement effect.
(C) shaping.
(D) second-order conditioning.
(E) a token economy.

Use the following information to answer questions 63–65.

Matt wants to contrast girls' and boys' views about leadership. He selects a random sample of 100 students from Northeastern High School in Maine and administers a standardized leadership survey. Scores range from 5 to 20.

63. What type of number will tell Matt whether or not there is a significant difference between how the boys and girls scored?
    - (A) standard deviation
    - (B) mean
    - (C) *p* value
    - (D) chi square value
    - (E) correlation coefficient

64. Matt's research design could best be classified as a (an)
    - (A) experimental.
    - (B) ex-post facto study.
    - (C) case study.
    - (D) naturalistic observation.
    - (E) content analysis.

65. What was the population in Matt's study?
    - (A) the 100 students who took the survey
    - (B) American students
    - (C) high school students in Maine
    - (D) students at Northeastern High School
    - (E) high school students throughout the world

---

66. Which part of the brain was thought to play the most important role in the Cannon-Bard theory of emotion?
    - (A) thalamus
    - (B) hippocampus
    - (C) medulla
    - (D) association areas
    - (E) hypothalamus

67. One month before finals, Conrad makes a study schedule and begins to review his notes. Two weeks before finals, Conrad is studying for hours each day to prepare. Right after finals at the start of summer vacation, Conrad comes down with the flu. Which of the following theories best explains this chain of events?
    - (A) Selye's general adaptation syndrome
    - (B) Yerkes-Dodson law
    - (C) Thorndike's law of effect
    - (D) Festinger's cognitive dissonance theory
    - (E) James-Lange theory of emotion

68. Learned helplessness is most likely to be directly related to
    - (A) the Barnum effect.
    - (B) self-serving bias.
    - (C) an external locus of control.
    - (D) unconditional positive regard.
    - (E) an Oedipal complex.

69. Which of the following are found in Jung's collective unconscious?
    - (A) fictional finalisms
    - (B) complexes
    - (C) archetypes
    - (D) feelings of inferiority
    - (E) bad memories

70. What color are the shortest electromagnetic waves humans can see?
    - (A) green
    - (B) violet
    - (C) red
    - (D) orange
    - (E) yellow

71. Which of the following drugs is best classified as a stimulant?
    (A) heroin
    (B) nicotine
    (C) alcohol
    (D) codeine
    (E) ecstasy

72. Due to brain damage, 10-year-old Genna underwent surgery to remove nearly the entire right hemisphere of her brain. Which of the following observations the day after the operation best illustrates the brain's plasticity?
    (A) Genna was able to understand what was said to her.
    (B) Genna was able to speak.
    (C) Genna was able to move her left hand.
    (D) Genna was able to move her right leg.
    (E) Genna was able to solve a logic problem.

73. Which of the following is the strongest piece of evidence for the idea that animals are capable of developing and using a sophisticated language?
    (A) The discovery of physical structures in animal brains are analogous to the language acquisition device in humans.
    (B) Primates quickly learn words that result in food rewards.
    (C) Systems of communication have been documented in species from honeybees to dolphins.
    (D) Apes have been able to use the words they know to express novel concepts.
    (E) Young apes and young humans pick up new vocabulary at similar rates.

74. Research has shown that people who read a job description written only with male pronouns (e.g., he, his) are more likely to think of an employee as male than people who read a description that uses gender-neutral language (e.g., he or she). This finding is most closely linked to
    (A) the linguistic relativity hypothesis.
    (B) gender schema theory.
    (C) the social role hypothesis.
    (D) modeling.
    (E) ethnocentrism.

75. In the nature versus nurture debate, nature is most closely associated with
    (A) environment.
    (B) culture.
    (C) learning.
    (D) temperament.
    (E) family.

76. If the College Board neglected to put any questions that had to do with neuroscience on the AP Psychology exam one year, the test would lack
    (A) construct validity.
    (B) predictive validity.
    (C) concurrent validity.
    (D) content validity.
    (E) face validity.

77. Kohler's studies with apes are seen as demonstrating
    (A) the apes' ability to communicate.
    (B) that apes are able to use objects from their natural environment as tools.
    (C) latent learning in primates.
    (D) that learning can occur via insight.
    (E) Thorndike's law of effect.

78. Mr. Maji gives a test to his class of 25 students. All but three students score between 82 and 94. The other three students score 47, 55, and 62. These scores are potential

(A) modes.
(B) skewers.
(C) outliers.
(D) variances.
(E) standard deviations.

79. What area of psychology focuses on the study of subjective well-being, optimism, and happiness?

(A) psychometrics
(B) human factors psychology
(C) social psychology
(D) positive psychology
(E) health psychology

80. After taking AP Psychology and doing well in the class and on the exam, Donald goes to college. If Donald is interested in psychology and has high achievement motivation, as a first-year student, he is most likely to

(A) take an introductory psychology class in which he knows that he will excel.
(B) enroll in an upper-level graduate seminar in which he will be exposed to a lot of new information but is likely to struggle to pass.
(C) avoid psychology classes since he has already mastered the material.
(D) sign up for an upper-level undergraduate course in which he will have to work hard to succeed and will learn new things.
(E) take the AP test again and see if he can earn an even better score.

81. Which of the following models of personality is the least deterministic?

(A) humanistic
(B) biological
(C) evolutionary
(D) behaviorist
(E) psychoanalytic

82. Vance's therapist believes Vance is psychotic. From which of the following medications would he most likely believe Vance would benefit?

(A) L-Dopa
(B) neuroleptics
(C) benzodiazepines
(D) SSRIs
(E) lithium

83. Sperling's partial report technique was designed to test the

(A) serial position effect.
(B) capacity of sensory memory.
(C) duration of working memory.
(D) difference between STM and LTM.
(E) misinformation effect.

84. Which of the following has been linked to a deficit of dopamine?

(A) major depressive disorder
(B) autism
(C) Parkinson's disease
(D) Alzheimer's disease
(E) schizophrenia

85. Runners in a park were found to pick up their pace when another runner came into view; this finding illustrates the phenomenon of

(A) social facilitation.
(B) conformity.
(C) deindividuation.
(D) norms.
(E) roles.

86. The Rosenhan study of mental institutions showed that

(A) treatment at private institutions tends to be better than treatment at public institutions.
(B) men are diagnosed at higher rates than women reporting the same symptoms.
(C) it is difficult to convince medical professionals that one has a disorder when one does not.
(D) people are overly concerned about the stickiness of diagnostic labels.
(E) confirmation bias may influence clinicians' views and treatments of mental patients.

87. An American teenager's prototype of a chair is most likely to include

(A) a desk and/or table.
(B) four legs and a seat.
(C) a feeling of anxiety associated with school.
(D) an armchair, a chairlift, and a wheelchair.
(E) pens, pencils, books, and a computer.

88. According to Kohlberg, in order to reason at the postconventional level, people must

(A) be generous.
(B) believe in God.
(C) be able to take another person's perspective.
(D) have had a successful resolution of the integrity versus despair stage.
(E) have been exposed to good, moral role models.

89. The incidence of schizophrenia in the population is closest to

(A) 1 in 10.
(B) 1 in 100.
(C) 1 in 1,000.
(D) 1 in 10,000.
(E) 1 in 100,000.

90. It has been suggested that learned helplessness may be related to

(A) major depressive disorder.
(B) paranoia.
(C) obsessive-compulsive disorder.
(D) paraphilias.
(E) somatic symptom disorder.

91. Tired after a long, hard day at school, Cyrus decides to take a nap. An hour later, his Dad wakes him to let him know it's time for dinner. Cyrus feels worse than when he went to bed and can hardly drag himself to the table. An EEG of Cyrus right before he was awoken would most likely have shown a preponderance of

(A) alpha waves.
(B) beta waves.
(C) delta waves.
(D) sleep spindles.
(E) K complex waves.

92. En route to the brain, information from the two eyes' retinas crosses at the

(A) optic nerve.
(B) optic chiasm.
(C) fovea.
(D) lateral geniculate nucleus.
(E) basal ganglia.

93. In studying for the AP Psychology exam, good advice would be to

(A) store as much as possible in your short-term memory.
(B) read this book over and over as many times as you can.
(C) rely heavily on the serial position effect.
(D) study from multiple sources.
(E) minimize interference by staying up the night before the exam to study.

94. A lesson from Janis's research on groupthink is that

(A) unanimity is important.
(B) small groups function better than large ones.
(C) groups function well under pressure.
(D) it is important for people to voice dissent.
(E) homogeneous groups come to better decisions than diverse groups.

95. Information from the optic nerve is initially processed in what part of the brain?

(A) occipital lobe
(B) hypothalamus
(C) thalamus
(D) hippocampus
(E) cerebellum

96. Which theory of emotion are cognitive psychologists most likely to support?

(A) social facilitation theory
(B) two-factor theory
(C) thalamic theory
(D) James-Lange theory
(E) opponent process theory

97. Odette is nearing her 70th birthday. Over the last year, she has suffered a loss of appetite and began to experience difficulty sleeping. She has lost interest in her favorite pastimes, gardening and bridge. Odette is most likely to be diagnosed as having

(A) Alzheimer's disease.
(B) seasonal affective disorder.
(C) insomnia and bulimia.
(D) major depressive disorder.
(E) antisocial personality disorder.

98. One cause of the deinstitutionalization of many psychiatric patients in the mid-1900s was

(A) an increase in government funding.
(B) the movement for the rights of the mentally ill.
(C) the creation of new medications.
(D) an improvement in psychotherapy.
(E) the recognition that too many healthy people had been institutionalized.

99. What part of Phineas Gage's brain was damaged by his accident while laying the railroad track?

(A) corpus callosum
(B) temporal lobe
(C) medulla oblongata
(D) prefrontal cortex
(E) midbrain

100. Approximately what percentage of participants in Milgram's obedience experiments thought they delivered the maximum amount of shock possible?

(A) 0
(B) 20
(C) 40
(D) 60
(E) 80

If there is still time remaining, you may review your answers.

PART II—FREE-RESPONSE QUESTIONS

50 minutes

DIRECTIONS: You have 50 minutes to answer the TWO questions that follow. Your answer should present an argument rather than a list of facts. Make sure to incorporate psychological terminology into your answers whenever possible.

1. Two-year-old Eli dislikes green vegetables and often refuses to eat them.

   (A) How could each of the following theories help explain Eli's behavior?

   - Evolutionary psychology
   - Erikson's psychosocial stage theory

   (B) How could Eli's parents use each of the following psychological phenomena to increase Eli's consumption of green vegetables?

   - Mere exposure effect
   - Eli's lack of Piagetian conservation
   - Conformity
   - Modeling
   - Positive reinforcement

2. Ten-year-old Pooja plays the trumpet. Her school band teacher assigns the students to practice at least 20 minutes a night and to keep a log of their practice time. At her weekly group lesson at school, Pooja notices that some students improve much more rapidly than others, and she decides to conduct a study for the 5th grade science fair to see why that might be. She surveys the other five students in her lesson group and finds a correlation between time spent practicing and improvement as measured by a rating from 1 (little improvement) to 10 (tremendous improvement) that she gives the students based on listening to their monthly playing tests. The data appear in the chart below.

Student	Average Weekly Practice Time (in hours)	Playing Test Score (1-10)
Kevin	8	9
Amy	1	1
Ling	2	4
Daniel	4	6
Mahip	3	3

   (A) - Draw and label a scatter plot to show this finding.
   - Describe the type of correlation Pooja found.

(B) Pooja decides to do a follow-up study in which she surveys all 42 members of her elementary school band and rates their performance on the monthly playing tests. In addition to asking how long they practice, Pooja asks about whether they take private lessons, how they divide their practice time over the week, and how nervous they feel during their playing tests.

Explain how Pooja could relate each of the following phenomena to her research topic or findings when presenting at the science fair.

1. Distributed practice
2. Experimenter bias
3. Social desirability
4. Yerkes-Dodson law

(C) One of Pooja's findings was that students who take private lessons average a score of 4.7 on their monthly playing test, while students who do not take private lessons average a score of 4.5. Pooja concludes that taking private lessons accelerates improvement.

- Draw and label a bar graph to show this result.
- Explain why you agree or disagree with Pooja's conclusion.

ANSWER KEY

Part I: Multiple-Choice Questions

1. **D**
2. **A**
3. **E**
4. **A**
5. **E**
6. **C**
7. **E**
8. **A**
9. **B**
10. **C**
11. **C**
12. **E**
13. **C**
14. **D**
15. **D**
16. **B**
17. **D**
18. **B**
19. **C**
20. **D**
21. **D**
22. **D**
23. **B**
24. **E**
25. **D**
26. **C**
27. **B**
28. **B**
29. **E**
30. **B**
31. **B**
32. **B**
33. **A**
34. **A**
35. **E**
36. **D**
37. **B**
38. **D**
39. **A**
40. **E**
41. **B**
42. **B**
43. **A**
44. **C**
45. **D**
46. **E**
47. **B**
48. **A**
49. **E**
50. **B**
51. **D**
52. **C**
53. **D**
54. **D**
55. **B**
56. **E**
57. **C**
58. **A**
59. **B**
60. **E**
61. **B**
62. **C**
63. **C**
64. **B**
65. **D**
66. **A**
67. **A**
68. **C**
69. **C**
70. **B**
71. **B**
72. **C**
73. **D**
74. **A**
75. **D**
76. **D**
77. **D**
78. **C**
79. **D**
80. **D**
81. **A**
82. **B**
83. **B**
84. **C**
85. **A**
86. **E**
87. **B**
88. **C**
89. **B**
90. **A**
91. **C**
92. **B**
93. **D**
94. **D**
95. **C**
96. **B**
97. **D**
98. **C**
99. **D**
100. **D**

ANSWERS EXPLAINED

Part I

1. **(D)** Myelin is a fatty tissue that surrounds the axons of some neurons and helps speed the movement of the action potential (essentially an electric charge) down the neuron. Neurotransmitters are chemicals that are stored in the terminal buttons and ultimately released into the synapse. Hormones are part of the endocrine system and are not involved in neural transmission.

2. **(A)** The sound made by the "c" in the word *cat* is best described as a phoneme. Phonemes are the smallest units of sound in a language. Morphemes are the smallest units of meaning in a language; the entire word cat is a morpheme as it cannot be broken down into smaller meaningful units. Holophrases are single words that toddlers use to express more complex ideas as they first learn language. A toddler might say "cat," meaning "look, there's a cat" or "I'd like to pet that cat." Like phonemes, syllables are units of sound, but they are often composed of multiple phonemes; for instance, the word cat contains three phonemes but only one syllable. A grapheme is a written symbol for a sound in a language; letters are graphemes but so are the letter combinations that make up multiletter phonemes, for instance, "ph."

3. **(E)** When first born, humans' dominant sense is hearing. In fact, research shows that fetuses are able to hear in the womb. By the age of about 6 months, sight replaces hearing as a typical baby's dominant sense.

4. **(A)** Ryan is most likely to be classified as suffering from GAD, generalized anxiety disorder. As described in the question, GAD involves a nearly constant low-level arousal of the autonomic nervous system. Major depressive disorder is a mood disorder rather than an anxiety disorder. In somatic symptom disorder, sufferers fear that typical body sensations are indicative of medical problems. People who have obsessive-compulsive personality disorder tend to be inflexible and overly concerned with things like neatness, routine, and perfection. PTSD (post-traumatic stress disorder) follows some kind of trauma and is usually marked by anxiety caused by memories, flashbacks, and nightmares having to do with the trauma.

5. **(E)** The psychoanalytic perspective was popular at the turn of the 20th century in Western Europe. The neuroscience, evolutionary, and cognitive perspectives had yet to capture most people's interest, largely because of the lack of technological resources to study people from these perspectives. While the behaviorist perspective was beginning to gain followers in the United States during this time, Western Europeans remained more interested in Freud's psychoanalytic approach.

6. **(C)** Pascale would best be classified as a cognitive psychologist due to his interest in children's processing strategies. Sociocultural psychologists focus on the role of various societal factors in shaping people. Clinical psychologists treat clients or research psychological disorders or therapies. Behaviorists would reject the importance of mentalistic concepts like "processing" strategies. Personality psychologists focus on questions concerning the development of people's personalities.

7. **(E)** Cyan's test would be classified as an aptitude test because it is intended to show a person's potential to be a good civil rights attorney. A speed test is comprised of many items and is meant to demonstrate how quickly a person can answer questions.

An achievement test measures people's knowledge of a given area. An EQ test would measure emotional intelligence, whereas an IQ test would measure intelligence.

8. **(A)** The learning process described would best be labeled classical conditioning because Marva's children have come to associate the sound of a car door slamming and their mother's screaming. Instrumental learning and operant conditioning are similar in that they involve learning to pair a consequence with a behavior. Observational learning, or modeling, is learning via observation and imitation. Latent learning is learning that is not evidenced until a reward is offered.

9. **(B)** The fact that the children now cringe when they hear any car door slam is an example of generalization since the children have generalized their response (CR) to the sound of their mother's car door slamming to the sound of all car doors slamming. Discrimination would be the opposite phenomenon—if the children learned to cringe only to the sound of their mother's car door and not other car doors. Acquisition in this example is when the children began to cringe to the sound of their mother's slamming car door. Extinction is the opposite of acquisition—if Marva learned to manage her anger and stop screaming at her children, they would eventually unlearn the cringing response to the sound of her car door. Spontaneous recovery would be if, after extinguishing the cringe response, the children at a later date cringed again upon hearing a slamming car door.

10. **(C)** Your friend's comment is a product of hindsight bias, also known as the "I knew it all along" phenomenon. Overconfidence is people's tendency to believe they have performed better than they have. A theory is a statement that seeks to explain some set of observations and is used to generate hypotheses. A hypothesis is a testable prediction. Response bias refers to any one of a host of factors that cause people to answer questions in ways that do not reflect their actual opinions or beliefs.

11. **(C)** A low level of glucose in Sam's bloodstream is most likely to make him want to eat a meal. Low blood sugar levels are an important cue that one is hungry. None of the other choices are tied directly to blood sugar rates.

12. **(E)** A trait theorist would be most interested in the results of the MMPI. The MMPI (Minnesota Multiphasic Personality Inventory) is a self-report instrument. Trait theorists use such inventories to help describe personality. Psychoanalytic theorists would not put much stock in people's conscious reports of their own traits since psychoanalysts believe important motivations are largely inaccessible in the patient's unconscious. Humanistic psychologists would prefer a more in-depth interview/conversation with a client in order to understand fully the unique features of each person. Behaviorists are far less interested in what people say than what they do. Finally, biological theorists are more interested in physiological factors than one's self-reported characteristics.

13. **(C)** Light enters the eye through an opening in the iris. The iris, the colored part of the eye, is a muscle that controls the size of the pupil, the hole through which light enters the eye. After passing through the pupil, the light is refracted by the lens and ultimately lands on the retina at the back of the eye. The blind spot is the part of the retina where the axons of the ganglion cells exit the eye en route to the brain; it is known as the blind spot because there are no photoreceptors there. The fovea is the part of the retina in which you have highest visual acuity due to the lack of summation there.

14. **(D)** In people, rods, unlike cones, have a lower absolute threshold for light; that is, rods function in conditions of dimmer light than do cones. Rods are located on the periphery of the retina, do not respond to color, and are good at detecting motion. Both rods and cones synapse with bipolar cells.

15. **(D)** The term group polarization describes the phenomenon of groups taking more extreme positions than the individuals that comprise the group. Social facilitation is the finding that the presence of others improves performance on well-learned tasks. Deindividuation is the loss of self-restraint that occurs in groups under conditions of high arousal and relative anonymity. Groupthink is the tendency of groups to suppress dissent and make bad decisions. Conformity is when one alters one's attitudes or behaviors to go along with a group.

16. **(B)** The siblings have different circadian rhythms, approximately 24-hour cycles in biological and behavioral processes including those that regulate alertness, body temperature, and heart rate. Sleep cycles are an example of an ultradian rhythm, a cycle that happens multiple times a day. The sleep cycle is approximately 90 minutes long, and we cycle through it several times over the course of a night's sleep. Even though the siblings may differ in terms of their daily activities and personalities, these are unlikely to account for their consistent differences in peak alertness time.

17. **(D)** The feeding tubes represent a somatic treatment, the discussion of how her beliefs are irrational involves a cognitive approach, and the belief that her early family relationships are important belies a psychoanalytic bent. The combination of these three different perspectives signals that an eclectic approach is being used.

18. **(B)** Counterconditioning lies at the heart of systematic desensitization. Counterconditioning is a type of classical conditioning that involves replacing one's initial reaction to a stimulus with a new reaction. Systematic desensitization is often used to treat phobias by replacing the fear response to the stimulus with a relaxation response. Flooding is based on extinction. REBT and stress inoculation are cognitive therapies, and token economies make use of operant, as opposed to classical, conditioning principles.

19. **(C)** Humanistic personality theory is criticized for having an unrealistically optimistic view of human nature. Humanistic psychologists generally believe that all people are innately good and motivated to fulfill their own unique potential, ideas that some critique as overly optimistic. None of the other perspectives listed have quite as positive a view of human nature.

20. **(D)** Superordinate goals have been found to decrease prejudice, perhaps most notably in Sherif's camp study and Aronson's use of the jigsaw classroom. All the other phenomena help contribute to prejudice. Stereotypes are specific ideas about a group applied to all its members. Scapegoating is the practice of blaming members of a disliked group for one's own misfortunes; it can serve to rationalize one's prejudice. Out-group homogeneity is the belief that members of one's out-groups are essentially all the same, thus facilitating prejudice. Discrimination is acting on one's prejudices; through the process of cognitive dissonance, discrimination may serve to amplify one's prejudices.

21. **(D)** One of the hallmarks of the experimental method is the ability to control for various confounding variables, while naturalistic observation is primarily a descriptive method that tried to convey a realistic picture of a phenomenon rather than artificially manipulate and control it. Experiments typically yield quantitative data; naturalistic observation often yields both quantitative and qualitative data. Naturalistic observation involves observation, not surveys; in experiments, the dependent variable measured may or may not be behavioral. While naturalistic observation typically takes place in something we could describe as the field, experiments may take place in either the lab or the field. Finally, both experiments and naturalistic observation may yield statistically significant results.

22. **(D)** According to humanistic psychologists, psychological disorders are most likely caused by unfilled needs. Humanistic psychologists believe that people are naturally good and that as long as their needs are met, they will develop into healthy individuals. However, if their needs (physical, emotional, etc.) are not met, psychological disturbances may result. Psychologists adhering to the biological perspective would be most likely to name neurochemical imbalances as the cause of psychological disorders. An unhealthy attributional style is a cognitive explanation. The phrase "learned associations" implies a behaviorist perspective, and the phrase "genetic predispositions" suggests an evolutionary approach.

23. **(B)** A fetus with the genotype XXY will most likely suffer from sterility as an adult. The XXY genotype is known as Klinefelter's syndrome and is one of the few chromosomal abnormalities that does not typically result in a miscarriage. Men with Klinefelter's syndrome are somewhat less likely to be color blind than other men since the trait for color blindness is recessive and carried on the X chromosome; therefore, these men would have to have a copy of the gene on each of the X chromosomes to express it. Depression is not associated with Klinefelter's syndrome, and everyone who has Klinefelter's syndrome is a male due to the presence of the Y chromosome.

24. **(E)** Most children will develop the ability to clap their hands before any of the other skills listed. Typically, infants learn to clap hands in the second half of their first year. In general, gross motor skills (e.g., clapping) tend to develop before fine motor skills (for example, writing, cutting with a knife, turning pages of a book). Most children do not speak in anything resembling full sentences until they are well over 2 years old.

25. **(D)** Antonia has a cat. The first time she sees a rabbit, she calls it a cat. Her error results from the process of assimilation. Assimilation, as defined by Piaget, is the ability to take in new information using one's existing schemas. Antonia had a schema for a cat and used it to make sense of a new animal, a rabbit. Accommodation will occur if Antonia is corrected and told that this new animal with longer ears and a shorter tail is a rabbit, and she then creates a new schema for rabbits. Discrimination and generalization are terms used together in discussing learning. Discrimination is when one can tell the difference between a stimulus and similar stimuli, and generalization is when one responds the same way to similar stimuli as one did to the stimulus with which one was originally trained. Habituation is a decrease in response to a repeated stimulus.

26. **(C)** *Divergent thinking* is a term closely associated with creativity. Convergent thinking involves looking for a single correct answer or using one prescribed method of problem solving; divergent thinking typically involves more open-ended problems. Hypothesis testing can absolutely have creative elements but is not synonymous with creativity as is divergent thinking. Contextual intelligence is a kind of practical intelligence described by Robert Sternberg. Habituation is a decrease in response to a repeated stimulus. Echoic memory is the auditory portion of sensory memory that lasts a few seconds.

27. **(B)** The somatic nervous system is part of the peripheral nervous system. The peripheral nervous system is comprised of the somatic (or skeletal) nervous system and the autonomic nervous system and collectively contains all parts of the nervous system outside of the central nervous system. The central nervous system contains the brain and spinal cord. The autonomic nervous system has two parts: the parasympathetic and sympathetic nervous systems.

28. **(B)** As animals evolved and became more advanced, their brains typically became larger, relative to the size of their bodies. However, the part of the brain that has increased the most in size and a part that is not even present in many animals is the cerebral cortex. This change makes sense given that the cortex is the seat of high-level thought. The pons and reticular formation are both part of the brainstem, an older part of the brain. The forebrain includes the cortex as well as less advanced structures like the hypothalamus.

29. **(E)** Of the disorders listed, major depressive disorder would respond best to cognitive behavioral therapy. Cognitive behavioral therapy (CBT) is a type of talk therapy in which the clinician tries to reason with the client. Given the disorganized thought and difficulties with oral expression of schizophrenics, they are poor candidates for such an approach. Dissociative identity disorder (DID) might also be difficult to treat from this perspective because cognitive psychologists focus on conscious thought and might be skeptical about the unconscious and the existence of DID. Alzheimer's disease would not respond well to CBT since it is a degenerative brain issue. Finally, while CBT might help someone with bipolar disorder while in the depressed phase, it would probably be less effective in dealing with people in the manic phase as they are typically not thinking logically nor receptive to rational arguments.

30. **(B)** The basilar membrane is found in the inner ear. The basilar membrane is in the cochlea, and the hair cells are embedded in this membrane. The hammer is one of the ossicles in the middle ear. The tympanic membrane, or eardrum, divides the outer and middle ears. The pinna and auditory canal make up the outer ear.

31. **(B)** An evolutionary psychologist or sociobiologist would assert that a key motivation for people is the desire to spread their genetic material. Cognitive psychologists believe that thoughts are at the core of motivation. Humanistic psychologists assert that people are motivated to fulfill their needs. Psychodynamic psychologists believe unconscious thoughts are important motivators. Behaviorists believe we are motivated by the contingencies of reinforcement to which we have been exposed.

32. **(B)** Psychodynamic theorists would say that Max is sublimating. Sublimation is a Freudian defense mechanism that involves taking inappropriate emotions (for example, fury) or desires and redirecting them toward more socially acceptable behaviors

(for example, artwork). The other choices are all other defense mechanisms. If Max used displacement, he would take his anger out on a less threatening target than Dylan. If Max used rationalization, he might think to himself that he can get a better prom date. If Max repressed his fury, he would basically forget about the event by pushing the memories into his unconscious. Finally, if Max used projection, he might claim that Dylan and/or Suzy were angry with him when, in fact, it is he who is angry.

33. **(A)** The relationship between arousal and performance is known as the Yerkes-Dodson law and is expressed by a graph that looks like an inverted "U." As arousal increases, so does performance—up to a point. When arousal becomes too high, performance suffers.

34. **(A)** Measures of variability (e.g., variance, standard deviation, range) show how spread out a distribution of scores is. The range (the highest score minus the lowest score) is less informative than the variance or standard deviation, which shows the average distance of all scores in a distribution from the mean. The mean, median, and mode are measures of central tendency; their aim is to mark the center of a distribution, not to say how spread out the distribution is.

35. **(E)** Since Coach Peterson takes away playing time that Jake usually has, the technique described is omission training. An example of positive punishment would have been if the coach had Jake run laps (added something unpleasant). Neither negative reinforcement nor positive reinforcement would have been a good tactic for the coach to use on Jake's lateness, since, by definition, they would have encouraged Jake to be late again. However, the coach could reinforce Jake's future appropriate behaviors toward the same end. He could praise Jake when he arrives on time (positive reinforcement) or excuse Jake from the laps run at the end of practice when he is on time (negative reinforcement). Modeling is learning via observation and imitation; the coach could model being on time himself.

36. **(D)** Gardner, Sternberg, and a host of other contemporary intelligence researchers believe that schools focus too much on traditional subjects and methods. Gardner has proposed that people have multiple abilities that ought to be considered intelligences, including bodily-kinesthetic intelligence, musical intelligence, and interpersonal intelligence. Sternberg believes schools should encourage students' creative and practical abilities as well as their analytical ones.

37. **(B)** Delusions of grandeur are most characteristic of schizophrenia. An example of a delusion of grandeur would be the belief that one was a god or a king. Along with delusions of persecution, delusions of grandeur are amongst the most common schizophrenic delusions.

38. **(D)** Faye believes that victims of natural disasters are foolish because they didn't develop better advance detection and warning systems. Faye is manifesting the just-world bias, the belief that because the world is a fair place, good things happen to good people and bad things happen to bad people. The false consensus effect is our tendency to overestimate the number of people whose views are similar to our own. The self-fulfilling prophecy effect is the ability of one person's expectations to elicit behavioral confirmation in another. Self-serving bias is the tendency to take more credit for good outcomes and less credit for bad outcomes than one deserves. The Barnum effect is people's willingness to see themselves in vague, stock descriptions.

39. **(A)** Four-year-old Kate positions herself squarely in front of all the other kids to watch a magician. Piaget would attribute this to Kate's egocentrism. Piaget would say that Kate does not have the cognitive capacity to realize that she is blocking others' view; she is only capable of seeing things from her own perspective. Piaget believed infants develop object permanence, the understanding that an object still exists even when no longer in view, toward the end of the first year. According to Piaget, children learn to conserve around age 7, when they enter concrete operations. Conservation is the knowledge that a change in the form of matter does not change the amount of matter that exists. Animism and artificialism are limitations in the thought of the preoperational child. Animism is when one attributes life or consciousness to inanimate objects, and artificialism is the belief that everything has been created by people.

40. **(E)** The inability to encode new memories is known as anterograde amnesia. The prefix *ante* means "before," and the "ante" in anterograde indicates that the trauma causing the memory problem preceded the memories with which it is interfering.

41. **(B)** The brainstem is comprised of the hindbrain and midbrain. The brainstem houses some of the most basic functions of the body and is present in similar form in less complex animals, such as reptiles.

42. **(B)** The limbic system plays an important role in regulating emotion. The amygdala is part of the limbic system and is vital in terms of regulating emotion. Maintaining balance is associated more with the cerebellum. Monitoring arousal is the job of the reticular activating system, also known as the reticular formation. The thalamus is important in the initial processing of most sensory information, and the prefrontal cortex is the part of the brain most associated with planning for the future.

43. **(A)** Loftus's work shows that memory is reconstructed; that is, a memory is not like an exact replica of what happened but rather is built each time a person thinks about it and is therefore affected by all sorts of extraneous information. The serial position effect refers to the tendency to remember the first and last items in a list better than the ones in the middle. While there is a predictable rate at which information is lost from short-term memory, it is not relevant to this question. Similarly, while the cerebellum plays a role in procedural memory, that fact is not the focus of this question. Finally, hindsight bias, the tendency to think you knew an answer all along after hearing it, does not relate directly to this question.

44. **(C)** Erikson's initiative versus guilt stage is most closely related to Freud's phallic stage. Both occur between the ages of roughly 3 to 5 and are the third stage in their respective theories. Freud's oral stage corresponds to Erikson's trust versus mistrust stage. Freud's anal stage corresponds with Erikson's autonomy versus shame and doubt stage. Freud's concept of latency is akin to Erikson's industry versus inferiority stage. While Freud's final stage is the adult genital stage and it lasts from puberty on, Erikson divided adolescence and adulthood into several stages: identity versus role confusion, intimacy versus isolation, generativity versus stagnation, and ego integrity versus despair.

45. **(D)** Daniel is most likely to be diagnosed with autistic spectrum disorder, an impairment of social development. Common symptoms include delayed speech, avoiding eye contact, and a preference for routine. A description of Down syndrome, or trisomy 21, is likely to mention an extra chromosome on the 21st pair and a degree of intellectual

impairment. A description of fetal alcohol syndrome would probably include mention of a mother who drank while pregnant and would likely also mention intellectual impairment. The hallmark of intellectual disability is intellectual functioning that is significantly below average. Klinefelter's syndrome results from a chromosomal abnormality of the sex chromosomes; boys with Klinefelter's syndrome have an XXY genotype. Signs of Klinefelter's syndrome include small testes, atypical secondary sex development, and infertility.

46. **(E)** Approximately 95 percent of the population scores between 70 and 130 on the WISC. The WISC has a mean of 100 and a standard deviation of 15, which means that the scores between 70 and 130 represent all the scores within two standard deviations of the mean. By definition, in a normal distribution, about 95 percent of scores fall within two standard deviations of the mean.

47. **(B)** The school librarian's system of giving students a prize for every five books they read uses a fixed ratio reinforcement schedule. The schedule is fixed (as opposed to variable) because students are rewarded for every five books they read—a fixed or constant number. The schedule is a ratio (as opposed to interval) schedule because what controls the reinforcement is the number of responses the person makes and not the passage of time.

48. **(A)** The fact that students read more books in the summer but fewer books in the fall is probably due to the overjustification effect, the finding that extrinsic rewards can undermine intrinsic motivation. Students who previously read because they liked to read may have come to think they read for the prizes and not because they liked reading. As a result, when the prizes are withdrawn, they no longer had a reason to read and therefore may have read less.

49. **(E)** It is impossible to prove a theory. Experiments and other research methods, even when they yield statistically significant results and those results are replicated, can garner support for a theory but not proof. It isn't really even possible to prove a hypothesis because the term proof implies that you are absolutely sure about something and given the role of probability in hypothesis testing, we can never really be 100 percent certain about anything.

50. **(B)** Lupe's situation with Craig represents an approach-avoidance conflict. She is attracted to certain aspects of Craig but not to others. In an approach-approach conflict, one has to choose between two desirable options—for instance, if Lupe was attracted both to Craig and his brother Greg. In an avoidance-avoidance conflict, one has to choose between two undesirable options; imagine Lupe's parents and Craig and Greg's parents had agreed their children would wed. If Lupe disliked both Craig and Greg but had to marry one of them, she would face an avoidance-avoidance conflict. In a multiple approach-avoidance conflict, one has to choose between several options, each of which has attractive and unattractive features. If Lupe thought Craig was attractive but boring and Greg was interesting but not attractive to her, she would face a multiple approach-avoidance conflict.

51. **(D)** Ani's belief that her attitudes and behavior play a central role in what happens to her is associated with an internal locus of control. While people with an external locus of control feel fate and luck play a large role in their lives, people with an internal locus

of control believe they control their destinies. A strong superego is associated with a being concerned with morals and ethics. People with low self-esteem have negative thoughts about themselves. People with low self-efficacy doubt their ability to get things done. Extraverted people are friendly and outgoing.

52. **(C)** The fact that people's ears are located on opposite sides of their heads is most adaptive because it helps us identify the origin of a sound. We locate sound by comparing the time it takes a sound wave to reach each ear and the intensity of the sound wave when it hits each ear. Sounds that come from our right reach our right ears more quickly and with greater intensity than sounds that come from the left and vice versa. The location of our ears does not increase the range of frequencies we can hear or help us gauge sound intensity, respond to noises behind us, or figure out what sounds to ignore.

53. **(D)** Young Tina had never seen the space shuttle until her parents pointed out a picture of it ready to launch. When she next saw a picture of it flying, she had difficulty recognizing it. Tina's problem can best be explained by shape constancy. Shape constancy is a perceptual constancy that we learn from experience. An unfamiliar object looks different from different angles, and we have to learn that it is the same. Until we do, we make errors like Tina's. The autokinetic effect is when a spot of light in a dark room appears to move on its own. Dishabituation refers to an increase in response that occurs to a novel stimulus. Summation refers to the way the layers of the retina are set up: multiple rods and cones synapse with one bipolar cell and multiple bipolar cells synapse with a single ganglion cell. Egocentrism is one of the cognitive limitations of the preoperational child, according to Piaget.

54. **(D)** Sal's conclusion that Petunia is a funny person after their brief meeting is best explained by the fundamental attribution error, the tendency for people to underestimate the role of the situation in explaining the behavior of others. The mere-exposure effect would hold that the more time Sal spent with Petunia, the more he would like her; it says that exposure to a person or thing increases liking. Self-serving bias is the tendency to take more credit for positive outcomes than negative ones. Equipotentiality is a learning principle, the belief that we have an equal opportunity to teach all organisms all things. Cognitive dissonance is the mental tension that arises from holding two contradictory thoughts or when people's thoughts don't mesh with their behavior.

55. **(B)** Since Edy is giving the cookies out herself and they have her name on them, the act of distributing will increase the student body's familiarity with her. According to the mere-exposure effect, increased exposure increases liking. Foot-in-the-door is a compliance technique that involves getting someone to agree to a small request in order to increase the likelihood they will agree to a larger, subsequent request. Edy's technique utilizes the peripheral route more than the central route; the central route to persuasion would involve Edy explaining why she is the best candidate. Pluralistic ignorance is one explanation for the bystander effect. Deindividuation is a loss of self-restraint under conditions of heightened arousal and relative anonymity.

56. **(E)** Alyssa is testing the impact of framing; milk that is 1 percent fat is the same as milk that is 99 percent fat free; the only difference is how the milk is framed. Representativeness heuristic is when people judge the likelihood of an event by comparing it to something they believe to be similar and assuming the probabilities of the events will be the

same. Confirmation bias is the tendency to pay more attention to information that supports our preexisting beliefs than information that contradicts it. Schema are cognitive structures that influence how we process information. The mere-exposure effect shows that exposure to something increases our liking for it.

57. **(C)** Eli, if developing typically and 6 months old, is probably just beginning to sit up. Infants develop in a predictable sequence and a fairly predictable rate: at about one month, most infants can lift their head; by 3 months, most can hold their heads steady; by 6 months, most can sit up; by 9 months, most are beginning to try to stand up while holding on to something; and by a year, most infants begin to stand on their own and take a step or two.

58. **(A)** Harlow's monkey experiment illustrated the importance of physical contact to development. Harlow compared infant monkeys' attachment to a surrogate mother made out of cloth or one made of wire that was attached to a bottle so "she" could feed the baby. He found the infant monkeys preferred the soft "mothers." His study did not involve language or tools. Even though the infant monkeys were separated from their natural parents, the goal was not to study the impact of that separation, and the study also did not look at the heritability of shyness.

59. **(B)** Disorganized language including the use of clang associations and neologisms is a common symptom of schizophrenia. These communication problems are thought to reflect disordered thought.

60. **(E)** In correlating the two sets of results, Jupiter is measuring the test's reliability. This type of reliability is known as test-retest reliability. Since perfectionism should not change over the course of the month, a low correlation would indicate that the test was not reliable. Outliers are extreme scores, and Jupiter does not appear to be looking for them. To standardize the test, Jupiter would have to give it to a standardization sample and then look to assemble a group of questions that yielded a normal distribution of scores. Nothing in the question suggests Jupiter believes the mean level of perfectionism should have changed, and the correlation will not necessarily show whether it has. Finally, even though Jupiter's work will show whether or not the test is reliable, it will not show whether or not it is valid. Validity is a measure of accuracy—in this case, whether the test actually measures perfectionism.

61. **(B)** Bandura showed that people learn by observing and then imitating others, a phenomenon known as modeling. Instrumental learning, named by Thorndike, is when people or animals learn that their behaviors are instrumental in bringing about specific consequences. The *copycat effect* is a term made up to sound like it fits the behavior described but not, in fact, used to do so. Thanatos is the name Freud gave to the supposed death instinct that drives people to commit aggressive and destructive acts. Sublimation is a Freudian defense mechanism in which people take the energy from impulses they view as unacceptable and redirect them toward more socially acceptable pursuits.

62. **(C)** The technique Coach Perry is using is called shaping. Shaping is defined as rewarding successive approximations of a desired behavior. Coach Perry would love 5-year-old Lana to be able to stop his hardest kick, but he knows that in order to reach that goal he must begin by letting her stop slow-moving balls. The law of effect is

Thorndike's pronouncement that pleasant consequences will increase the likelihood of a behavior and unpleasant consequences will decrease the likelihood of a behavior. The partial reinforcement effect is the finding that partial reinforcement schedules are more resistant to extinction than continuous reinforcement. Second-order conditioning is when, in classical conditioning, you use something that was initially a CS as a US to condition a new CS. A token economy is a method of promoting desired behaviors by rewarding such behaviors with tokens, redeemable at a future time for any of a range of items.

63. **(C)** A *p* value of .05 or less indicates that a difference is statistically significant. *p* stands for probability, and a *p* value gives the probability that the result occurred by chance. To compute the *p* value in this case, Matt will have to use both the standard deviation and the mean, but neither of those alone will tell him whether or not the difference is significant. Given the type of data with which Matt is working, he would have to run a t-test rather than a chi square test or a Pearson correlation to find a *p* value.

64. **(B)** Matt's research design is best classified as an ex-post facto study. In an ex-post facto study, what the researcher conceives of as the independent variable has already been predetermined. Student gender is predetermined; Matt cannot randomly assign students to be either girls or boys; hence, the study is an ex-post facto study. Random assignment of participants is required in an experiment. A case study looks closely at only one or a small group of people. Naturalistic observation uses unobtrusive observation rather than a survey. A content analysis studies the coverage of various topics in a communications medium (e.g., television, textbooks).

65. **(D)** The population in Matt's study is the Northeastern High School student body. The population is defined as anyone who could have been in the study. Since Matt took a random sample of the whole student body, they all had a chance to be in the study. The group of 100 students who actually took the survey is known as the sample. American students, high school students in Maine, and high school students throughout the world are all groups that Matt might be interested in, and they might be closer to what you think of when you think of the word "population," but they are not the population in this study because no one who was not attending Northeastern High School had the chance to be in Matt's study.

66. **(A)** The part of the brain thought to play the most important role in the Cannon-Bard theory of emotion was the thalamus. These psychologists thought the thalamus received information from the environment and simultaneously sent signals to the cortex and autonomic nervous system.

67. **(A)** Selye's general adaptation syndrome explains how the body deals with stressors. It has three stages: alarm, resistance, and exhaustion. After working so hard to deal with the stress of finals, Conrad reached what Selye termed exhaustion and succumbed to illness. The Yerkes-Dodson law explains the relationship between arousal and performance. The law of effect explains the relationship between the consequences of an action and repetition of that action. Cognitive dissonance theory proposes that we are motivated to maintain consistent attitudes. The James-Lange theory of emotion states that specific physiological changes in the body are indicative of specific emotions.

68. **(C)** Learned helplessness is most likely to be linked to an external locus of control. Learned helplessness is when exposure to circumstances one cannot control leads one to believe that one cannot control later events that are, in fact, within one's control. Similarly, someone with an external locus of control believes that factors such as luck and fate determine what happens to them as opposed to internal factors like effort or skill. The Barnum effect is that people believe vague, stock personality descriptions describe them. Self-serving bias is the tendency to take more credit for positive outcomes as opposed to negative ones. You have unconditional positive regard when someone accepts you regardless of your faults; humanistic theorist Carl Rogers thought it essential for a person to be psychologically healthy. An Oedipal complex is the Freudian idea that boys are in love with their mothers.

69. **(C)** Jung's collective unconscious contains archetypes, which are universal thought forms he believed were passed down through the species. Fictional finalisms and feelings of inferiority are terms more closely associated with Alfred Adler, another neo-Freudian. Jung believed complexes and bad memories would be stored in the personal unconscious.

70. **(B)** The shortest electromagnetic waves humans can see are violet. The acronym *Roy G. Biv* makes it easy to remember the order of the colors in the visible spectrum. The red waves are the longest followed by orange, yellow, green, blue, indigo, and finally violet.

71. **(B)** Nicotine is a stimulant because it has an arousing effect on the central nervous system, increasing heart rate, respiratory rate, and alertness. Alcohol, on the other hand, has the opposite effect and therefore is classified as a depressant. Both heroin and codeine are opiates, which means that their primary effect is to relieve pain. Finally, ecstasy is a hallucinogen, which means that it distorts perceptions.

72. **(C)** The right hemisphere controls the left side of the body and is important in recognizing faces, doing spatial tasks, and all sorts of creative pursuits. The left hemisphere plays a larger role in speech and language, logical problems, and controlling the right side of the body. Plasticity is the brain's ability to change as the result of experience, and one way it is illustrated is when the functions of a damaged part of a brain are taken over by another part of the brain. Since most of Genna's right hemisphere was damaged and removed, plasticity is shown by her ability to perform functions associated with that hemisphere after the surgery. The only behavior associated with the right hemisphere is moving her left hand.

73. **(D)** One of the more impressive feats cited by those who believe that animals are capable of true language is that some apes have been able to use words they were taught to express novel concepts. For instance, Washoe, who didn't know the word for refrigerator, was able to describe it as a "cold box." Chomsky speaks of a language acquisition device, but the term does not refer to a physical structure in the brain. Even though primates are able to learn words that result in food rewards, critics of the idea that animals have language say these words are merely the result of operant conditioning and do not evidence true language. There is no doubt that animals including honeybees and dolphins can communicate with one another and with people to some extent; however, there is much debate over what should be considered "language." Young apes are much slower to pick up new vocabulary than are young humans.

74. **(A)** The finding that people who read a job description written only with male pronouns (e.g., he) are more likely to think of an employee as male than people who read a description that uses gender-neutral language (e.g., he or she) is most closely linked to the linguistic relativity hypothesis. The linguistic-relativity or Sapir-Whorf hypothesis holds that language influences thought. Therefore, people who read a job description written using only male pronouns are influenced to think of the person who holds the job in a particular way. Gender schema theory holds that children learn about the gender roles of their culture and that the expectations they develop then guide their behavior. The social role hypothesis theorizes that society's expected roles can influence people to act in various ways. Modeling, or observational learning, is Bandura's theory that people learn by watching and imitating others. Ethnocentrism is the tendency to look at things from the perspective of one's own culture.

75. **(D)** In the nature versus nurture debate, nature is most closely associated with temperament. Nature refers to things that are innate. Temperament is one's inborn style of interacting with the world. Most of the other terms—environment, culture, and learning—are associated with nurture. One's family plays a role in both nature (e.g., via genes) and nurture (e.g., via the home environment).

76. **(D)** If the College Board neglected to put any questions that had to do with neuroscience on the AP Psychology exam one year, the test would lack content validity. A valid test measures what it is supposed to measure. A test with high content validity covers all the areas it is supposed to in the appropriate level of depth. Predictive and concurrent validity are two types of criterion validity. A test with predictive validity provides a measure of how someone will perform on a task in the future, whereas concurrent validity provides a measure of how someone will perform at the present time. Face validity is a shallow type of content validity; if a test is supposed to assess mathematical skill and contains math problems, it has face validity.

77. **(D)** Kohler's studies with apes involved setting up various problems to be solved such as how to retrieve bananas positioned out of reach. Kohler's observations led him to argue that the animals solved the problems by thinking about them—specifically, by having sudden insights about how to solve them.

78. **(C)** The scores of the three students who score much differently from the rest of the class are known as outliers or extreme scores. The mode is the most frequently occurring score in a distribution. Even though outliers skew a distribution, they are not called skewers. Variance is a measure of the variability in a distribution, as is standard deviation.

79. **(D)** Positive psychology focuses on the study of subjective well-being, optimism, and happiness. It is a relatively new area of psychology that grew out of the belief that too much of psychology focused on the negative aspects of the human condition (e.g., depression, prejudice, aggression). Psychometrics is the study of how to make tests. Human factors psychology melds psychology and engineering in an effort to make machines that are user-friendly. Social psychology is the study of how people interact with one another, and health psychology is an area that looks at how psychological factors impact physical health.

80. **(D)** After taking AP Psychology and doing well in the class and exam, Donald goes to college. If Donald is interested in psychology and has high achievement motivation, as a first-year student, he is most likely to sign up for an upper-level undergraduate course in which he will have to work hard to succeed and will learn new things. His interest in psychology will lead Donald to want to take more psychology classes and learn new things, while his high achievement motivation will lead him to select a class that will be challenging but not overly difficult.

81. **(A)** Humanistic models of personality reject the idea of determinism (that one's action and choices have been determined by factors outside of one's control) and embrace the idea of free will (that people are able to make their own choices). Biological models of personality tend to see human thought and behavior as determined by physiological factors. Evolutionary models view genes as the determining factor over most human behavior. Behaviorists believe one's history of reinforcement determines future choices, and psychoanalysts see the thoughts in one's unconscious as the factor that controls human behavior.

82. **(B)** Neuroleptics are commonly prescribed to treat schizophrenia, the most common psychotic disorder. L-Dopa is used to treat Parkinson's disease and would likely have an adverse effect on Vance since it would lead to an increase in dopamine and an excess of dopamine is a hypothesized cause of schizophrenia. Benzodiazepines are commonly used to treat anxiety. SSRIs (serotonin selective reuptake inhibitors) are used to treat major depressive disorder, and lithium is used to treat the manic phase of bipolar disorder.

83. **(B)** Sperling's partial report technique was designed to test the capacity of sensory memory. Sperling hypothesized that the reason people were only able to report about four items they were exposed to for a split second was not that more items didn't make it into the sensory register but that the memory decayed before the people could report them. He used the partial report technique to expose participants to a matrix of 12 letters (3 rows of 4) and showed that if cued on which line to report immediately after the matrix was removed from view, participants could usually recall the entire row correctly. This technique is not used to test the serial position effect, duration of working memory, difference between STM and LTM, or misinformation effect.

84. **(C)** Parkinson's disease has been linked to a deficit of dopamine. Major depressive disorder is associated with low levels of both serotonin and norepinephrine. The cause of autism is currently unknown. Similarly, the role of various neurotranmitters in Alzheimer's disease remains debated, but one view holds that shortages of acetylcholine are involved. Schizophrenia is associated with elevated levels of dopamine.

85. **(A)** Runners in a park were found to pick up their pace when another runner came into view; this finding illustrates the phenomenon of social facilitation since it shows that the presence of others improved performance. Conformity involves a change in attitude or behavior to fit in with a group; if a runner ran faster to keep up with her soccer teammates, conformity could be at work. Deindividuation is a loss of self-restraint under conditions of high arousal and anonymity. Norms are standards of expected behavior, and roles are sets of expected behaviors for different members of an organization.

86. **(E)** The Rosenhan study of mental institutions showed that confirmation bias, the tendency to pay more attention to information that supports one's views than challenges them, may influence clinicians' views and treatments of mental patients. In this study, a number of people checked themselves into a variety of mental institutions, including small private facilities and large public ones, reporting that they heard voices saying "empty," "hollow," and "thud." The otherwise normal people were admitted and then resumed their normal behavior. The study revealed that it took a long time for any of the hospitals' employees to realize that these patients were not in need of treatment, something that might be partly explained by the fact that the staff members tended to avoid contact with the patients. When the pseudopatients were released from the hospitals, they were diagnosed as schizophrenics in remission, which illustrates the stickiness of labels. The Rosenhan study showed that it can be difficult to discern who is mentally ill and who is well.

87. **(B)** An American teenager's prototype of a chair is most likely to include four legs and a seat. A prototype is the most typical example of category. Although there are many types of chairs such as the armchair, chairlift, and wheelchair listed in choice D, most chairs we encounter have the features described. We may commonly think of chairs with desks and tables or as a place to keep our pens, pencils, books, and computers. Through classical conditioning, someone may have come to associate certain types of chairs with anxiety.

88. **(C)** According to Kohlberg, in order to reason at a high moral level, people must be able to take another person's perspective. Kohlberg's theory includes three levels of moral development: preconventional, conventional, and postconventional. One of the hallmarks of postconventional thought is the ability to see things from multiple perspectives. Although we think of generosity as a good thing, it is conceivable that someone in the postconventional stage would decide that generosity, at least in some situations, should be avoided. Kohlberg's theory is not linked to any religious beliefs. Erikson's theory includes the integrity versus despair stage, but this idea is not tied to Kohlberg's theory. One could come to postconventional morality in a number of ways; one does not have to have learned one's moral beliefs from good role models.

89. **(B)** The incidence of schizophrenia in the population is closest to 1 in 100.

90. **(A)** *Learned helplessness,* a term coined by Martin Seligman, is when exposure to uncontrollable circumstances leads one to believe that he or she cannot exert control over other, controllable circumstances. Research has shown that learned helplessness is correlated with major depressive disorder.

91. **(C)** About an hour into one's first sleep cycle, people are typically in stage 3 or 4. In these stages, they experience deep, slow-wave sleep, which is marked by the presence of delta waves. Alpha waves indicate drowsiness, beta waves are present when one is awake and alert, and sleep spindles and K complex waves occur mostly in stage 2.

92. **(B)** Information from the eyes' retinas crosses at the optic chiasm. Each eye sends information to both hemispheres of the brain. Information from the left side of each retina goes to the left hemisphere of the brain, and information from the right side of each retina goes to the right side of the brain. The information is traveling via the optic

nerve. The fovea is the part of the retina that has the highest visual acuity. The lateral geniculate nucleus is the part of the thalamus where initial visual processing takes place. The basal ganglia are a group of nuclei that help coordinate different parts of the brain.

93. **(D)** In studying for the AP Psychology exam, good advice would be to study from multiple sources. Studying from your class notes, homework, old tests, and review book involves a fairly deep level of processing and will result in more elaborative encoding. Short-term memory only lasts about 20–30 seconds, so it's not a place to store information you're going to need hours later. Even though we hope you find our book helpful, reading any one source over and over again is a relatively shallow form of processing, and you would do better to study from multiple sources. Since what you need to know for the exam is not a long list of items, the serial position effect would not be particularly helpful. Finally, although minimizing interference is a good goal, you will perform better with a good night's sleep, and research shows that interference during sleep is actually minimal.

94. **(D)** A lesson from Janis's research on groupthink is that it is important for people to voice dissent. Groupthink occurs when dissent in a group is suppressed in order to preserve harmony, and bad decisions result. Classic examples include the Bay of Pigs fiasco and the *Challenger* explosion. Unanimity, pressure, and homogeneity are all factors that can promote groupthink. Groupthink can occur in groups of any size.

95. **(C)** Information from the optic nerve is initially processed in the thalamus, in the lateral geniculate nucleus (LGN). From the thalamus, information is sent to the primary visual cortex in the occipital lobe. The hypothalamus, hippocampus, and cerebellum are not thought to play a large role in the early processing of visual information.

96. **(B)** Cognitive psychologists would be most likely to support Schachter's two-factor theory of emotion. This theory holds that emotion results from the cognitive appraisal of a general physiological arousal. Social facilitation is the finding that people perform well-learned tasks better in the presence of others. The other three theories listed, while theories of emotion, do not give cognition a prominent role. Cannon-Bard's thalamic theory posits that the thalamus receives information from the environment and simultaneously sends signals to the cortex and autonomic nervous system. The James-Lange theory suggests that every emotion is associated with a unique physiological set of responses that tells us what emotion we feel. The opponent process theory of emotion states that the experience an emotion triggers is followed by the experience of its opposite.

97. **(D)** Odette has several classic symptoms of major depressive disorder—loss of appetite, disrupted sleep, and a loss of interest in her usual activities. Although Odette is at an age when many people sadly begin to suffer from Alzheimer's, she is not experiencing the rapid degeneration in memory and cognitive function associated with that disease. Since her problems began about a year ago, they do not seem to be associated with winter, and she is unlikely to be diagnosed with seasonal affective disorder. There is no indication that she is engaging in the binge-purge cycle associated with bulimia nor is there evidence that Odette evinces the major symptom of antisocial personality disorder, a disregard for and carelessness toward others.

98. **(C)** One cause of the deinstitutionalization of many psychiatric patients in the mid-1900s was the creation of new medications such as antipsychotic drugs. It was hoped that this movement would save the government money and enable people suffering from mental illness to have more freedom. Unfortunately, once released from the institutions, many people did not stay on their medication regimes, and without adequate systems in place to follow up on these people, many became homeless. Even though methods of psychotherapy may have improved, the former patients no longer had access to it. The deinstitutionalization movement was not the result of a belief that we had institutionalized healthy people.

99. **(D)** The prefrontal cortex of Phineas Gage's brain was damaged by his accident while laying the railroad track. This part of the brain plays a vital role in judgment and decision making, and the damage helps explain how Gage's personality changed from dependable and even-tempered to irascible and irresponsible. The corpus callosum is the band of neurons that links the brain's two hemispheres. The temporal lobes are located on the sides of the head just above the ears and house the auditory cortex. The medulla oblongata sits atop the spinal cord and helps regulate involuntary activities like heart rate. The midbrain is part of the brainstem and contains the reticular formation, which regulates arousal.

100. **(D)** Approximately 60 percent of participants in Milgram's obedience experiment thought they delivered the maximum amount of shock possible, a figure far in excess of what psychologists had predicted. Remember, no actual shocks were delivered; the "learner" was a confederate of the experimenter trained to act the part.

Multiple-Choice Error Analysis Sheet

After checking your answers on the practice test, you might want to gauge your areas of relative strength and weakness. This sheet will help you to classify your errors by topic area. By circling the numbers of the questions you answered incorrectly, you can get a picture of which areas you need to study the most.

Chapter	Question Numbers									
History and Approaches	5	6	31							
Methods	10	21	34	49	63	64	65	78		
Biological Bases of Behavior	1	27	23	28	41	42	72	95	99	
Sensation and Perception	3	13	14	30	52	53	70	92		
States of Consciousness	16	71	91							
Learning	8	9	35	47	48	61	62	77		
Cognition	2	26	40	43	56	73	74	83	87	93
Motivation and Emotion	11	33	50	66	67	79	80	96		
Developmental Psychology	24	25	39	44	57	58	75	88		
Personality	12	19	22	51	68	69	81			
Testing and Individual Differences	7	36	46	60	76	94				
Abnormal Psychology	4	22	37	45	59	84	89	90	97	
Treatment of Psychological Disorders	17	18	29	82	86	98				
Social Psychology	15	20	38	54	55	85	94	100		

Part II

Question 1 Scoring Rubric

This is an 8-point question with two distinct parts. Part A asks you to explain how the two terms provided might explain Eli's aversion to green vegetables. Part B asks you to discuss how the additional five terms might be used to encourage Eli to eat green vegetables.

1. Two year-old Eli dislikes green vegetables and often refuses to eat them.

Part A

Point 1

Evolutionary Psychology

Evolutionary psychologists believe that human behavior is motivated by the desire to ensure the survival and proliferation of our genes. By age two, children are able to move about on their own and will therefore encounter new plants, some of which may look like vegetables but, in fact, be dangerous to eat. Therefore, an evolutionary psychologist might say that Eli's refusal to eat green vegetables is due to a natural avoidance that arises about the time children become independent enough to eat things without supervision.

Point 2

Erickson's Psychosocial Stage Theory

According to Erikson, from ages one to three children are in a stage that revolves around a conflict between autonomy or shame and doubt. As such, children of this age often try to assert their will, and the word ***no*** becomes a common part of their vocabularies. Eli's refusal to eat the green vegetables his parents so desperately want him to eat may therefore just be a way of asserting his independence.

Part B

Point 3

Mere Exposure Effect

The mere exposure effect says that the more one is exposed to something, the more one comes to like it. Therefore, Eli's parents could simply serve him green vegetables frequently hoping that with repeated contact, he will come to like them more.

Point 4

Eli's Lack of Piagetian Conservation

According to Piaget, children learn to conserve upon entering the concrete operations stage around age six. Until then, children are typically unable to solve problems that ask them to compare quantities. Eli's parents may be able to take advantage of this cognitive limitation in how they present his vegetables. For instance, instead of serving Eli many small pieces of celery, they could ask Eli to eat just one (large) celery stalk.

Point 5

Conformity

People have a natural desire to fit in with others. If Eli's siblings or cousins or friends eat green vegetables, Eli's parents may be able to increase his consumption of vegetables by serving them to Eli among a group of people all of whom will eat their green vegetables.

Point 6

Modeling

Modeling is when someone observes someone else's behavior and then copies it. While conformity involves fitting into a group, modeling can be done by an individual. Eli's parents can model eating green vegetables themselves hoping that Eli will notice and copy them.

Point 7

Positive Reinforcement

A reinforcer is a consequence that increases the likelihood of a behavior. Eli's parents can use positive reinforcement by giving Eli something he wants when he eats his green vegetables. For instance, each day that Eli finishes his vegetables he could be rewarded with a half hour of watching television.

Question 2 Scoring Rubric

Note: On several exams in recent years, the AP Psychology Exam included a free-response question in which students were asked to create and label a bar graph. In this question, we included a bar graph to mimic that style of the question and also asked for a scatter plot in an effort to anticipate what the exam might include in years to come.

This is an 8-point question with three parts that focus on a student research project. Part A of the question asks you to graph a small data set in a scatter plot and describe the correlation found. Part B requires that you relate four psychological concepts to the research described in the question. Part C presents one of the findings of the research and asks that you graph it and evaluate the student researcher's conclusion.

Part A

Point 1

Draw and Label a Scatter Plot

No text is necessary to earn this point other than the axis labels on the graph below. A scatter plot is used to show a correlation; it depicts one variable on the *x*-axis (horizontal) and the other on the *y*-axis (vertical). Typically, the independent variable is plotted on the *x*-axis and the dependent variable on the *y*-axis. As you may remember, in a correlational study like this one, there is no true independent variable because neither variable is manipulated by the researcher. Thus, you would score the point regardless of which variable you plotted on either axis.

I used Excel to make the graph shown below. However, on your exam, you will not be expected to exhibit the precision of a graphing program. You will not even have graph paper. So long as you draw and label your axes and make a reasonable effort to plot the points in approximately the correct places, you will earn the point.

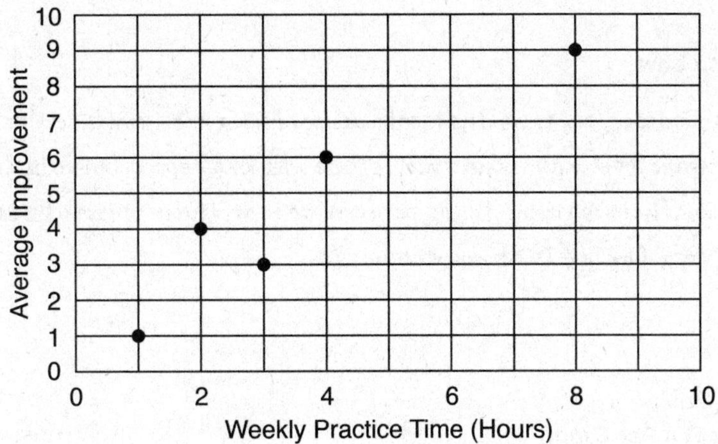

Point 2

Describe the Type of Correlation Pooja Found

Pooja found a positive correlation between weekly practice time and playing test score.

Part B

Point 3

Distributed Practice

Musicians who distribute (spread out) their practice time are more likely to improve than musicians who use massed practice.

Point 4

Experimenter Bias

A problem in Pooja's study was experimenter bias—the tendency of researchers to inadvertently influence their work in such a way as to confirm their hypotheses. If Pooja is aware of how much practice time the students have reported as she listens to their playing tests, she may be subconsciously inclined to interpret what she hears so as to support her predictions.

Point 5

Social Desirability

Social desirability is the tendency of people to report the "right" kind of data. In Pooja's case, the students all know they are supposed to practice, and may, therefore, not be entirely honest in their reports of their practice time.

Point 6

Yerkes-Dodson Law

The Yerkes-Dodson law says that optimal performance is related to moderate levels of arousal. Pooja may find that students who report being a little nervous during their playing tests perform better than students who report very high or very low levels of nervousness.

Part C

Point 7

Draw and Label a Bar Graph

Again, you don't need a ruler to earn this point. Just draw the two bars and label the axes as shown below.

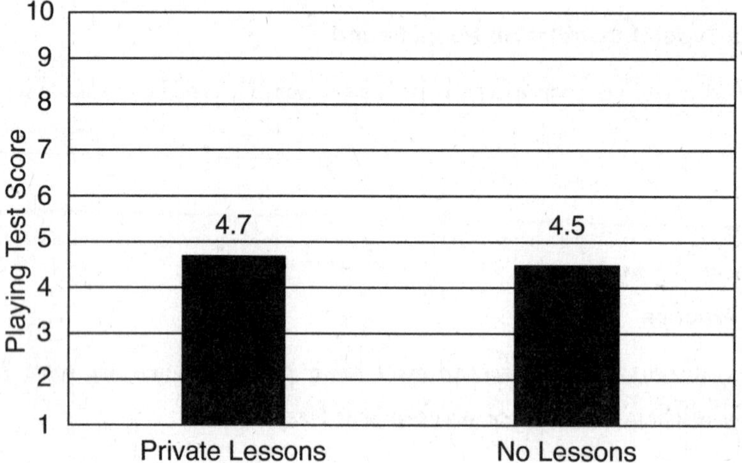

Point 8

Explain Why You Agree or Disagree with Pooja's Conclusion

You should not agree with Pooja's conclusion, but to earn the point you need to say something about why you do not agree. There are two main problems with Pooja's conclusion, and describing either one would earn you the point. One problem is that Pooja confuses causation with correlation, and you could score this point by explaining that problem in one of two ways. It may be that taking private lessons causes students to improve, but it also may be that students who are improving are more likely to seek out private lessons. Alternatively, you could explain that because Pooja does not run an experiment and randomly assign students to take private lessons or not, it could also be that some third factor (such as, practice time) is responsible both for the improvement and for the decision to take private lessons.

The second major problem with Pooja's conclusion is the size of the difference between the groups—4.5 versus 4.7. This small difference is unlikely to be statistically significant—that is, such a small difference is very likely to be due to chance.

ANSWER SHEET
Practice Test 2

1. Ⓐ Ⓑ Ⓒ Ⓓ Ⓔ	26. Ⓐ Ⓑ Ⓒ Ⓓ Ⓔ	51. Ⓐ Ⓑ Ⓒ Ⓓ Ⓔ	76. Ⓐ Ⓑ Ⓒ Ⓓ Ⓔ
2. Ⓐ Ⓑ Ⓒ Ⓓ Ⓔ	27. Ⓐ Ⓑ Ⓒ Ⓓ Ⓔ	52. Ⓐ Ⓑ Ⓒ Ⓓ Ⓔ	77. Ⓐ Ⓑ Ⓒ Ⓓ Ⓔ
3. Ⓐ Ⓑ Ⓒ Ⓓ Ⓔ	28. Ⓐ Ⓑ Ⓒ Ⓓ Ⓔ	53. Ⓐ Ⓑ Ⓒ Ⓓ Ⓔ	78. Ⓐ Ⓑ Ⓒ Ⓓ Ⓔ
4. Ⓐ Ⓑ Ⓒ Ⓓ Ⓔ	29. Ⓐ Ⓑ Ⓒ Ⓓ Ⓔ	54. Ⓐ Ⓑ Ⓒ Ⓓ Ⓔ	79. Ⓐ Ⓑ Ⓒ Ⓓ Ⓔ
5. Ⓐ Ⓑ Ⓒ Ⓓ Ⓔ	30. Ⓐ Ⓑ Ⓒ Ⓓ Ⓔ	55. Ⓐ Ⓑ Ⓒ Ⓓ Ⓔ	80. Ⓐ Ⓑ Ⓒ Ⓓ Ⓔ
6. Ⓐ Ⓑ Ⓒ Ⓓ Ⓔ	31. Ⓐ Ⓑ Ⓒ Ⓓ Ⓔ	56. Ⓐ Ⓑ Ⓒ Ⓓ Ⓔ	81. Ⓐ Ⓑ Ⓒ Ⓓ Ⓔ
7. Ⓐ Ⓑ Ⓒ Ⓓ Ⓔ	32. Ⓐ Ⓑ Ⓒ Ⓓ Ⓔ	57. Ⓐ Ⓑ Ⓒ Ⓓ Ⓔ	82. Ⓐ Ⓑ Ⓒ Ⓓ Ⓔ
8. Ⓐ Ⓑ Ⓒ Ⓓ Ⓔ	33. Ⓐ Ⓑ Ⓒ Ⓓ Ⓔ	58. Ⓐ Ⓑ Ⓒ Ⓓ Ⓔ	83. Ⓐ Ⓑ Ⓒ Ⓓ Ⓔ
9. Ⓐ Ⓑ Ⓒ Ⓓ Ⓔ	34. Ⓐ Ⓑ Ⓒ Ⓓ Ⓔ	59. Ⓐ Ⓑ Ⓒ Ⓓ Ⓔ	84. Ⓐ Ⓑ Ⓒ Ⓓ Ⓔ
10. Ⓐ Ⓑ Ⓒ Ⓓ Ⓔ	35. Ⓐ Ⓑ Ⓒ Ⓓ Ⓔ	60. Ⓐ Ⓑ Ⓒ Ⓓ Ⓔ	85. Ⓐ Ⓑ Ⓒ Ⓓ Ⓔ
11. Ⓐ Ⓑ Ⓒ Ⓓ Ⓔ	36. Ⓐ Ⓑ Ⓒ Ⓓ Ⓔ	61. Ⓐ Ⓑ Ⓒ Ⓓ Ⓔ	86. Ⓐ Ⓑ Ⓒ Ⓓ Ⓔ
12. Ⓐ Ⓑ Ⓒ Ⓓ Ⓔ	37. Ⓐ Ⓑ Ⓒ Ⓓ Ⓔ	62. Ⓐ Ⓑ Ⓒ Ⓓ Ⓔ	87. Ⓐ Ⓑ Ⓒ Ⓓ Ⓔ
13. Ⓐ Ⓑ Ⓒ Ⓓ Ⓔ	38. Ⓐ Ⓑ Ⓒ Ⓓ Ⓔ	63. Ⓐ Ⓑ Ⓒ Ⓓ Ⓔ	88. Ⓐ Ⓑ Ⓒ Ⓓ Ⓔ
14. Ⓐ Ⓑ Ⓒ Ⓓ Ⓔ	39. Ⓐ Ⓑ Ⓒ Ⓓ Ⓔ	64. Ⓐ Ⓑ Ⓒ Ⓓ Ⓔ	89. Ⓐ Ⓑ Ⓒ Ⓓ Ⓔ
15. Ⓐ Ⓑ Ⓒ Ⓓ Ⓔ	40. Ⓐ Ⓑ Ⓒ Ⓓ Ⓔ	65. Ⓐ Ⓑ Ⓒ Ⓓ Ⓔ	90. Ⓐ Ⓑ Ⓒ Ⓓ Ⓔ
16. Ⓐ Ⓑ Ⓒ Ⓓ Ⓔ	41. Ⓐ Ⓑ Ⓒ Ⓓ Ⓔ	66. Ⓐ Ⓑ Ⓒ Ⓓ Ⓔ	91. Ⓐ Ⓑ Ⓒ Ⓓ Ⓔ
17. Ⓐ Ⓑ Ⓒ Ⓓ Ⓔ	42. Ⓐ Ⓑ Ⓒ Ⓓ Ⓔ	67. Ⓐ Ⓑ Ⓒ Ⓓ Ⓔ	92. Ⓐ Ⓑ Ⓒ Ⓓ Ⓔ
18. Ⓐ Ⓑ Ⓒ Ⓓ Ⓔ	43. Ⓐ Ⓑ Ⓒ Ⓓ Ⓔ	68. Ⓐ Ⓑ Ⓒ Ⓓ Ⓔ	93. Ⓐ Ⓑ Ⓒ Ⓓ Ⓔ
19. Ⓐ Ⓑ Ⓒ Ⓓ Ⓔ	44. Ⓐ Ⓑ Ⓒ Ⓓ Ⓔ	69. Ⓐ Ⓑ Ⓒ Ⓓ Ⓔ	94. Ⓐ Ⓑ Ⓒ Ⓓ Ⓔ
20. Ⓐ Ⓑ Ⓒ Ⓓ Ⓔ	45. Ⓐ Ⓑ Ⓒ Ⓓ Ⓔ	70. Ⓐ Ⓑ Ⓒ Ⓓ Ⓔ	95. Ⓐ Ⓑ Ⓒ Ⓓ Ⓔ
21. Ⓐ Ⓑ Ⓒ Ⓓ Ⓔ	46. Ⓐ Ⓑ Ⓒ Ⓓ Ⓔ	71. Ⓐ Ⓑ Ⓒ Ⓓ Ⓔ	96. Ⓐ Ⓑ Ⓒ Ⓓ Ⓔ
22. Ⓐ Ⓑ Ⓒ Ⓓ Ⓔ	47. Ⓐ Ⓑ Ⓒ Ⓓ Ⓔ	72. Ⓐ Ⓑ Ⓒ Ⓓ Ⓔ	97. Ⓐ Ⓑ Ⓒ Ⓓ Ⓔ
23. Ⓐ Ⓑ Ⓒ Ⓓ Ⓔ	48. Ⓐ Ⓑ Ⓒ Ⓓ Ⓔ	73. Ⓐ Ⓑ Ⓒ Ⓓ Ⓔ	98. Ⓐ Ⓑ Ⓒ Ⓓ Ⓔ
24. Ⓐ Ⓑ Ⓒ Ⓓ Ⓔ	49. Ⓐ Ⓑ Ⓒ Ⓓ Ⓔ	74. Ⓐ Ⓑ Ⓒ Ⓓ Ⓔ	99. Ⓐ Ⓑ Ⓒ Ⓓ Ⓔ
25. Ⓐ Ⓑ Ⓒ Ⓓ Ⓔ	50. Ⓐ Ⓑ Ⓒ Ⓓ Ⓔ	75. Ⓐ Ⓑ Ⓒ Ⓓ Ⓔ	100. Ⓐ Ⓑ Ⓒ Ⓓ Ⓔ

Practice Test 2

PART I: MULTIPLE-CHOICE QUESTIONS

1 Hour and 10 Minutes

DIRECTIONS: Each of the questions or incomplete statements below is followed by five suggested answers or completions. Select the one that is best in each case.

1. Which of the following is the most important detail of Wundt's early research that established the psychology as a science?
   (A) Wundt was a member of the upper class, which helped his credibility.
   (B) Wundt wrote well and communicated results to large numbers of people effectively.
   (C) Wundt set up a laboratory and focused on empirical evidence that could be replicated.
   (D) Wundt worked outside the university system and was seen as an independent thinker.
   (E) Wundt focused exclusively on observable behavior, not unobservable events like thinking and consciousness.

2. Which of the following psychologists would most likely agree with the following statement: behavior is a result of the combination of reinforcers and punishers?
   (A) William James
   (B) Wilhelm Wundt
   (C) B. F. Skinner
   (D) Carl Rogers
   (E) Albert Bandura

3. Choosing 20 people at random from a large lecture class of 400 people is an example of which of the following?
   (A) random assignment
   (B) random sampling
   (C) representative assignment
   (D) representative sampling
   (E) assignment to conditions

4. Which technique controls for both experimenter and subject bias?
   (A) demand characteristics
   (B) double blind study
   (C) single blind study
   (D) Hawthorne effect
   (E) counterbalancing

5. Damage to the occipital lobes of the brain would most likely affect which of the senses?
   (A) hearing
   (B) touch
   (C) balance
   (D) sight
   (E) smell

6. A medication prescribed by a psychiatrist for major depressive disorder would most likely influence the balance of which of the following neurotransmitters?

(A) serotonin
(B) dopamine
(C) acetylcholine
(D) thorazine
(E) adrenaline

7. A doctor examining a car crash victim in order to determine whether the crash caused structural damage to the brain would use what kind of brain scan?

(A) MRI
(B) PET
(C) EEG
(D) fMRI
(E) EKG

8. Physiological reactions to surprise or shocks are most controlled by which of the following parts of the nervous system?

(A) somatic nervous system
(B) sympathetic nervous system
(C) endocrine system
(D) serotonin system
(E) contralateral control

9. Children who suffer brain damage may be able to regain their physical and mental abilities more quickly than older brain damage patients due to which of the following properties of the brain?

(A) contralateral control
(B) Klinefelter's syndrome
(C) effective psychological environment
(D) brain lateralization
(E) brain plasticity

10. Which of the following kinds of brain scans would be most useful in disproving the statement: "Most people only use 10 percent of their brains"?

(A) CAT
(B) MRI
(C) EEG
(D) PET
(E) EKG

11. Which of the following structures in the eye is most specifically responsible for color vision?

(A) rods
(B) optic nerve
(C) cornea
(D) cones
(E) lens

12. Human senses can be divided into which two major categories based on what the senses gather from the outside world?

(A) sensation and perception
(B) conduction and transduction
(C) energy and chemical
(D) bichromatic and trichromatic
(E) opponent and process

13. Turning up the volume on a music player changes which aspect of sound?

(A) amplitude of the wave
(B) frequency of the wave
(C) pitch of the tone
(D) transduction of the tone
(E) energy of the sound

14. A research study establishes that most people can taste one gram of salt in one quart of water. Which of the following concepts is most closely related to the goal of this study?

(A) difference threshold
(B) absolute threshold
(C) taste constancy
(D) sensory adaptation
(E) perceptual adaptation

15. A musician's ability to make a distinction between two very similar pitches depends on which of the following concepts?
   (A) absolute threshold
   (B) signal detection theory
   (C) bottom-up processing
   (D) difference threshold
   (E) frequency theory

16. Our ability to perceive depth depends primarily on what other perceptual abilities?
   (A) proximity and similarity
   (B) top-down processing and bottom-up processing
   (C) binocular and monocular cues
   (D) size and shape constancy
   (E) vestibular and kinesthic senses

17. REM sleep deprivation generally causes what kinds of side effects?
   (A) intense, prolonged periods of stage 3 and 4 sleep
   (B) interference with memory tasks
   (C) decreased sleep onset episodes
   (D) sleep apnea and night terrors
   (E) heightened manifest dream content

18. Adrian dreams she has discovered a new restaurant in the city with really good salads. Her analyst suggests that the dream reflects Adrian's discontent with her current life situation and her desire for change. The analyst's interpretation best exemplifies a
   (A) cognitive perspective
   (B) psychoanalytic perspective
   (C) sociocultural perspective
   (D) behaviorist perspective
   (E) biological perspective

19. What is the first step in any example of classical conditioning?
   (A) following a response with a reinforcement or a punishment
   (B) reinforcing an organism for a behavior similar to the desired behavior
   (C) pairing an unconditioned stimulus with a conditioned stimulus
   (D) rewarding a behavior with an unconditioned stimulus, such as food
   (E) punishing behaviors other than the target behavior

20. An "A+" course grade is which kind of reinforcer?
   (A) primary
   (B) secondary
   (C) continuous
   (D) partial
   (E) interval

21. A researcher who concludes that "people who watch graphic violence in films are more likely to behave in violent ways than people who don't" is probably researching which kind of learning?
   (A) latent
   (B) behavioral
   (C) observational
   (D) insight
   (E) abstract

22. In the three-box information processing model, what is the first place memories are stored?
   (A) short-term memory
   (B) eidetic memory
   (C) semantic memory
   (D) sensory memory
   (E) procedural memory

23. Memory research indicates that memories may be physically stored in the brain through strengthened connections between brain neurons. What is this process called?

(A) proactive interference
(B) long-term potentiation
(C) state-dependent memory
(D) semantic memory
(E) information-processing model

24. Most mnemonic devices (like learning the notes on the staff by memorizing the sentence "Every Good Boy Does Fine" and using the first letter of each word) are examples of which memory enhancement technique?

(A) semantic encoding
(B) potentiation
(C) recognition
(D) chunking
(E) proactive interference

25. Seeing someone in line at the grocery store and remembering her or his name is an example of which kind of retrieval?

(A) recognition
(B) recall
(C) episodic
(D) semantic
(E) retroactive

26. Which of the following is most likely to lead to a constructed memory?

(A) brain injury
(B) serial position effect
(C) leading questions
(D) proactive interference
(E) relearning effect

27. Abraham Maslow's hierarachy of needs theorizes that each person is motivated by what?

(A) desire to achieve in the eyes of others
(B) satisfying needs from the next step in the hierarchy
(C) primary (physical) and secondary (emotional) needs
(D) homeostasis needs determined by our inner self
(E) sex, thirst, hunger, and safety, in that order

28. Which of the following brain structures is most centrally involved in hunger motivation?

(A) cerebellum
(B) medulla
(C) amygdala
(D) hypothalamus
(E) corpus callosum

29. Which kinds of motivations best encourage positive behaviors to persist over long periods of time?

(A) primary drives
(B) secondary drives
(C) achievement motivation
(D) intrinsic motivation
(E) extrinsic motivation

30. A researcher tests the problem-solving skills of twenty 10-year-old, twenty 20-year-old, and twenty 30-year-old participants for a study on age and problem solving. What research method is this researcher using?

(A) longitudinal
(B) stage
(C) developmental
(D) cross-sectional
(E) social-cognitive

31. Which of the following newborn reflexes help infants find and eat food?

(A) Babinski
(B) Moro
(C) atttachment
(D) conservation
(E) rooting

32. Mary Ainsworth placed babies into a strange situation and observed the babies' reactions when the parents left and then returned. What developmental concept was Ainsworth studying?

(A) parenting style
(B) motor development
(C) infant reflexes
(D) attachment
(E) assimilation

33. Which developmental stage theory explained how experiences in infancy, childhood, adolescence, adulthood, and old age influence later personality characteristics?

(A) Piaget's cognitive development theory
(B) Erikson's psychosocial stage theory
(C) Kohlberg's moral development theory
(D) Ainsworth's social attachment theory
(E) Harlow's social attachment theory

34. What would Piaget test in order to determine whether a child is in the pre-operational or concrete operational stage of cognitive development?

(A) object permanence
(B) attachment
(C) concepts of conservation
(D) hypothesis testing
(E) universal ethical principles

35. According to Sigmund Freud, what is the dominant factor determining our personality traits?

(A) secondary drives and needs
(B) genetic and nutritional factors
(C) unconscious conflicts
(D) parenting styles
(E) positive and negative reinforcements

36. Which of the following is a common way to categorize personality traits?

(A) the Big Five
(B) Erikson's 8 traits
(C) Piaget's 4 stages
(D) the Nine Defense Mechanisms
(E) the Top Two

37. A pencil and paper personality test that places a person in one of several personality categories (such as extrovert/introvert, etc.) is based on which personality theory?

(A) psychodynamic
(B) trait
(C) biological
(D) behaviorist
(E) social cognitive

38. Which of the following was an important technique used by Abraham Maslow and the humanistic psychologists during therapy?

(A) defense mechanisms
(B) factor analysis
(C) unconditional positive regard
(D) somatotype theory
(E) secondary central dispositions

39. Which of the following kinds of personality theorists is the most likely to use a projective test?

(A) social-cognitive
(B) behaviorist
(C) humanist
(D) psychoanalyst
(E) trait

40. Which of the following kinds of tests is most likely to be an achievement test?

(A) an IQ test
(B) a classroom test over a chapter in a textbook
(C) an entrance exam for law school
(D) a personality test based on the Big Five personality traits
(E) a projective test

41. The ability to solve a new computer game based on logical puzzles probably depends on which kind of intelligence?

(A) fluid intelligence
(B) crystallized intelligence
(C) aptitude intelligence
(D) achievement intelligence
(E) multiple intelligence

42. Which of the following terms applies to IQ tests?

(A) achievement
(B) standardized
(C) projective
(D) triarchic
(E) crystallized

43. A person who experiences flashbacks and nightmares after being involved in a serious car accident is likely to be diagnosed with which psychological disorder?

(A) dissociative identity disorder
(B) bipolar disorder
(C) schizophrenia
(D) post-traumatic stress disorder
(E) panic disorder

44. What kind of symptom is common among all the somatic symptom disorders?

(A) inappropriate affect
(B) disconnection from reality and delusions related to personal identity
(C) maladaptive ways of behaving that prevent a person from accomplishing goals
(D) substance dependence
(E) experiencing a physical problem without a physical cause

45. Psychogenic amnesia is an indication of which kind of psychological disorder?

(A) schizophrenic
(B) anxiety
(C) mood
(D) dissociative
(E) personality

46. People who suffer from major depressive disorder often have very low levels of which neurotransmitter?

(A) thyroxin
(B) endocrine
(C) acetylcholine
(D) serotonin
(E) lithium

47. In what way would a person diagnosed with schizophrenia most likely differ from a person diagnosed with a dissociative disorder?

(A) A person with schizophrenia is likely to have more than one personality.
(B) A person diagnosed with a dissociative disorder is likely to have delusions.
(C) A person diagnosed with schizophrenia is likely to experience hallucinations.
(D) A person diagnosed with a dissociative disorder may have difficulty keeping a job.
(E) A person with schizophrenia is likely to be split from reality.

48. What is the principal tool used in all forms of psychotherapy?

(A) talking to a patient
(B) cognitive/behavioral interventions
(C) biomedical/cognitive treatments
(D) somatic therapies
(E) secondary preventions

49. Why are psychoanalysts sometimes interested in talking with a patient about dreams?

(A) Psychoanalysts discovered that neurotransmitter abnormalities sometimes cause dream disturbances.
(B) Since all people are striving for self-actualization, psychoanalysts look at the cognitive obstacles in dreams.
(C) Nonproductive counterconditioning behaviors are sometimes revealed in dreams.
(D) Some psychoanalysts believe that dream symbols represent unconscious conflicts.
(E) Dreams reflect variations in brain waves during REM sleep.

50. Which of the following kinds of therapies would most likely be used by a somatic therapist?

(A) counterconditioning
(B) systematic desensitization
(C) rational emotive behavior therapies
(D) in vivo desensitization
(E) chemotherapy

51. Which of the therapies listed below is no longer used to treat patients?

(A) electroconvulsive shock therapy
(B) implosive therapy
(C) free association
(D) Gestalt therapy
(E) prefrontal lobotomy

52. Which of the following kinds of therapists is most likely to prescribe lithium for a patient diagnosed with bipolar disorder?

(A) psychoanalyst
(B) psychiatrist
(C) clinical psychologist
(D) cognitive psychotherapist
(E) Gestalt psychologist

53. A nonprofit environmental group includes a free gift of address labels in a letter asking for contributions. Which social psychological principle is the nonprofit group trying to use to increase contributions?

(A) self-fulfilling prophecy
(B) stable attribution
(C) compliance strategy
(D) fundamental attribution error
(E) out-group homogeneity

54. A math teacher refuses to look at the grades her students received in the past in math classes. The teacher is worried that looking at their past grades might influence the ways she reacts to her students. What effect is the teacher trying to avoid?

(A) cognitive dissonance
(B) self-fulfilling prophecy
(C) fundamental attribution error
(D) false-consensus effects
(E) self-serving bias

55. What kinds of factors are ignored or de-emphasized when people commit the fundamental attribution error?

(A) dispositional
(B) situational
(C) social
(D) cognitive
(E) behavioral

56. Which social psychological principle best explains prejudice?

(A) individualism
(B) collectivism
(C) self-serving bias
(D) in-group bias
(E) compliance strategies

57. Sherif's Robbers Cave study indicated that which of the following principles best helps reduce tensions between groups?

(A) superordinate goals
(B) diffusion of responsibility
(C) group polarization
(D) deindividuation
(E) groupthink

58. Milgram's obedience study was criticized based on what ethical grounds?

(A) lack of informed consent
(B) nonrandom sampling procedures
(C) violation of anonymity
(D) risk of psychological harm
(E) lack of debriefing

59. What makes the psychoanalytic perspective different from the other psychological perspectives?

(A) Psychoanalysts focus on the unconscious mind.
(B) Psychoanalysis relies on the scientific method.
(C) The process of psychoanalysis takes a long time and is focused on individuals, not groups.
(D) The research psychoanalysis is based on primarily involves people with psychological disorders.
(E) Psychoanalysis is the only perspective to involve treatment of psychological disorders.

60. If a distribution of scores includes one or more outliers, which of the following measures of central tendency should be used?

(A) standard deviation
(B) range
(C) median
(D) mean
(E) normal curve

61. Which of the following would a researcher need to use to determine if the difference between the mean scores of experimental and control groups was significant?

(A) descriptive statistics
(B) inferential statistics
(C) field experiment
(D) standard deviation
(E) counterbalancing

62. Which sentence most accurately describes how neurons communicate?

(A) Neurons communicate through physical contact between dendrites of one cell and the next cell.
(B) Electricity passes between neurons, which carries messages between one neuron and another.
(C) Chemicals travel from one neuron to another, influencing whether a neuron will fire or not.
(D) Neurons send messages up the spinal cord to the cerebral cortex through neural reflexes.
(E) Axons of neurons wrap around each other and communicate messages through hormones.

63. Someone with brain damage who has difficulty making the muscle movements needed to produce accurate speech might have damage to which area of the brain?

(A) Wernicke's area
(B) hippocampus
(C) Broca's area
(D) amygdala
(E) Gage's area

64. Which of the following structures is located at the most central and protected part of the brain?

(A) somato-sensory cortex
(B) cerebellum
(C) cerebral cortex
(D) Broca's area
(E) medulla

65. The case study of Phineas Gage's brain injury was significant for which of the following reasons?

(A) Gage's accident was one of the first to be treated with drugs that alter the neurotransmitters in the brain.
(B) It was one of the first well-documented examples of a specific brain area being associated with a set of physical and emotional changes.
(C) This accident provided psychiatrists with one of the first opportunities to treat a brain-damaged patient with psychotherapeutic techniques.
(D) The CAT scan was used for the first time in the Phineas Gage case to document the extent of brain injury.
(E) The case of Phineas Gage demonstrated that brain injury primarily affects physical abilities, not mood or our emotions.

66. An artist doing a pencil drawing could use which of the following techniques to add depth to her or his drawing?

(A) retinal disparity
(B) convergence
(C) closure
(D) olfaction
(E) linear perspective

67. Which classical conditioning term best describes the following scenario? Later in his classical conditioning experiments, Ivan Pavlov's dogs began to salivate whenever they heard any sound similar to a bell, such as a doorbell or someone accidentally clinking a water glass.

(A) discrimination
(B) spontaneous recovery
(C) trace conditioning
(D) generalization
(E) unconditioned response

68. Garcia and Koelling's research regarding learned aversions established that which of the following US and CS pairs are the most powerful and learned most quickly?

(A) performing a task and receiving a food reward
(B) nausea and food or drink
(C) movement and shock
(D) punishments and rewards
(E) administration of a punishment and aversion

69. Why might a researcher use a variable ratio of reinforcement rather than a fixed ratio?

(A) Fixed ratio schedules of reinforcements are more time intensive.
(B) Variable ratio schedules of reinforcements produce results more quickly.
(C) Variable ratio schedules of reinforcements avoid problems such as generalization and the Premack principle.
(D) Variable ratio schedules of reinforcements allow researchers to use both classical and operant conditioning.
(E) Variable ratio schedules of reinforcement are more resistant to extinction than fixed schedules.

70. Knowledge of different categories of trees and where they grow best is an example of what kind of long-term memory?

(A) episodic memory
(B) semantic memory
(C) procedural memory
(D) eidetic memory
(E) mnemonic memory

71. Which of the following is an example of an implicit memory?

(A) describing the taste of the cake at your last birthday party
(B) remembering how to tie a tie
(C) recalling the name of your junior high school shop teacher
(D) recognizing a celebrity
(E) repeating the name of your first pet

72. Research indicates that which of the following factors most influence a person's sexual orientation?

(A) parenting style
(B) masculine/feminine personality traits
(C) hormones released in the womb
(D) sexual orientation of parents
(E) traumatic childhood experiences

73. A psychology teacher who believes that all students want to learn and creates a classroom culture that encourages this intrinsic motivation is using which kind of management style?

(A) approach-avoidance
(B) James-Lange
(C) Cannon-Bard
(D) theory X
(E) theory Y

74. Which of the following factors impacts the speed of motor development the most?

(A) early gross motor practice and experiences
(B) concrete operational exercises soon after birth
(C) myelination of brain neurons
(D) secure attachments with parents
(E) secure parenting styles

75. Which of the following statements best describes an important difference between authoritarian and authoritative parenting styles?

(A) Authoritarian parents use clear rules and enforce those rules consistently.
(B) Parents using the authoritative style allow children to set and enforce their own rules in order to encourage independence.
(C) Authoritative parents set and enforce rules, but explain and emphasize the rationale behind the rules.
(D) Children who grow up in authoritative households are likely to be less independent as adults because they are not used to making decisions.
(E) Authoritative parents set fewer rules than Authoritarian parents do, but they are more likely to enforce the rules with stricter punishments and more extensive rewards.

76. What kind of question would be most useful in a study testing Lawrence Kohlberg's concepts of pre- and post-conventional stages?

(A) How many objects remain if 3 objects are taken away from a group of 12 objects?
(B) Should someone tell a small lie in order to prevent someone's feelings from being hurt?
(C) What is the most effective way to respond to a child crying in her or his crib?
(D) Which type of parenting style most quickly establishes a parenting style that encourages secure attachment?
(E) At what age can children reason abstractly and think about different hypotheses?

77. Which of the following is a common criticism of Freud's personality theory?

(A) Freud's research was based mainly on students in his classes and wasn't representative.
(B) The theory was focused on the psychologically healthy and did not apply well to people with psychological disorders.
(C) Personality is too complex to be studied using the scientific experiments Freud used.
(D) Genetics theory was not advanced enough in Freud's time to be used as he tried to.
(E) The evidence for Freud's method was based only on his therapy sessions and was not tested scientifically.

78. Someone who fails an important exam and reacts by spending more time studying in the library and less time socializing probably has which kind of locus of control?

(A) internal
(B) external
(C) subconscious
(D) unconscious
(E) fundamental

79. How would a psychometrician interpret an IQ score of 145?

(A) This score is slightly above the average score on most IQ tests.
(B) This score is well below the standard average of 200 on IQ tests.
(C) This score indicates that the person has high verbal intelligence but low logical intelligence.
(D) This score is three standard deviations above the average score of 100.
(E) This score is high for a child, but is considered average or low for an adult.

80. Which of the following is the most complete list of the common characteristics of psychological disorders?

(A) humanistic, behavioral, cognitive, biomedical
(B) maladaptive, disturbing, unusual, irrational
(C) anxiety, dissociative, affective, schizophrenic
(D) disorganized, paranoid, catatonic, undifferentiated
(E) dependent, narcissistic, histrionic, obsessive

81. Which of the following is one of the key factors that differentiate major depressive disorder from periods of sadness that everyone experiences?

(A) Major depression is indicated by specific changes in the brain.
(B) People who experience major depression are sad for longer than two weeks without an obvious cause.
(C) Individuals diagnosed with major depression experience sadness along with episodes of heightened emotions and mania.
(D) All mood disorders, like major depression, involve tolerance and withdrawal of controlled substances.
(E) Normal periods of sadness are much less intense than the sadness associated with major depression.

82. Which of the following techniques would be most helpful in avoiding the problems associated with groupthink?

(A) responding to deindividuation among group members
(B) encouraging contrary opinions within the group
(C) increasing group polarization within different groups
(D) identifying approach-avoidance conflicts
(E) promoting similarity, proximity, and reciprocal liking

83. Which of the following was one of the factors that increased conformity in Asch's studies?

(A) presence of the authority figure
(B) level of shock administered
(C) placebo effect
(D) size of the group
(E) expectations about conformity

84. A psychologist who advises a patient to write about his depressed thoughts and prescribes an antidepressant medication is using a combination of which of the following perspectives?

(A) therapeutic and psychoanalytic
(B) behavioral and socio-cultural
(C) humanist and evolutionary
(D) cognitive and biopsychology
(E) structuralist and empiricist

85. Why can experiments determine causal relationships when no other research method can?

(A) Experiments are more precise than the other research methods.
(B) Experiments isolate the effects of independent variables on dependent variables.
(C) Experiments typically involve more participants than other research methods do.
(D) Experiments take place in more realistic, real-life settings.
(E) Experiments involve precise descriptive and inferential statistical methods.

86. Which research method would most likely be used to test the following hypothesis? People who conserve energy by buying hybrid cars are more likely to spend more money on organic foods.

(A) experiment
(B) naturalistic observation
(C) case study
(D) correlation
(E) ethnography

87. Professor Ek is interested in studying online bullying behaviors of middle school students. Which of the following research method choices (and the rationale for the choice) is the most appropriate?

(A) Experiment—the most convenient and ethical way to study online bullying is to randomly assign half of the participants to a group who experiences the independent variable (online bullying).
(B) Correlation—it would be unethical to purposefully expose middle school students to bullying behaviors, so Professor Ek should examine variables that correlate with existing instances of online bullying.
(C) Naturalistic observation—observing instances of online bullying by monitoring middle school students' social networking behavior would provide the most accurate data and not raise important privacy concerns, because social networks are considered "public" space.
(D) Survey—self-reports about online bullying behaviors and responses to these behaviors would likely provide the most accurate descriptions of bullying and its impact.
(E) Case study—Professor Ek should examine one real example of online bullying in detail because data and conclusions from this single case would generalize best to the general population.

88. A person suffering from a skin rash finds her pain is temporarily relieved by vigorous scratching. She does not perceive the pain from the rash while she is scratching, but the pain returns soon after she stops scratching. Which concept best explains this temporary pain relief?

(A) opponent-process theory
(B) amplitude and frequency theories
(C) transduction theory
(D) gustation theory
(E) gate-control theory

89. Withdrawal symptoms are most directly caused by which of the following processes?

   (A) tolerance
   (B) dissociation
   (C) activation-synthesis
   (D) role theory
   (E) antagonists

90. What is the major difference between classical and operant conditioning?

   (A) Operant conditioning was established well before classical conditioning.
   (B) Classical conditioning involves pairing stimuli, and operant conditioning involves pairing a response with a stimulus.
   (C) Operant conditioning is used to train organisms to perform specific acts, and classical conditioning is used to get organisms to stop performing specific acts.
   (D) Classical conditioning is more difficult to use but more effective than operant conditioning.
   (E) Operant conditioning involves biological responses, and classical conditioning involves rewards and punishments.

91. What is the major difference between negative reinforcement and punishment?

   (A) Punishments are used with nonhuman animals, and negative reinforcements are used with humans.
   (B) Negative reinforcements are used in classical conditioning, and punishments are used in operant conditioning.
   (C) Punishments are primarily used when training an organism to perform a behavior and negative reinforcements are used to train an organism to stop performing a behavior.
   (D) Negative reinforcements are more effective than punishments but take longer to use.
   (E) Punishments decrease the frequency of a behavior and negative reinforcements increase the frequency of a behavior.

92. Noam Chomsky and B. F. Skinner disagreed about how children acquire language. Which of the following concepts is most relevant to the differences between their theories?

   (A) phonemes
   (B) morphemes
   (C) linguistic relativity hypothesis
   (D) language acquisition device
   (E) serial position effect

93. A research participant eats half a bowl of M&M candies, and then stops eating. How would a motivation researcher using drive reduction theory explain this participant's behavior?

   (A) Humans are instinctively driven to eat sugar and fat when presented to them.
   (B) The Yerkes-Dodson law explains that people will eat food when presented to them, but usually in moderate amounts in order to avoid being perceived as selfish.
   (C) The primary drive of hunger motivated the person to eat, and then stop when she/he regained homeostasis.
   (D) The research participant was satisfying the second step on the hierarchy of needs: Food needs.
   (E) Each person uses incentives in order to determine what to be motivated to do. This person decided on a hunger incentive and ate half the candies.

94. Which of the following is the best summary of Stanley Schacter's two-factor theory of emotion?

(A) An external event causes us to experience a specific emotion, and this emotion triggers certain physiological changes to occur.
(B) When our body responds to an external event, our brain interprets the biological changes as a specific emotion.
(C) Each person follows a predictable pattern of changes in response to stress, including alarm, resistance, and exhaustion.
(D) Perceived control over life events reduces stress, which in turn cause specific emotions.
(E) A combination of psychological changes and our cognitive interpretations combine to produce our emotional experiences.

95. How would Piaget describe the process of learning something new using terminology from his cognitive development theory?

(A) When we can't assimilate new information, we change our schemas through accommodation.
(B) As we encounter new social situations, we either develop healthy or unhealthy personality characteristics in order to cope with social demands.
(C) Humans develop increasing abilities to think about moral choices, and our ability to think about the rights of others develops over time.
(D) Rewards and punishments for behaviors are the major influence on learning in humans.
(E) The interaction between nature and nurture determines that genetic influences are a major cause of the pace of learning and learning difficulties.

96. Albert Bandura and the social-cognitive personality theorists believe that personality results from the interaction of which factors?

(A) genetics, the unconscious, and social
(B) id, ego, and superego
(C) rewards, punishments, and reinforcements
(D) traits, the environment, and behavior
(E) humanism, behaviorism, and cognition

97. What would a psychometrician conclude about a personality test that tells a person she is an extreme extrovert the first time she takes the test and an extreme introvert the next time she takes it?

(A) This personality test has low reliability but high validity.
(B) The test is probably high in construct validity but isn't very predictive.
(C) These test norms and standardization probably need improvement.
(D) The results indicate that the test has low test-retest reliability.
(E) Like most personality tests, this test is most likely an aptitude rather than an achievement test.

98. Which of the following statements is true about the relationship between reliability and validity?

(A) Reliability and validity are mutually exclusive: a test can be reliable or valid, but it can't be both.
(B) If a test is reliable, then it is valid, but if a test is not reliable, it cannot be valid.
(C) Validity is a concept related to achievement tests, and reliability is the corresponding concept related to aptitude tests.
(D) A test can be valid but not reliable.
(E) A test can be reliable but not valid.

99. What is the purpose of the *Diagnostic and Statistical Manual of Mental Disorders*?

(A) to describe the causes of psychological disorders
(B) to explain the biomedical symptoms, causes, and cures related to psychological disorders
(C) to list diagnoses and symptoms so that psychologists and others can help diagnose psychological disorders
(D) to summarize research studies regarding psychological disorders and how these diagnoses relate to one another
(E) to discuss theories related to the causes of psychological disorders and how the theories lead to cures

100. What kind of therapy involves both behavioral and cognitive interventions?

(A) counterconditioning
(B) symptom substitution
(C) primary preventions
(D) rational emotive behavior therapy
(E) systematic desensitization

PART II: FREE-RESPONSE QUESTIONS

50 minutes

DIRECTIONS: You have 50 minutes to answer the TWO questions that follow. Your answer should present an argument rather than a list of facts. Make sure to incorporate psychological terminology into your answers whenever possible.

1. Many different kinds of psychological researchers spend their careers studying the process of attitude formation.

   (A) Explain how the following psychological principles influence attitudes:

   - Cognitive dissonance
   - Schema
   - Reciprocal determinism
   - Locus of control
   - Belief bias
   - Fundamental attribution error

   (B) Describe two interventions a psychologist might use to change a prejudiced attitude. One intervention should be based on the behaviorist perspective and one intervention should use the cognitive perspective.

2. Professor Kester, a developmental psychologist, is investigating the long-term effects of different parenting styles. Her hypothesis is: Children of parents who use the permissive parenting style will be more independent as adults than children of authoritarian or authoritative parents.

   (A) Describe how Professor Kester could test this hypothesis. Include the following elements in your description:

   - Identify the two key variables in this hypothesis and explain a possible operational definition for each variable.
   - Briefly describe two studies that could test this hypothesis, one using the cross-sectional method and one using the longitudinal method.
   - Explain how Professor Kester could ensure that her study will meet at least 3 of the 5 ethical requirements for research involving human participants.

   (B) Predict what Professor Kester might discover based on your knowledge of parenting style research.

ANSWER KEY

Part I: Multiple-Choice Questions

1. **C**
2. **C**
3. **B**
4. **B**
5. **D**
6. **A**
7. **A**
8. **B**
9. **E**
10. **D**
11. **D**
12. **C**
13. **A**
14. **B**
15. **D**
16. **C**
17. **B**
18. **B**
19. **C**
20. **B**
21. **C**
22. **D**
23. **B**
24. **D**
25. **B**
26. **C**
27. **B**
28. **D**
29. **D**
30. **D**
31. **E**
32. **D**
33. **B**
34. **C**
35. **C**
36. **A**
37. **B**
38. **C**
39. **D**
40. **B**
41. **A**
42. **B**
43. **D**
44. **E**
45. **D**
46. **D**
47. **C**
48. **A**
49. **D**
50. **E**
51. **E**
52. **B**
53. **C**
54. **B**
55. **B**
56. **D**
57. **A**
58. **D**
59. **A**
60. **C**
61. **B**
62. **C**
63. **C**
64. **E**
65. **B**
66. **E**
67. **D**
68. **B**
69. **E**
70. **B**
71. **B**
72. **C**
73. **E**
74. **C**
75. **C**
76. **B**
77. **E**
78. **A**
79. **D**
80. **B**
81. **B**
82. **B**
83. **D**
84. **D**
85. **B**
86. **D**
87. **B**
88. **E**
89. **A**
90. **B**
91. **E**
92. **D**
93. **C**
94. **E**
95. **A**
96. **D**
97. **D**
98. **E**
99. **C**
100. **E**

ANSWERS EXPLAINED

Part I

1. **(C)** Wundt set up the first psychological laboratory and his empirical, replicable experiments are the reason he is called the father of the science of psychology.

2. **(C)** Skinner focused on operant conditioning within the perspective of behaviorism, which specifically addresses the impact of reinforcers and punishers on behavior. The other theorists listed did not specifically focus on operant conditioning in their research.

3. **(B)** Choosing participants at random for a study is random sampling. Assignment occurs when participants are assigned to control and experimental groups. Representative sampling and assignment involve purposefully making groups that represent a larger population.

4. **(B)** A double blind study controls for both experimenter and subject bias since neither the researchers nor the participants know who is assigned to the experimental and the control groups while the study is taking place. The other concepts listed as possible answers do not relate directly to both experimenter and subject bias.

5. **(D)** Impulses from the eyes travel to the occipital lobe where they are perceived as vision. If the occipital lobe is damaged, vision would most likely be affected.

6. **(A)** Low levels of serotonin are associated with clinical depression, so a medication prescribed to treat depression will most likely affect serotonin levels, rather than any of the other neurotransmitters or other options listed.

7. **(A)** MRI and CAT scans provide detailed information about the structure of the brain (and other body parts). These scans would reveal any structural brain damage caused by the car crash. The PET, EEG, and fMRI scans are primarily used to detect brain function, not structure (although the fMRI would also provide structural details). An EKG scan is unrelated to brain function.

8. **(B)** The sympathetic nervous system is responsible for the "fight or flight" response—mobilizing our body in response to stress (such as surprise or shock). The other terms in the question do not relate to this response.

9. **(E)** Dendrites grow more quickly in children, so brains of younger people are more "plastic," or changeable. A young person who suffers brain damage is more able to make new connections in nondamaged parts of the brain and regain lost functions. The other brain-related concepts listed are not related to brain plasticity.

10. **(D)** PET scans provide information about which parts of the brain are most active, which would reveal that all parts of the brain are used (although different areas of the cerebral cortex are more active than others on different tasks). CAT and MRI scans only provide information on the structure of the brain, not brain activity. An EEG scan does provide information about brain wave activity, but does not tie this activity to specific areas of the brain. And EKG is a scan of heart function, not related to brain activity.

11. **(D)** Although all the structures listed are involved in vision (including color vision), cones are uniquely involved. Cones are cells in the retina that respond to wavelengths of light that we perceive as color.

12. **(C)** Vision, hearing, and touch can be categorized as energy senses, since they gather energy (in the form of either light or sound waves). Taste and smell can be categorized as chemical senses since they gather chemicals (through the mouth or nose) and turn them into smell and taste perceptions.

13. **(A)** Volume is determined by the amplitude (height) of the sound wave. Wave frequency determines the pitch of the sound.

14. **(B)** The absolute threshold represents the minimum amount of stimulus we can usually detect, such as the minimum amount of salt we can taste in water.

15. **(D)** Detecting the difference between two very similar pitches depends on the difference threshold, the minimum difference between two stimuli that we can perceive.

16. **(C)** Depth perception depends on monocular cues (like linear perspective) and binocular cues (like retinal disparity).

17. **(B)** People deprived of REM sleep have difficulty with memory tasks. REM sleep deprivation does not increase stage 3 and 4 sleep (in fact, people deprived of REM sleep more easily slip into sleep onset and REM sleep, not deeper sleep stages like stage 3 and 4). REM deprivation is not related to sleep apnea, night terrors, or manifest dream content.

18. **(B)** Psychoanalysts would view the salad restaurant as the manifest content of the dreaming masking the more important latent content. Clinicians from other perspectives tend not analyze dreams.

19. **(C)** Classical conditioning always starts with pairing a conditioned stimulus (like a bell) with an unconditioned stimulus (like food). All the other possible answers involve reinforcements and punishments, which are involved in operant conditioning, not classical conditioning.

20. **(B)** A course grade is a secondary reinforcer because (most of us) learn to value high course grades. We do not need to learn to value primary reinforcers because they are related to basic needs and are rewarding (e.g., food, water, sleep).

21. **(C)** Observational learning theorists, like Albert Bandura, were primarily concerned with how we learn through observing the actions of others (rather than learning through direct rewards and punishments).

22. **(D)** In the three-box model, sensations are stored first in sensory memory. Sensations are only stored in sensory memory for a split second and then are either encoded into short term memory or are forgotten.

23. **(B)** Long-term potentiation is the process of strengthened connections between brain neurons. After repeated firings, the connection is strengthened, and the receiving neuron becomes more sensitive to the neurotransmitters from the sending neuron.

24. **(D)** The average capacity of short-term memory is about seven items. Grouping items into groups (chunking) increases the capacity of short-term memory.

25. **(B)** Recognition is the process of matching a current stimuli to something already in memory (e.g., seeing someone and recognizing whether you've ever seen her or him before). Recall is retrieving information from memory with an external cue (e.g., looking at someone and remembering her or his name).

26. **(C)** Researchers (like Elizabeth Loftus) demonstrated that leading questions can cause us to incorporate false details into our memories of events. For example, a question like "How fast was the car going when it went through the red light?" might cause a person to incorporate a red light into the memory even if a red light wasn't actually present.

27. **(B)** Maslow's hierarchy of needs predicts that people are motivated to achieve the next step in the hierarchy of needs. The order of the hierarchy is physiological needs, safety needs, love needs, esteem needs, and finally self-actualization.

28. **(D)** Stimulation of the lateral hypothalamus causes an organism to be hungry, and stimulation of the ventromedial hypothalamus causes an organism to stop eating. The other brain structures listed are not centrally involved in hunger motivation.

29. **(D)** Intrinsic motives (such as enjoyment or satisfaction) are associated with behaviors that continue over a long period of time. Extrinsic motivations (e.g., rewards, such as money) are effective in the short term, but behaviors slow down or stop after some time since most extrinsic rewards are temporary.

30. **(D)** Cross-sectional studies use groups of subjects of different ages in order to infer the impact of age on a variable. Longitudinal studies follow one group of people over a long period of time in order to infer the impact of age on a variable.

31. **(E)** Infants are born with the rooting reflex, which causes a baby to turn her or his head toward something that touches the cheek. This reflex can help a baby find the mother's nipple in order to eat.

32. **(D)** Ainsworth categorized three different types of attachment (secure, avoidant, and anxious/ambivalent) by observing infant reactions after parents left and returned while the infant was in a "strange situation" (a room the infant had not been in before).

33. **(B)** Erikson examined the major social experiences at all stages of life and theorized how these major experiences (which he described in eight stages) impact personality.

34. **(C)** Children in the concrete operational stage of development understand concepts of conservation (that the physical properties of object, such as number, area, and volume) do not change when objects are rearranged or reshaped. Children in the preoperational stage do not understand these concepts and will perform differently on related tasks.

35. **(C)** Freud believed that unconscious conflicts (such as fixations and defense mechanisms) determine our personalities.

36. **(A)** Many current personality trait theorists believe that our personalities can be described through a combination of the Big Five personality traits: extraversion, agreeableness, conscientiousness, openness to experience, and emotional stability.

37. **(B)** Trait theorists believe that personalities can be described through a combination of a small number of factors, or traits. Trait theorists often use pencil and paper tests to assess personality, and the results of these tests indicate that the person falls in a specific personality category.

38. **(C)** Maslow and the humanists believed that all people are working toward self-actualization and will become more mentally healthy if they are given the right environment. Maslow and the humanistic therapists provided unconditional positive regard to their clients in order to help clients discover for themselves how to best move toward self-actualization.

39. **(D)** Psychoanalysts might use a projective test in order to try to uncover unconscious conflicts and motive. The theory of the projective test is that a person will "project" his or her unconscious conflicts and desires on to vague and ambiguous stimuli (such as ink blots).

40. **(B)** Achievement tests measure what a person has learned, either knowledge or skill. IQ tests and most entrance exams are aptitude tests, measuring ability or potential (such as the potential to complete law school successfully). Personality tests and projective tests are neither aptitude or achievement tests: they both measure aspects of a person's personality (either conscious or unconscious).

41. **(A)** Fluid intelligence is the ability to solve novel, abstract problems. A new logic-based computer game probably depends on this kind of intelligence, rather than crystallized intelligence, which is the ability to use previously acquired knowledge to solve problems.

42. **(B)** IQ tests are standardized. Test items and test administration are kept standard for different groups of test takers and IQ test results are compared to a norm group (a standardization sample).

43. **(D)** The symptoms described best match PTSD, post-traumatic stress disorder.

44. **(E)** Somatic symptom disorders, like conversion disorder, are manifestations of psychological stresses/problems through physical problems.

45. **(D)** Psychogenic amnesia is categorized as a dissociative disorder. All dissociative disorders involve disruptions in our consciousness, such as the loss of memory that occurs during amnesia.

46. **(D)** People with depression often have low levels of serotonin, and drugs used to treat depression usually affect the serotonin system in the brain.

47. **(C)** Schizophrenia is associated with hallucinations and delusions. Both schizophrenia and dissociative disorders involve splits from reality, and both disorders are very disruptive and may interfere with a career and jobs.

48. **(A)** Psychotherapies all involve talk therapy, rather than behavioral or biomedical (somatic) treatments.

49. **(D)** Psychoanalysts, like Sigmund Freud, feel that dreams consist of symbols that reveal unconscious conflicts. This kind of analysis is seen as useful because psychotherapists believe that personality and personality difficulties are caused by unconscious conflicts.

50. **(E)** Somatic therapists view psychological disorders as biomedical issues, caused by either genetic or brain chemistry issues. Somatic therapists are likely to use chemotherapies (using psychoactive medications) rather than any of the behavioral or cognitive therapies listed.

51. **(E)** Lobotomies were used at one time to treat a variety of disorders, but this kind of serious psychosurgery was stopped when drug therapies because more common and precise.

52. **(B)** Psychiatrists are required to train for a medical degree and can prescribe medication. The other kinds of therapists listed do not necessarily receive medical training and are less likely to be able to prescribe medication.

53. **(C)** Including the free address labels is an example of norm of reciprocity, one of the compliance strategies. People are more likely to help if they feel someone has done them a favor, such as including a gift in a letter asking for contributions.

54. **(B)** Self-fulfilling prophecies occur when our preconceived ideas about someone influences the ways we act toward them, which may increase the likelihood that our preconceived ideas about the person may seem to be confirmed.

55. **(B)** When people commit the fundamental attribution error, they ignore the situational factors that may influence another person's behavior and instead attribute the person's behaviors to their inner disposition.

56. **(D)** We tend to see members of our own group (the in-group) as more diverse and more favorable than people outside our group (the out-group). This bias could contribute to discrimination and prejudice.

57. **(A)** Superordinate goals (goals that all groups need to work together on to accomplish) reduce tensions between groups. The other concepts listed do not relate to group tensions.

58. **(D)** Milgram's participants believed they were delivering shocks to strangers during his obedience studies. Some researchers think the participants were at serious risk for potential psychological harm because the study indicated they would have harmed a stranger by obeying an authority figure.

59. **(A)** Psychoanalysis is based on the study of the unconscious mind, a part of our consciousness that we are not consciously aware of. The other possible answers are not unique to psychoanalysis as compared to the other perspectives.

60. **(C)** The median is the measure of central tendency least affected by extreme scores (or outliers). Outliers can dramatically impact the mean. Standard deviation and range are measures of variability of the distribution. The normal curve is a graph of a normally distributed set of scores.

61. **(B)** Inferential statistics are used to examine distributions of scores in order to find statistically significant differences. Descriptive statistics (like standard deviation) describe sets of scores, but used alone cannot help make judgments about the significance of differences between sets of scores. Field experiments and counterbalancing are terms related to research methodology and aren't relevant to the question.

62. **(C)** Chemicals (neurotransmitters) move between neurons. These neurotransmitters either increase the likelihood the next neuron will fire (excitatory neurotransmitters) or decrease the chance the next neuron will fire (inhibitory neurotransmitters).

63. **(C)** Broca's area of the brain (located in the left frontal lobe in most people) helps control the muscles in the jaw, throat, and tongue needed to produce speech. Wernicke's area is also involved in spoken language but primarily with meaning and interpretation of language. The hippocampus and amygdala areas of the brain are not involved in spoken language. Gage's area is not an area of the brain. (Phineas Gage was a famous case study in brain function, but is not related to a specific area of the brain.)

64. **(E)** The medulla is located at the top of the spinal cord where it enters the brain. This is the area of the brain that controls blood pressure, heart rate, and breathing, and it is in one of the most protected parts of the brain.

65. **(B)** The doctors who treated Phineas Gage documented what areas of the brain were damaged and how Gage's physical and emotional characteristics changed after the accident. This was one of the first cases to tie a specific brain area to a specific function.

66. **(E)** Only monocular depth cues (like linear perspective) can be used in a pencil drawing, since binocular depth cues (like retinal disparity and convergence) depend on the different sensations we receive from two eyes.

67. **(D)** Generalization occurs in classical conditioning when an organism responds to any stimuli similar to the conditioned stimuli, such as salivating to any sound similar to a bell.

68. **(B)** Garcia and Koelling's research in learned taste aversions established that when any organisms become nauseous, they are very likely to associate the nausea with what they just ate or drank, and will avoid that food or drink in the future.

69. **(E)** Organisms trained using variable ratio schedules of reinforcements will continue to perform the desired behavior for a long time after reinforcement is stopped (i.e., extinction of the behavior is delayed).

70. **(B)** Semantic memories are general knowledge about the world. Procedural memories are memories of skills and how to perform them, and episodic memories are memories of specific events. Eidetic and mnemonic are not specific kinds of long-term memories.

71. **(B)** Explicit memories are memories of facts and events. Implicit memories (or nondeclarative memories) are memories of procedures or skills that we may not even realize we have, such as the skill of tying a tie.

72. **(C)** Research indicates that biological factors, such as hormones released to the developing fetus in the womb, may influence later sexual orientation. Research indicates that the other factors listed as possible answers do not influence sexual orientation.

73. **(E)** Theory Y managers believe that workers want to do good work and set policies in order to support worker efforts to improve and do quality work. Theory X managers believe that workers will only produce if given rewards and punishments. The other options listed as answers are not associated with management style theory.

74. **(C)** Motor development occurs in predictable stages as brain neurons mature and are further myelinated (thus improving communication between neurons).

75. **(C)** Authoritative parents set and enforce rules for children, but they talk about the reasons behind and the importance of the rules and help children understand the rules and participate in discussions about good and bad behavior.

76. **(B)** Kohlberg's theory dealt with the development of moral thinking. He would have been interested in how children of different ages responded to this question about the ethics of lying.

77. **(E)** Freud's theory was built on case studies from his psychoanalytic practice and was not tested empirically. In fact, his claims about the unconscious could not be tested experimentally because the unconscious by definition is not accessible to conscious investigation.

78. **(A)** A person who buckles down and studies more after failing an exam must believe that her studying will benefit her and that she will do better on the next exam because of her efforts. This is the definition of an internal locus of control: the belief that our actions have impact and that we are in control of what happens to us.

79. **(D)** 100 is the average score on IQ tests, with a standard deviation of 15. A score of 145 is three standard deviations above the average, and is a very high IQ score.

80. **(B)** In order to be diagnosed with a psychological disorder, a person's behavior is maladaptive (harmful to themselves or others), disturbing (disturbs others), unusual (atypical, not common), and irrational (not based in reality).

81. **(B)** In order to be diagnosed with major depression a person has to have a depressed mood that lasts for longer than two weeks without an obvious cause.

82. **(B)** Groupthink occurs when a group makes a bad decision because members of the group did not want to contradict each other (often due to mutual admiration of group members). Any techniques used to encourage contrary opinions within the group will work against this groupthink tendency.

83. **(D)** Asch found that conformity increased if the group was made up of three or more people.

84. **(D)** This psychologist is advising the patient to examine her or his own thinking (cognitive perspective) and prescribing a psychoactive medication (biopsychology perspective).

85. **(B)** Experiments use experimental and control groups to isolate what happens when a specific variable (independent variable) is changed and to measure the impact on the variable that changes as a result (dependent variable). The other options listed are either not true about the experimental method or are not unique to the experimental method.

86. **(D)** This study would most likely be done by comparing the average amount spent on organic food between people who own hybird cars and people who don't. This study could not be performed as an experiment. (There is no practical way to randomly assign

people to "own hybrid cars" and "don't own hybrid cars" groups.) The other research methods listed would not allow researchers to conclude about the likelihood of spending money on organic food.

87. **(B)** Purposely exposing middle school students to online bullying, or monitoring private social network interactions, would be unethical. In addition, self-reports about this sensitive topic may not be reliable, and conclusions from a single case would not necessarily generalize to the general population. Therefore, Professor Ek should look at correlations between online bullying and other variables.

88. **(E)** According to gate-control theory, higher-priority touch sensations (e.g., vigorous itching) will be perceived instead of lower-priority touch sensations (e.g., low-level pain related to the skin rash). So this person does not perceive the low-priority rash pain sensations while she is scratching vigorously (a higher-priority sensation), but the pain returns after she stops scratching.

89. **(A)** Most drugs produce increased tolerance with repeated uses—the need for increasing amounts of a drug in order to produce the same physiological effects. This tolerance gradually changes the levels of specific neurotransmitters in the brain, so when a person stops using the drug, withdrawal symptoms occur as the body and brain readjust and compensate for altered levels of these neurotransmitters. The other concepts listed in the answers are not related to the tolerance-withdrawal cause-effect cycle.

90. **(B)** Classical conditioning involves pairing conditioned stimuli with unconditioned stimuli, producing a conditioned response. Operant conditioning involves providing a stimuli (a reinforcer or a punishment) after a specific response is performed. The other possible answers provided about classical and operant conditioning are not accurate.

91. **(E)** Punishments are defined as stimuli that decrease the likelihood that an organism will perform the behavior that preceded the punishments. Negative reinforcements reinforce a behavior, increasing the likelihood the behavior will be repeated. They reinforce the behavior by taking away an aversive stimulus (e.g., an aspirin takes away a headache, which makes the person more likely to take an aspirin in the future).

92. **(D)** Chomsky and Skinner disagreed about how children acquire language. Skinner's behaviorist theory held that children learn language like they learn everything else: through rewards and punishments. Chomsky pointed out that language acquisition occurs too quickly to be explained by reward and punishment. Chomsky hypothesized that humans must be born with a language acquisition device that enables us to learn language quickly during a certain window of opportunity during childhood.

93. **(C)** Drive Reduction theory states that we are motivated by primary drives (like hunger) and secondary drives, and that we act to satisfy these drives until we regain a state of homeostasis (balance—in this case, we are no longer hungry). The other options each relate to a different motivation theory.

94. **(E)** Options A and B describe James-Lange's and Cannon-Bard's theories of emotion, respectively. Schacter's two-factor theory holds that a combination of biological changes and mental interpretations (cognitive labels) combined are what we call "emotion."

95. **(A)** Piaget described schemas (the ways we think about the world) as going through a process of assimilation and accommodation. When we encounter something new in the world, we first try to use our existing schemas to understand it (assimilation). If that doesn't work, we may have to change or expand our schemas in order to deal with the new object, event, or idea (accommodation). We learn through accommodation, as our schemas change and become more sophisticated.

96. **(D)** The social cognitive theorists described personality through reciprocal determinism, meaning that our personality traits interact with our environment, and these both interact with our behaviors. Each of these factors influences the others, and our personality is a result of these interactions.

97. **(D)** Test-retest reliability is a measure of a test's ability to deliver similar results each time it is administered to the same person.

98. **(E)** A test can be reliable (can provide the same results each time it is administered) but may not be valid (those consistent results may not accurately measure what the test claims to measure).

99. **(C)** The DSM lists the official names of diagnoses and exact symptoms associated with these diagnoses so that psychologists and psychiatrists can reliably diagnose patients. The DSM does not address causes of psychological disorders.

100. **(E)** Patients using systematic desensitization try to replace anxiety with relaxation. Patients place themselves in somewhat stressful situations and use relaxation techniques (calming thoughts, deep breathing, etc.) to reduce their stress reactions until they are no longer stressed in this situation. Patients then move up to the next level of the "fear hierarchy" and place themselves in a slightly more stressful situation and use the relaxation techniques. The other therapies listed are either strictly behavioral (counterconditioning) or cognitive (rational emotive behavior therapy).

Multiple-Choice Error Analysis Sheet

After checking your answers on the practice test, you might want to gauge your areas of relative strength and weakness. This sheet will help you to classify your errors by topic area. By circling the numbers of the questions you answered incorrectly, you can get a picture of which areas you need to study the most.

Chapter	Question Numbers										
History and Approaches	1	2	59	84							
Methods	3	4	60	61	85	86	87				
Biological Bases of Behavior	5	6	7	8	9	10	62	63	64	65	
Sensation and Perception	11	12	13	14	15	16	66	88			
States of Consciousness	17	18	89								
Learning	19	20	21	67	68	69	90	91			
Cognition	22	23	24	25	26	70	71	92			
Motivation and Emotion	27	28	29	72	73	93	94				
Developmental Psychology	30	31	32	33	34	74	75	76	95		
Personality	35	36	37	38	39	77	78	96			
Testing and Individual Differences	40	41	42	79	97	98					
Abnormal Psychology	43	44	45	46	47	80	81	99			
Treatment of Psychological Disorders	48	49	50	51	52	100					
Social Psychology	53	54	55	56	57	58	82	83			

Part II

Question 1 Scoring Rubric

This is an 8-point question. Each application of a term in part A is worth one point (6 points possible) and each description of an intervention in part B is worth 1 point (2 points possible).

Many different kinds of psychological researchers spend their careers studying the process of attitude formation.

(A) Explain how the following psychological principles influence attitudes.

Point 1

Students should explain how the motivation to have consistent attitudes and behaviors influences attitudes. Students can describe this general influence or use a specific example. Students could describe how an action that is inconsistent with a specific attitude causes dissonance that is reduced when the attitude is changed.

Point 2

Students should explain how the internal cognitive rules we use to understand the world influences attitudes. Students can describe this general influence or use a specific example. The student essay could describe how one of the mental rules we use establishes or changes an attitude, such as a stereotype about a specific type of person.

Point 3

Students should explain how the process of reciprocal determinism impacts attitude. Students can describe this general influence or use a specific example. This explanation or example should explain the reciprocal relationship between personality, environment, and behavior, and how these interactions relate to attitude.

Point 4

Students should explain how the concept of locus of control describes types of attitudes. Students can describe this general influence or use a specific example. The explanation should include the attitude that our actions determine what happens to us (internal locus of control) and/or the attitude that influences outside our control determines what happens to us (external locus of control). Students could go on to describe how internal or external locus of controls might lead to other attitudes (e.g., optimism or pessimism).

Point 5

Students should explain how belief bias influences attitude. Students can describe this general influence or use a specific example. This explanation or example should include the idea that we might not change our attitudes in the face of contradictory evidence, and some attitudes might represent an illogical conclusion in order to confirm our preexisting beliefs.

Point 6

Students should explain how the fundamental attribution error contributes to attitude formation. Students can describe this general influence or use a specific example. The explanation or example should describe how the mental act of attributing a person's behavior to their internal disposition rather than to the situation reflects and establishes an attitude toward that person.

(B) Describe two interventions a psychologist might use to change a prejudiced attitude. One intervention should be based on the behaviorist perspective and one intervention should use the cognitive perspective.

Point 7

In part B, students need to describe two interventions a psychologist might use to change an attitude. In order to earn point 7, students need to describe an intervention based on the behavioral perspective. This intervention needs to clearly use either an operant or classical conditioning technique in order to change an attitude.

Point 8

In order to earn point 8, students need to describe an intervention based on the cognitive perspective. This intervention needs to clearly involve how we interpret, process, or remember events. Using the perspective, the psychologist would try to intervene in the ways a person mentally interprets or remembers an event and this change results in a change in attitude.

Question 2 Scoring Rubric

This is an 8-point question. Part A is worth a total of 7 points and part B is worth 1 point. Students need to describe how Professor Kester could test her hypothesis in part A and make a clear prediction about the results in part B.

Points 1 and 2

Students should identify parenting style and "independence" as the key variables in this hypothesis. Students can refer to "parenting style" in general as the variable or can specifically refer to authoritarian, authoritative, and permissive styles as variables. In order to receive points 1 and 2, students need to both identify these variables and provide a possible operational definition for each. Possible operational definitions are listed below (not an exhaustive list—students may score these points for other reasonable operational definitions).

Point 3

Students need to briefly describe a cross-sectional study that tests the hypothesis. In this brief description, students need to include the idea that people of different ages are being tested at the same time (a cross-sectional study). Students could describe a study in which groups of children, young adults, older adults, and the elderly are given measures of independence, and these results are compared with self-report inventories that measure parenting style in order to test the hypothesis.

Point 4

Students need to briefly describe a longitudinal study that tests the hypothesis. In this brief description, students need to include the idea that one group of children is being tested over a long period of time (a longitudinal study). Students could describe a study in which a group of children is observed interacting with their parents, and a dominant parenting style is established for each child. Then the independence of these children is tested over a number of years in order to establish a relationship between parenting style and independence.

PRACTICE TEST 2

Parenting style	Observational studies of parents measuring relevant factors, such as rule setting, rule enforcement, and levels of communication Self-reports of parenting style Instruments that measure parenting styles
Independence	Self-reports of perceived independence Observational checklists of independent and dependent behaviors Other data describing independent/dependent behaviors, such as living independent from parents, economic independence, etc.
Informed consent	Students need to describe how Professor Kester described the goals of the study to participants and received their consent (either through signatures on a consent form or consent of parents for the participation of children).
Coercion	Students need to indicate that the participants were involved in the study voluntarily and no coercive methods were used to ensure continued participation.
Anonymity	Students need to describe how Professor Kester ensured participants' anonymity, through the use of codes for participants or the use of fictional names when results were communicated to others.
Risk	Students need to describe how Professor Kester made sure none of the participants experienced mental or physical risk as a result of participation in the study.
Debriefing	Students need to describe how Professor Kester informed the participants of all the research procedures after the study was completed and how to obtain results of the study when they are available.

Points 5, 6, and 7

In order to earn points 5, 6, and 7 students need to describe how Professor Kester's study meets at least three of the five ethical criteria for research involving human participants. Students can describe more than three of the criteria, but only 3 points maximum are awarded.

Point 8

In order to earn point 8, students need to predict that Professor Kester's results will indicate that children raised in permissive households will be *less* (not more) independent than children raised in households where other parenting styles are the norm. Past parenting style research indicates that the permissive parenting style generally results in more dependence among children and young adults. The authoritative parenting style is generally associated with higher levels of independence.

Sample Student Response Essay 2

Professor Kester needs to identify the right variables in her hypothesis. Two of the more important variables are parenting styles and age. Then the professor needs to go on and operationalize these variables. The operational definition of parenting styles are how parenting styles affects the independence of children who grow up in households where different parenting styles are used. The operational definition of age is obvious: how old people are.

There are at least two studies that Professor Kester could do to test this hypothesis. One study might use the cross-sectional method: this is when you take a cross-section of people, in this case people of different ages, and you test them all at once. You could figure out which people grew up with permissive parents and which didn't, then look at the people in different age groups and figure out if the "permissive" groups were more independent than the other groups or not. Or Professor Kester could use the longitudinal method. This one would take longer: Professor Kester would have to find one group of people as kids, then figure out which ones were growing up with permissive parents and which weren't. Then the professor would have to wait until the kids grew up a little, then test their independence again. Then wait a few years, and test again. Over the years, the professor might be able to figure out whether being a kid of permissive parents has anything to do with independence.

Ethical considerations are very important to researchers, and Professor Kester might have trouble meeting the ethical requirements for this hypothesis. First, she would have to get the participants' permission to even be involved in the study in the first place. This would mean the parents' permission and their permission for their kids to be involved. Along with this, Professor Kester would have to make sure that no one was going to be hurt because of the study. Independence is a tricky thing to measure, and the professor would have to make sure that no one was making any risky choices with this independence. Finally, Professor Kester would have to make certain that the results of the study are only published in real psychological journals that are reviewed and edited by other psychologists, and not just in popular magazines or newspapers.

If Professor Kester overcomes all these obstacles, she might figure out some interesting results through this study. During the study, I believe that the professor will figure out that kids who grow up with permissive parents will actually be less independent than other kids. Permissive parents don't teach their kids anything about rules, and this might make it harder for kids to have rules later on in life.

Sample Student Response Essay 2 Scoring Explanation

Points 1 and 2

The student's essay doesn't score either point 1 or point 2. The student correctly identifies parenting styles as one of the key variables, but the student's operational definition of parenting style is not specific (it is basically a restatement of the hypothesis). The student misidentifies age as one of the key variables in the hypothesis. Age is a variable involved in the study, but the other key variable in this hypothesis is independence.

Point 3

The student scores this point at "the cross-sectional method: this is when you take a cross-section of people, in this case people of different ages, and you test them all at once." The student clearly establishes that this study would use people of different ages, testing them all at once and comparing groups of different ages.

Point 4

The student scores this point at "find one group of people as kids, then figure out which ones were growing up with permissive parents and which weren't. Then the professor would have to wait until the kids grew up a little, then test their independence again." This indicates that the professor is following one group of participants over a number of years.

Points 5, 6, and 7

The student scores 2 of these 3 points. Point 5 scores at "get the partipants' permission to even be involved in the study in the first place" (informed consent). Point 6 scores at "make sure that no one was going to be hurt because of the study." (risk). The student does not score point 7 because the last ethical consideration the student discusses (where the study results are published) is not one of the five ethical requirements for research involving human participants.

Point 8

The student scores this point at: "kids who grow up with permissive parents will actually be less independent than other kids." This prediction matches the research on parenting styles: children who grow up in households with authoritative parents are more independent than either permissive households or authoritarian households.

Index

C

N

O

P

R

T